The Treasures and Pleasures of the Caribbean, Bermuda, and The Bahamas

IMPACT GUIDES

THE TREASURES AND PLEASURES OF THE

Caribbean

Bermuda and the Bahamas

BEST OF THE BEST

JOHN AND NANCY EDMISTON

IMPACT PUBLICATIONS
MANASSAS PARK, VA

Second Edition

Previous edition published as ***Shopping and Traveling the Exotic Caribbean***

Library of Congress Cataloging-in-Publication Data

Edmiston, John W.
The treasures and pleasures of the Caribbean / John W. Edmiston, Nancy B. Edmiston. — 2nd ed.
p. cm.
"Previous edition published as Shopping and traveling the exotic Caribbean"—T.p. verso.
Includes bibliographical references and index.
ISBN 1-57023-046-3 (alk. paper)
1. Shopping—Caribbean Area—Guidebooks. 2. Caribbean Area—Guidebooks. I. Edmiston, Nancy B., 1942-. II. Edmiston, John W., 1941- Shopping and traveling the exotic Caribbean.
III. Title.
TX337.C27.E362 1995
380. 1'45'00025729—dc20 95—41135
CIP

For information on distribution or quantity discount rates, Tel. 703/361-7300, FAX 703/335-9486, or write to: Sales Department, IMPACT PUBLICATIONS, 9104-N Manassas Drive, Manassas Park, VA 22111-5211. Distributed to the trade by National Book Network, 4720 Boston Way, Suite A, Lanham, MD 20706, Tel. 301/459-8696 or 900/462-6420.

Contents

Acknowledgments

This book would not have been possible without the help of many people—friends, strangers, and new acquaintances both at home and throughout the Caribbean.

A special thank you first to Ron and Caryl Krannich for giving us the opportunity to contribute to the Impact Guides travel series, and for their endless hours of assistance in formatting, editing, and proofreading the manuscript.

We are grateful to the countless shop owners, artists, and craftspeople who took the time to speak with us about shopping; as well as the cruise ship lines who supplied us with data on ship accommodations and special tips for passengers who want to shop and participate in other activities while in port.

A special thanks also goes to the tourism representatives of St. Lucia and Martinique, and to all the other island tourist bureaus for providing us with assistance and information about their countries. Henky Looman is responsible for taking the unique cover photo depicting the bird on the cactus which appeared in the first issue of *Curaçao Now!* published by Curaçao Tourism Publications, Curaçao, Netherlands Antilles. It represents one of this region's many surprises which seasoned travelers have long discovered in this delightful part of the world—much of the Caribbean is arid. Bruce Bennett, who assisted with the chapter on the Bahamas in the previous edition, drew most of the maps appearing in this book.

Liabilities and Warranties

While the authors have attempted to provide accurate and up-to-date information in this book, please be advised that names, addresses, and phone numbers do change; shops, restaurants, and hotels do move, go out of business, change ownership and management; and the islands occasionally become victims of devastating hurricanes which can significantly alter the local tourist infrastructure. Such changes are a constant fact of life in the Caribbean. We regret any inconvenience such changes may cause to your travel plans.

Inclusion of shops, restaurants, hotels, and other hospitality providers in this book in no way implies guarantees nor endorsements by either the authors or publisher. The information and recommendations appearing in this book are provided solely for your reference. The honesty and reliability of shops and shippers is best ensured by **you**—always ask the right questions and request proper receipts and documents.

The Treasures and Pleasures of the Caribbean, Bermuda, and the Bahamas provides numerous tips on how you can best experience a trouble-free adventure as well as lessen the likelihood of encountering dishonesty, misrepresentation, and misunderstanding when traveling and shopping in the Caribbean Bermuda, and the Bahamas. As in any unfamiliar place or situation, or regardless of how trusting strangers may appear, the watch-words are always the same—watch your wallet! If it's too good to be true, it probably is.

Preface

The Caribbean, Bermuda, and the Bahamas offer some of the world's most exciting treasures and pleasures for those who know what to look for and where to go. For more than 25 years, we have repeatedly discovered unique places in the islands, stayed in outstanding hotels, enjoyed its many fine restaurants, and returned again and again to visit artists, gallery owners, and the many shops, arcades, factories, and market-places. Each year more visitors find their way to the ever changing, or never changing, intoxicating islands. Some cruise through the entire chain, while others fly directly to a destination and enjoy the islands one at a time.

The Caribbean, Bermuda, and the Bahamas offer many opportunities to acquire fashions, jewelry, gems, arts, crafts, and imported European goods. The mixture of European and African cultures have resulted in arts and crafts unique to the area. In addition, numerous duty-free shops offer opportunities to purchase exquisite items from France, England, and Ireland at a fraction of the cost you would pay either in North America or Europe. From each trip we return home with truly unique and quality items to enhance our homes and wardrobes. If approached properly, the Caribbean, Bermuda, and the Bahamas may well become your favorite island destinations.

The Caribbean, Bermuda, and the Bahamas have grown rapidly in the past ten to fifteen years. As tourism has increased, so too has the kind and quality of merchandise available throughout the region. Most islands are clean, convenient, comfortable, modern, orderly, and safe. While political unrest does occasionally arise in area, it's usually very sporadic and short-lived.

This is a convenient area to visit: English is spoken most everywhere; the food is outstanding; accommodations come in every size, shape, and price range imaginable; most any type of water related activity is available year round; and the people are delightful. There are, however, a few island countries, such as the Dominican Republic and Haiti, where visitors should not drink the local water, and travel outside the major cities is for the adventuresome tourist only. But these areas only add to the exotic nature of the Caribbean, and can be thoroughly enjoyed with a little extra planning and local assistance.

As we go to press, several hurricanes have raked the Caribbean, leaving in their aftermath millions of dollars in property damage. While some of our favorite hotels, restaurants, and shops in the islands have sustained damage, we expect them to be back in business shortly. Be sure to check with your travel agent or write, call, or fax ahead to check on local conditions. Hurricanes are a fact of life in the Caribbean that can significantly alter travel plans.

The chapters that follow present a particular perspective on traveling to selected island countries in the Caribbean. Like other volumes in the Impact Guides travel series, we focus on the best of the best. This book is purposefully written to present more than just another descriptive travel guide primarily focusing on hotels, restaurants, and sightseeing and with only a few pages devoted to shopping. While our primary focus is on shopping, the book goes beyond other shopping guides that only concentrate on the "whats" and "wheres" of shopping.

Our experience convinces us that there is a need for a book that outlines the "how-tos" of shopping in the Caribbean along with the "whats" and "wheres." Such a book should both educate and guide you through the shopping maze in the nine areas we explore. Consequently, this book focuses on the shopping process as well as provides you with the necessary details for making informed shopping choices in specific shopping areas, arcades, centers, galleries, shops, and marketplaces.

Rather than just describe the "what" and "where" of travel and shopping, we include the critical "how"—what to do before you depart on your trip as well as while you are on the various islands. We believe you and others are best served with a book which leads to both understanding and action. Therefore, you will find very little on the history, economics, and politics of the Caribbean, Bermuda, and the Bahamas; these topics are covered well in other types of travel books.

The perspective we develop throughout this book is based on our belief that traveling should be more the just another adventure in eating, sleeping, sightseeing, and taking pictures in unfamiliar places. Whenever possible, we attempt to bring to life the fact that the Caribbean, Bermuda, and the Bahamas are important centers of talented artists, craftspeople, traders, and entrepreneurs who offer you some wonderful opportunities to participate in their societies through their shopping process. When you leave these islands, you will take with you not only some unique experiences and memories but also quality products that you can appreciate for years to come.

We do not hesitate to make qualitative judgments about shopping in the island destinations we cover here. If we just presented you with shopping information, we would do you a disservice by not sharing our discoveries, both good and bad. While we know that our judgments may not be valid for everyone, we offer them as reference points from which you can make your own decisions. Our major emphasis throughout this book is on quality shopping. If you share our concern for quality shopping, you will find many of our recommendations useful to your own shopping.

Buying quality items does not mean you must spend a great deal of money on shopping. It means that you have taste, you are selective, and you buy what fits your home or wardrobe. If you shop in the right places, you will find quality products. If you understand the shopping process, you will get good value for your money. While shopping for quality may not be cheap, it need not be expensive. But most important, shopping for quality in the Caribbean, Bermuda, and the Bahamas is fun and the results can be enjoyed for many years.

Throughout this book we include "tried and tested" shopping and traveling information. We make judgments based upon our experience and research approach: stayed at different hotels, ate in a variety of restaurants, visited many places and shops, talked with numerous people, and simply shopped.

We wish you well as you travel the Caribbean, Bermuda, and the Bahamas. The book is designed to be used on the streets of the various areas presented. If you plan your journey and handle the shopping process according to the first five chapters, and navigate the streets and shops based on the remaining chapters, you should have a marvelous shopping and remaining chapters, you should have a marvelous shopping and travel experience. You will discover some exciting places, acquire some choice items, and return home with fond memories of these exotic places. If you put this book to use, it will become your passport to enjoying the best of the treasures and pleasures of the Caribbean, Bermuda, and the Bahamas!

John Edmiston
Nancy Edmiston

The Treasures and Pleasures of the Caribbean, Bermuda, and The Bahamas

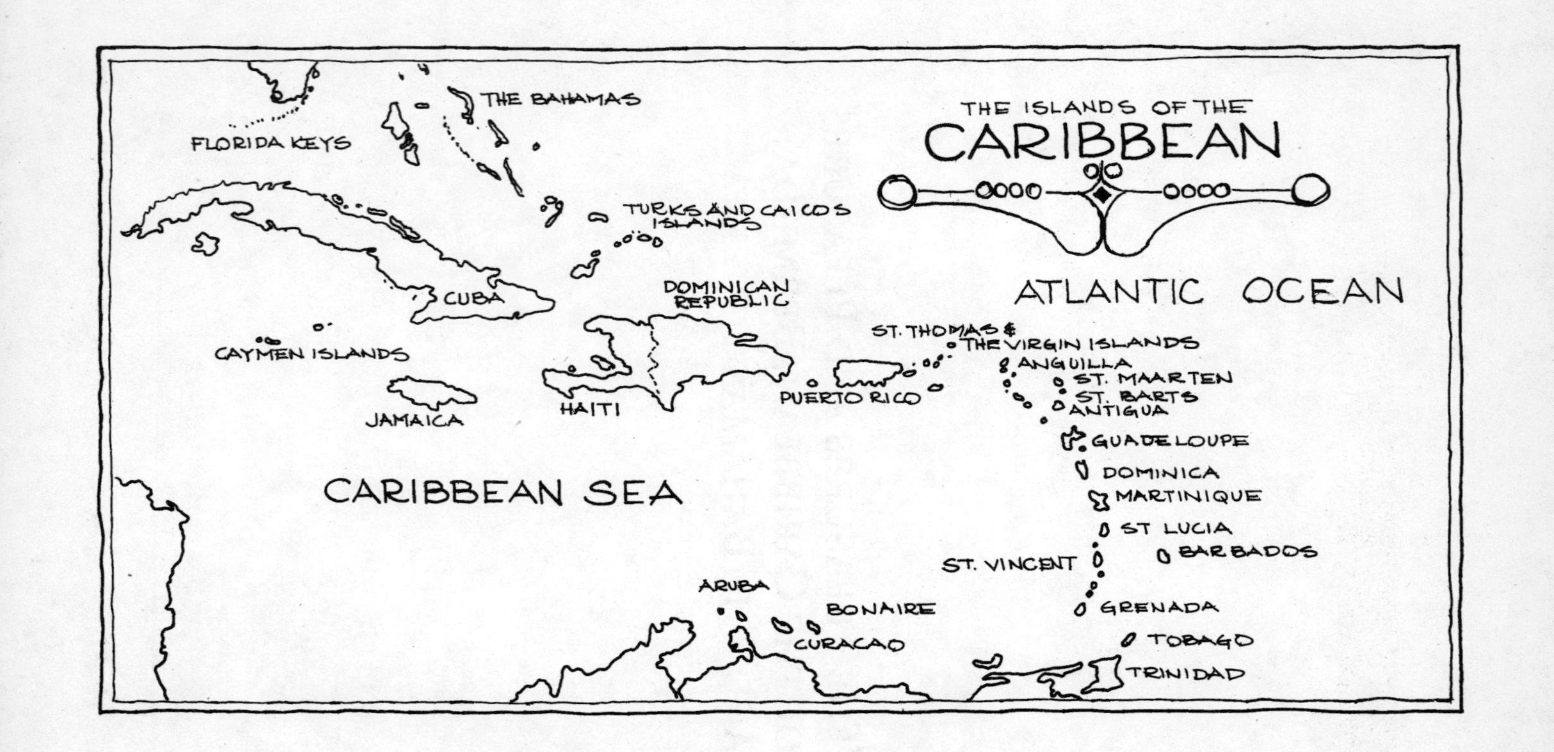
THE ISLANDS OF THE
CARIBBEAN
THE BAHAMAS
FLORIDA KEYS
TURKS AND CAICOS ISLANDS
CUBA
DOMINICAN REPUBLIC
ATLANTIC OCEAN
CAYMEN ISLANDS
ST. THOMAS & THE VIRGIN ISLANDS
ANGUILLA
ST. MAARTEN
ST. BARTS
ANTIGUA
JAMAICA
HAITI
PUERTO RICO
GUADELOUPE
DOMINICA
MARTINIQUE
CARIBBEAN SEA
ST LUCIA
BARBADOS
ST. VINCENT
ARUBA
BONAIRE
CURACAO
GRENADA
TOBAGO
TRINIDAD

1

Welcome to the Caribbean, Bermuda, and the Bahamas

Welcome to the treasures and pleasures of the Caribbean, Bermuda, and the Bahamas. Stretching through hundreds of islands for thousands of miles, this is one of the world's most expansive and exotic shopping areas. Second only to Europe as the favorite foreign destination for U.S. citizens, and a choice playground for residents from many other countries, the Caribbean offers sun, blue skies, beautiful clean clear waters, idyllic beaches, friendly and gracious people, bustling marketplaces, colorful festivals, fascinating cultures, and unparalleled shopping. It's an area where you can literally "shop 'til you drop" and still want to come back for more.

An Enticing World

The Caribbean will surely touch you forever with its beauty, people, products, and prices. Once you experience the Caribbean, you, like millions of other people, will come back time and time again to experience its many and varied pleasures.

From the fashionable boutiques, dazzling jewelry stores, unique art galleries, and exquisite displays of china and crystal of Aruba, Barbados, Bermuda, Martinique, Puerto Rico, St.

Lucia, St. Martin/Sint Maarten, and St. Thomas, to the colorful street vendors and crowded market places of Haiti, Dominican Republic, Jamaica, and The Bahamas, let us take you on a fascinating adventure as we fly, sail, drive, and walk in search of the Caribbean's many treasures and pleasures. Come with us and we will share with you some places largely absent in the enticing tourist brochures, travel books, and advertisements. We'll take you on an intriguing adventure that literally begins less than an hour from the East Coast of the United States. Within minutes you'll discover the unique treasures and pleasures of the Caribbean.

Treasures and Pleasures

Travel to the Caribbean can be both a rewarding and trying experience. Many people visit the islands to vacation and relax. Others stop over during business trips to or from South America. And still others go to the Caribbean only to shop. Whatever your reason for visiting these beautiful and inviting islands, you will undoubtedly discover many unique shopping opportunities while experiencing an extremely rewarding travel adventure.

The Caribbean rewards travelers who seek new experiences, set specific goals, plan well, remain flexible, are open toserendipity, and have good luck. The rewards are found in enjoying the travel process itself, acquiring new experiences and friends, and returning home with a treasure trove of wonderful memories recorded on film, savored in funny anecdotes, and reflected in wonderful Caribbean purchases.

Yet, travel is not all pleasure. At times it is hard work and can be a challenging experience. The best laid plans can go awry. Canceled flights, crowded airports, missing luggage, long lines, poor service, illness, sunburn, overpricing and cheating, unhealthy environments, and disastrous weather can spoil what was otherwise planned as a dream vacation. We have experienced both the joys and sorrows of travel, and will most likely continue to do so in the future regardless of how well we plan our trips. But we are committed travelers who embrace adventure, discovery, new experiences, and the other joys that accompany travel to the Caribbean and other places in the world.

Above all, we love to travel and shop at the same time. And as we get older and wiser from trial and error learning, we have become much more discriminating travelers. We seek to minimize the pain and maximize the pleasure of traveling outside the U.S. by constantly upgrading the quality of our accommodations, food, transportation, and service, and thereby minimize many of the hassles—especially wasted time—attendant with a great deal of budget travel.

This is not to say that we travel primarily to shop, spend a great deal of money, and encourage others to do so. Indeed not. Rather, we enjoy traveling, budget according to our means, know how to get a good bargain on what is important to us, and find shopping to be one of the great rewards in our varied itinerary of visiting historical sites and museums, enjoying good hotels and restaurants, lying on the beaches, sailing, meeting new people, and thoroughly immersing ourselves in different cultures.

We love to shop while we travel, because we find wonderful items, get good bargains, and enjoy the challenge and serendipity of the shopping process. Finding beautiful British and Irish woolens in Bermuda and Barbados, locating unique home decorative items in the hundreds of shops in St. Thomas and Puerto Rico, discovering exquisite handcrafted objects in small out-of-the-way shops in Jamaica, discovering the latest perfumes in Martinique finding the latest European fashions in St. Martin/Sint Maarten, and designing our own Haitian painting and Dominican jewelry are only a few of the many treasures we've uncovered from our many trips to the exotic Caribbean.

- **The Caribbean offers sun, blue skies, beautiful clear waters, idyllic beaches, friendly and gracious people, bustling marketplaces, colorful festivals, fascinating cultures, and unparalleled shopping.**
- **The islands throughout the Caribbean offer quality at both ends of the spectrum.**
- **We have learned what and where not to buy along with what best to buy, where best to buy, and how best to buy.**
- **Avoid the tacky, buy quality at the lowest price, and acquire purchases with the least hassle.**

Focus on Quality and Value

We assume you seek unique and quality goods at the best prices possible. If you are like us, you want to return home with treasures that complement your home and wardrobe, make nice gifts, generate fond memories of a wonderful trip to the Caribbean, and can be admired for years to come.

When you visit the Caribbean, do so with a discriminating eye for quality and good prices. You will find that the islands throughout the Caribbean offer quality at both ends of the spectrum—from ordinary and mediocre goods dominating the marketplaces to the finest quality products accenting the exclusive stores in the main shopping areas as well as the glamorous boutiques and jewelry shops in deluxe hotels and arcades.

It is not easy for everyone to do what we now do successfully. It took us many years of traveling in the Caribbean, the Bahamas, and Bermuda to discover the many treasures and pleasures of these enticing islands. We have certainly made our share of mistakes on the road to successful shopping outside the U.S. Like so many other travelers, we have languished in tourist shops wondering whatever possessed someone to produce such tacky items. We have, indeed, purchased that *"Don't Worry Be Happy"* T-shirt only to have all the lettering completely disappear with the first washing! We have chided ourselves on being poorly prepared and deplored the fact that we were not always able to discriminate quality merchandise from junk. We wish we had known many years ago what we now know about shopping in the Caribbean. We hope that our lessons will be your gain as you explore the rest of this book.

Most important, we have learned what and where not to buy along with what best to buy, where best to buy, and how best to buy. In short, we have learned to become discriminating shoppers by being able to sort the good from the bad. By learning how to go beyond the tourist shops, touts, and tour leaders, we have discovered a wonderful world of quality shopping everywhere we visit.

If you seek quality, as we do, shopping becomes extremely rewarding yet hard work requiring specific knowledge and skills. You become selective, seeking reputable shops which have the type of products you most desire. Avoiding the typical tourist knickknack shops, we primarily look for products which we will appreciate for years to come.

Each of the Caribbean islands possesses a unique set of shopping strengths and weaknesses. Accordingly, we organize ourselves to benefit from the strengths of each. To be able to distinguish good quality from poor; to know what will fit into your environment back home; to know the "what," "where," and "how" of buying on a particular island; and to get everything at a reasonable price and shipped home in good condition requires specific knowledge and skills not normally found in the typical travel book nor through a tour. It is this knowledge and ability to shop well and enjoy shopping treasures that we wish to share with you, the discriminating reader.

The Treasures and Pleasures of the Caribbean, Bermuda, and the Bahamas is designed to provide you with the necessary knowledge and skills to become an effective shopper in the islands whether you arrive by air or cruise ship. We especially designed the book with three major considerations in mind:

- Target the largest and most accessible shopping areas.
- Focus on quality shopping.
- Find unique items.

This is not a book on how to find cheap merchandise in the Caribbean. Rather, the book primarily focuses on quality shopping for unique items. While we do outline many of the general "whats," "wheres," and "hows" of shopping found in other travel guides, we do so with one major difference: we assume you wish to avoid the tacky, buy quality at the lowest price, and acquire purchases with the least hassle. Based on this assumption and our latest research and experience, we outline in the following chapters what we have found to be the necessary rules of shopping for quality, price, and convenience. As such, we describe in how-to terms the best methods of preparing for shopping in the Caribbean and then specify the most rewarding methods for acquiring quality products in the different islands. Each chapter is designed to lead you through the shopping process as painlessly as possible. Most important, the book is designed to enhance your travel experience with wonderful and rewarding shopping experiences which will be remembered and relived for many years to come!

FEATURED ISLANDS

We chose our destinations—including Bermuda and The Bahamas which technically lie outside the Caribbean—for several reasons. First, we concentrated on what we believe are the largest shopping destinations in the islands. We did this based upon the size and variety of the shopping areas, primary airline hubs, the main ports of call for cruise ship lines, and the most popular vacation spots for millions of travelers.

Second, Bermuda and The Bahamas are included because they both certainly fit all of the above criteria. Furthermore, most travelers think of them as being part of the Caribbean, even though geographically, neither is. Although either of these islands could be the subject of a separate book on shopping, we decided to cover them here and thus orient the book to the **travel region** as a whole.

Third, and probably most important, is our personal experience in shopping and traveling the Caribbean. Spending many years traveling throughout the region, we find our selected islands offer the most comprehensive shopping opportunities available in the Caribbean.

This is not to say that you won't find treasures elsewhere in the Caribbean, and we certainly do not intend our selection to infer that these are the only places to shop. In fact, you'll discover unique shopping on many of the other islands. Visit them if you can. We hope to include many of these, such as the Cayman Islands, in future editions of this book.

APPROACHING THE SUBJECT

The chapters that follow explore the best treasures and pleasures of the Caribbean. In so doing, we have attempted to construct a complete user-friendly guide that first focuses on the shopping process and then offers extensive details on the "how," "what," and "where" of shopping and enjoying your stay.

The chapters are organized in the order one would plan a trip to these islands. Each chapter incorporates the necessary details, including names and addresses, to get you started in some of the best shopping areas and shops on each of the islands covered.

The remainder of this book is divided into two parts and sixteen additional chapters which look at both the process and content of finding Caribbean treasures and pleasures. The next four chapters in Part I—**"Traveling Smart"**—assist you in preparing for your Caribbean adventure by focusing on the how-to of traveling and shopping in the Caribbean. Chapter 2, "Choosing Your Island Paradise for Shopping," basically covers what merchandise is available on the islands, with details on product lines and the best buys on each. Chapter 3, "Planning Your Adventure," examines how to best prepare for your trip to the Caribbean, including what is best to pack, health and customs tips, money matters, as well as how to identify your shopping needs and ship your purchases home with ease. Chapter 4, "Shopping the Islands," concentrates on the type of shopping you can expect to encounter, including pricing, bargaining, and bargains. Chapter 5, "Tips for Cruise Ship Passengers," prepares the cruise ship passenger for quality shopping even though you may only have part of a day, or even an hour, in port.

The chapters in Part II—**"Island to Island Shopping"**—examine in detail the "how," "what," and "where" of shopping in Aruba, The Bahamas, Barbados, Bermuda, Dominican Republic, Haiti, Jamaica, Martinique, St. Lucia, St. Martin/Sint Maarten, The U.S. Virgin Islands, and Puerto Rico.

RECOMMENDED SHOPS

We hesitate to recommend specific shops since we know the pitfalls of doing so. Shops that once offered us excellent products and service, for example, may change ownership, personnel, and policies. In addition, our shopping preferences may not be the same as your preferences.

Our major concern is to outline your shopping options in these particular islands of the Caribbean, show you where to locate the best shopping areas, and share some useful shopping strategies that you can use anywhere in the Caribbean, regardless of particular shops we or others recommend. Armed with this knowledge and some basic shopping skills, you will be better prepared to locate your own shops and artists, and determine which ones offer the best products and service in relation to you own shopping and travel goals.

However, we also recognize the "need to know" when shopping in exotic places. Therefore, throughout this book we list names and locations of shops and galleries we have found to offer good quality products. In some cases we have purchased items in these shops and galleries and can also recommend them for service and reliability. But in most cases we surveyed shops to determine the quality of products offered without making purchases. To shop in all of these places would be beyond our budget, as well as our home display and storage capabilities! Treat our names and addresses as **orientation points** from which to identify your own products and shops. If you rely solely on our listings, you will miss out on some of the great pleasures of shopping in an exotic place such as the Caribbean—discovering your own artists, galleries, or special shops that offer unique items and exceptional value and service.

EXPECT A REWARDING ADVENTURE

Whatever you do, enjoy your shopping and travel adventure to the Caribbean. This is one of the most interesting parts of the world, and the islands are surprisingly easy and enjoyable to get to and get around in. Better still, the islands offer many unique items that can be purchased and integrated well into many homes and wardrobes outside the Caribbean.

So arrange your accommodations, flight schedules, or cruise ship passage; pack your credit cards and travelers checks; and head for some of the world's most delightful shopping and travel destinations. One or two weeks later you should return home with much more than a set of photos and travel brochures. You will have some wonderful purchases reflecting the Caribbean's many cultures and unique crafts as well as numerous shopping tales that can be enjoyed and relived for a lifetime.

Shopping and traveling in the Caribbean only takes time, money, and a sense of adventure. Take the time, be willing to part with some of your money, and open yourself to a whole new world of shopping in truly exotic and unique places. If you are like us, your shopping adventure will introduce you to an exciting world of quality products, friendly people, and interesting places that you might have otherwise missed had you just passed through these places to eat, sleep, see sights, lie on the beach, and take pictures. When you shop and travel the Caribbean, you learn about the places through the people and products that define these island cultures.

PART I

Traveling Smart

2

Choosing Your Island Paradise For Shopping

Given hundreds of diverse islands spread over an area of more than one million square miles, you have numerous choices from which to select the perfect island. Include Bermuda and the Bahamas—which technically lie outside the Caribbean—and your choices are even greater. Do you, for example, romanticize about escaping to an island paradise to revitalize your soul? Do you dream of lying on a sandy beach listening to the waves break near the shore? Do you want to "shop 'til you drop" in chic boutiques for magnificent jewelry and designer fashions, all at fantastic prices? What about shopping in local marketplaces for native handicrafts or visiting homes and studios of local artists who produce everything from colorful paintings to interesting sculptures? All of these possibilities exist in the islands of the Caribbean, but not all options exist on the same island.

Follow Your Dreams

We strongly recommend that you determine your priorities and then select the island or islands that best fulfill your dreams. Do you envision something right out of the South Seas with lush foliage and palm trees lining the beaches? That's the dream Errol Flynn fulfilled when he put in at Port Antonio, Jamaica. Are you looking for a relatively private and deserted island away from the hub-bub, where time slows to an unreal pace? You can capture that mood on several long beaches, such as in Anguilla or Jamaica. Is shopping more important than getting a great tan? St. Thomas and Sint Maarten should be on the top of your list. If you want an exotic foreign flavor along with adventure, consider Haiti. If you want a European resort with all facilities available at a moment's notice, try L'Habitation in St. Martin. Acquire the latest perfumes several months before your friends at home in Roger Albert's shops in Fort-de-France, Martinique. Must everything be neat, clean, and picturesque, such as the freshly washed walls of Bermuda homes? The Bermuda Islands have all this and more to offer.

The islands of the Caribbean are many things to many different people. They have small towns and cosmopolitan cities. Each has its own distinct cultures with its own unique travel and shopping environments. Whether you go primarily to relax in the sun or splash in the surf, you should spend at least a few hours shopping the many wonderful shops and marketplaces for bargains or unique items. It's all there. Join us on a thrilling adventure as we discover the many treasures and pleasures of the Caribbean!

Best Places and Buys

Traveling in the Caribbean can be a great deal of fun and bargains can be found in many places. You'll enjoy meeting people at the marketplaces and bargaining for the local straw, wood, jewelry, and food items. You'll be able to visit artisans in their studios or homes and watch them at work producing lovely art. Or you'll shop the many chic boutiques or plush jewelry stores for fabulous items not found back home. Often you will buy because the price makes the purchase a real bargain. Other times you purchase something simply because it is unique and beautiful, and you probably won't find it elsewhere. You'll discover many different types of shopping available to fit any budget.

The U.S. Virgin Islands offers the freedom of not having to convert U.S. dollars and figure prices in foreign currencies, and it offers the highest duty-free allowances when returning to the U.S. In Charlotte Amalie, the capital, you can easily spend the entire day shopping and still not cover all of the shops.

You will encounter a large range of both locally produced

and imported products when you shop these islands. Prices and selections in St. Thomas, for example, reflect the fact that many products are imported or created especially for visitors. St. Martin/Sint Maarten also has a wide variety of merchandise that is imported and duty-free, and the prices there are better on some items, such as perfumes and watches, than in St. Thomas. It's especially fun to shop for perfume in both Marigot (the French Side) and Philipsburg (the Dutch side) where you can get the latest scents—even before they arrive in the U.S. French luxury imports are the very best buys in Martinique, and unique silk screens can be found at Bagshaws in St. Lucia.

- ❑ **The islands of the Caribbean are many things to many different people.**
- ❑ **St. Thomas, The U.S. Virgin Islands, is the duty-free haven of the Caribbean.**
- ❑ **In-bond shopping is the name of the game in Barbados.**
- ❑ **The best deals in Bermuda are found by shopping for sales.**
- ❑ **Look for primitive art in Haiti.**
- ❑ **In Puerto Rico bargaining is primarily confined to shopping for arts and crafts.**
- ❑ **French fashions are excellent buys in St. Martin.**

Some of the most exotic shopping is found in Port-au-Prince, Haiti where French history and a rich local culture are reflected in the primitive paintings. This art is increasingly recognized and collected in international circles. Since most items purchased here are made locally (more than 65% local content), they qualify as duty-free items when re-entering the U.S.

Don't forget the shopping on the other side of the island of Hispaniola in Santo Domingo where the rare amber and the newly discovered larimar stones are widely available along with many primitive paintings and carnival masks.

THE ISLANDS

The islands included in this book have numerous shopping strengths:

- **Aruba**: Aruba is not technically a free port, but the duty on fine Dutch porcelain, pottery; Dutch, Swedish and Danish silver and pewter; Swiss watches; French perfumes; British woolens and many other imported items is quite low. The prices are, therefore, much lower than in the U.S. Shopping here is hassle-free, with bargaining not considered appropriate. Best buys: jewelry, resortwear, handicrafts.

- **The Bahamas**: The Bahamas offer some excellent buys. This is a duty-free port so prices on imported items can be

25% to 40% cheaper then in the U.S. You should especially look for imported watches, perfumes, crystal, and British china. This is a wonderful place to haggle at the straw markets, especially the largest one in Nassau on Bay Street near the cruise ship docks. It is always well stocked and has and endless display of various shell necklaces (including conch) that are unusual, along with numerous straw products. In Freeport the straw market is located at the International Bazaar, which also houses a series of import shops with a wide variety of items. Best buys: shell jewelry, straw products from the markets in both Freeport and Nassau, and crystal.

- **Barbados:** In-bond shopping is the name of the game here. This is another British heritage island where the bulk of the shopping is found in downtown Bridgetown on Broad and Bond streets. Clothing is well priced with a wide selection of chic fashions available. You'll find boutiques with original designs that can be quickly made-to-order. Watches are an excellent buy along with British cashmere and wool products. Jewelry, especially gold, is a superb value. Local items are found at Pelican Village, about a mile outside of Bridgetown toward Deep Water Harbor where the cruise ships dock. Here you will find a large variety of handicrafts; woodcarvings are the best buy. You'll also find some tortoise shell jewelry, but remember tortoise shell is prohibited from entry into the U.S. Barbados rum is an excellent buy and it makes a good gift for friends back home. Best buys: in-bond liquor, English china and sweaters, and mahogany woodcarvings.

- **Bermuda:** The main shopping areas are downtown Hamilton and St. Georges. While you'll find some shopping in other quaint areas and at large hotels, most shops tend to be outlets of the main downtown shops. Bermuda is clean and neat and has a department store shopping atmosphere. The best deals here are found by shopping for sales rather than trying to "bargain" for a better price. There are many British items here as well as liquor. The in-bond pricing can be 50% less than back home, depending on your local tax structure. Interesting local products include items made from cedar and tubes of shark oil, used to predict the weather. However, these are becoming increasingly difficult to find. Best buys: anything British, including china and woolens.

- **Dominican Republic:** Outstanding buys include amber jewelry and items made from larimar stone—a form of turquoise. An unusual shopping and cultural experience is the Mercado Modelo market for arts and crafts. Here you can buy everything from paintings to coffee. Cash lowers the price considerably. It's a very busy hustle-bustle place with high sales pressure. Other good buys in the Dominican Republic include perfume and liquor. Best buys: local arts and crafts.

- **Haiti:** Look for primitive art here. Art dealers are everywhere—even greeting you in your hotel lobby. Make an appointment to meet an artist and have a work commissioned. Even though prices have increased on paintings by the better known artists, there are still many new artists waiting to be discovered. Haitian Voodoo Flags are becoming increasingly popular. A unique and somewhat overwhelming experience is shopping at the Iron Market in Port-au-Prince. The largest selection of Voodoo dolls is found here among all the iron and stone sculptures, straw goods, and woodcarvings. Haggling is a must. A drive to Petionville is rewarded with numerous hidden treasures amongst its unique boutiques and small craft shops. You may fall in love with the painted primitive boxes of Gauthier. Best buys: primitive art, stone and metal sculptures.

- **Jamaica:** In-bond prices abound on Swiss watches, Japanese and German cameras, British china, and French perfumes. Jamaica's local rum liqueurs are world famous as is its Blue Mountain Coffee. Local crafts, such as straw items, wood carved statues, black coral and shell jewelry, abound here. Shopping is widespread throughout this large island. In-bond shopping is available around tourist hotels, in malls, and near cruise ship docks for convenience. The largest straw market is found in Kingston which sells local and international items. Shops will need to see your ID to determine that you are indeed a tourist so you can carry all In-bond items with you—except liquor which can be purchased at the airport or cruise dock. Best buys: in-bond perfumes, coffee, rum, cigars, and shell jewelry.

- **Martinique:** All French luxury goods are excellent purchases here. French perfumes reach these French citizens about six months before the U.S. stores. The main shopping is in Fort-de-France or Pointe du Bout just across the bay by ferry. Foie Grass in earth color pottery is a great

Christmas purchase here and fine French rum by St. James is world renowned. Lalique crystal, fashions from the best known houses in Paris, and Limoges dinnerware are just some of the wonderful finds. A wide selection of French cosmetics, even for children, are found here. Cruise ships create huge crowds in the streets, something you may wish to avoid by checking with your hotel or the tourist office. Most shops close between 12:30 PM and 2:30 PM daily except Roger Albert. Best buys: perfumes and French fashions.

- **Puerto Rico:** While shopping is everywhere on the island, the most famous area is Old San Juan. Caribbean art is especially popular here, with Haitian art being hot at present. Puerto Rico has some outstanding contemporary artists. Bacardi Rum and cigars are also good buys. You'll find many unique shops here offering products not found elsewhere. Don't miss the butterfly collections at The Butterfly People. Crystal and bone china in Puerto Rico can be purchased at the same low prices as in St. Thomas. Bargaining is primarily confined to shopping for arts and crafts. Santos, small wood carved religious figures, are an island specialty, as well as carnival masks. Best buys: local crafts and one-of-a-kind jewelry.

- **St. Croix:** The main area of shopping is in Christiansted. Known for one-of-a-kind items in their many tiny shops. Original jewelry from Sonyas as well as leather bags from Nancee are just two of many handmade purchases to be found. There is also the assortment of merchandise for the home, sports wear, Java wraps, island arts and crafts. Low duty-free prices allow U.S. Citizens to take home up to $1200 worth of "goodies" with them tax free. Best buys: jewelry and local art.

- **St. Lucia:** A free port, St. Lucia, has one very exclusive shop called Bagshaws. It is world famous for its brightly colored handmade silk-screen printed fabrics made into everything from place mats to clothing. The island is also famous for its original batik artwork. Pointe Seraphine houses a collection of shops convenient to the cruise-ship passenger, but other shops exist in Castries, at hotels, and around the island. Best buys: fabrics and local art.

- **Sint Maarten:** Since this Dutch side of the island has free port status, look for good buys on Delfware and all international items such as fashions, crystal, watches, perfumes, and jewelry. You'll find some of the lowest prices in the Caribbean here. Best buys: Italian fashions, perfume, china, jewelry, and crystal.

- **St. Martin:** This French side of the island has the very latest in perfumes from France—stocking new scents about six months ahead of stores in the U.S. No taxes make this a free port which means good buys on French items. French fashions are excellent buys—much cheaper than at home. Expect to save 40% on famous silk ties and signature scarves. Best buys: anything French.

- **St. Thomas:** This is the duty-free shopping haven of the Caribbean. Most products are 30% to 50% below U.S. prices, and you receive a higher duty-free allowance to encourage you to buy. Old warehouses converted into shops invite you to fill your shopping bags with china, porcelain, crystal, clothing, jewelry, leather goods, watches, and even furs. While you will find many good bargains, you'll have to watch for great buys. Best buys: liquor, china, and jewelry.

3

Planning Your Adventure

Preparation is one of the most important ingredients to ensuring a successful shopping trip to the Caribbean. But preparation involves much more than just examining maps, reading travel literature, making airline and hotel reservations, or booking tours on or between the islands. Preparation, at the very least, is a process of minimizing uncertainty by learning how to develop a shopping plan, manage your money, determine the value of products, handle Customs, pack for the occasion, and ship or hand-carry the items home with ease. It involves knowing what products are good deals and where and how to buy them. Most important of all, preparation helps organize and ensure all the successful aspects of a shopping adventure.

Getting There By Air

Flying to the Caribbean is by far the most expedient way to get to an island paradise. We have left on many trips by 8am, had lunch beside a pool or the beach, and been shopping by 1pm! While numerous flights service the Caribbean, you may have to make one or two connections in order to get to islands other than Puerto Rico and the U.S. Virgin Islands.

With the advent of deregulation, it is almost impossible to know with certainty all the airlines that fly from the United States or elsewhere to the Caribbean. However, American Airlines, Air Canada, Air France, ALM, Bahamas Air, Air Jamaica, Delta, Continental, Carnival Paradise Islands, Gulfstream International and USAir normally have daily service from many U.S. east coast cities. Airfares continue to fluctuate. The best way to plan for a trip to the Caribbean by air is to contact a specific airline or your local travel agent. Your travel agent should be aware of special airfares as well as the seasonal hotel situation. There's nothing more frustrating than to spend hours planning your flights and then discover that no accommodations are available on an island for months! Indeed, many hotels in the Caribbean are rather reluctant to book rooms for people without firm airline reservations.

What's the best time of the year to visit the Caribbean? While "high season" in many parts of the United States is during the summer months, the most difficult time to get to the Caribbean is from December 15 through April 15. This is the Caribbean's "high season." At this time of the year most flights will be booked far in advance and you will pay the highest room rates—if you can find a vacancy. If you plan to use frequent flyer miles, be sure to check for any blackout periods. The most common blackout periods occur during Christmas, New Years, and Easter as well as near the more popular college spring breaks.

In addition to travel agents, check with local clubs about excursions to the Caribbean. Many employee organizations of government agencies, civic groups, and social clubs plan trips to specific islands. You might be able to save as much as $300-400 on your airfare and hotel bill by shopping around for the best deal.

You should also contact airlines about their special travel packages. These specials often include airfare, hotel, and "extras" such as social activities or excursions to various destinations. We frequently take advantage of these specials, but we normally skip the "extras." We set our own itinerary and spend our time shopping or relaxing rather than participating in an organized excursion to the beaches or mountains. If you separate from the group during most of your stay, make sure you meet them at the proper time and place for your return flight.

LAST MINUTE PLANNING

Although most people travel to the Caribbean for a family vacation or for rest and relaxation, many people from New York, Washington, Miami, and other destinations come here only to shop. Do not be dissuaded from planning a last minute shopping trip. On many occasions we have been told by an airline that we were sold the last two seats into the Dominican Republic, Haiti, or St. Thomas only to learn that the plane took off with at least 15 empty seats. If you need to purchase a ticket at the last minute, you may have to fly standby, since on many occasions all seats will be booked. This especially happens when traveling in and out of Haiti and the Dominican Republic, because of the few flights and small aircraft used. While hotel space may be found at the last minute, during the high season most major hotels may be filled. For example, at times most hotels in Sint Maarten/St. Martin will be filled. If this happens, take a 20-minute boat trip to the island of Anguilla where you can get a beautiful cottage on the beach at about half the price. And you'll only be one half hour away from shopping.

- **The most difficult time to get to the Caribbean is from December 15 through April 15, the Caribbean's "high season."**
- **Flying from one island to another will often involve the use of small local airlines.**
- **Sometimes baggage is left behind because of weight restrictions on small airlines. So travel light.**
- **Be sure to check in at the counter very early since some flights may leave early.**
- **Most departure taxes range from $5 to $15. To avoid delays, have the correct amount or use small bills.**

If you need to make last minute reservations for accommodations, try some of these direct dial numbers for assistance:

Anguilla	800-553-4939
Aruba	800-862-7822
Bahamas	800-327-0787
Barbados	809-426-5041
Bermuda	809-292-0023
Dominican Republic	809-532-2907
Haiti	(011) 509-5-2551
Jamaica	809-926-3635
Martinique	596-63-79-60
Puerto Rico	809-723-2944
St. Lucia	212-867-2950
Sint Maarten	(011) 599-5-3133
St. Martin	(011) 586-87-54-52
U.S. Virgin Islands	212-582-4520

ISLAND HOPPING

While major international airlines will get you to the islands, flying from one island to another will often involve the use of small local airlines. Since the Caribbean is spread out over such a vast area, travel between the islands is most conveniently done by air.

Several small airlines now service the various islands of the Caribbean: American Eagle, Air Aruba, Air Martinique, Air Guadeloupe, Air St. Barthelemy, WINIAR, Eastern Metro, and LAIT. At times one of the most efficient ways to get from island to island is by the smaller charter carriers. We have, for example, used Caribe Aviation, a charter company based in Antigua.

Traveling on smaller airlines, however, is not the same as traveling on an A-300 airbus. First of all, you will have greater baggage limitations. You will be charged for luggage weighing in excess of 44 pounds. Also, since people take priority over baggage and the weight on the aircraft is carefully checked, the passenger gets first priority on the plane. Sometimes baggage is left behind because of weight restrictions. The best way to travel efficiently between islands is to pack very lightly. Be prepared to ship any large purchases home rather than carry them on the aircraft. Some aircraft are so small that carry-on luggage is taken from you at the steps and put in baggage lockers.

Be sure to check in at the counter very early since some flights may leave early—especially if all the other passengers have arrived and are ready to go. While this does not happen often, it nonetheless occurs. We recommend checking in at least one hour before scheduled flight time, even though the flight may be only 20 or 30 minutes in length. Also, always reconfirm inter-island flights to ensure that the flight will depart as scheduled. If at all possible, purchase your tickets prior to leaving home. Flights are normally cheaper if booked in advance as part of your regular ticketing.

The departure lounges for the inter-island airlines are usually smaller than those for the major carriers, and departure procedures may be handled differently. For example, even in Puerto Rico at the American Eagle terminal, some departure announcements are made by personnel at the door taking tickets rather than over loudspeakers. You should check departure times at the counter and stay alert close to departure time so that you are not left behind.

One other tip that will make your travel more comfortable

and certainly keep you in better graces with your fellow travelers is to be ready to board when the announcement is made. Many small planes do not have air conditioning, and since the weather is normally warm, sitting on a small aircraft waiting for a lagging passenger is not a pleasant experience.

AIRPORTS, ARRIVAL, AND DEPARTURE TAXES

With few exceptions, most airports throughout the Caribbean are small, open-air structures. In all cases, you will depart the plane by stairs and walk across the tarmac in order to get to the terminal.

When arriving at the airports, closely follow directions for entering the building. This will help you get through Immigration and Customs without too much delay. Be sure you have appropriate documents completed and proof of citizenship available before arriving at the Immigration desk. Also, pay close attention to the signs and the size of lines.

On some islands, Immigration officials are very strict and prohibit visitors in lines reserved for residents. In other airports, such as Bermuda, if the visitors' line is long but the line for residents is nearly empty, the Immigration officers at the desks reserved for residents will be happy to assist tourists. By paying close attention, we are often able to get through Immigration within minutes.

Please keep in mind that the pace of life is a little slower in the Caribbean than you may be used to. Few officials are in a hurry, and they may occasionally stop to talk to passengers or to one another. This can be exasperating for some travelers. It's best to take it easy in the Caribbean and learn to "go with the flow."

After completing Immigration, gather your bags and go through Customs. In many islands, Customs officials generally ask questions and conduct bag searches. One of the most extensive checks we've encountered is in Haiti where nearly every bag—both checked-through and carry-on—was thoroughly examined by Customs officials. Customs personnel in most islands are extremely friendly and will help you with any questions you may have.

Departure taxes are required in most of the islands. These taxes range from $5 to $15. Payment methods vary. In the Dominican Republic, for example, the departure tax must be paid in U.S. dollars. They will not take local currency even though you are technically still in the Dominican Republic.

Many other islands accept either U.S. dollars or the local currency. However, one tip can save you a lot of time—do not show up at the departure tax counter or ticket counter with large bills. We have seen people delayed because they tried to pay a $10 departure tax with a $100 traveler's check.

GETTING THERE BY SEA

One of the best ways to see the Caribbean is from the deck of a cruise ship. The beautiful waters, sunny skies, and small isolated islands are best appreciated from sea. Most cruise ships offer all the benefits of island hopping without the inconvenience of packing and unpacking as well as changing flight schedules. In addition, cruise lines call at several ports on a single voyage—a real treat for avid shoppers seeking treasures in Puerto Rico, St. Thomas, and Sint Maarten all on one trip.

Although the ports may change, at present the following cruise ships service the islands and ports included in this book:

- **Aruba**: (Oranjestad) Carnival, Celebrity, Crystal, Cunard, Dophin, Holland America, Norwegian, Regency, Royal, Royal Caribbean, Seawind, Sun, and Windstar.

- **The Bahamas**: (Freeport) Majesty, Royal Caribbean, and Windjammer. (Nassau) Carnival, Celebrity, Costa, Cunard, Dolphin, Holland American, Majesty, Norwegian, Premier, Royal, Royal Caribbean, and Windjammer.

- **Barbados**: (Bridgetown) Carnival, Celebrity, Costa, Crystal, Cunard, Diamond, Dolphin, Holland American, Norwegian, Princess, Regency, Royal, Royal Caribbean, Seawind, Silversea, Windjammer, and Windstar.

- **Bermuda**: Celebrity, Cunard, Holland America, Majesty, Norwegian, Royal Caribbean, and Silversea.

- **Dominican Republic**: Costa and Cunard.

- **Haiti**: (Labadee) Royal Caribbean.

- **Jamaica**: (Montego Bay) Commodore, Dolphin, Princess, Regency. (Ocho Rios) Carnival, Celebrity, Crystal, Cunard, Holland American, Norwegian, Princess, Regency, Royal, and Royal Caribbean.

- **Martinique:** (Fort-de-France) Carnival, Celebrity, Commodore, Costa, Cunard, Diamond, Dolphin, Holland America, Norwegian, Princess, Regency, Royal, Royal Caribbean, Silversea, Windjammer, and Windstar.

- **Puerto Rico:** (San Juan) Carnival, Celebrity, Costa, Crystal, Cunard, Diamond, Holland America, Norwegian, Princess, Regency, Royal, Royal Caribbean, and Sun.

- **St. Croix:** Commodore, Cunard, Holland America, Princess, Regency, and Royal Caribbean.

- **St. John:** (Cruz Bay) American Canadian, Costa, Cunard, Dolphin, Holland America, Norwegian, Princess, Regency, Royal, and Royal Caribbean.

- **St. Lucia:** (Casteries) Celebrity, Commodore, Cunard, Diamond, Holland America, Norwegian, Regency, Royal, Seawind, Silversea, Windjammer, and Windstar.

- **Sint Maarten/St. Martin:** Carnival, Celebrity, Commodore, Costa, Cunard, Dolphin, Holland American, Norwegian, Princess, Regency, Royal, Royal Caribbean, Silversea, Windjammer, and Windstar.

- **St. Thomas:** (Charlotte Amalie) American Canadian, Carnival, Celebrity, Commodore, Costa, Crystal, Cunard, Diamond, Dolphin, Holland American, Norwegian, Princess, Regency, Royal, and Royal Caribbean.

Cruise lines depart from many major East Coast cities as well as some West Coast cities for travel through the Panama Canal. Many airlines also have air/cruise packages which enable you to fly one way and cruise the other. Check with your local travel agent on these options. You'll find a great deal of literature on the various cruise lines indicating their specific itinerary. You'll also find a wealth of information in certain magazines such as ***Cruise Travel Magazine*, *Travel and Leisure***, and ***Travel/Holiday***.

Since the Caribbean is usually calm year around, cruises are available throughout most of the year. However, September, October and November are hurricane months, and thus cruise ships may change itineraries should a tropical storm occur.

YACHTING TIPS AND PORTS OF ENTRY

Chartering your own yacht either with or without a crew is a popular way to visit the islands. All sizes are available for charter and for virtually any length of time, but most are limited to a week or longer.

Several companies specialize in chartering or outfitting yachts. Among the many are: Caribbean Sailing Yachts Limited, Box 491, Tenafly, NJ 07670 (201-568-3039 or 800-631-1593); Nicholson Yacht Charters, 9 Chauncey Street, Cambridge, MA 02138 (617-661-0181); West Indies Yacht Charters, 2190 Southeast 17th Street, Ft. Lauderdale, FL 33316 (800-327-2290); Tortolla Yacht Charters, 5825 Sunset Drive, South Miami, FL 33143 (800-243-2455); The Moorings Limited, 1305 U.S. 19 South, Suite 402, Clearwater, FL 33546 (800-535-7289); Worldwide Yacht Charters, 145 King Street, West, Toronto, Ontario M5H 1J8 (416-365-1950); and World Yacht Enterprises, Pier 62, West 23rd Street, Hudson River, New York, NY 10011 (212-929-7090).

While this mode of transportation is very relaxing and enjoyable, the responsibility is yours or the crews to inquire how to arrive and disembark at the various ports of entry. In some cases, such as Haiti, very specific planning is a must. You may have to be receive permission several days prior to arrival to enter a particular port. The chartering companies will have all of this information. However, if you are planning to arrive on your own, check with the tourist information offices of the specific islands prior to your departure.

TOURIST INFORMATION SERVICE

You'll find a tremendous amount of literature available on hotels and shopping in the Caribbean. In addition to information found in many magazines, such as ***Caribbean Travel and Life***, all islands have tourist offices. The Caribbean Tourism Authority (200 East 46th Street, New York, NY 10017, 212-682-0435), for example, provides a great deal of information as do many of the following island tourist offices:

- **Anquilla:** Anquilla Tourist Information and Reservation Office, c/o Medhurst & Associates, 775 Park Ave., Huntington, NY 11743 (516-425-0900 or 800-553-4939).

- **Aruba:** Aruba Tourism Authority, 1000 Harbor Blvd., Weehawken, NJ 07087 (201-330-0800 or 800-862-7822); 2344 Salzedo St., Miami, FL 33134 (305-567-2720); 86 Bloor St. W., Suite 204, Toronto, Ontario M5S 1M5 (416-975-1950).

- **The Bahamas:** Bahamas Tourist Office: Headquarters—150 E. 52nd Street, New York, NY 10022 (212-758-2777). Other offices—120 Bloor Street, Suite 1101, Toronto, Ontario M4W 3M5 (416-968-2999); 1255 Phillips Square, Montreal, Quebec H3B 3G1 (514-861-6797); 2957 Clairmont Road, Suite 150, Atlanta, GA 30345 (404-633-1793); 1027 Statler Office Building, Boston, MA 02116 (617-426-3144); 875 North Michigan Avenue, Suite 1816, Chicago, IL 60611 (312-787-8203); World Trade Center, Suite 186, Stemmons Freeway, Dallas, TX 75258-1408 (214-742-1886); 5177 Richmond Avenue, Suite 755, Houston, TX 77056 (713-626-1566); 26400 Lahser Road, Suite 309, Smithfield, MI 48034 (313-357-2940); 255 Alhambra Circle, Suite 425, Coral Gables, FL 33134 (305-442-4860); 3450 Wilshire Boulevard, Los Angeles, CA 90010 (213-385-0033); 44 Montgomery Center, Suite 503, San Francisco, CA 94104 (415-398-5502); 1730 Rhode Island Avenue, NW, Washington, DC 20036 (202-659-9135); Lafayette Building, 437 Chestnut Street, Room 212, Philadelphia, PA 19106 (215-925-0871); 470 Grandville Street, Suite 129, Vancouver, British Columbia V6C 1V5 (604-688-8334).

- **Barbados:** Barbados Board of Tourism, 800 Second Avenue, New York, NY 10017 (212-986-6516); 3440 Wilshire Boulevard, Suite 1215, Los Angeles, CA 90010 (213-380-2198); 20 Queens Street, West, Suite 1508, Box 11, Toronto, Ontario M5H 3R3 (416-979-2137); 615 Dorchester Boulevard, West, Suite 960, Montreal, Quebec H3B 1P5 (514-861-0085 or 800-268-9122).

- **Bermuda:** Bermuda Department of Tourism, 310 Madison Avenue, Suite 201, New York, NY 10017 (212-818-9800); 44 School Street, Suite 1010, Boston, MA 02108 (617-742-0405); 150 North Wacker Drive, Suite 1070, Chicago, IL 60606 (312-782-5468); 235 Peachtree Street, NE, Suite 2001, Atlanta, GA 30303 (404-524-1541); 1200 Bay Street, Suite 1004, Toronto, Ontario M5R 2A5 (416-923-9600).

- **Dominican Republic:** Dominican Tourist Information Center, 1 Times Square, New York, NY 10022 (212-768-2480); and the Dominican Republic Tourist Office, 2355 Sanzedo Street, Coral Gables, FL 23134 (305-444-4592); 1464 Crescent St., Montreal, Quebec, H3A 2B6 (514-933-6126).

- **Haiti:** Haiti National Office of Tourism, 488 Madison Avenue, Suite 1505, New York, NY 10022 (212-757-6492); 17620 Northeast Second Court, North Miami Beach, FL 33162 (305-651-3487); Consulate General of Haiti, 60 East 42nd Street, 13th Floor, New York, NY 10165 (212-697-9767); 330 Biscayne Boulevard, Suite 808, Miami, FL 33132 (305-377-3547); 919 North Michigan Avenue, Chicago, IL 60611 (312-337-1603); 2311 Massachusetts Avenue, NW, Washington, DC 20008 (202-332-4090). Also represented by consulates at: 71 Dunmurray Boulevard, Toronto-Scarborough, Ontario M1T 2K2 (416-886-3398); 44 Fundy Etage F, Pl. Bonadventure, Montreal, Quebec H5A 1A9 (514-871-8893). The Haitian government does not keep all of these offices open all of the time. If you find an office closed, write directly to the Washington, DC address. This office seems to provide the most thorough and helpful information on Haiti—including everything that's also available upon arrival in Haiti.

- **Jamaica:** Jamaica Tourist Board, 801 Second Avenue, 10th Floor, New York, NY 10017 (212-856-9727); 1320 South Dixie Highway, Coral Gables, FL 33146 (305-665-0557); 500 N. Michigan Ave., Suite 1030, Chicago, IL 60611 (312-527-1296); 8215 Westchester, Suite 500, Dallas, TX 75225 (214-361-8778); 3440 Wilshire Boulevard, Suite 1207, Los Angeles, CA 90010 (213-384-1123); 1110 Sherbrooke Street, West, Montreal, Quebec H3A 1G9 (514-849-6387); 1 Eglinton Avenue, East, Suite 616, Toronto, Ontario M4P 3A1 (416-482-7850).

- **Martinique:** French West Indies Tourist Board, 610 Fifth Ave., New York, NY 10020 (212-757-1125); 9401 Wilshire Blvd., Beverly Hills, CA 90212 (310-271-6665); 656 N. Michigan Ave., Suite 430, Chicago, IL 60611 (312-751-7800); 2305 Cedar Spring Rd., Dallas, TX 75201 (214-720-4010); 1981 Ave. McGill College, Suite 90, Montreal, Quebec H3A 2W9 (514-288-4264);

1 Dundas St., W., Suite 2405, Toronto, Ontario M5G 1Z3 (416-593-4723 or 800-361-9099).

- **Puerto Rico:** Government of Puerto Rico Tourism Company, 575 5th Avenue, New York, NY 10017 (212-599-6262); 4301 Spruce Street, Suite B201; Philadelphia, PA 19104 (215-387-2913); P.O. Box 8053, Falls Church, VA 22041-8053 (703-671-0930); 11 East Adams Street, Chicago, IL 60603 (312-922-9701); 2635 Century Parkway, Suite 780, Atlanta, GA 30345 (404-279-0042); 200 Southeast First Street, Suite 903, Miami, FL 33131 (305-381-8915); 8724 Tall Pine Lane, Orlando, FL 32817 (407-273-0383); 501 Brandon Street, Grand Prairie (Dallas), TX 75051 (214-262-2903); 12893 Westheimer Street, Suite 230, Houston, TX 77077 (713-870-9202); 1161 South Birch Street, Suite 208, Denver, CO 80222 (303-759-1539); 2043 East Broadway, Long Beach, CA 90803 (213-433-4431); 2504 Maryland Circle, Petaluma, CA 94952 (707-762-3468); 3575 West Cahuenga Boulevard, Suite 248, Los Angeles, CA 90068 (213-874-5991).

- **St. Lucia:** St. Lucia Tourist Board, 820 2nd Ave., 9th Floor, New York, NY 10017 (212-867-2950 or 800-456-3984); 4975 Dundas St. W., Suite 457, Etobicoke D, Islington, Ontario M9A 4X4 (800-456-3984).

- **Sint Maarten:** Sint Maarten Tourist Office, 275 Seventh Avenue, 19th Floor, New York, NY 10001-6788 (212-989-0000) or 243 Ellerslie Avenue, Willowdale-Toronto, Ontario M2N 1Y4 (416-223-3501).

- **St. Martin:** French West Indies Tourist Board, 610 Fifth Ave., New York, NY 10020 (212-757-1125); 9401 Wilshire Blvd, Beverly Hills, CA 90212 (310-271-2358); 656 N. Michigan Ave., Suite 430, Chicago, IL 60611 (312-751-7800); 2305 Cedar Spring Rd., Dallas, TX 75201 (214-720-4010); 1981 Ave. McGill College, Suite 490, Montreal, Quebec H3A 2W9 (514-288-4264); 1 Dundas Street, West, Suite 2405, Toronto, Ontario M5G 1Z3 (416-593-4723 or 800-361-9099).

- **U.S. Virgin Islands:** U.S. Virgin Islands Division of Tourism, 1270 Avenue of the Americas, New York, NY 10020 (212-332-2222); 7270 Northwest 12th Street, Suite 620, Miami, FL 33126 (305-591-2070); 900 17th

St., Washington, DC 20006 (202-293-3707); 122 S. Michigan Avenue, Suite 1270, Chicago, IL 60603 (312-461-0180); 235 Peachtree Center, Suite 1420, Atlanta, GA 30303 (404-688-0906); 2655 Le June Rd., Suite 907, Coral Gables, FL (305-442-7200); 3460 Wilshire Boulevard, Suite 412, Los Angeles, CA 90010 (213-739-0138); 1300 Ashford Avenue, Condado, Santurce, Puerto Rico 00907 (809-724-3816).

Once arriving in the islands, check for information at the airports, cruise ship terminals, and various hotels. Some local papers, small tourist booklets, and travel books list the latest activities as well as new shopping opportunities. Many will mention special sales taking place during your stay.

Immigration Tips

Every island requires you to fill out some sort of Immigration form, and proof of citizenship is required in all islands. Driver's license and other forms of identification are insufficient. Although a certified copy of a birth certificate (not the hospital certificate) will suffice in most cases, a passport is most convenient. Traveling with a passport eliminates all questions of citizenship and speeds the entry process.

Upon arrival at any island airport, be prepared to show proof of citizenship and present your completed Immigration form. The form will normally ask for your destination—where you plan to stay. In most cases a general statement identifying a hotel or area will suffice. You will receive a copy of this form. Be sure you safeguard it along with your proof of citizenship. Your copy must be returned when you leave. Losing it can greatly delay your departure.

Many islands require an on-going or return ticket. We have been asked to show this on islands such as Anguilla, even if passing through on our way to Sint Maarten to shop, and in the Bahamas. If you can not show such proof, you may be asked to post a bond to ensure that you will have enough money for your return trip.

The immigration process in most islands is fairly casual and normally very swift. The only exception will be at some of the larger airports such as Sint Maarten or San Juan when a number of jumbo jets arrive at the same time. When this happens, the lines can become extremely long. Pay close attention to the directions and signs; try to get to the Immigration desk as soon after you depart the plane as possible.

UNITED STATES CUSTOMS

Although you will frequently see the words "duty-free" throughout the Caribbean, keep in mind what "duty-free" really means. In most cases, the term indicates that duty was not paid on goods brought into that island for resale. It does not mean that you may take those items back home duty-free. Upon returning to the U.S., you are allowed to bring in $400 or $600 (depending on the island) worth of goods of any kind as long as you have been out of the country for at least 48 hours and have not claimed this personal exemption within the last 30 days. The limit is higher for the U.S. Virgin Islands—$1000 per person rather than the normal $400. There are specific limitations on certain items, such as liquor and wine, even if they are within your exemption limit. The best source of the current regulations is a booklet published by the U.S. Customs Service entitled ***Know Before You Go***. This may be obtained from any local U.S. Custom Service office (check under the U.S. Department of Treasury in your telephone book) or by mail: U.S. Customs Service, Box 7407, Washington, DC 20044.

It's always good to know before you go the exact amounts charged by Customs on certain items you are likely to purchase in the Caribbean. For most items, the duty charged on the first $1,000 over your limit is a flat 10% rate. A purchase may still be a good bargain if you buy it at a price which is 30-50% below the normal U.S. price. However, some of the Customs duties after the first $1400 may be quite high—up to 20% for crystal, 26% for certain china tableware, and 27.5% for silver. If you have purchased that beautiful set of dishes at an excellent price—20% off the price back home—but then have to pay 26% duty on it, such an excellent buy becomes expensive. You may decide to purchase that beautiful piece of crystal anyway, however, because you can't find it at home at any price. Our point is to know what you are doing and make a decision based on knowledge. Also, avoid the game of having an invoice or receipt made in an amount lower than you actually paid. U.S. Customs inspectors know what prices are charged for jewelry, china, crystal, silver, and gold in the Caribbean.

You should also be aware that in some instances you may have no duty to pay at all. Some items, for example, are indeed duty-free:

- Original Caribbean art work, whether paintings or sculptures.

- Hand-made Caribbean furniture.
- Antiques that are more than 100 years old.
- Handwoven textile products produced in the Caribbean.
- Certain unset precious stones, such as diamonds, emeralds, and sapphires.

Upon re-entering the US with any of these items, be prepared to **prove** the duty-free status. We have found that a certificate from the shopkeeper, a written statement of authenticity from a gallery, or even a handwritten note signed by the artist will normally suffice. Indeed, we've returned with original art on many occasions with no problem, but we prepared for Customs. We found the most expedient way to handle items that are valued far above the exemption is to declare the full value on the front of the Customs form, and then explain the exemption on the reverse side. , Our best record for one trip was four pieces of original Haitian art (one 6 feet by 10 feet!), five Voodoo flags, six stone sculptures, and 15 hand-carved wood figures—all entered the U.S. duty-free.

Being knowledgeable about duty requirements can save you time and money. Such knowledge may also save you a long delay and prevent you from actually losing a treasure. The U.S. Customs regulations, in addition to setting duties, also list items that you may not bring into the country. Most notable are many animal products, food products, live plants, tortoise shell items, ivory products, and many counterfeit products such as fashions, watches, cameras and electronics which are covered by the U.S. trademarks laws. Customs officials can confiscate prohibited items. Do not listen to a shopkeeper in regard to prohibited items since they are more interested in making a sale than in what will happen when you try to get the item through Customs back home.

Again, the best plan for worry-free shopping in the Caribbean is to **know before you go**.

CUSTOMS REGULATIONS IN THE CARIBBEAN

Other countries also have custom regulations, and the countries of the Caribbean are no exception. This only presents a problem for you if you plan to island hop. Remember, if you enter a country—even if only for a day or two on your way elsewhere —you are subject to the Customs regulations of that country. Most islands allow visitors to bring in all wearing apparel and articles for personal use, including sports equipment, cameras, and golf bags. In addition, you may claim a gift allowance (normally $25-100). Firearms are prohibited on most islands. Normally a limit is placed on the amount of liquor and wine, tobacco products, foodstuffs, and meats. It is possible you might have to pay duty on some items you purchased elsewhere. Even on the islands that are ostensibly "duty-free," regulations do protect local merchants. While not a major problem, you may want to check on local regulations if you plan to stop on your way home after doing serious shopping on another island.

CLIMATE

Although the climate varies from island to island and sometimes from one side of the island to the other, the Caribbean is generally warm most of the year. In the winter, temperatures throughout the Caribbean range somewhere between 70 and 80 degrees with slightly cooler temperatures in the higher elevations. It may also be approximately five to ten degrees cooler at night. In the summer, the temperatures rarely go above 90 degrees which makes most of the islands in the Caribbean actually slightly cooler during the summer than many U.S. cities. In addition to not having 100 degree temperatures, most of the islands will feel cooler because of the ever-present tradewinds.

- ❑ **The Caribbean is generally warm most of the year. Winter temperatures range between 70 and 80 degrees. Summer temperatures rarely go above 90 degrees.**
- ❑ **Keep in mind that autumn is the hurricane season throughout the Caribbean.**
- ❑ **The "off season" runs from late April to early December —a time for good savings on air travel packages and hotels and a great time to shop without crowds.**

Technically located outside the Caribbean, Bermuda's weather differs from the other islands. Its temperatures are much cooler. We have been in Bermuda in November and found that a light jacket or sweater is necessary most of the time. On rainy days, a heavier jacket may be required. However, even though the winter months are slightly cooler, Bermuda can be delightful any time, especially for shopping. In fact, the ideal month to travel to some islands, such as Bermuda, is November. This is not normally a high travel month for families, and you are ahead of the seasonal rush which starts around mid-December. At this time of year shopkeepers are more relaxed, have more time to spend with you, restaurants are readily available, and hotel accommodations are seldom a problem.

Keep in mind that autumn is the hurricane season throughout the Caribbean. However, even though hurricanes and storms may occur, it certainly should not dissuade you from traveling during those months. Just be sure to check weather service reports on any impending storms that could affect your travel plans.

THE "OFF SEASON"

Since most travelers go to the Caribbean to escape cold winter months, the heaviest travel occurs from mid-December to mid-April. The rest of the year is commonly known throughout the Caribbean as the "off season." Lower fares are available for air travel as well as hotel accommodations at this time. You will find good savings on air travel packages, and hotel prices are between 30% to 60% lower during the off season. In addition, you will find many islands have properties and villas available during the off season that are virtually booked solid for years in advance during the winter months. It is not unusual to find special promotions available such as free bottles of spirits, many discount coupons and booklets for meals and shopping, and good fees for recreational activities.

Since the off season is approximately twice as long as the high season, you'll have many opportunities to visit and shop virtually any island on your list. During this time of the year we can leisurely shop and talk with shopkeepers since we are often the only customers in the store. During the winter months, some of those shops may be very difficult to approach. Many of the popular and famous restaurants that require reservations three or four nights in advance during the winter months are readily available during the off season for last minute diners. The quality the food also differs during the off season. Since the kitchens are not rushed, the chefs—and in some smaller restaurants the owners—take more time to prepare a delightful meal.

LANGUAGE

Although Spanish is the official language for the Dominican Republic and Puerto Rico, French for Haiti, Martinique, and Sint Maarten, and Dutch for St. Martin, English is readily spoken and understood everywhere in the Caribbean. Although spoken English may take many forms, you will have no problem conversing. However, if you do not speak Spanish or French and plan to shop in remote areas outside the major cities in the Dominican Republic or Haiti, a guide should prove most helpful. In both countries, if you are dealing with a local artisan or a shopkeeper outside the major areas, much gets lost in the translation when bargaining. Although we have put great faith in our guides at various times, if you do not speak the local language, you'll have difficulty knowing what is included in the price—which may include a tip for your guide.

CURRENCY, TRAVELER'S CHECKS, AND CREDIT CARDS

U.S. currency is readily accepted everywhere in the Caribbean. However, you may find the local currency has advantages in certain bargaining situations. When you bargain with the local currency, for example, you don't have to negotiate an exchange rate after settling on a price.

Because U.S. dollars are readily accepted, you will find many prices stated in dollars. But be sure to inquire whether prices are stated in U.S., Bahamian, Bermudian, or Barbadian dollars or any other local currency. This is not a problem on islands such as the Bahamas or Bermuda where the local dollars are roughly equivalent to the U.S. dollar. However, if a price in Barbados is stated as $50 and you think this is in U.S. dollars but the shopkeeper actually expects 50 Barbadian dollars, you'll pay twice the local price by paying US$50.

The exchange rate throughout the Caribbean fluctuates little. You'll find the following official currencies and exchange rates for the islands: Eastern Caribbean Dollar (2.70 EC to US#1) (Anguilla); Bahamian dollar ($1 to US$1); Bermudian dollar ($1 to US$1); Barbadian dollar (approximately $2-$2.20 to US$1); Dominican Republic gold peso ($12.30 to 12.50 pesos to US$1); Haitian gourde (5 gourdes to US$1); French franc (approximately 4.5 francs to US$1) (St. Martin and Martinique); Jamaican dollar (approximately 22 to 30 Jamaican dollars to US$1); Netherlands Antillies florin or guilder (1.8 Naf to US#1) (Aruba and Sint Maarten). The U.S. dollar is the official currency in both Puerto Rico and the U.S. Virgin Islands.

While we do not advise carrying large amounts of cash on any trip, in some out-of-the-way places, cash is best. Although most of the larger shops will take traveler's checks or credit cards, many of the small shops and artisans outside the main cities do not. Be sure to have plenty of small cash for tipping and taxi fairs ($1 or $5 denominations) as well as for small shops ($25 and $50 denominations). Take traveler's checks for large purchases in major shopping areas, but cash checks as you go so you always have cash for small purchases and getting around town. Do not assume that the smaller shops will be able to cash a $100 traveler's check unless your purchase is for nearly that amount. When exchanging traveler's checks at a shop, bank, exchange counter, or hotel, be sure to ask if they have that amount of currency available prior to countersigning the check. If you want U.S. dollars, you must specify this currency before making the transaction. In most cases, you will be given local currency for traveler's checks—unless you specify otherwise.

Exchange rates and service charges vary depending on where you convert your money. Hotels and shops will give you less than banks. You may have to pay a separate fee for the transaction. Many exchange places are not open 24-hours a day. Even in some major hotels, the exchange desk may be open only a few hours a day. It is virtually impossible to convert traveler's checks to local currency in the evening.

Traveler's checks most readily accepted in the Caribbean are issued by American Express, Bank of America, Citicorp, MasterCard, or Visa.

Credit cards are most convenient for paying hotel and restaurant bills as well as for making major purchases. Cash is better when making smaller purchases. Indeed, your bargaining power is best when you offer to pay in cash. If you try to use a credit card, many merchants will add a 10% fee to the bargained price to defray their banking costs. The most widely accepted credit cards are American Express, Visa, MasterCard, Diners Club, and Carte Blanche.

You may want to use your credit cards for large purchases since some of these companies automatically insure purchases against breakage when you use their card. Also, if you later discover something you purchased was misrepresented, your credit card company may assist you in resolving the problem. Check with your credit card company as to their policies.

Some shops will accept personal checks if you present proper identification—your passport or a major credit card. Personal checks are generally accepted by local artists and small shops.

One word of caution when exchanging money. We recommend using the standard places of exchange such as a bank, a specifically designated exchange, your hotel, or the major shops. Beware if you are approached by people offering a much higher exchange rate for local currency. It is not uncommon to receive counterfeit currency from these people. This black market exchange is illegal in most countries.

It's also good to take an extra personal check or two to handle any customs duties you may have to pay when returning home.

TIPPING AND COMMISSIONS

Many hotels and restaurants add a 10% to 15% service charge to your bills. While this is not a universal practice, ask if it is included before tipping. Tipping on cruise ships is a different matter. Please read your cruise literature carefully to understand the tipping procedures. Some ships provide passengers with good directions on how much and whom to tip. When in doubt, ask the purser who will be glad to give you guidelines.

While you may be used to tipping porters, bellmen, chambermaids, and waiters, in the Caribbean many taxi drivers and guides also expect tips. Since taxis are not metered in most islands, you must settle on a fare prior to entering the cab. Most taxi drivers throughout the Caribbean are honest, and many associations controlling the cabs or the hotels have standard posted rates. It is common, however, to include an additional 10% to 15% tip for the taxi driver. This is not mandatory nor always expected, but it is appreciated.

Many guides who help you shop also expect tips. The two islands where such guides are most available, and often a necessity, are the Dominican Republic and Haiti. When shopping in parts of Santo Domingo, a guide will immediately approach you upon entering some of the shopping districts. If you decide to use their services, you should immediately agree on how the guide will be compensated. In Santo Domingo most guides in the downtown area are paid by the shopkeepers. That, of course, means their "commission" fee is included in whatever price you pay the merchant. Such guides should not be tipped. Haiti, however, is another case. In places like the Iron Market in Port-au-Prince, for example, some guides are reimbursed by the shopkeeper but others are not. In those cases, it is acceptable to initially ask how their services will be compensated. In Haiti the acceptable amount is 10% of the purchases, whether the guide be in Port-au-Prince, Petionville, Cap Haitian or in Jacmel. In some countries, if an individual has made special arrangements for you to meet with a specific artist or artisan, and that individual is not associated with a travel association or a tour group, you may be asked to compensate the guide at the rate of 5% to 10% of your purchase.

HEALTH TIPS

Your major health concerns in the Caribbean will be sunburn, insects, diarrhea, and upset stomach. Since the entire Caribbean is located near the equator, you can quickly burn after only an hour or two in the sun. You should be prepared with appropriate suntan products which you should bring with you to the Caribbean. In some areas it is virtually impossible to find anything other than a local product, often priced much higher than products available in the U.S.

Although the insect problem, especially mosquitos, has been lessened on most islands by spraying, these little pests can still be annoying. You should definitely pack a good insect repellent and some bug spray. These products are not readily available in the islands and are a necessity—especially if you are near the water at sundown. Many islands also have small gnats known as "noseeums." They are virtually impossible to see, but you will recognize their ankle bites the next morning. The best way to avoid this problem is to use an insect repellent—especially if you do not have air-conditioned accommodations. If your hotel is air-conditioned, turn the thermostat down slightly since both mosquitos and other bugs avoid cold temperatures.

The most troublesome health problems are diarrhea and upset stomach. The best way to avoid these problems is to avoid drinking local water unless you known it is purified. On some islands, such as the U.S. Virgin Islands, Bermuda and the Bahamas, tap water is okay to drink. In other countries the water is definitely not potable. In fact, in both Haiti and the Dominican Republic many local people drink bottled or boiled water. Check with your doctor for medications, but we find Imodium AD or Kaopectate to be two of the best over-the-counter products. There are also prescription remedies available if you believe you may need something stronger. Keep in mind that prolonged diarrhea and upset stomach can cause lasting problems. If the problem persists for more than a day or two, you should seek medical help. However, if you consume only boiled, bottled, and sealed drinks and avoid eating unpeeled fruits or uncooked vegetables, you should have no such health problems.

POWER FAILURES

Power failures have become a way of life in some islands. They occur almost daily in some places. Be sure to pack a small pocket flashlight for such occasions. In some larger hotels, power outages will go virtually unnoticed since these hotels have their own backup generators. Many shops also have generators that can be turned on during power failures.

You may also want to pack a candle and matches for occasional power outages at night. In some areas you can purchase candles. But, again, it's best to have these items with you when you most need them. Shopping for candles in the dark is not our idea of adventure!

PACKING FOR YOUR TRIP

Since your main goal is to be comfortable when you travel and shop, you should pack as little as possible yet organize your wardrobe so you can dress properly for most social occasions. The best way to do this in the Caribbean is to:

- Organize your travel wardrobe around a single color or very few colors. Obviously whites are acceptable virtually any time of the year, and a white skirt or white trousers can go with any color blouse or shirt. Do not feel that you have to bring a separate outfit for every day since most of the hotels and resort facilities throughout the Caribbean do have laundry facilities.

- Cottons or any natural fabrics are much more comfortable than synthetics. Since synthetic fibers do not breathe, you may quickly become uncomfortable wearing such clothing in hot and humid temperatures.

- If you visit such places as Bermuda during the summer months, you should take light-weight summer clothes, including a light jacket or sweater. Take a heavier coat or jacket during the winter months.

- For the Bahamas and most of the islands, spring or summer clothing is acceptable and practical during most of the year.

- Pack clothes that have pockets so that you can easily carry your traveler's checks, passports, and other documents. Do not leave such items in your hotel room. They are much safer with you.

We have traveled throughout the Caribbean for two weeks at a time and only needed one suitcase and a carry on. If you carefully select colors, types of clothing, and keep in mind that most dress is casual, you can eliminate a lot of extra weight. By taking fewer items, you'll have more room to carry home your new shopping treasures. Traveling light also will be more convenient if you decide to island-hop using some of the smaller aircraft. You'll avoid excess baggage charges for clothing you didn't use.

Dress and Local Protocol

Normal daytime wear for shopping is a lightweight dress or skirt and blouse or long pants and a sport shirt. In most islands, bathing suits are not acceptable in the shopping areas.

Since the islanders are extremely conservative people, beach apparel is not appropriate in town or in shopping districts or stores. Larger restaurants and resort hotels may recommend a jacket and tie. However, during the last few years ties have virtually disappeared—except in Bermuda—and jackets are recommended rather than required in most cases. A lightweight dress for the women and either white pants or light grey pants with a summer weight blue blazer is all that's necessary even in the finest restaurants and hotels.

If you travel by cruise ship, the dress code for your particular ship will suffice for shopping in the islands. Again, some cruise ships do have some activities that require more formal wear than a bathing suit and a sport shirt. On cruise ships men are appropriately dressed in a lightweight sport coat worn over a sport shirt and women are fine wearing a lightweight dress. Cruising through the Caribbean is more informal than cruising to Europe.

Shipping or Hand-Carrying Your Treasures Home

The joys of shopping and finding something special should also be accompanied by knowledge of how you will get your purchases home. Since the Caribbean is so close to the U.S. mainland, some of the nightmares of shipping from Europe or Asia, especially time delays, are not at issue.

In most countries in the Caribbean you will have three alternatives available to you for shipping or bringing goods home:

- Do it yourself through the postal services or international shipping companies such as DHL, UPS, or Federal Express.
- Let a local shipper or the shops ship your purchases.
- Pack or wrap the items so they may be carried on board your cruise ship or airplane, or checked as baggage.

We've tried all three alternatives with varying results. Arranging to ship the goods yourself may be cheaper, but doing so may take an inordinate amount of time in some locations. Many islands do not have large postal facilities with convenient hours nor have numerous outlets for international shippers. In some cases, you will have to locate packing materials and tape. Indeed, we have actually paid more in taxi fares to get to a post office or shipping company than we would have paid to have the shopkeeper do the shipping. In addition, regulations as to size and weight are different in each location. On the plus side, however, we have successfully sent many items through the mail from St. Thomas, San Juan, Freeport, Nassau, and Bermuda. We also have found the offices of DHL, UPS, and Federal Express in such places as Haiti and the Dominican Republic to be easy to find and most helpful.

On the other hand, most of the shops specializing in exquisite china or crystal are skilled at packing the more delicate items. They often pack the items free and only charge you for the actual postage or air freight charges. If you choose to have them ship your goods, insist upon a receipt specifying when they will ship the item. Also, stress the importance of packing the item well to avoid possible damage. If they cannot insure the item against breakage or loss, find another shipper. Invariably a version of Murphy's Law operates when shipping delicate or expensive items: **If it is not insured and has the potential to break or get lost, it will surely break or get lost!** Unless you are definitely planning to carry the item with you, shipping more than one or two items is best arranged by a reputable shop.

If you plan to purchase large items, such as wrought iron or mahogany furniture in Haiti, or a large antique piece elsewhere, use a local shipper. Shipping charges are usually figured by volume, and the shipping can be done either by air or sea. While air freight is more expensive than sea transport for large and heavy items, the shipping time for air freight is a matter of days rather than weeks. It is relatively easy to get information on local companies either through the place of purchase or the local Yellow Pages. If you buy from a very small vendor, or even from a street vendor, you will have to make all shipping arrangements yourself. You should definitely check on this before committing to purchase any large item in Haiti or the Dominican Republic since many small shops or street vendors do not have telephones, let alone shipping capabilities.

When shipping or mailing from the islands, you must prepare the appropriate shipping and Customs documents, and, of course, arrange for Customs clearance back home. You may send yourself or others gifts not exceeding $50 as long as no more than one package arrives on the same day ($100 from the U.S. Virgin Islands); all other items are subject to duty. Remember, items not carried through Customs do not qualify as "duty free" items when shipped.

Cruise ship passengers may be forced to ship purchases home. Most ship cabins are small, and some ships limit what you can bring on board to store in your cabin. Some vessels have other storage facilities, but it is best to check with the purser if you are contemplating purchasing a large or bulky item that will not fit into your baggage. The same is true if you are thinking about purchasing an additional suitcase or bag.

Since many beautiful and treasured items you will find in the Caribbean are not large, your luggage should satisfy your shipping needs. But occasionally you may purchase large items which do not fit into your luggage, or fragile items which require special packing and handling. We normally pack two extra soft-sided bags, brown wrapping paper, a roll of strong strapping tape, a small roll of twine, and a few sheets of plastic bubble-wrap. These items lessen the probability of damage and save us time by not having to find such items on the local market. The bubble-wrap will protect your delicate purchases, such as china items or small sculptures, from damage caused by baggage handling. A nylon strap or two, extra luggage tags, and a small handle that can be taped to a box or slipped under the twine often come in handy.

If you buy large paintings, the safest and most convenient way to carry them is to remove them from the frame, cover the surface with polyethylene or a good grade of thin paper used by many galleries, roll them around a sturdy tube, and then wrap them with brown shipping paper and tape.

Finding packing materials in some locations is a real problem if not nearly impossible. Taking a few items with you will not only save you time, but will go a long way toward ensuring that your purchases arrive home intact.

GATHER THE RIGHT INFORMATION

Depending on what you plan to buy, you should take all the necessary information you need to make those important shopping decisions. If you are looking for home furnishings, along with your "wish list" you should include room measurements to help determine if the item will fit into your home. You might take photographs and wall measurements of particular rooms you hope to furnish. Be sure to include measurements of dining tables and beds since you will find wonderful table linens and bedspreads in many locations throughout the Caribbean.

Comparison shop before you depart if you are considering cameras, watches, or electronic items. You may find wonderful prices in many areas, but these still may be slightly higher than you will find at many discount outlets at home.

Jewelry is another item you will need to price as well as learn more about if you are not an expert. Read about how to determine quality, and learn about color, clarity, carat weight, and cuts. Visit jewelry stores at home to learn how to identify quality and compare prices. Ask salespeople questions, especially about craftsmanship, settings, quality and discounts. You can get terrific buys on jewelry, gems, and watches in the Caribbean if you know what you are doing. Most people, however, are simply overwhelmed by the choices confronting them in St. Thomas, Sint Maarten, Bermuda, The Bahamas, and Barbados. Novices shopping for fine jewelry in the Caribbean often end up with much less than they had bargained for. Although most shops in the islands are very reputable, some shoppers think they were getting a **steal** and then later discover it was the shop that got the real steal!

4

Shopping the Islands

While you'll fall in love with the many exquisite products in the Caribbean, knowing how to shop can be equally as important as knowing what to buy. Some items are the same or similar to what you could find at home, but with a significantly lower price tag. Others are one-of-a-kind items that may be difficult to compare; their uniqueness rather than price may be your foremost consideration.

Do Your Homework

How do you know if you're getting a good deal or acquiring quality products? Chances are you don't, unless you've done some basic homework prior to departing on your Caribbean adventure. Once you're in Caribbean shops, you'll discover how important it is to know the price of similar merchandise at home as well as what to look for to determine the quality of jewelry, designer clothing, or other products you may purchase. If you've not done your homework, you won't know if a seemingly great price is a bargain or not.

Since the turnover of stock in the Islands is rapid, you should find the latest merchandise in most shops. Sizes should not pose a problem since most clothing is in U.S. sizes—ordered especially for the numerous buyers from the States—except on some of the French Islands, and these sizes are easy to convert.

Timing of your trip can make a difference in the prices and quality of merchandise. Most sales occur during the off-season when the merchandise is cleared for the large shipments arriving for the next high tourist season. So you decide whether you would prefer the additional discounts of the off-season or the larger, perhaps fresher, selection of the peak season.

TAX FREE SHOPPING

There are many terms given to the various types of tax free shopping found in the Caribbean. The three most common are duty-free, in-bond, and freeport shopping.

Duty-free shops sell goods that are imported without the imposition of many taxes. You can purchase such items at lower prices because the taxes are very low or non-existent.

In-bond shopping is a version of duty-free purchasing. Items are held in bonded warehouses where they are treated as if they never actually entered the country. Therefore, no duty is charged on the import. When an item is purchased in-bond, delivery is made directly to the airport or cruise ship. Some islands now also allow the items to be hand carried by the purchaser if proper documentation is shown to indicate that the purchaser is a visitor and is traveling on to other islands or back to the U.S.

Freeport shopping relates to items made in the motherland that are not taxed. A good example are French perfumes that are tax free in St. Martin and Martinique.

Duty-free also refers to cases where no duty is charged by the U.S. on certain items purchased in the islands. This is especially true for locally produced arts and crafts, such as most straw goods, local spices, art, and carved wood items. This is due to the Generalized System of Preferences (GSP) which is intended to encourage cottage industries and help the economies of particular countries.

U.S. Customs allows citizens to bring back from U.S. Territories $1200 worth of duty-free items. This includes up to five liters of liquor per adult. If your purchases exceed the dollar allowance, only 10% duty is charged on the next $1000. Gifts may also be mailed home daily as long as only one arrives at a single address on the same day and the value is $100 or less. U.S. Customs allows $400 or $600 (depending on the island) of duty-free items from islands that are not U.S. territories (plus a $50 dollar a day allowance for mailed gifts), one liter of liquor plus a normal supply of cigarettes for personal use.

Since customs regulations do change, it's a good idea to check the specific regulations in effect **before** you depart on your trip.

WHERE TO BARGAIN

We would like to think that bargaining exists everywhere and to some extent it does. Some high ticket items such as gemstones are always open to negotiation. Art can often be purchased directly from the artists at a fraction of what you would pay from a dealer.

Straw markets are good places to bargain. Most street vendors will reduce the price about 25% after a little bargaining, even in Charlotte Amalie, St Thomas. This is especially true in the summertime when there are fewer tourists around and business is slower. In the Bahamas, Martinique and Jamaica try to visit the straw markets when the cruise ships are not in town. Not only will you avoid heavy crowds, your negotiations will result in better prices. You should always bargain at roadside stands—especially in Jamaica and the Dominican Republic. A visit to a factory will also give you an opportunity to test your bargaining skills.

HOW TO BARGAIN

In Bermuda bargains are primarily found at sales. If you try to negotiate here, the shopkeeper will politely let you know that everything is tagged and prices are fixed. But make an appointment with an artist either at the studio or through the Bermuda Department of Tourism, and there is room for traditional bargaining. This is usually about 20% to 25% off the requested price especially in the winter which is off season here.

On the other hand, in the Dominican Republic and Haiti—at the famous Mercado Modelo and Iron Market—you will see few if any items priced. If you show any interest in a product or ask "How much?", the bargaining process will begin. Always start bargaining at one half or less of the requested price and work up to a compromise that is comfortable or acceptable to you.

If you are willing to spend a little time bargaining, even during high season, you can get excellent prices on many truly unique and one-of-a-kind pieces of art or sculpture. If you speak

Spanish in Santa Domingo or French in Port au Prince, your bargaining skills will go even further. If you cannot reach a satisfactory arrangement, tell the vendor politely that you want to think about it as well as look around; then gently turn away and start walking. This will generally bring the shopkeeper on your heels asking "What price do you want to pay—give me a price!" If you do not wish to continue, ignore him and keep on walking.

If you do find yourself at an impasse because of the language difference, but you're still interested in a particular item, you can usually find guides at street corners or taxi drivers willing to help you. But they don't come free; they will expect a commission from either you or the seller on everything you purchase. However, these same people may also lead you to some good shops as well as introduce you to local artists.

- **Art can often be purchased directly from the artists at a fraction of what you would pay from a dealer.**
- **Straw markets are good places to bargain.**
- **Always start bargaining at one half or less of the requested price.**
- **The off season is the best time to get the better buys.**

In St. Thomas most shopkeepers prefer fixed prices and mark most merchandise accordingly. However, some shops will bargain in Charlotte Amalie. It never hurts in the smaller shops and jewelry stores to ask about a better price. You will be pleasantly surprised how often such a request produces a price reduction. Again, the off season is the best time to get the better buys.

In Jamaica, especially in Kingston, when approached by strangers on the street, it's best not to be too open or engaging unless you are serious about buying. Hustlers are very persistent, and it is difficult to leave them behind.

Barbados is like shopping in any city with department stores and mini malls. While you will find many sales here, prices are marked on everything.

Good buys are not necessarily bargained buys. Remember, goods purchased as duty-free, in-bond, or free ports can be excellent buys.

SHOPPING FOR QUALITY PRODUCTS

You may be overwhelmed by the shopping choices available in the Caribbean. You may wish you were better able to determine whether that opera length string of pearls or that beautiful Cartier watch is really a good deal compared to prices back home. Prepare for your shopping adventure by learning as much about the products you may wish to buy before you leave home. If you want to shop for jewelry in the Caribbean, for example, visit several jewelry stores at home. Talk to jewelers not only about prices but ask questions that give you an opportunity to learn about quality. Ask why one 24-inch strand of pearls is several hundred dollars more than the one next to it. Question the differences between the two l carat diamond rings you have in front of you. This shopping homework will help you make more informed decisions once you set out on your shopping adventure.

WATCHES

You'll find all types of watches in the Caribbean, from automatic to quartz and digital. Watch prices range from less than $10 to more than $100,000! The most expensive watches are made with precious metals such as gold or platinum as well as hand made by master watchmakers. If you are buying an expensive watch, look for a familiar brand name, and always buy from a reputable dealer. Watches are a very popular item in the Caribbean, and you'll find many excellent shops and dealers. Be sure to get an international warranty with every purchase, since there are hundreds of copies of just about every make imaginable. Some copy watches, such as Rolex, do get confiscated by U.S. Customs. If the deal looks too good to be true, it probably is, and should be avoided if you are looking for a quality product.

PEARLS

Much time and care should be given in selecting good quality pearls. Size, color, luster, symmetry, and smoothness of surface all interact to determine the value of a pearl. How well the pearls are matched on all these factors is an important consideration in a necklace or bracelet. The size of a pearl is a major determinant of its value. Luster is also a prized quality. Always view away from direct light to catch the glow within a pearl's shadow area. The greater the pearl's symmetry, the better. The surface will look like satin, and it may look irregular under glass. Expect a quality necklace to be strung with individual knotting between each pearl since ordinary wear may weaken and stretch the threads. Knotting between the pearls will keep you from losing your pearls if the strand should break.

Standard strand lengths are as follows:

▪ Choker	14-16 inches
▪ Matinee	20-24 inches
▪ Opera	28-30 inches
▪ Rope or Sautoir	any additional length.

Saltwater pearls most widely available in the Caribbean are the Akoya pearls. Eighty-five percent of the cultured pearls sold are grown in Akoya oysters off the coast of Japan and are famous for their intense luster, fine grain, and warm color. They range from 2mm to 9mm in diameter and cost approximately $2,500 for a good 14 inch strand of 8mm pearls. South Sea pearls are among the largest pearls cultivated. They are grown in the Pacific Southwest and often have a silver color. The sizes range from 10mm to 17mm in diameter and cost between $25,000 to $100,000 for a 14 inch strand of 15mm pearls. Burmese pearls are grown in Burma and have the same structure as the South Seas pearls, but have a pink cast. They are 10mm to 17mm and cost $60,000 to $70,000 for a 14 inch strand of 14mm pearls. Mobé pearls, cultivated in western Japan, Australia, and the Philippines cannot be strung because of their hemispherical shape. They are 10mm to 15mm across and are made into rings and other pieces of jewelry. You'll find these in St. Thomas. They cost one-third the price of an Akoya pearl.

Freshwater pearls grow in oysters that live in lakes and streams. They can be purchased throughout the Caribbean islands as well as the Bahamas and Bermuda. The strong muscles of the oyster produce a flat, elongated pearl. There are two varieties. The Chinese freshwater pearl is the most common and are grown in mainland China. They are known for their crinkly surface, wide color range, and opaqueness. They cost about $35 for a 14 inch strand. Biwa pearls are lustrous and smooth, and the most expensive freshwater pearls. They are named from Japan's Lake Biwa and are sometimes cultivated to be round. They cost about $500 for a good 14 inch strand.

GOLD

Gold is universally accepted and treasured since it does not tarnish or corrode and is a lifetime investment. It has a luster and can be further enhanced and strengthened by combining it with other metals which give it various shades of color. Yellow, pink, green, and white golds are all made with this process. Gold is rare because of the amount of ore it takes and the expense of getting it out of the ground. It takes two to three tons to extract one ounce of this precious metal. It is easy to work with and can be stretched or hammered because it is so soft. It is sold by weight and purity. When buying gold jewelry always look for a karat mark such as 18K, 14K 10K, etc, plus the manufacturer's trademark stamped somewhere. This indicates you are buying real gold. 24K gold is too soft and normally always must be alloyed with some other metal. Another easy way to remember the formula is using 24K as 100%, then 18K is 18 parts gold and 6 parts other metal. 14K will be 14 parts gold and 10 parts other metal. Anything less than 10K cannot be marked as gold. It must then state gold-filled or gold-plated.

The shading of the gold should also be noted, with 24K gold having a more golden color than gold of fewer karats. Always remember to compare one piece to another, and always buy expensive pieces from a reputable dealer. Beware that the clasp may indicate 18K but the rest of the rope may be something else. If you purchase a gold ingot charm or ring, be sure to ask for the paperwork that substantiates the authenticity. Prize goldsmiths are located in St. Thomas and Sint Maarten where just about any jewelry piece can be made. The Dominican Republic has artists who create a delicate Spanish style in their gold works. The Bahamas, St. Thomas, St. Martin, Sint Maarten, and Puerto Rico have excellent buys on gold. Barbados has low priced gold from South American that is not always authenticated.

PERFUMES

One of the best buys in the Caribbean is perfume. Many of the islands have their own fragrances at reasonable prices, and they are nice gifts to take home to friends. The international perfumes, especially those from Europe, are an excellent buy and are usually 25% to 40% below U.S. prices. A plus factor in purchasing perfumes in the islands is that many new scents are introduced in the Caribbean six months or more before their introduction in the US.

Different methods are used to make perfumes. For example, Lili perfume manufactured since 1929 in Bermuda uses an ancient method called "effleurage" which originated in France. The essential oils of the flowers are extracted by the use of solvent and a distillation unit. The extract is fortified by the addition of flower oils. A fixative is added which enables the alcohol to retain the fragrance for a long period of time. This could be Civet from the Civet cat of Ethiopia, Musk from the Musk deer of Tibet, or Ambergris from the Sperm Whale. The perfume is aged for one year so ingredients become harmonious.

In perfumes, the mixture is 80% spirit. In toilet water it is 10% to 14%, and in cologne only 5%. Perfume is different on each person, as the acid content in a person's skin will make the fragrance slightly different.

DIAMONDS

Diamonds are rare, beautiful, durable, retain their value, and, in fact, are the hardest substance known to man. Even with more discoveries around the world, only 20% of all rough diamonds are suitable for cutting and polishing into gems. The value of any diamond is determined by considering the four "C's"—Carat, Color, Clarity, and Cut.

- **Carat:** Carat refers to the unit of weight, 1/5 of a gram or 1/142 of an ounce. Carats are subdivided into points, 100 points equal a carat. Since large diamonds are rare they have higher value per carat. Diamonds just short of a carat are much less valuable than a one carat stone. Beware of that trap.
- **Color:** Stones are graded from D to Z (colorless to yellow). Completely colorless, icy-white diamonds are rare. White diamonds with a tint of blue are even more rare. The best way to see a true color of a diamond is to look at it against a white surface. Although most diamonds are a shade of white they come in all colors. These colors are called "fancies" and are valued for their depth of color.
- **Clarity:** There are inclusions in all diamonds. Flawless means there are no imperfections visible under a microscope that magnifies ten times. These marks make each stone unique. As long as the flaws do not interfere with the light passage through the stone, they do not affect its beauty. VVS1 and VVS2 are considered slight flaws and are sound investments. The lower VS1 or VS2 stones are much more plentiful and are considered shaky investments. But that doesn't mean you wouldn't be happy to have one in a piece of jewelry as long as the price is right.
- **Cut:** The cut of the diamond is considered extremely important in determining its value. Diamonds are cut to an exact formula. The greatest demand is for the round brilliant cut stones. That is the most traditional shape.

Emerald, marquise, pear, oval and heart are other frequent shapes. These are sometimes called fancy cuts. Other terms that are of helpful to know when selecting a stone are: **Baguette**, a rectangular shaped small diamond often used to enhance the setting of a larger stone; **Channel setting** used to mount a number of smaller stones of uniform size in a row (stones are not held by individual prongs, but in continuous strips of metal); and **Pave**—small stones set closely together to appear as an all diamond surface without any metal showing. Solitaire is simply the mounting of a single gem stone. A Tiffany setting is a four or six prong setting that flares out from the base to long slender prongs that hold the stone.

OTHER GEM STONES

Colored gems are more speculative as an investment, although rubies, emeralds and sapphires have appreciated in about the same percentage over the past few years as diamonds. Even though there is no uniform grading system, some investors believe that the scarcity of colored gemstones may eventually make them an even better investment than diamonds. Many of the same cuts are used, and color along with clarity and carat weight also affect their value. Always buy from a reputable dealer and get a warranty. Many emeralds found in the shops of the Bahamas and Caribbean come from South America.

GOLD COINS

Gold coins have become a very popular investment during the past five years. They are easy to find in shops all over the Caribbean, both new and ancient coins, but are a popular buy in Bermuda, St. Thomas, St. Martin, and Jamaica. The output of counterfeit coins has risen sharply along with the popularity. Knowledge is the best strategy for purchase. Study examples of the coin or coins you are trying to purchase, and buy only from the accredited dealers. Experienced dealers will be able to spot even the best counterfeits. Always get a warranty or be sure that you have the ability to return the coin. After a purchase, have it analyzed by another coin dealer in the area if possible. If there is any question, the American Numismatic Association Certification Services (818 N. Cascade, Colorado Springs, CO 80903) can authenticate your coin. Be sure to always check the latest U.S. regulations when importing gold.

FASHIONS

Since the majority of visitors to the Caribbean are from the U.S. and Canada, most merchants offer local produced and imported fashions that appeal to these groups. When shopping the French and Italian designers on St. Martin and Martinique be sure of the fit since the cut and sizing of the garments are slightly different.

KNITS

For the best value in knit, buy a sweater made of natural fibers—cotton or wool. These breathe and hence keep the wearer more comfortable and the garment will have a longer life. Be sure to check the quality by looking at the label carefully. "Shetland wool" is not trademark protected. *"Made in Shetland"* is. Handknit sweaters are the best and have a more substantial feel, not the flat texture of a machine knit. The price reflects the added time to produce. Bermuda has a wonderful selection of British Isle knits as well as Icelandic knits. Barbados is another good spot to check.

ART AND SCULPTURE

It's always exciting to find an original work of art or sculpture to take home as a wonderful remembrance of that glorious Caribbean vacation. While the finest art is usually found at a reputable dealer or gallery, street art can be fun and result in a decent and treasured purchase. If you're looking for a good investment as well as treasure, it's best to go directly to the source—the artist. You will find that many artists have studios open to the public—especially in Bermuda, Barbados, Haiti, and sometimes Jamaica. The local tourist office may have information on where to find local artists or ask at your hotel. For example, we found an excellent source for Voodoo Flags at the Hotel Olffson in Port au Prince.

One of the best and most adventuresome places to find artists and purchase art is Haiti. Small private galleries and sources for art and sculpture abound here. You will probably need a guide or a driver to take you to the artists, since many are located in areas not readily found on any map. The 10% or more you will have to pay as a commission is well worth it if you get a work of art to grace your home and remind you of your exotic vacation in the Caribbean. When commissioning art in most islands, expect to pay 50% down, with the balance due upon delivery. Remember to always get proof of authenticity and a receipt. Both will be extremely important to you when clearing Customs back home, since original and authenticated art from the Caribbean should be duty-free when entering the U.S.

ANTIQUES

Mahogany antiques and imported period furniture are found on most every island. In recent years, some of the best reproductions of West Indian colonial pieces and exquisite cane furniture you can find in the world are available in many shops—especially in Barbados.

5

Tips For Cruise Ship Passengers

We're not sure how much shopping the first cruise ship passengers and their captain—the crew and Christopher Columbus—were able to accomplish. But we do know that ships and shoppers have been calling on the Caribbean islands in unbelievable numbers ever since. Indeed, the Caribbean can boast that more than 40% of all cruises in the world visit these sunny islands, with over 50 ships of 20-plus cruise lines carrying passengers to sun, relaxation, fun, and exquisite shopping.

Documents

If you are a U.S. citizen, be sure to take with you proof of citizenship: a passport, certified birth certificate, certified naturalization documents, or a voter's registration card, along with a valid driver's license, but you will need it if you plan to rent an automobile. A driver's license normally is not proof of citizenship. While you probably won't have to show these documents if you don't leave the ship, you may have to show some proof of citizenship if you are embarking or re-entering Miami, Los Angeles, or Puerto Rico. Purchasing items in shops on some islands, or cashing a traveler's check, necessitates some proof of citizenship or identification. Whether flying between islands or sailing by cruise ship, a passport is by far the best document to carry with you for easy and acceptable identification.

Alien residents who are permanent residents of the U.S. are normally required to have a valid Alien Registration Card, and in some instances a special sailing permit. In addition, alien residents may need visas to enter some of the countries in the Caribbean. You should check with your local Immigration office and the respective embassies and consulates prior to your trip. These are very important matters to check into, since most cruise lines will not refund your fare if you are denied boarding by U.S. Immigration officials for lack of proper documentation.

You should also check to determine if you need any additional documents if you plan to leave the ship somewhere and return to the U.S. by air.

TIME IN PORT

In most cases, you will only be in port for a day or less. This will limit shopping time because of several factors. First, the larger ships may not be able to pull along side the docks at some Caribbean islands. In such situations you will be transported by tender or launch back and forth to the pier. While the amount of time this takes will depend on the number of passengers going ashore, you should plan on a least an hour each way.

Second, you should check to determine how long before sailing you must embark since some cruise lines like to have everyone aboard a few hours before departure. This, of course, will limit your time even more.

Third, if you are planning to arrange for shipping of some purchases, this may require a few extra minutes on some of the islands.

Some of the smaller cruise ships can dock at most islands. If time in port for shopping is important to you, you may want to consider the size of cruise ship before you book your trip.

EXCURSIONS ASHORE

You will be able to go ashore at most ports. The cruise director will be able to make all arrangements. Some planned tours will primarily include history and sightseeing, but you should ask about shopping opportunities. Some islands may have organized shopping tours. However, you will probably do better shopping on your own. Many cruise directors will also have information on shopping, such as maps or recommended shops. Try to get these materials early in your cruise so you can plan how to best use your limited time. If you plan to rent an automobile, you should check about reserving one through your travel agent prior to the cruise. Trying to rent a car upon arrival is not always successful.

- ❑ **Be sure to take with you proof of citizenship. A driver's license normally is not proof of citizenship.**
- ❑ **In most ports U.S. currency, traveler's checks, and credit cards will be accepted in shops close to the cruise ship.**
- ❑ **Most rooms are extremely small and contain little or no closet space.**
- ❑ **If you make large purchases, consider shipping them.**
- ❑ **Most cruise lines close their on-board shops when in port.**
- ❑ **Shopping in most ports is literally steps away from the ship.**
- ❑ **Bathing suites, brief tops, or short shorts are not acceptable in public anywhere in the conservative Caribbean.**

When planning your shopping itinerary, keep in mind where you plan to eat. For example, do you want to have lunch on board, if lunch is provided while you are in port, or do you plan to have lunch ashore? And what about embarkation requirements? Your answers these questions will affect how long you will have for shopping.

Prior to going ashore to shop, be sure to inquire about currency requirements. All monetary transactions on board will be in U.S. currency. In most ports U.S. currency, traveler's checks, and credit cards will be accepted in shops close to the cruise ships. There may well be occasions, however, when only local currency will be accepted or will net a better bargain. Prepare for these occasions by exchanging a small amount of local currency. You may receive change in local currency from small shopkeepers or street vendors who do not keep small denomination U.S. bills or coins. If you are given local currency, you should try to use it before returning to the ship, since it will not be accepted on board.

Your choice of clothing should be comfortable and casual. Since shopping in most ports involves some walking, be sure to pack a pair of good walking shoes. Open-toe shoes and sandals may not be the best for some places, such as Old San Juan's cobble stone streets. Keep in mind that bathing suits, brief tops, or short shorts are not acceptable in public anywhere in the conservative Caribbean. Wear them at the beach or in the recreational areas of your hotel or resort. However, since the weather will be warm and humid, loose-fitting casual cotton blouses, skirts, shirts, and trousers are best for all around comfort and acceptability.

ACCOMMODATIONS

When booking your cruise, keep in mind the size of your room—especially if you plan to purchase items such as china, crystal, or art. Most rooms are extremely small and contain little or no closet space. If you get a very small room, which is likely, plan to ship your larger purchases home. Most travel agents can determine the size of your room. Although you may specify a room, some cruise lines only assign cabins at the port of embarkation. It's usually difficult to change rooms, especially if the ship is full.

BAGGAGE

Although some cruise lines do not limit the amount of baggage allowed on board, other lines may limit by weight or by the number of bags. If you fly home from the port of disembarkation, the airlines may charge for more than two checked bags and limit your carry-on baggage. If you make large purchases, consider shipping them. Shipping charges may actually be less than the excess baggage charges.

VALUABLES

Most cruise lines limit their liability for lost or stolen items, usually to $100 to $300. If you do purchase jewelry, gems, or an expensive watch, ask the purser about a safety deposit box or other safekeeping arrangements. However, there may be a charge—usually referred to as a declared value charge—for this service. There may also be a limit as to the liability even if you do use a safety deposit box.

If you plan to make expensive purchases, you may want to check your present insurance coverage before departure. If necessary, purchase any additional insurance prior to your departure.

LEAVING THE SHIP

If you purchase fragile or expensive items, inquire about the final disembarkation procedures. Some cruise lines require all baggage, except a small bag you will carry with you, be placed outside your room the night before arrival. The baggage will be taken directly to Customs where you must claim it as well as pay any required duties. This procedure presents problems for shoppers who have fragile and important items they do not want out of their sight for extended periods of time. If such a protocol is required during your cruise, be sure to have shops pack your purchases accordingly. The safest way to handle this situation is to have everything packed as though you were going to have it shipped.

The best way to protect valuable jewelry, gems, or watches is to keep them with you at all times during disembarkation.

ON-BOARD SHOPS AND SHOPPING IN PORTS

Most cruise ships have shops on board where you will find many wonderful gifts, luxury items, and everyday necessities at duty-free prices. Most cruise lines, however, do not want to compete with the shops in port. In fact, they may close while in port. We suggest that you shop on board for essentials, such as toothpaste, books, film, suntan products, or candies. Always compare the prices on shore for the expensive items such as fashions, perfumes, and jewelry. Many shopkeepers we know have suggested that you not rely on the "port lectures" exclusively for your shopping information. When in a port, do look beyond the various promotional maps that will be provided. Pick up the local literature and try to explore the entire area for some shops that are not on the "recommended list." Of course, we recommend that you beware of the less than reputable stores, and try to pay by credit card if at all possible.

LIQUOR AND WINE

The cost of alcoholic beverages on board are usually not included in your ticket price. However, the cost of drinks on board are usually below what you will have to pay at a restaurant on shore. The lower prices are possible because the cruise lines are able to purchase the liquor at duty-free prices. Even though you will also be able to purchase liquor and wine at very good prices in the Caribbean, most ships will not let you bring your own liquor or wine into the dining rooms or most other public areas.

TIPS FOR SPECIFIC ISLANDS

Shopping in most ports is literally steps away from the ship. Every port has its own unique shopping streets and centers. Since every island covered in this book is different, we have included a special section in each chapter which gives you particulars on shopping if you have limited time. Be sure to do research on what is available in each port, how to get there easily, and where to go first if you only have an hour or so for shopping. If you do this, you will be able to quickly discover some unique treasures that go beyond the typical tourist shops.

PART II

Island to Island Shopping

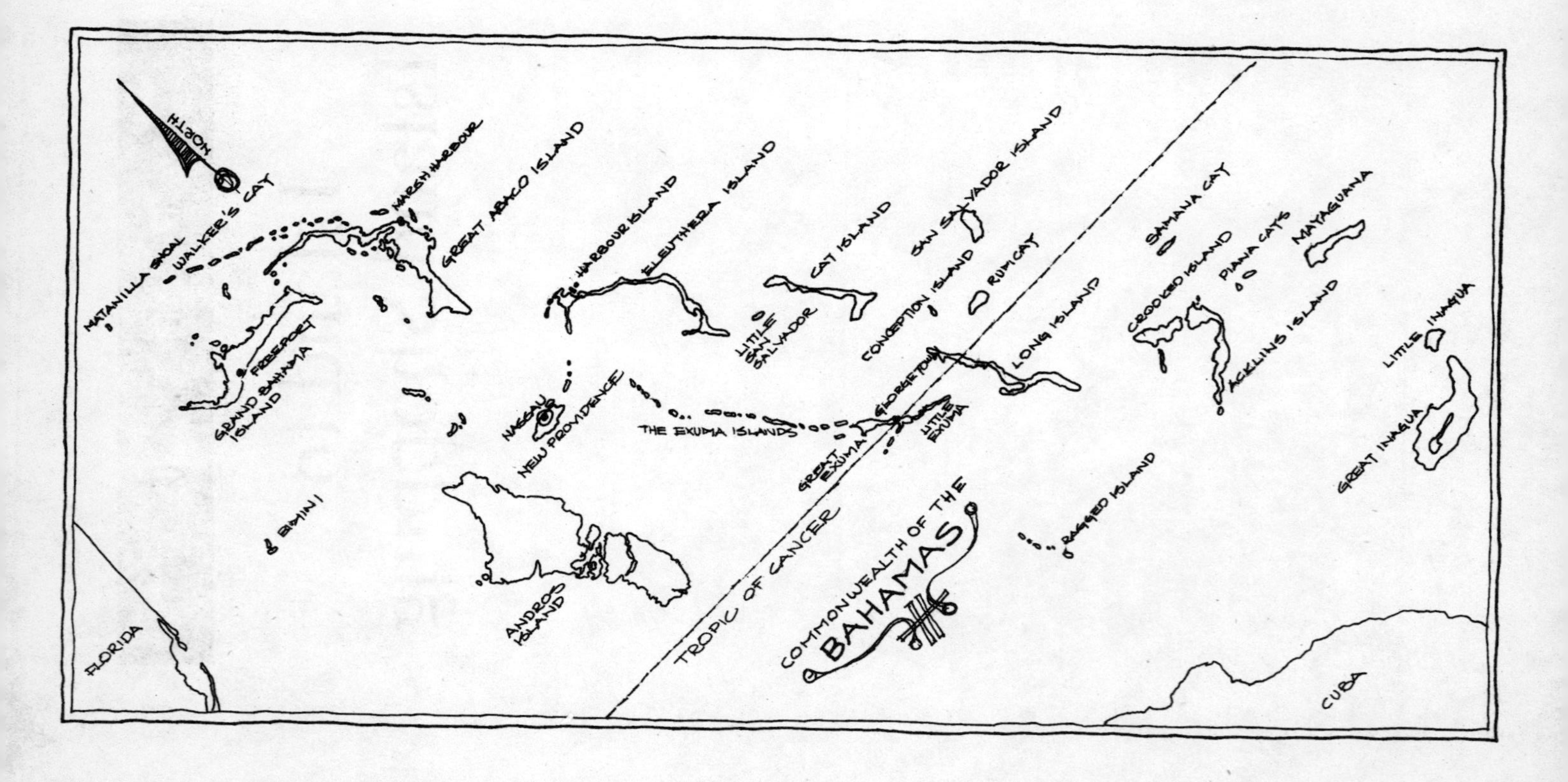
NORTH
MATANILLA SHOAL
WALKER'S CAY
MARSH HARBOUR
GREAT ABACO ISLAND
GRAND BAHAMA ISLAND
FREEPORT
BIMINI
HARBOUR ISLAND
ELEUTHERA ISLAND
NASSAU
NEW PROVIDENCE
ANDROS ISLAND
THE EXUMA ISLANDS
LITTLE SAN SALVADOR
CAT ISLAND
SAN SALVADOR ISLAND
CONCEPTION ISLAND
RUM CAY
GREAT EXUMA
GEORGETOWN
LITTLE EXUMA
LONG ISLAND
TROPIC OF CANCER
COMMONWEALTH OF THE
BAHAMAS
RAGGED ISLAND
SAMANA CAY
CROOKED ISLAND
PIANA CAYS
MAYAGUANA
ACKLINS ISLAND
LITTLE INAGUA
GREAT INAGUA
FLORIDA
CUBA

6

The Bahamas

Welcome to one of the world's most popular "warm weather" destinations. For U.S. citizens, the Bahamas is close, inexpensive, and exotic. Located only 55 miles off the Florida coast at its closest point, the more than 700 islands comprising The Commonwealth of the Bahamas stretch some 600 miles south toward the Caribbean.

Getting to Know You

While there is much more to the Bahamas than the two major tourist distinations—Nassau (Island of New Providence) and Freeport (Grand Bahama Island)—most shopping and related tourist infrastructure are concentrated in these two cities and islands. The "other Bahamas," consisting of the Family Islands, has some interesting shopping for adventurous travelers. You'll find on the two major Family Islands, the Abacos and Eleuthera, artist colonies creating unique pottery, paintings, and metal sculptures, as well as villages of boat builders producing beautiful wooden sailing vessels and ship models.

NASSAU

Nassau, the capital of the Bahamas, is located on the Island of New Providence. This small island, 21 miles long and 7 miles wide, is home to two-thirds of the Bahamian population.

Nassau has a charm that immediately captures your attention. A city more than 300 years old, the delightful colonial architecture transports one to a different place in time. In its back streets, or even on Bay Street, in the evenings after shoppers have dispersed, it's easy to imagine pirates walking the streets or swashbuckling blockade runners of the U.S. Civil War or bootleggers during the Roaring Twenties who used this place as their base of operations.

Nassau is a walking city. A good place to start your shopping adventure is the Ministry of Tourism, which is conveniently located near the Straw Market. This office can provide you with a map and itinerary. From here you should explore the old forts, experience the wonderful downtown colonial architecture, and wander through the open air markets as you get ready to explore Nassau's many shops.

FREEPORT

As late as 1960, Grand Bahama Island was a quiet backwater. Freeport was largely nonexistent except as a concept in the mind of American real estate developer Wallace Groves.

All this changed as Grand Bahama Island underwent dramatic transformations. Today, Grand Bahama Island is an industrial, commercial, and tourist complex, with a thriving economy and over 40,000 residents. Its location in relation to Florida makes it a major cruise ship destination with several departures daily for Port Everglades, Florida.

THE BASICS

LOCATION AND GEOGRAPHY

Strictly speaking, the Bahamas is not part of the Caribbean. However, it is normally associated with the Caribbean because of its island culture and proximity to the Caribbean islands.

The Commonwealth of the Bahamas is comprised of over 700 islands and at least 2,000 small islets called Cays (pronounced "Keys"). The northern-most island, Walkers Cay, lies 115 miles east of Stuart, Florida. From this point the islands stretch 600 miles southeast to Great Inagua Island, located only

50 miles east of Cuba, at the northern reaches of the Caribbean. The Bahamas thus lie entirely within the Atlantic Ocean. At their closest point, Bimini, they are only 55 miles east of Miami.

The two major tourist destinations, Nassau and Freeport, are also very close to the U.S. mainland. Nassau, the capital of the Bahamas, is only 170 miles from Florida, and Freeport is only 80 miles from Florida. From Miami by jet, the flight time to Nassau is less than 25 minutes!

Most visitors to the Bahamas stop in Nassau on New Providence or Freeport on Grand Bahama Island. But there are over 698 more islands! These islands, the Family Islands or the "out islands," are defined as everything but Nassau and Freeport.

The Tropic of Cancer divides the Bahamas making the lower half of the island chain "sub-tropical." Two other major climatic influences affect the islands. The Gulf stream, whose warming waters parallel the western most islands, and the trade winds which blow out of the south east, bring year round warmth.

The Bahamanian islands are coral-limestone and generally very flat with the highest elevation being 206 feet above sea level. The countless miles of white and pink sand beaches, crystal clear waters, and swaying palms make for a vacation paradise.

POPULATION

The Bahamas has a total population of approximately 250,000. The majority of people are concentrated in the two major urban areas, Nassau and Freeport. The population mix is approximately 85% black and 15% white, with both groups tracing their ancestry back several hundred years. Neither group is in any way related to the original inhabitants of the islands, the Lucayan Indians, who disappeared as a race soon after the discovery of the Bahamas in 1492.

CLIMATE, WHEN TO GO, WHAT TO WEAR

Peak season in the Bahamas is generally mid-December through mid-April. This is a wonderful time to visit the Bahamas. Mixed in with the hundreds of thousands of other visitors are a cross section of the world's rich and famous, who add a distinctive flair to the social, cultural and shopping activities of the islands.

The weather during the peak season is generally quite good with temperatures ranging from 65-80 degrees. However, there are no guarantees. If a cold front, known locally as a "norther," pushes through during your visit, you can be faced with a few days of high winds, clouds, and temperatures dipping into the 50's.

- Peak season is mid-December through mid-April.
- Peak hurricane season is August through October, but hurricanes reach the Bahamas only once every 10-15 years.
- Shops and restaurants shut down on Sunday.
- The major taboo is swim wear which is definitely limited to the beach and pool and is inappropriate elsewhere.

The "second season," generally from mid-April to mid-December, is also called "Goombay Summer." This is a more relaxed, casual, and less expensive time to visit, with accommodations discounted 20% to 50%. The islands are still very active with sailing regattas, fishing tournaments, and countless social and cultural activities during this time of the year. The weather is warmer, and the beaches and their cooling sea breezes become magnetic. There is also more rain during this period, but it comes in the form of showers, rarely lasting more than an hour, and frequently not even interrupting the sunshine.

Peak hurricane season is August, September, and October. However, the unique geographic location of the Bahamas affords it excellent protection, and hurricanes reach the Bahamas only once every 10 or 15 years.

The wonderful weather puts the focus on cool and casual clothing. Evening wear in Nassau and Freeport can go toward the dressy side of casual, and a few establishments do require a coat and tie. It is always best to ask when making reservations. The casinos are a mix of all forms of dress in the evenings. The best advice is to be modest in how you dress. The major taboo is swim wear which is definitely limited to the beach and pool and is inappropriate elsewhere.

It's good to pack a sweater for the cool evenings as well as for air-conditioned rooms. And don't forget to take your sunglasses and plenty of sunscreen.

GETTING THERE

Given the proximity to Florida, you have numerous ways to get to the Bahamas. Seaplanes, cruise ships, sailing ships and regular scheduled air all cross the short distance from Florida countless times a day. Miami, Fort Lauderdale, and West Palm Beach are the major gateways to the Bahamas.

Bahamas Air, the nation's flag carrier, offers numerous direct flights from many U.S. destinations direct to Nassau and

Freeport. It also operates connecting flights to the Family Islands.

Several U.S. carriers, including American Eagle, Delta and USAir, offer direct service to the Family Islands from Miami, Fort Lauderdale, and Palm Beach. Smaller carriers offering extensive service throughout the islands include Carnival Airlines, COMAIR, Paradise Island Airways, Laker Airways, Odyssy and Air Canada. Some of these flights are on smaller aircraft which may not leave from the main terminals. If you plan to connect with one of these flights, we recommend checking your bags only as far as Florida. Retrieve them there and then recheck them with your island carrier. It is usually possible to double check when getting on the plane that the bags are there. This all takes time, so be sure your travel agent gives you at least a 90 minute layover in Florida.

If you need to make hotel reservations, the Bahamas Reservation Service (BRS) (800-327-0787) books many hotels in the Family Islands, and some in Nassau and Freeport. This is a fast, easy, and reliable way to book a room.

DOCUMENTS

Since the Commonwealth of the Bahamas has made every effort to keep formal requirements to a minimum, you should have little difficulty in entering. U.S. citizens, for example, do not need a passport or visa to enter the Bahamas for periods of up to eight months. The only requirement is that you carry "sufficient identification." Passports, birth certificates, a naturalization card, voter's registration card, or military identification card fill this requirement.

To re-enter the U.S., you need a document clearly showing your U.S. citizenship such as a passport. Any other form of identification must be an original or certified copy, and it must be accompanied by a photo identification. There is no guarantee that you will get back into the U.S. with the driver's license that you used to gain entry to the Bahamas!

Canadian citizens and citizens of the United Kingdom do not require a passport or visa for stays of up to three weeks. Passports are required to re-enter the U.K.

The regulations for persons carrying passports from other countries are not as straight forward. Generally passports are required, but there are few visa requirements. A quick call to your nearest Bahamian Embassy will clarify any questions.

ARRIVAL AND DEPARTURE

The Bahamas

Upon entering the Bahamas, every visitor is given an Immigration card to complete and sign. You will be given the carbon copy which should be kept in your possession until departure, when you will be required to turn it into the Immigration Officials. Don't lose it!

Upon arrival, you need to have "onward passage." Meeting a friend with a boat for a ride home? It doesn't matter; you will still be required to have an onward air ticket.

If departing by air, each adult must pay a $13 departure tax. This must be paid in cash. It is wise to have the correct change. Although the people collecting this tax do seem to make an effort to give change in U.S. currency, the occasional visitor does end up with a handful of Bahamian dollars for a last minute souvenir.

It is fairly easy to bring your pets. Contact the Ministry of Agriculture, Trade, and Industry, P.O. Box N-3028, Nassau, Bahamas (809-322-1277/9).

Nassau

Every day of the week cruise ships off load hundreds of passengers at Prince George Wharf to get a taste of Nassau. At the head of the wharf is Rawson Square and Bay Street, the main shopping area. On most cruise ships itineraries, this is about all you will have time for.

The majority of the other arrivals are through the international airport which is to the west of town. Don't expect jetways. It is a brief walk from your plane to the new arrivals hall which generally makes quick work of processing passengers. Have your Immigration card filled out and your identification ready.

Once outside the airport, it's a brief and convenient taxi ride to the Cable Beach Resort area. Downtown and Paradise Island are further with a downtown taxi ride costing $15 to $20 and Paradise Island $20 to $30. Many taxis are large station wagons or limos, so don't be rushed into one by yourself. Getting a few people together with the same general destination makes the fare far more reasonable. There is no bus service from the International Airport.

Freeport

Arriving on Grand Bahama Island by cruise ships puts you at the commercial harbour, a brief taxi ride from the Grand Bahama's main city and resort center, Freeport. The taxis are well organized to bring you into town to the International Bazaar. Charging by the person, they are the easiest and best way to get into town and back out to the boat.

If you are arriving by air, Freeport International Airport is very convenient to downtown and is once again easiest reached by taxi. For this ride to downtown or to your resort, the taxi will be metered and we found the rates quite reasonable.

CUSTOMS AND IMMIGRATION

Bahamian Customs inbound is "no problem" as long as you aren't bringing in anything for resale.

Most visitors departing Nassau International Airport, Freeport International for U.S. destinations will clear U.S. Customs and Immigration prior to departure. No further formalities are required at your U.S. destination.

Visitors departing for all other destinations must clear Customs and Immigration at their destination.

U.S. visitors returning after a stay of over 48 hours in the Bahamas are allowed $600 for each member of the family regardless of age. This exemption may only be used once every 30 days.

After your basic $600 allowance, the next $1,000 is dutiable at the rate of 10% and from there on at the discretion of the officer. Family members over 21 may each bring back 1 liter of alcohol, 100 cigars, and 200 cigarettes.

The Bahamas is a GSP (Generalized System of Preferences) country. This allows U.S. residents to import unlimited quantities of Bahamian manufactured goods free of all duty. Imported goods purchased in the Bahamas but not made there are dutiable.

There are a few items for sale in the Bahamas which are illegal to bring into the U.S. These include Cuban cigars, tortoise shell jewelry, plants, and fruits.

Canadian residents are allowed similar allowances which are outlined in the Canadian Customs brochure *"I Declare."*

CURRENCY AND CREDIT CARDS

The Bahamian dollar is on par with the U.S. dollar. The two currencies are used interchangeably throughout the islands, with change often given as a mixture of the two currencies. Traveler's checks in U.S. dollars are accepted throughout the islands. Canadian dollars and other foreign currencies are not widely accepted.

Credit cards are accepted universally at all major resorts, shops, and restaurants in Nassau and Freeport. However, it is best to inquire first since there are exceptions and occasionally limits are placed on the maximum amount that may be charged. This can be due to the inability of the more isolated resorts to verify large charges.

When purchasing an item to be shipped home, always use a credit card. If anything goes wrong or the item is broken, the credit card company can be your greatest ally.

SECURITY

Nassau and Freeport are relatively safe cities for travelers. But one must take the normal precautions of not inviting trouble.

Be sure to keep your traveler's checks, credit cards and cash, in a safe place along with your travel documents and other valuables. Money belts do provide good security, but they are really too uncomfortable and bulky for the hot climate in the Bahamas. Our best advice is for women to carry money and documents in a bag that can be securely closed and with a long shoulder strap so it can conveniently be kept with you at all times. For men, keep your money and credit cards in your wallet. When in heavy crowds, it pays to shift your wallet to your front pocket. If this is uncomfortable, you probably need to clean it out.

You may also want to use the hotel safety deposit box for your cash and other valuables. If one is not provided in your room, ask the cashier to assign you a private box in their vault.

Expensive jewelry has little place in the Bahamas. Leave it at home and avoid any problems.

Under no circumstances should you leave your money and valuables unattended; not in your room, at a restaurant table, in a dressing room, and not on the beach. If you get robbed, chances are it will be in part, your own fault, because you invited someone to take advantage by not being cautious in securing your valuables.

TIPPING

Many Bahamian restaurants automatically include a 10% or 15% gratuity, but this is by no means universal. You should take care to examine first the menu and then the bill. For those without absolutely perfect eyesight or a ready command of the system of hieroglyphics used on restaurants bills, it is best to ask. Use your own discretion in any additional gratuity for exceptional service.

When no gratuity has been added to the check, 15% is considered the standard. This applies to restaurants, bars, nightclubs, hotel service, taxis, barbers, and beauty operators.

LANGUAGE

English is the language here and it is spoken in a wide a range of accents and dialects. Don't be surprised or embarrassed when you find yourself asking someone to repeat something for the third or fourth time. Sometimes sign language works even better than this wonderful common language of ours.

BUSINESS HOURS

Never on Sunday! The Bahamians are very religious, and do not allow commercialism to intrude on a day of worship and family relaxation. Not only are shops not open, it is even difficult to find a restaurant open outside the major resort areas.

As a rule of thumb, expect shops to be open 9am to 5pm, Monday through Saturday, in Nassau and Freeport. Shops in the major hotels will have longer hours.

ELECTRICITY

The electricity is U.S. standard 120 volts, 60 cycles, and compatible with all American appliances. European visitors with 220 volt appliances should bring along the necessary converters as they may not be available even in the major resorts.

TRANSPORTATION

Taxis in Nassau and Freeport are generally plentiful and in relatively good repair. The overall condition of the taxi fleet gets worse the further you get from these major areas. The poorer quality of roads takes its toll and this is compounded by the difficulty in getting repairs. Major repairs are only accomplished in Nassau or Freeport. This requires a long and expensive ride by ship from the other islands. Obviously this ride tends to get put off.

Nassau and Freeport both have extensive inexpensive private bus systems. Your hotel can provide you with information on the routes to fit your needs.

Bahamas Air, the nation's flag carrier, offers an extensive network of inter-island connections on well maintained equipment. They also have international service offering direct flights from many U.S. cities.

Traveling by "mail boats" are for those who have time on their hands. These vessels connect to even the most isolated corners of the Bahamas. The quality of the accommodations aboard varies, but they are well worth checking out if your time allows the luxury of slow passage. Contact the Dock Master at Potter's Cay, Nassau, under the Paradise Island Bridge. (809-323-1064)

If you are adventuresome, the perfect way to see the Bahamas is by boat. There are three major "bareboat" charter organizations in the Bahamas ready to fill your requirements. Since each is also capable of providing you with an experienced captain, lack of boating experience should not hold you back. Contact: Abaco Bahamas Charters (800-626-5690), Sunsail (305-484-5246), or Eleuthera Bahamas Charters (508-255-8930).

Many sailing and sport fishing boats in Florida can be hired to take you to your island destinations. Information on these services can be found by reading the major sailing magazines—***Yachting, Sailing,*** and ***Cruising World***. All have a classified section in the back listing many companies ready to fill your specific needs. One of our favorites is sailing aboard "Witt's End," a 51-foot ketch captained by Greg and his wife B.J. Witt (305-451-3354).

Rental cars are available in Nassau and Freeport at the airports and at most major hotels. In the Family Islands, it is a little more difficult but any major resort can solve your transportation needs. Driving in the Bahamas is a bit of a trick. It is British style (left hand side of the road) in U.S. style autos. "Think Left"! And buy all the insurance you can if it is your first adventure at this style of driving.

If you are thinking of renting a moped or motorcycle, our recommendation in Nassau is **don't do it**! Moped rentals are fine in the Family Islands or even in Freeport, but avoid mopeds in Nassau. There are over 50,000 automobiles on New Providence Island, which is only 21 miles long and 7 miles wide. The speed limits are not particularly low, and we have never noticed the drivers paying any particular attention or courtesy to the moped traffic.

Late night taxis in Nassau frequently do not use meters, and occasionally they are not taxis. Fixed fare prices we have been charged are generally in line with daytime fares, but be careful and negotiate the price before accepting a ride. Many "second shift" drivers are moonlighting illegally in "Uncle Joe's" taxi to pick up a few extra bucks.

FOOD AND DRINK

Since the drinking water in Nassau and Freeport is filtered and chlorinated, it should present no problem for you. Water in the Family Islands is rarely a problem. Most facilities are served by central water systems supplied by central wells. It is the rare guest house or restaurant still served by a rainwater cistern system.

The food in the Bahamas is wonderful! As a world class international destination, the finest in French, German, Italian, and other cuisines is available, but the Bahamian cuisine is also well worth trying.

Native restaurants abound throughout the islands, and many native dishes are available at the international restaurants. Many of the dishes are very simple, made from only the freshest ingredients.

Conch (pronounced "konk") is (or was) the resident of the beautiful large pink shells seen everywhere around the islands. It is a staple in the Bahamian diet. It can be eaten raw, minced in soup, broiled as a burger and served on a bun, or deep fried in a delicious batter served as "conch fritters."

Grouper is the staple fish and has an excellent flavor. It is also prepared by a variety of methods, as is the local lobster which is really a large crayfish (also called spiny lobster). It has a flavor very different from the northern cold water lobster tails served in the U.S. and Canada.

"Peas and rice" accompanies most meals. It is a delicious blend of pigeon peas (beans), white rice, and spices.

For dessert try the heavenly coconut creme pie. There are other desserts such as key lime pie, coconut custard, and various cakes. We have rarely been disappointed with any of the desserts.

RESOURCES

The Bahamas Ministry of Tourism (BMT) is a great source for information on the Bahamas. They have many offices throughout the United States and Canada. In Nassau they are located at the Straw Market on Bay Street, at Prince George Wharf where the cruise ships dock, and at Fort Charlotte. In Freeport they are located at the International Bazaar, the International Airport, and at the cruise ship docks.

We recommend contacting BMT as you formulate your plans for a visit to the Bahamas. They can be very helpful with information on "what's happening," maps, and brochures of the islands you hope to visit.

Prior to arriving in the Bahamas, you may want to look at a few books on the Bahamas. The APA Insight Guide, ***Bahamas***, provides a good overview of Bahamian history, society, and culture, as well as a few travel tips. Like other books in this series, read this book before you arrive in the Bahamas; it's not a good travel companion given its size and photographic format. Fodor's also produces a useful guide to the Bahamas.

If you are interested in a more in depth look at the culture and history of the Bahamas try ***A History of the Bahamas*** by Michael Craton.

While visiting Nassau, you will see ***Best Buys in the Bahamas***, a great little magazine published by the local businesses. In addition to general information on the Bahamas, it contains advertisements from major shops and restaurants, and locator maps. It is published twice yearly and is given out free in the shops of most participating retailers. ***What-to-do, Nassau, Cable Beach & Paradise Island*** is a similar publication, and well worth picking up.

Tourist News, Nassau Bahamas is a monthly newspaper also given free to tourists. It contains articles on up coming events as well as advertising for local businesses and restaurants.

What-to-do, Freeport—Lucaya is the same format as their Nassau publication, containing general information on the Bahamas, advertisements for the major shops and restaurants, and locator maps. It is published twice a year and is given out free in the shops of participating retailers.

The Freeport Shoppers Guide and Map has five excellent maps including shop by shop listings for the International Bazaar and Port Lucaya. It makes finding what you are looking for quick and easy.

SHOPPING IN THE BAHAMAS

The Bahamas is truly "duty-free." Additionally, the Bahamas has no sales tax or value added tax (VAT) and this helps keep the islands very competitive on the world market.

The key to a successful shopping adventure in the Bahamas is doing your homework—comparative shopping. After a brief look at this chapter, you will know the kinds of things you will be looking for, even if you have never been to the Bahamas.

Make a list of the things you might be interested in before you go and do some window shopping. Visit your local stores, examine wholesale catalogues, and telephone major discount houses. If, for example, your list includes cameras or electronic equipment, you should check the prices for comparable items found in stores and discount houses back home. In the U.S., call the toll-free numbers of mail-order discount houses in New York City for phone quotes on cameras, film, computers, and electronic equipment. Bi-Rite (800-221-7774), 47th Street Photo (800-221-7774), and Executive (800-223-7323) are just a few of the many places you can contact to quickly comparative shop by phone. The Sunday and Wednesday editions of ***The New York Times*** include ads from these highly competitive firms. You will quickly discover their prices may be 10% to 30% cheaper than the best price you can find in your local discount houses. Some of these New York firms will even bargain over the phone when you inform them of a competitor's better price!

So, do your homework before you go! There is nothing more deflating to your shopping enthusiasm than to return home with your newly acquired Bahamian bargain and to discover you could have purchased the same item for less at home. We were recently trying to replace a camera, and the best price we could negotiate in the Bahamas was 20% higher than our New York quote. There are some excellent deals, but you must do your homework to be able to spot them!

Jewelry is another item that requires comparative shopping and some minimal level of expertise in determining authenticity and quality. Read as much as you can on different qualities of jewelry, and visit jewelry stores at home where you can learn a great deal by asking salespeople questions about craftsmanship, settings, quality, and discounts.

If you are in the market for name brand watches, china, crystal, and flatware, comparison shopping is also easy. With a quick trip to your local shopping areas and a few calls, you should be able to get good pricing information for getting the best deal in the Bahamas.

When purchasing anything in the Bahamas, make sure you get a receipt, and keep it! If the receipt is not clear, have the merchant write out on the receipt a description of the item purchased. Make sure any representations as to grade, quality, or guarantees are made in writing. In addition to helping document your purchase should any problems arise, this written receipt will make clearing Customs much easier.

Most major stores in Nassau and Freeport want you to believe that they are fixed price. Generally speaking they are, as the individual salespeople are not authorized to accept anything but the marked price. If you pay cash, you should ask for, and may receive, an additional 5% discount, since you save the merchant this amount in credit card costs. While this practice is discouraged by credit card companies, it occurs nonetheless. If you have the time and patience to negotiate with the manager, you should be able to get discounts on major purchases. As any good negotiator knows, once the door is opened, everything is negotiable. Fixed pricing is a myth invented by retailers to make more money and to make their lives easier, but we would never buy anything without giving a try at getting a discount. This is particularly easy if you have done your homework and can quote a price that you can buy the item for elsewhere. Frequently discounts are there just for the asking. An additional 10% to 20% makes the difference between a good deal and a great deal!

The straw markets are a good place to practice your negotiating skills. Indeed, you're expected to negotiate there!

NASSAU—ISLAND OF NEW PROVIDENCE

The major shopping area of Nassau is **Bay Street**. Most of the major stores are located between Rawson Square, where the cruise ships dock, and The British Colonial, the huge pink hotel complex. The delightful old buildings that line this street overflow with fine products from all over the world.

Numerous stores also spill into the side streets, but most of the good shops are within one block of Bay Street. Two alley ways between Bay Street and the harbour have been developed into delightful meandering shopping and architectural experiences. Watch for Prince George Plaza and The International Bazaar on your right side while walking toward the British Colonial Hotel.

Paradise Island is a brief taxi or water taxi ride from downtown. Merv Griffin owns several major hotels and the casino on Paradise Island. Much is going on in Paradise Island, with new construction and remodeling everywhere. There is a shopping center on your right hand side, just after you cross the toll bridge. It recently underwent major expansion and now includes many of the same stores found downtown. When approaching Paradise Island by taxi, be prepared to pay the $2 toll. This toll is collected on the way in—not on the way out.

The best local fruit and vegetable market is located underneath the **Paradise Island Bridge** on the mainland side—Potters Island. This wonderfully photogenic market offers an incredible array of tropical fruit in season and gives the novice

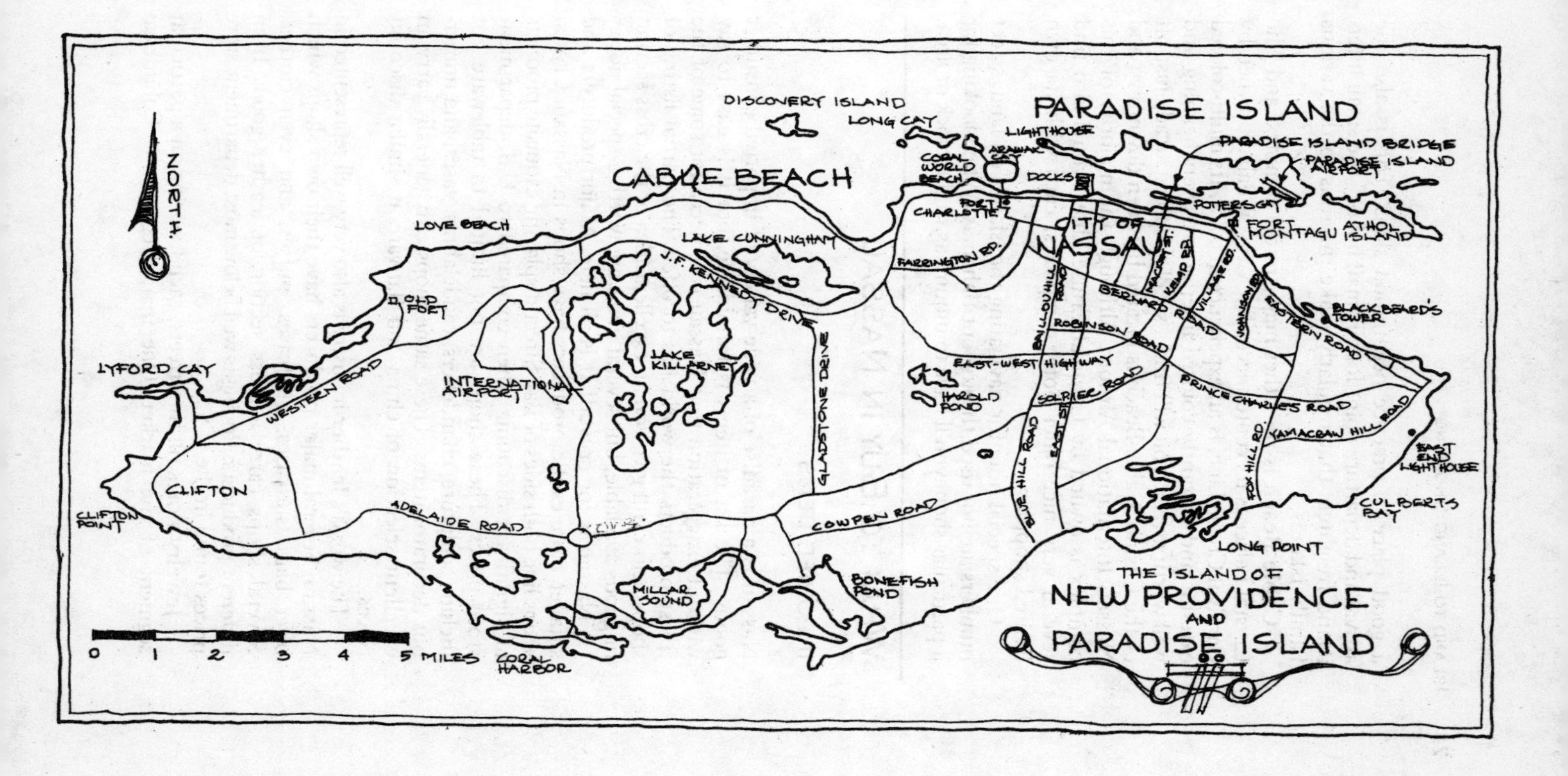
THE ISLAND OF
NEW PROVIDENCE
AND
PARADISE ISLAND
PARADISE ISLAND
DISCOVERY ISLAND
LONG CAY
CABLE BEACH
LIGHTHOUSE
ARAWAK CAY
CORAL WORLD BEACH
DOCKS
PARADISE ISLAND BRIDGE
PARADISE ISLAND AIRPORT
POTTERS CAY
FORT MONTAGU
ATHOL ISLAND
FORT CHARLOTTE
CITY OF NASSAU
LOVE BEACH
LAKE CUNNINGHAM
FARRINGTON RD.
J.F. KENNEDY DRIVE
BALLOU HILL ROAD
MACKEY ST.
KEMP RD.
VILLAGE RD.
JOHNSON RD.
BERNARD ROAD
EASTERN ROAD
BLACKBEARD'S TOWER
ROBINSON ROAD
OLD FORT
LAKE KILLARNEY
LYFORD CAY
INTERNATIONAL AIRPORT
WESTERN ROAD
GLADSTONE DRIVE
EAST-WEST HIGHWAY
HAROLD POND
PRINCE CHARLES ROAD
YAMACRAW HILL ROAD
FOX HILL RD.
BLUE HILL ROAD
EAST ST.
EAST END LIGHTHOUSE
CLIFTON
CLIFTON POINT
ADELAIDE ROAD
COWPEN ROAD
CULBERTS BAY
LONG POINT
BONEFISH POND
MILLAR SOUND
CORAL HARBOR
NORTH.
0 1 2 3 4 5 MILES

a good place to practice negotiation skills. This is also the arrival and departure point for all "mail boats," the small inter-island freighters that regularly make the runs to the various Family Islands.

Cable Beach is the other major resort complex, and The Crystal Palace is its centerpiece. The Crystal Palace, owned by Carnival Cruise Line, is an experience in color. Its multi-colored exterior and vibrantly colored interior are overwhelming and well worth a visit. You will find a small shopping arcade just off of the Casino. Cable Beach is located between downtown and Nassau International Airport. Although the majority of this complex is owned by Carnival Cruise Lines, you'll also find several very nice older hotel complexes, each with its own limited shopping.

One special note for navigating the islands on land: street numbers are not used throughout Bahamas. When looking for a particular shop, you'll have to inquire as to the block or area.

WHAT TO BUY IN NASSAU

IMPORTED ITEMS

Nassau is a paradise of a wide variety of imported consumer goods. The list of items is formidable, but it is easy to say without exaggeration that Nassau is a mecca for some of the finest products the world has to offer. The partial listing of shops below will give you an excellent idea of the cross section of goods available, but several items are worth a special note.

Nassau is for **crystal**! It is all here. Major producers and smaller more exotic producers have shops in Nassau. Crystal shops line both sides of Bay Street displaying exquisite products at significant discounts when compared to U.S. department store prices. These shops are not limited to tableware but include sculpture, chandeliers, candelabras, vases, and numerous decorator items. These same shops also generally carry an excellent selection of china and flatware at similar discount prices.

The world's **leather** industry is also very well represented in Nassau. Several major producers have their own shops which offer bags, suitcases, briefcases, purses, and even clothes. Several shops carry a cross section of leather goods from different producers. Pricing is well below most department store prices found in the U.S.

Jewelry stores fill the streets, each focusing on a particular segment of the market. One major segment is Columbian emeralds. Several stores offer this gem in all forms—raw, uncut, finished, and both mounted and unmounted. These beautiful stones are offered in a selection not generally seen outside the Caribbean. They are well priced and stunning.

Most **watches** produced in the world seem to be for sale in Nassau. This is one area where doing your homework is very easy and important. The prices on watches are good, but it's best to know comparative prices back home before making such a purchase in Nassau.

While you will find a wide array of **clothing** for sale in Nassau, the only real deals seem to be on sweaters. Cashmere, Shetland, and Scandinavian sweaters are all available at substantial discounts.

Cameras are not a good buy in Nassau compared to what you can purchase them for at discount houses in the United States.

LOCAL ART AND CRAFTS

Nassau is also the center for Bahamian art and crafts. You'll find a wide selection of unique products in various shops.

The Bahamas is home to several world caliber **artists**, and their work is frequently displayed in Nassau. The most renowned living artist in the Bahamas is Amos Fergerson. He paints in a "primitive" style. If his style and price range are not what you had in mind, you'll find several artists who paint in a more contemporary style. Of particular note are Brent Malone, Dorman Stubbs, and Maxwell Taylor. These three artists produce pieces in the $200 to $5,000 price range. While their paintings may turn out to be excellent investments, our advice is to buy because you like it rather than for investment. They all produce stunning pieces with strong composition and excellent use of color.

The Bahamas produces a wide array of **local jewelry**. The spectrum goes from the inexpensive shell necklaces sold at the straw market to fine work in conch shell and coral sold at the best jewelry stores and in specialty shops. These beautiful and unique pieces make excellent gifts.

WHERE TO SHOP IN NASSAU

BAY STREET

Most of the best shopping in Nassau is concentrated along Bay Street and its side streets between Rawson Square and The

British Colonial Hotel. All of the shops listed below are found in this area.

Leaving Rawson Square headed for the British Colonial, you will find on your left hand side several wonderful stores. **Little Switzerland** is a chain of stores found throughout the Caribbean. There are three other branches here along Bay Street and another one at Paradise Island. This store has a fine selection of crystal, ceramics, jewelry, perfume, and a large selection of watches. Their extensive inventory includes Gucci, Ebel, Heuer, Rado and Omega. This store also has a display of Bahamian crafts, including model ships and ceramic fish in iridescent colors.

Pipe of Peace is noteworthy for its selection of tobacco including the finest in cigars. They also have Cuba's finest, but U.S. residents must smoke them in the Bahamas because they are still illegal in the U.S.

Bernard's has one of Nassau's finest collections of china and crystal. They stock Baccarat Crystal, Lalique Crystal, Daum Crystal, Wedgwood, Royal Copenhagen, Royal Worchester, Royal Crown Derby, Crown Staffordshire, and Coalport. Additionally, they stock several lesser known labels that are unique and exquisite. They also have a reliable mail-order department.

Greenfire Emeralds Jewelry has beautiful raw and finished stones. Only in the Caribbean will you find a jewelry store with this extensive a selection of emeralds.

Further down Bay Street is **Johnson Brothers, Ltd.** They specialize in locally produced conch and coral jewelry. Their items cover a wide price range and make excellent gifts. But be careful here; they also sell tortoise shell jewelry which is illegal to bring into the U.S.

The **Island Shop** is one of Nassau's oldest shops. It carries a wide variety of items in an atmosphere that feels more like an old drugstore. They are particularly noted for their upstairs bookstore. In addition to general literature, they carry the best selection of books on the Bahamas that we have found anywhere.

The **Nassau Shop** is a wonderful place to browse. It's an old-fashioned department store that carries men's and women's wear as well as a nice selection of Ballantyne, Pringle and Braemar cashmere, lambs wool and Shetland sweaters. It also carries Piagat, Concord, Baume and Mercier, Movado, Orient, Nivada, and Swatch watches along with leather, linen, jewelry, and gift items.

Gold Ltd. offers what its name implies—gold jewelry of all descriptions. Gold chains, earrings, and pins are all sold by weight based on the daily gold price, "fix." **Valentines** is another shop specializing in gold.

Discount Warehouse has a wide selection of jewelry, gold, and watches. Of particular note is their selection of locally produced conch and coral jewelry.

If you are in the market for high end jewelry or diamonds in particular, you will find Nassau does not have much to offer since most of its jewelry sells for under $5000. **Guccini**, at the corner of Bay Street and the International Bazaar is the single exception. They have the most upscale collection in Nassau. While their ads mention an additional 10% discount, once again this is a starting point for negotiations.

Alexander's Gold has some very unique pieces, big and bold, crafted in gold, silver and shell. They also have some beautiful leather pieces.

Vanite' has Hummel figurines and David Winter villages, while **Cotton Ginny** carries a line women's fashions ideal for island wear.

Treasure Traders has one of Nassau's finer selections of collectibles, such as Baccaret, Lalique, and Rosenthal. In addition to the major feature items of crystal and china, they stock the locally produced Abaco Ceramics. These simple poured ceramics are done in shell and starfish motifs and are finished in a fine quality double white glaze. They make excellent gifts.

Last, but certainly not least on Bay Street, is the famous **Straw Market**. This two-story extravaganza of T-shirts, coconut carvings, shell jewelry, wood carvings, straw hats, straw bags, straw placemats, and straw just-about-anything-else-you-can-think-of, is another "must" see and do. You can not go home without a T-shirt saying "It is better in the Bahamas," bargained for in the Straw Market. Go ahead and do it, it's lots of fun!

THE SIDE STREETS

The International Bazaar and **Prince George Plaza** run off of Bay Street to the harbor. These winding little passages are architecturally very "cute" and also have some shops worthy of note. **Las Tiendas** has leather goods and gifts from South America. They also offer some very beautiful and unique sweaters. The **Island of Mycanos**, a store loaded with gifts from Greece, and **Mora's Linen Closet**, are both worth a visit.

Island Gallery is also located in The International Bazaar. This is the smaller and less expensive of two galleries run by Dorman Stubbs, one of the Bahamas best young artists. He displays works by several local artists as well as a limited selection of his own works. It is well worth the visit to get a feel for what some young Bahamian artists are doing. But don't miss **Artist Gallery**, located only a few blocks away where the truly impressive (and more expensive) pieces are located. Artist Gallery is located on Bay Street across the street from the west end of the British Colonial Hotel.

The **English Shop** on Parliament Street has some wonderful antiques, linen, and lace, but their collection of antique oil paintings (most with a nautical theme) is worthy of a fine gallery. Stop in if only to window shop.

MCM.This is the only MCM outlet in the Caribbean, and has excellent discount prices.

Leather and Things Ltd. stocks some very fine pieces from Dodney & Booney Inc., US, and Gucci.

The **Brass and Leather Shops Ltd.**, carries Land Leather of Miami, a few Italian pieces, and Fendi. They also offer a limited selection of brass and some Scrimshaw reproductions. At their second shop, **Galeria Cano**, they also have a wonderful collection of exotic jewelry. Both shops are on Charlotte Street.

Coins of the Realm on Charlotte Street, in addition to coins and stamps, has some beautiful silver jewelry, with some of the more interesting pieces coming from Spain. You'll find an interesting mix of merchandise here.

The **Scottish Shop**, also on Charlotte Street, has a few nice cashmere sweaters by Dean, Delmont and Barrie and a small collection of silver jewelry.

Marlborough Antiques Art and Gifts is a five-star shopping "must." Located across the street from the main entrance to the British Colonial Hotel, this wonderful shop is owned in part by Brent Malone, one of the Bahamas' most renowned artists. You'll usually find an excellent selection of his work on display. The shop also displays Max Taylor, prints by Antoine Chapon, and watercolors by David White. They have some British antiques, a fantastic collection of antique ship models, old prints, pottery, books, and art work by Sue Bennett Williams and Dennise Knight. The list of outstanding offerings goes on and on. Be sure to visit this shop.

EAST OF RAWSON SQUARE

John Bull is one-stop-shopping for jewelry, watches, crystal, china, etc. They are one of the oldest shops, and they truly have it all. But watch your prices here.

The **Gold Mine** is another shop selling gold by weight. They also have jewelry and watches.

FURTHER EAST OF TOWN

A "must" on any shopping agenda with an interest in arts and crafts is a trip east of town. Bahamian Arts and Crafts is located on Bay Street between downtown and the Paradise Island Bridge. This wonderful shop is run by Eunice Sands and is a treasure house of woodwork, shell pendants with gold trim, beautiful shell trimmed mirrors, prints, and hand painted shirts.

On this same end of town is **The Nassau Glass Company**. This is one of the strangest art galleries we have ever seen. Mixed in with the light fixtures, vanities, medicine cabinets and various electrical supplies is the best collection of local Bahamian painters to be found anywhere in the islands. Nassau Glass is located on Mackey Street and is only a short taxi ride from downtown and a brief detour if you are taking a taxi between Paradise Island and downtown.

The Nassau Gallery is run by the Wasile Family. Elyse Wasile in conjunction with Kaiser of West Germany has produced a series of fine porcelain plates, vases, and boxes. In addition the shop also handles a series of prints and other art work. The shop is located in the East Bay Shopping Center which is on the foot of the Nassau side of the Paradise Island Bridge.

CRUISE SHIP PASSENGERS

If your stay in Nassau is short, do not despair—shopping is only a few steps from your ship. If you have a half a day, head for Bay Street from the Prince George Wharf. At Bay Street, turn right and continue to the British Colonial Hotel, cross over, and come back the other side of the street to where you started. You will cover most of the main shopping area in these few blocks and will be exposed to the best Nassau has to offer. Even if you have only an hour, you can visit a few shops in the first block or two of Bay Street.

FREEPORT—GRAND BAHAMA ISLAND

The diamond in Freeport's crown has always been The Princess Casino and its attached International Bazaar. Located in town, this complex is a brief taxi ride from most beach resorts.

The International Bazaar and Casino take architectural "cute" to new levels. The Casino, the anchor of the complex, is done in Moorish style. The associated arcades lead to a shopping complex where it changes to a delightful undulating

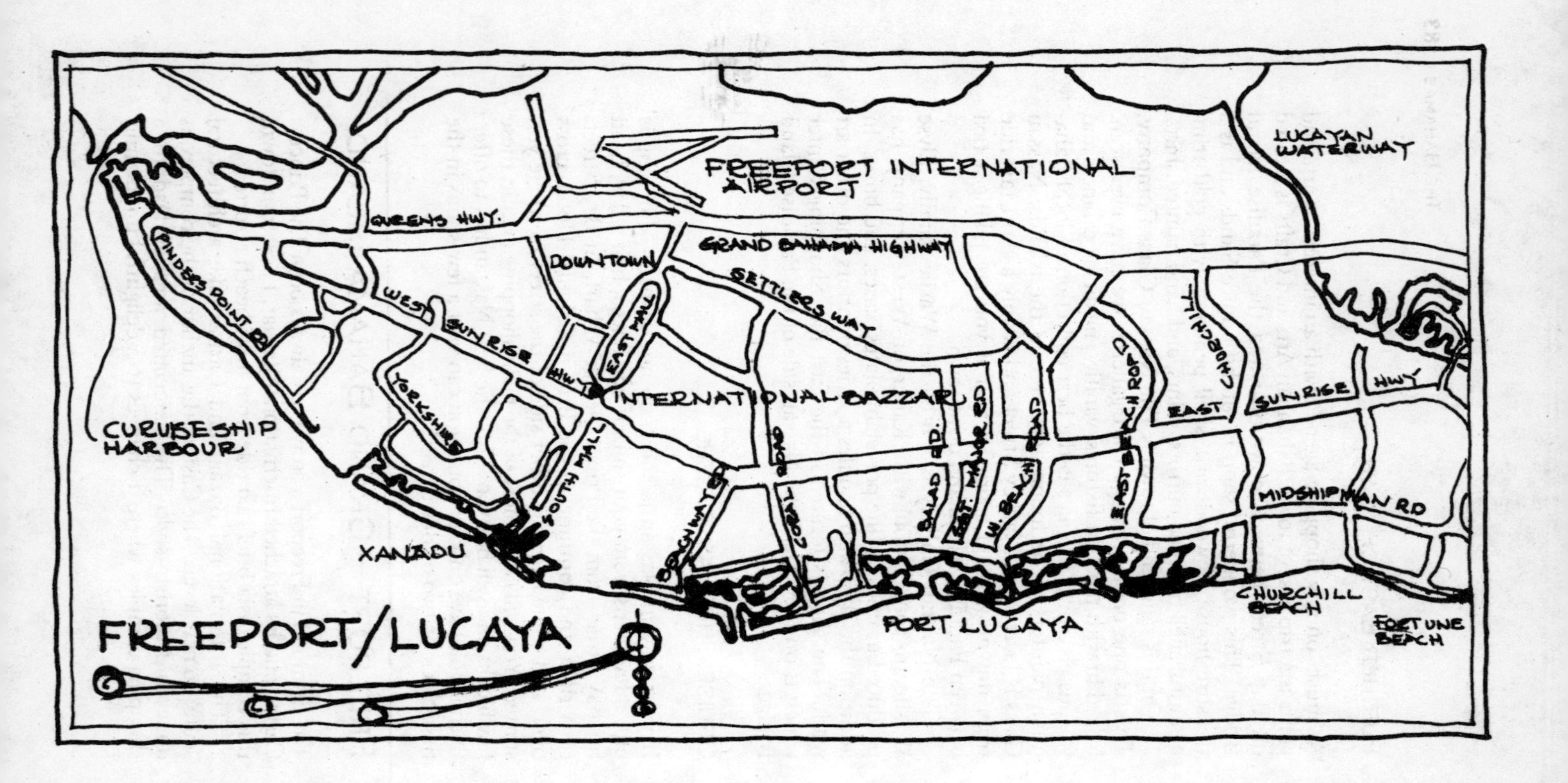
FREEPORT INTERNATIONAL AIRPORT
LUCAYAN WATERWAY
QUEENS HWY.
GRAND BAHAMA HIGHWAY
DOWNTOWN
SETTLERS WAY
PINDERS POINT RD
WEST SUNRISE HWY
EAST MALL
INTERNATIONAL BAZZAR
YORKSHIRE
SOUTH MALL
CURUISESHIP HARBOUR
XANADU
CORAL ROAD
SALAD RD.
W. BEACH ROAD
EAST BEACH ROAD
CHURCHILL
EAST SUNRISE HWY
MIDSHIPMAN RD
CHURCHILL BEACH
FORTUNE BEACH
PORT LUCAYA
FREEPORT/LUCAYA

complex of eclectic Chinese, Mid-Eastern, Scandinavian, French, and South American architecture. Sound like a maze? It is, and a delightful one, a not-quite-so-well-kept Disneyland for shoppers.

You'll find a Tourist Information Center and straw market immediately next to the Bazaar complex.

The largest of the beach resort areas is Lucaya. Here you will find the Lucayan Beach Hotel and Casino as well as the Lucayan Marina Hotel, Atlantic Beach Hotel, and Holiday Inn.

Port Lucaya is a the new shopping and marina complex recently completed in Lucaya. Most of the major shops represented in the Bazaar are also found at Port Lucaya.

And, yes, there is a straw market at Port Lucaya.

The other major beach resort is Xanadu, formerly the exclusive enclave of Howard Hughes.

WHAT TO BUY IN FREEPORT

Like Nassau, Freeport is home of the "duty-free", and if you've done your homework, you can find some deals.

Freeport and Nassau have many of the same larger shops. On first impression, Freeport seems to have many small shops. However, appearances are somewhat deceptive. At both the International Bazaar and Port Lucaya, the major shops have "pumped up" the number of shops by operating under many different names. They give shoppers the impression of a greater variety of shopping. For example, according to which door you enter to the Island Galleria at Port Lucaya, you may think you are in **Ciro, Linens of Lucaya, Lucaya Knits, Columbian Emeralds, Parfum de Paris,** or even **Island Galleria**. They are all the same shop.

Imported goods available in Freeport are the same as those found in Nassau.

Arts and crafts found in Freeport are imported from the rest of the islands since there are no major Bahamian artists in residence. The selection of local arts and crafts at the International Bazaar and at Port Lucaya is good.

WHERE TO SHOP IN FREEPORT

THE INTERNATIONAL BAZAAR

The International Bazaar is truly an extravaganza. It is a "must" for any shopper with the patience to look between and beyond all the T-shirts. Some of the most noteworthy shops include the following:

- **The International Arcade: Island Galleria** has a most interesting selection of merchandise, with a noteworthy collection of local arts and crafts, including work by Eileen Seitz, Ann Green, and Melissa Maura. **Oasis** (also a part of the Island Galleria organization) has perfume from Parfum de Paris, cosmetics, and jewelry and watches from Columbian Emeralds International. The interconnections continue. They also have a Pharmacy which is open late till 11pm, Monday through Saturday, and from 10am to 6pm on Sunday. **El Fendi** has an excellent selection of leather accessories.

- **The Scandinavian Section: Tivoli Danish Designs** has some beautiful wool sweaters at excellent prices. **Midnight Sun** has some very nice crystal and porcelain. **Little Switzerland** is a much smaller shop than the one in Nassau, with a small display of jewelry and some crystal and porcelain.

- **The French Section: Les Parisians** carries an excellent selection of Gucci products. **La Fandalle** has a collection of look alike watches and some interesting jewelry.

- **The South American Section: Columbian Emeralds** is always worth a stop. This chain of fine jewelry stores is well represented throughout the Caribbean, but in the Bahamas they have shops only in the International Bazaar and Port Lucaya. They carry an extensive array of watches and other jewelry in addition to their beautiful namesake. **Casa Simpatica Discount Warehouse** is not particularly noteworthy, but upstairs is a shell shop with some very interesting floral arrangements made out of local shells. **Casa Miro** has Lladro and Goebel crystal, while **El Gallion** has some nice inexpensive coral and conch jewelry. **The Unusual Center** (TUC) has some women's fashions, jewelry, and very nice eel skin accessories.

- **The Chinese Section: The Ginza** (John Bull) offers cameras, watches, jewelry, and perfume. It is much smaller than the John Bull shop in Nassau, but we feel the prices are a little better here.

- **The Mid-East Section:** The **Far East Shop** has a very nice collection of linen and lace at about 50% off of U.S. department store prices. The **Jade Dolphin** carries Barrie sweaters and a small but nice linen collection.

Located in the rear of the International Bazaar, the **Continental Pavilion** allows you to do one-stop T-shirt shopping. They seem to have them all or at least enough that the ones they don't have should not make any difference.

We also found fake Rolex watches for sale, but they are expensive—to $150! Since these are illegal to bring into the U.S., you may want to pass on this purchase.

Located in front of the International Bazaar is the **Straw Market**. It is similar to the one found in Nassau. Be sure to bargain here as you would in other straw markets.

PORT LUCAYA

The **Island Galleria** tops our list for interesting shopping at good values. This delightful shop, managed by Kay Saunders, has many interesting collectibles and many doors. Behind those doors are watercolors by J.C. Hunt and Kathy Moore, Kaiser Porcelain, David Winter Cottages, lace, and knit sportswear. Take a look at the hand painted silk scarves by Armelle. They make excellent gifts!

Oasis has a pharmacy open Monday through Saturday from 10am to 8pm in addition to a stock of jewelry, cosmetics, perfume, and watches.

Caribama has some very nice shell jewelry and decorator pieces by Marilyn Smith hidden among the T-shirts and less desirable items.

If you are looking for crystal or china, **Midnight Sun** should have it in their extensive collection.

The **Glass Menagerie** has a few nice paintings and sketches. **The Strap** offers some nice leather by Lapidus of Paris.

And yes, there is another **Straw Market** here where you can practice your negotiation skills.

CRUISE SHIP PASSENGERS WITH LIMITED TIME

The main shopping areas in Freeport are a short taxi ride from where the cruise ships dock. If you have five or more hours of free time, take a taxi to the International Bazaar first. After shopping there, take another taxi to the new shopping center at Port Lucaya. However, if you only have two or three hours, plan to go the International Bazaar only.

ENJOYING YOUR STAY

ACCOMMODATIONS

The easiest way to get a reservation in the Bahamas is by calling Bahamas Reservation Service (BRS): 800-327-0787. They book many hotels in the Family Islands as well as some in Nassau and Freeport.

In Nassau:

- **Coral World Villas** is located on the private isle of Silver Cay. Very luxurious and private, each villa has its own pool. It has 22 suites and a private beach. (Tel. 809-328-1036, 800-328-8814).

- **Graycliff** is a small, elegant hotel overlooking Nassau. It has 12 guest rooms, pool, sauna, restaurant, and excellent service. (Tel. 809-322-2796, 800-633-7411).

Paradise Island:

- The centerpiece of Paradise Islands is the **Paradise Island Resort and Casino**, now owned by Merv Griffin. It has 1200 rooms and operated by Resorts International.(Tel. 809-363-3000 or 800-321-3000).

- **Atlantis Paradise Island** is a 14 acre waterscape, including the largest open-air aquarium in the world. The Beach Tower has 424 guest rooms; the Coral Tower offers 574 rooms and suites; and the Reef Club features 94 luxurious rooms with VIP concierge services. There are 12 restaurants and lounges, a casino and an 18 hole championship golf course. (Tel. 809-363-3000, 800-321-3000)

- **Pirates Cove Holiday Inn**, with a beach on a small protected cove, has 564 rooms, 86 suites and 3 restaurants. It features an outside bar that is a replica of a pirate ship. (Tel. 809-363-2100, 800-234-6835).

- **Ocean Clib Gold and Tennis Resort** is located on 35 acres along a white sand beach. It is considered one of the most beautiful resorts, with 71 quiet rooms. (Tel. 809-363-2501, 800-321-3000, Fax 809-363-2424).

Cable Beach:

- At Cable Beach the largest complex is **Carnival's Crystal Palace Resort and Casino** (Tel. 809-327-6200, 800-222-7466). Also worth noting at Cable Beach is the **Wyndham Ambassador Beach** (Tel. 809-327-8231 or 800-822-4200).

In Freeport:

- Directly across from the International Bazaar and Casino is the **Bahamian Princess Resort** (Tel. 809-352-9661 or 800-223-1818). This very large and nice facility has a huge pool complex, golf course, and a free shuttle service to the beach at the Xanadu Beach Hotel.

- Also located across from the Bazaar is **Castaways Resort** (Tel. 804-352-6682). A less expensive alternative to the Princess, it is conveniently located for shopping at the International Bazaars.

- On the beach at Lucaya is **The Lucayan Beach Resort & Casino** (Tel. 809-373-7777 or 800-772-1227), **The Atlantic Beach Hotel** (Tel. 809-373-1444), and the **Holiday Inn** (Tel. 809-373-1333).

- A less expensive alternative in the **Lucayan Marina Hotel**. Located across the harbour from the beach front resorts it is connected by a complimentary water taxi that runs every 30 minutes (Tel. 800-772-1227).

- Three miles east of Lucaya is **Club Fortuna.** It is an all-inclusive Mediterranean style Italian resort with 204 rooms and a restaurant. (Tel. 809-373-4000).

- Several miles further west along the coast is **Xanadu Beach Hotel**. This is the former residence of recluse Howard Hughes. In addition to the normal rooms and oceanside villas, the present owner, Land'Or International, has divided Mr. Hughes' former residence into four luxury suits (Tel. 809-352-6782).

RESTAURANTS

In Nassau:

- When shopping downtown, you'll find several places for lunch. **Pick-a-dilly** (Tel. 322-2836) is located on Parliament Street, just off of Bay Street and Rawson Square. This is a wonderful outdoor restaurant. The menu is excellent, and the daiquiri bar is addictive. They claim to make the world's best daiquiris, and we believe them.

- Further up Parliament Street, away from the dock, is **Green Shutters** (Tel. 325-5702), a taste of the English past. Reservations are advised.

- Also worthy of note for the truly hungry is the buffet at the **Bayside** (Tel. 322-7479). The food is good, the harbor view is fantastic, and it is open late. The Bayside is in the shopping arcade associated with the British Colonial Hotel. After dinner, enjoy strolling the grounds of this monument of days past.

- For dinner with true British elegance, served in the former manor of Lord Dudley is **Graycliff**. It features continental cuisine with a touch of Bahamian seasoning, and an extensive wine collection. (Tel. 322-2796).

- For that special night out, try the **Sun and...**, considered by many to be the best restaurant in Nassau. Located in a quiet residential neighborhood just east of town, this is truly a world class establishment with both indoor and outdoor dining. Although a bit expensive, it is still an excellent value. Reservations are a must, and patrons are expected to be well dressed (Tel. 323-1205).

Paradise Island:

- There are many restaurants in the casinos on Paradise Island. Two that we believe are set apart are the **Bahamian Club** (363-3000, ext. 5608) and the **Coyaba** (Tel. 363-3000), both located in Merv Griffin's Paradise Island Resort and Casino. One has an exclusive British gentlemen's club atmosphere with dark paneled walls, while the other specializes in Chinese cuisine with a South Seas flavor.

In Freeport:

- If you need to take a break from shopping in the International Bazaar, **The Pub On The Mall**,(Tel. 352-2700)directly across the street, offers an excellent international menu, including fish and chips.

- **Lucianno's** overlooks the waterway and features fine French and Italian dishes. Jackets may be required in the evening. (Tel. 373-9100).

- Located in the Lucayan Beach Resort and Casino, **Les Oursins**, features elegant continental dining. Reservations and jackets required. (Tel. 373-7777).

- **The Stoned Crab** is nice for that special night out. Located directly on Taino Beach, the lobster, crabs, and steaks are excellent. Reservations are recommended (Tel. 373-1442).

- **Harry's American Bar**, (Tel. 348-2660) made famous by Hemingway, is located at Deadman's Reef. It should be included as a lunch stop on a day excursion to the west of town. No credit cards are accepted.

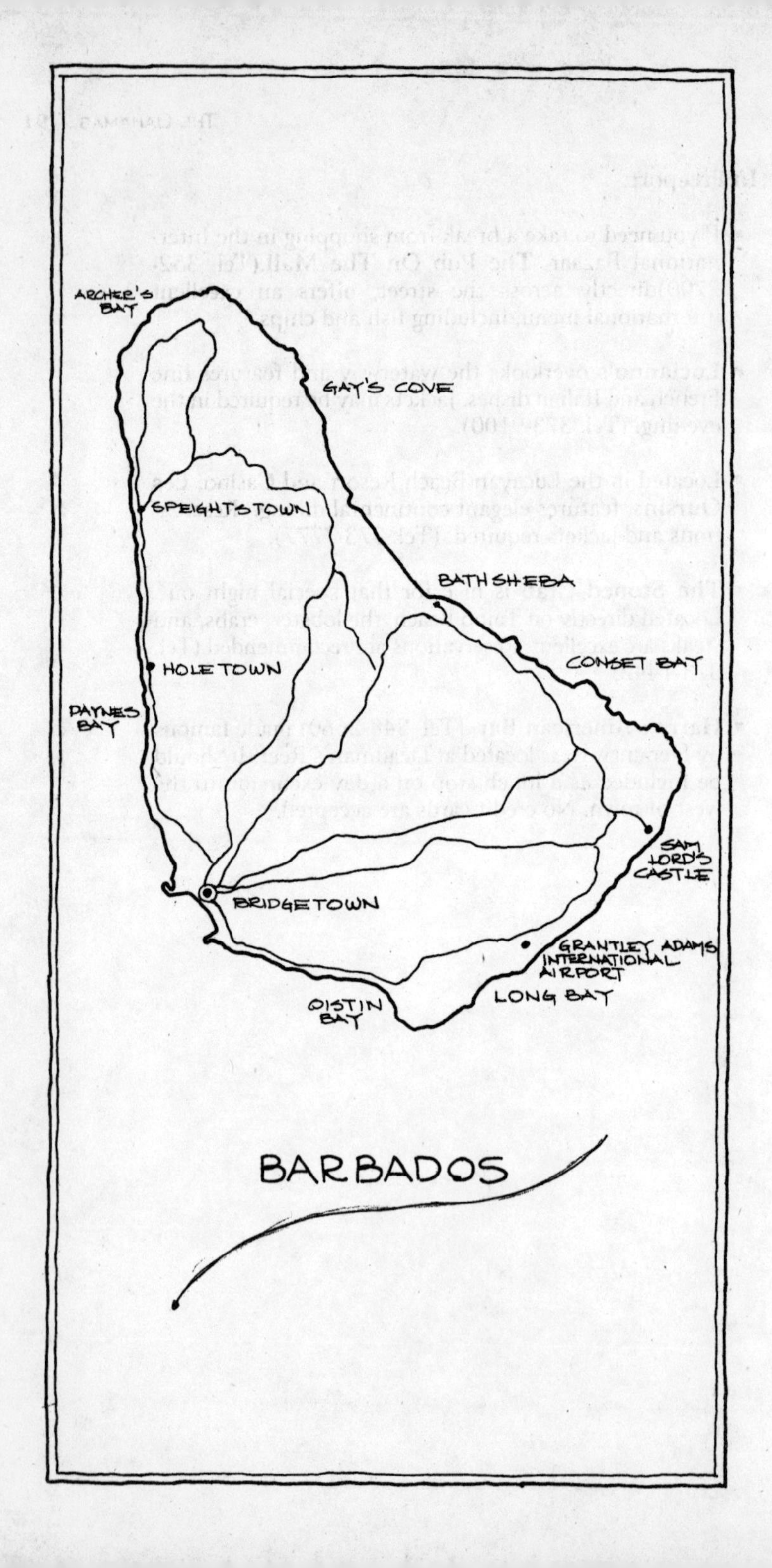
ARCHER'S BAY
GAY'S COVE
SPEIGHTSTOWN
BATHSHEBA
HOLETOWN
CONSET BAY
PAYNES BAY
SAM LORD'S CASTLE
BRIDGETOWN
GRANTLEY ADAMS INTERNATIONAL AIRPORT
LONG BAY
OISTIN BAY
BARBADOS

7

Barbados

The natural beauty of Barbados is legendary. It seems as if someone sat down and designed the perfect Caribbean island. With the Atlantic Ocean on one side and the Caribbean Sea on the other, this 21 by 14 mile island seems much larger than it is. The island is dotted with seaside villages, English country churches, beautiful plantation houses, miles of sugar cane fields, chicken hatcheries, and dairy farms. The French lacework on the pastel painted houses give Barbados a very graceful air.

Bajan Treasures

Barbados' greatest treasure is its people, who seem to treat all tourists as long lost relatives. Not only are the Bajans (as they call themselves) friendly, but they love their island and want to share it with visitors. They go out of their way to show them sights, shopping areas, and some good times.

Barbados has a long British heritage. Even though the island achieved independence in 1966, it still retains many British symbols. Cricket is the national pastime; Lord Nelson is perched in the middle of Bridgetown's square; the police band still plays concerts from the Victorian bandstand on the esplanade; and Bajans drive on the left side of the road.

Barbados is politically and economically very stable and it has a superb climate. Thousands of visitors return here year after year to savor the relaxation and beauty of this exotic island.

Shopping is a delight in Barbados. Each seaside village has its own quiet shopping area. Shopping in Bridgetown is cosmopolitan with a major department store and malls to explore. Many of the island's top artisans can be found working in the shops of Pelican Village.

GETTING TO KNOW YOU

Barbados is the eastern most island of the West Indies. Located at 13 degrees north latitude and 50 degrees west longitude, it lies just outside the Caribbean's windward chain of islands. Approximately 260,000 people inhabit the island with 65,000 Bajans living in Bridgetown alone. The rugged north side of the island faces the Atlantic and is reminiscent of northern Scotland. While dangerous to swim here, the area is well posted and several spots offer safe areas for swimming. The western Caribbean coast is smooth and usually calm.

Los Barbados was the name given the island in 1536 by its Portuguese discovers. It means "the bearded ones" because the Bajan trees have exposed roots that look like beards. Through an oversight, Portugal never claimed the island. The first English settlers arrived in 1605 after the Earl of Marborough was granted the island by the King. They established a settlement in Holetown. The island was controlled by the British until its independence.

Barbados' history has been more peaceful than most other islands in the Caribbean. The original settlers worked hard to establish large sugar plantations. Through their own efforts and with the labor of many African slaves, they created a very prosperous economy. Great Houses abound on this small island. Sam Lord built his own castle and lured many passing ships onto the reefs by hanging lights along the shore. Appropriating the cargo of shipwrecks, he helped enrich the island economy. Today his castle sits in the center of the Marriott Resort and is open to the public. Other representations of Chattel Houses unique to Barbados are seen along side the road. These colorful cottages were constructed by the workers to be moved from plantation to plantation for living quarters while they brought in the sugar cane crop. Sugar is still important to the Barbadian economy and you can visit a modern sugar cane factory from February to June during the grinding season.

Barbados is very diverse for its 166 square mile size. The island is hilly with jagged cliffs and bluffs as well as a long valley near the beach. Most resorts and villas face the Caribbean Sea. An inland web of narrow roads winds through sugar plantations and tiny colorful villages. Bridgetown is the capital and sits in the curve of the southwestern coast.

The main shopping destination on this island is the capital of **Bridgetown**. Its crowded downtown caters to all the shopping needs of visitors. You can easily shop this area in part of one day. Millions of dollars worth of renovations have taken place during the last few years, including a new duty-free shopping terminal at the harbor for cruise ships

Another major shopping area is **Pelican Village**. Located one mile out of town, it houses the artisans of Barbados. North of Bridgetown on Highway 1 is Holetown, which is where the British supposedly first landed on Barbados. Further north is the small village of Speightstown, an interesting old town which is particularly busy on Saturday mornings. Here, as well as in nearby Six Man's Bay, you can still see wooden fishing boats being built.

- ❑ **Each seaside village has its own quiet shopping area.**
- ❑ **The main shopping destination is the capital of Bridgetown.**
- ❑ **Most taxi drivers will take you sightseeing for a full or half-day.**
- ❑ **There is little different between the exchange rates offered by banks versus hotels, shops, and restaurants.**
- ❑ **Shops prices are normally stated in U.S. dollars.**
- ❑ **You may find shops less crowded in the early afternoon.**

Barbados has everything you expect on a tropical island—and then some. The cooling trade winds whisper through the palm and casuarina trees lining the shore. While the Caribbean gently caresses the western beaches, the Atlantic surf to the east rises majestically onto the beaches and rock pools. The sunrises over the Atlantic are pink spectaculars and sunsets are glorious explosions of crimsons and indigo. At certain times of the year the sunsets include a fine dust that blows across from the Sahara Desert.

Time is not considered as important here as it is elsewhere in the world. Indeed, the Bajans boast that the hands of the clock stand still on their island. They are efficient people, but they also would like you to enjoy a little of their unhurried island philosophy. The Bajans are friendly people and will lend a helping hand if you get lost or have a flat tire.

Barbados is one of the very few islands in the Caribbean

that has continuous and pervasive British influence. The British connection is evident in the Bajans culture, laws, religion, and manners. As in Britain, the police remain unarmed. Cricket is more than just a sport—it's both a national obsession and a way of life.

THE BASICS

LOCATION AND GEOGRAPHY

Barbados is situated in the eastern most portion of the Caribbean—east of St. Lucia and St. Vincent, two of the windward islands. Strictly speaking, Barbados is not in the Caribbean because it is located in the Atlantic Ocean. However, since most people consider Barbados to be a Caribbean Island and Bajans do too, by convention it is part of the Caribbean.

Barbados is located 118 miles from St. Lucia, 100 miles east of St. Vincent, and 155 miles northeast of Grenada. For many Americans who vacation here for a week or two, Barbados is just a short four and one half hour trip from New York City. For the British, it's a very popular Caribbean island because of its warm weather and eastern location.

A coral island measuring 14 by 21 miles, Barbados is flat compared to the somewhat wild volcanic terrain of many islands in the Antilles. It's shaped like a shoulder of lamb and from the air looks much larger than it really is. It is an island of hills and dales, but not mountains. The highest point on Barbados is Mt. Hillaby at 1,115 feet.

You will find most hotels and many villas on the west coast, usually right on the beach. This is the Caribbean side of the island where the gentle sea, in varying shades of blue and green, slosh against the shore. This coast has been taken over by tourism. By contrast, the eastern Atlantic side of the island has furious waves and man-made structures. Experienced surfers from all over the world come to surf this wild sea, but it's not recommended for amateur swimmers. Part of this coast is known as the Scotland District, because it strongly resembles the Highlands. The cluttered little capital of Bridgetown and large portion of the island's population is found on the southwestern coast.

CLIMATE, WHEN TO GO, WHAT TO WEAR

The climate of Barbados is one of the healthiest in the world, with no smokestack industries to pollute the air and with fresh sea breezes and an excellent mixture of sunshine and rain. The daytime temperatures range from 75 to 85 degrees throughout the year. The ever present trade winds keep the humidity down and sweeten the night air with aromas of hibiscus, bougainvillea, and Barbados' own special limonia. The island boasts 3,000 hours of sunshine a year, yet there is enough rainfall to guarantee an abundance of fruits and vegetables.

Barbados is beautiful all year long. Its high season is from December 15 to April 15. However, many people prefer visiting Barbados just before or after the high season when hotel and villa rentals drop as much as 30%. Beaches are nearly empty and the cooling sea breezes keep the island from getting too hot. The island does have a rainy season, usually from September through mid-November, but the rain usually comes and goes quickly.

Given the island's casual atmosphere, chances are you will live in shorts and simple tops. It is best to wear bathing suits only at the beach and the pool areas, however, since the islanders are fairly conservative. A few hotels require men to wear jackets in the evening. It is a good idea to pack a sweater or windbreaker for the boat rides. Walking shoes are a must and simple sandals are handy.

GETTING THERE

Daily flights to Barbados from New York are available on American Airlines and BWIA. The trip takes about four hours from New York. Airlines also have flights to Barbados from Miami, Boston, Chicago, Atlanta and Washington, DC. Some airlines connect through San Juan to the island. In addition to many small regional air carriers, Barbados is also serviced by LIAT and Air Martinique. British Air and Air Canada also provide service.

DOCUMENTS

U.S. citizens coming directly from the U.S. to Barbados for a period not exceeding three months must have proof of identity and citizenship. This can take the form of an original birth certificate, citizenship papers, or passport. You can provide proof of identity with a driver's license, university or school I.D. card, or a senior citizen's card as long as they include a photograph. For stays longer than three months, a passport is required. This is another island that may also ask for an ongoing or return ticket to be shown at Immigration.

ARRIVAL AND DEPARTURE

From the air, Barbados looks vast. From the harbor, Bridgetown looks bigger than it actually is. If you arrive by air, you will find the airport very efficient. Finished in 1979, the Bajans are very proud of the Grantly Adams International Airport. Immigration is fast and courteous, and everything is available at the airport to assist you. Although you can use U.S. money to get into town, be prepared to pay in Barbados Dollars. The airport money exchange is very convenient. The National Bank at the airport is open from 8am to noon every day, and you can actually exchange your money before you pass through Immigration.

After passing through Immigration and retrieving your bags, you proceed on to Customs which is very quick and efficient. You'll discover a great deal of traffic at the airport, because the Bajans, like residents of many other Caribbean Islands, love to visit the airport to watch all the activity. If you plan to rent a car, you'll see the car rental counters after you pass through Customs; all major companies are represented. It's best to reserve a car in advance to ensure its availability. One of the most delightful ways of getting around is to rent a minimoke—a small open jeep-like car. Many tourists and shoppers find the minimoke more exciting for exploring the island than a normal car. Although having your own car is certainly convenient, you might want to think twice before renting one. With donkey carts on the road, trucks stacked high with sugar cane, and left side rules of the road, driving can sometimes resemble an obstacle course rather than getting from one place to another on a highway.

If you choose not to rent a car or minimoke, you'll find plenty of taxis just outside the door of the airport. Some hotels also provide a pick up service. If you take a taxi to your hotel, the trip will take about 25 to 40 minutes and cost about $28 to $45 Barbados dollars depending on what part of the Island you are staying. Since taxis are not metered, be sure to confirm the fare beforehand. All the rates are set but tips are at your discretion.

Barbados also has a bus system and a privately owned minibus service. Both charge about 75 cents in Barbados currency and exact change is required. Buses usually run about five to ten minutes behind the posted schedule.

If you arrive by ship, your port will be about one mile from Bridgetown. It's very easy to get a taxi here for sightseeing and shopping. Some ship lines also have package deals with the Hilton Hotel for using the hotel beaches. The Hilton actually has two beaches which are located next to Bridgetown. You'll find a shopping arcade here that could serve as a nice one-stop shopping area if your time is limited.

You may want to take a taxi to the beach to enjoy the exquisite Caribbean waters. Vendors on the beach expect you to bargain.

Most taxi drivers will take you sightseeing. You can make arrangements with them for full or half-day tours.

If you have more than an hour or two, you might want to rent a minimoke or a car to drive around the island. The roads are not well marked, but maps are available; it is easy to find your way back to the port. The Barbados National Bank also operates an exchange bureau at the seaport.

All passengers departing from Barbados must pay a departure tax of $25 dollars Barbados or US$12.50. The tax may be paid in either currency. Children under 12 years of age are exempted and no departure tax is required if you have been on the island one day or less.

CURRENCY, TRAVELER'S CHECKS, CREDIT CARDS

The Barbados dollar is valued at approximately US$.50. This is a constant ratio since it is officially pegged to the US dollar. Most shops accept both US and Canadian dollars as well as traveler's checks. Some larger stores and several hotels and restaurants also honor American Express, Diners Club, VISA, and Mastercard. Stores do not offer discounts for payments made in US cash or traveler's checks. There is little difference between the exchange rate offered by banks versus hotels, shops, and restaurants. Although both currencies are accepted, it is more convenient to exchange your money into Barbadian dollars and use the local currency for shopping. If you use American currency, you will probably receive change in Barbados dollars.

Most banks are open Monday through Thursday from 9am to 3pm and Fridays from 9am to 1pm and 3-5pm. Barclay's Bank open one hour earlier (8am) than the other banks. All banks are closed on weekends and holidays. When shopping in Barbados, keep in mind that unless otherwise specified, prices are normally stated in U.S. dollars.

TIPPING

Most hotels and restaurants add a 10% service charge to your bill. You may, however, want to leave something extra for exceptional service. When a service charge is not included, it is customary to tip waiters 10-15%, hotel maids approximately one dollar per room per day, and bellboys 25 cents per day. In cases of special errands, a $1 or $1.50 tip is fine. Airport porters expect to receive about .50 cents per bag. Taxi drivers are normally tipped 10% of the fare.

LANGUAGE

As in many other Caribbean Islands, language here is no problem. Bajans speak English with their own musical lilt. This is one of the few islands where English has been the official language since the island was founded.

BUSINESS HOURS

The Bajans say their stores and shops open as early as 8am. However, we find most do not open before 9am. They also close around 4pm, and some shops close for lunch. Since the Bajans like to do most of their shopping in the morning, you may find shops less crowded in the early afternoon.

TRANSPORTATION AND TOURS

Barbados is a beautiful island with an exhausting list of attractions. If you rent a car to drive around the island, you'll find maps in magazines such as ***The Visitor*** or ***The Sun Seeker*** as well as at the rental agencies. Keep in mind, however, that you will need a temporary permit or an international driver's license. You can get a visitors driver's license with your own license and a fee of $10 Barbados dollars ($5 US) by filling out a form at the airport or at the police stations in Bridgetown, Hastings, Holetown, or Worthing. Again, keep in mind that driving is on the left side of the road, and pay particular attention to the one-way street signs in Bridgetown. Since street parking is more or less impossible, use parking lots which are not expensive. If you are fortunate enough to find a parking place on a Bridgetown street (the areas are marked with a large blue "P" sign), you will undoubtedly be accosted by a gentlemen who holds your door open as you get out and offers to "mind" your car. Although there is no set fee for this service nor are you obligated to accept it, the going rate is about two Barbados dollars.

If you prefer not driving, one of the best ways to see the island is to hire a taxi. Nearly all Bajan taxi drivers are familiar with the island and love to show it off to visitors. A six to eight hour day trip by taxi will cost $80-$100 for a party of up to four.

L. E. Williams (427-1043) and the United Taxi Owners Association (426-0284) offer day tours that cover the entire island as well as include lunch. Cosmic Tour (428-2050) offers a unique tour for viewing the island. Numerous other tours are also available. Be sure you know what the tour fees entail, including sites chosen for lunch.

Very special tours can be arranged by VIP (429-4617)Sally Shern slides you though the countryside in an air conditioned Mercedes Benz with an itinerary of your choice.

Bajan Helicopters (431-0069) can take you aloft to see the island.

RESOURCES

You will find plenty of local resources for keeping abreast of international and local events. ***The Barbados Advocate*** is the island's daily newspaper. ***The Nation*** is published daily, but Sunday's edition is known as ***The Sun***. They are sold on the curbs and almost every corner. A monthly magazine called ***The New Bajan*** is also good to read for local events.

The Visitor is a tourist publication highlighting nightspots, restaurants, and shopping specials. Published by ***The Nation***, it's available at hotels and information centers. ***The Sun Seeker*** is published weekly by the ***Advocate*** and is at all tourist areas. Both publications are free and very useful.

The Board of Tourism is located in Bridgetown at the Harbour Industrial Park (427-2623). The cruise ship pier at Deep Water Harbour and the airport also have information centers. Both places offer an ***Official Guide to Barbados*** and ***Things You Should Know***.

SHOPPING IN BARBADOS

Barbados may not have the skyscrapers of New York or the sophistication of London's Bond Street, but it has great merchandise and prices. Barbados is not only a paradise for visitors coming for sun and sea, it's a paradise for shoppers. It is by some standards arguably the best island in the Caribbean for style, quality, originality, variety, and price.

The name of the game here is duty-free shopping. With the liberal tax regulations of 1986, shopping is more attractive and easier than ever. There is much less red tape, which leaves more time to hunt out great bargains in the island boutiques and department stores. Shops, whether in Bridgetown or out of town, are filled with a wide range of quality goods at bargain prices: crystal, bone china, cameras, watches, jewelry, perfume, spirits and clothing—especially British woolens, tweeds, and cashmere.

Throughout the island there are a variety of **local handicrafts** for sale, which make excellent gifts as well as superb souvenirs. These include colorful and practical local pottery, some with designs based upon Arawak and Caribe Indian themes; sea based items such as coral and shell jewelry; original Barbadian designed and manufactured clothing; woodcarvings; straw works; and Barbadian prints and paintings.

Excellent **souvenirs** include rag dolls, in the form of wall hangings to pajama bags, sand dollars, Khus Khus aromatic root hangers for the closet, and an enormous array of mahogany and shell gift items, such as ashtrays, gift boxes, and desk sets.

Batik is also very popular. Originating in Indonesia, this hot wax and dye technique involves the application of brilliant patterns to fabrics. In Barbados batik has evolved into many original local designs and produced as dresses, blouses, shirts, scarves, beachwear and wall hangings; brilliant designs incorporate the flowers, birds and fish of the Caribbean.

An interesting and most unusual gift is a **tapestry kit** of Barbadian prints. These depict scenes native to Barbados in colorful patterns. They are available at Bests in Barbados shops which also features a great many gift items designed by artist Joel Walker.

Children's clothing and smocks beautifully embroidered by Barbadian women as a cottage industry are sold at very attractive prices and make practical as well as lovely gifts.

Modest sized shops of big department stores carry superb **famous name merchandise** from all the corners of the world: bone china from the great English potteries, Irish and Danish crystal, Thai and Chinese silks, French perfumes, watches from Switzerland, leather work from Spain and Italy, and more.

Shopping for quality antiques is a great pastime on the island. There are a number of shops specializing in original pieces as well as excellent reproductions of West Indian colonial furniture.

DUTY-FREE SHOPPING

Prior to May 1, 1986, duty-free goods had to be purchased "in bond" meaning that the goods were never actually brought into the country and could not be delivered to the customer in the store. The goods were held on the docks or international trade zone, the customer saw the product in the store, made the purchase, but received the item at the airport or on board ship. The normal disadvantage of this was timing. Normally, purchases had to be made at least 24 hours in advance. If you lost your claim check, you had a problem.

This situation has now changed. Duty-free items can be taken from the point of purchase. Exceptions include electronics(such as video games and computers), liquor, and tobacco. Shops will be happy to advise you on the current regulations. The duty-free list has also been expanded to include most imported goods. Clothing bought here duty-free can be worn immediately.

Even though "in bond" shopping is not required for most items, visitors buying duty-free goods must produce bonafide travel documents, such as air or cruise ship tickets, in order to "take away" the goods. You can, of course, buy duty-free goods without the documents in your possession, but those purchases must be delivered to the plane or ship.

In addition to the many shops on Broad Street in Bridgetown, you'll also find duty-free shops at Bridgetown Harbor and at Grantly Adams Airport. Although their selections may be limited compared to other shops, they come in handy for last minute shopping.

Prices, Discounts and Bargaining

Pricing in Barbados is very similar to Bermuda—mostly fixed with little room for bargaining. Except with beach vendors, you will have little opportunity to bargain here. At Pelican Village, where arts and crafts are available by local artisans, you can negotiate some since the craftspeople directly sell their own products. But even this shopping is not like bargaining elsewhere in the Caribbean. We frequently do receive up to 25% discount on some jewelry at Pelican Village, but only during the off season summer months.

You will find shopping in Bridgetown to be very much like shopping in the U.S. Bargain shopping primarily occurs when items are put on sale. At the same time, the stated prices on many items is still 30% to 50% below what the items sell for in the U.S.

The only real bargaining in Barbados is on the beaches where you will find hand made items and T-shirts galore. When dealing with beach vendors, always offer half of the initial asking price and work somewhere towards the middle of the difference. Some Antique dealers will negotiate.

WHAT TO BUY

Since shopping in Bridgetown is like shopping in most cities, it often lacks the quaint charm found when shopping in many other Caribbean locations. You will find some very good buys in Barbados. In fact, the best buys in the Caribbean for some items are found in Barbados.

- **The name of the game in Barbados is duty-free shopping.**
- **Most pricing is fixed with little room for bargaining. The only real bargaining takes places on the beaches for T-shirts and handmade items.**
- **The best buys are on original works and handmade items, mahogany sculptures, and pottery.**
- **The most unique purchase in Barbados is the flash frozen, vacuum sealed, flying fish.**

The stores and malls of Bridgetown contain everything from the latest perfumes to electronic items and antiques. Duty-free items, such as liquor, bone china, crystal, silver, cameras, watches, binoculars, and clothing are everywhere. Of course, there is no duty on art or local craft items.

The best shopping buys are found on original works and handmade items, mahogany sculptures, and pottery. Watches are among the best items to look for in jewelry. Javanese gold pieces, heavy and high in gold content, are not stamped with the gold content and thus may be difficult to authenticate. The prices on Lladro are the best in the Caribbean, but we find selections here somewhat limited. Rolex watches also rival St. Martin prices and are the lowest of any place outside of St. Martin. Barbadian antique shops sell pieces of island yesteryear, much of it originally from Great Britain. They also carry reproductions, so be sure to ask. Recently West Indies furniture is catching on outside of the Caribbean. It is made from mahogany wood and chairs are heavy with larger seats that are made from cane with an open weave for comfort. The rocking chair can be seen in many of the great houses and is the most popular piece sold.

The most unique purchase in Barbados is the flash frozen, vacuum sealed, flying fish. Take them home with you to relive those wonderful memories of dining in Barbados.

Don't forget the rum. Mt. Gay rum factory, a 175 year tradition in Bridgetown, gives guided tours, including samples, where you can see how it is blended, bottled, and tested. If you wish to purchase some rum, be sure to order it immediately so that the "in bond" process can work and you can actually take the rum home with you.

ARTS AND ANTIQUES

Antiques in Barbados have been imported many generations ago or are heirlooms that belonged to original Colonials. Most antiques here have been imported from England, but you'll find an impressive variety of furniture and objects of art collected from the 18th and 19th Century plantation houses. Local Bajan craftspeople also have created four poster beds, tables, and chairs long before turning to sculpturing for visitors. Both the original pieces of furniture and the excellent reproductions are made of mahogany, and the quality of the open cane weave pieces is exquisite.

Some suggested places to shop for arts and antiques are **Antiquaria**, located at Spring Garden Hwy., Grenwich House Antiques (most of the items predate 1910) located near the major resort area. St. Michael, and the **Women's Self-Help Handicraft and Flower Shop** on Broad Street. Antiquaria has many old maps, prints and paintings, as well as silver, crystal, and porcelain. The Women's Self-Help Handicraft and Flower Shop specializes in smaller antiques from the colonial period. There are others such as **Antiques and Collectibles** located in Hastings and **Greenwich House Antiques** and **La Galerie Antique** both located in St. James.

Period furniture is available throughout Barbados. The **London Gallery** in Holetown is one of the best sources for this furniture. Since there are a number of museums displaying rooms of furniture from the Colonial period, you may want to visit them to acquaint yourself with plantation life as well as gain background information to assist in shopping for the antiques.

There are also a number of auction sales which offer the opportunity to find unique antiques. The sales are most often listed in the Sunday newspaper.

JEWELRY AND WATCHES

Many shops in Bridgetown carry a varied collection of gold and silver jewelry, pearl necklaces, quartz watches, necklaces, bracelets, and earrings. Seiko watches are a specialty of **Correl's** on Broad Street. Raymond Weil, Paiget, Bravado, and Citizens can all be found at the **Royal Shop** on Broad Street. Prices on Rolex watches, in such places as **Lewis L. Bailey & Son** on Broad Street and other fine jewelry shops, are some of the best we have seen throughout the Caribbean with the exception of St. Martin. When purchasing any of the more expensive jewelry and watches, pay close attention to the gold content, the warranty supplied, and the certificate of authenticity.

PERFUME

Even though Barbados does not manufacture a local fragrance, you will find excellent buys on imported name brands. Lanvin, Yves St. Laurent, and Oscar de la Renta at **Da Costas** sell for up to 50% below US prices. **Cave Shepherd** and **Harrison's** have the widest selections.

FASHIONS

Barbados is a shopper's paradise for reasonably priced men's and women's fashion wear. Barbados often sets the style for casual wear as well as cool elegant fashions for evening wear in the Caribbean.

Certainly the number one department store in Barbados—for sheer size as well as variety—is **Cave Shepherd** on Broad Street in Bridgetown. Among the vast variety of merchandise available, you will find the exclusive boutique dresses, sarongs, and beachwear by Clarabelle Boutique, plus the well known designer T-shirts from Kokonuts of St. Lucia. The store also carries a number of other leading Barbadian designers plus imports from other Caribbean countries. Here, too, you will find the exclusive collection of Jensen's sportswear.

For a truly fine selection of shoes, you should try **Mademoiselle** on Broad Street. Here you will find a unique range of leather and synthetic footwear in high style imported from Spain, Brazil, Italy and England. The store carries the famous Clark's brand as well as Bandilino. Quality leather handbags are available in many stores. Mademoiselle also carries a limited amount of fashion clothing.

In the new **Da Costas Mall** on Broad Street look for branches of such fashionable boutiques as Paris Dreams, Top Mode, and Pilgrims Shoe Shop. Many of these shops carry all sorts of casual wear and some of the more popular Rosco Tees and Cotton Club line of T-shirts.

If you like batik, try **Boutique Caribe** on Broad Street and at the Hilton Hotel Arcade. This shop offers original batik designs created in Barbados, Trinidad, and Tobago as well as small gift items. The selections include everything from swim wear to casual clothes to beautiful designer evening wear.

Lindsay Corbin's screen prints and hand painted cotton

fabrics, featured in Vogue, are available at **Dover** in Christ Church. Two of the most original and extensive lines of special T-shirts found in Barbados, under both the Rosco Tees and Cotton Club labels, are available in many shops including the one owned by Rosco Tees called "In Transit." The Top Mode label, which is known for its comprehensive and unusual T-shirts, beach, and 100% cotton casual wear, is well known throughout the world. They are available in many shops but are featured in the **Top Mode** shop in Mall 34 and now at De Costas. Swim wear, T-shirts, dresses, men's shirts and trousers, and sportswear can be found at Top Mode. They also carry such other popular brands as Dragon Lady and Surf and Sound. Two other well known fashion collections—Naf-Naf and Tout Fou—are also available in a number of stores. The boutique in Mall 34 and the Hilton Hotel, **Paris Dreams**, handles both of these lines.

Many shops carry a unique collection of fashions and accessories as well as hand-painted, printed, embroidered, and appliqued clothing by local designers. You will find quality imports for day and evening wear, and many selections are made of 100% cotton. Two good sources for unique items are **Origins** in the Careenage in Bridgetown and in Holetown, St. James and Cotton Days Design. Carol Codogan has her design studio at Rose Cottage, lower Bay Street and her sportswear at Bridge House, Cavans Lane.

LINENS

Harrison's and **Cave Shepherd** are excellent hunting grounds for Oriental or European linens, but the **Women's Self-Help Shop** in Bridgetown is where you will find local handmade lace and embroidered items. You can even have linens made to order and shipped to you at home.

FOOD

The most famous delicacy is **flying fish**. It is flash frozen and vacuum packed along with a favorite local recipe. Fly Fish, Inc. packages the fish so major airlines will approve it for carry-on and it will pass U.S. Customs. You should also try to enjoy it at the many restaurants on the Island.

Bajans have their own style of **hot sauce**, and it is very hot. It is made from Scotch Bonnet peppers, and a little bit goes a long way.

SPIRITS

Barbados has numerous distilleries producing rum and beer. The most famous is **Mount Gay** for good quality rum. This is the island for the best planter's punch using dark rum, lime juice and syrup topped with fresh nutmeg. Bajan's say the secret to the finest rum is the mountain water. They certainly create a wide variety of drinks such as **Falernum** which is a sweet syrupy rum based drink. It is mixed with pure rum and lime and poured over ice. A Bajan boilermaker consists of a pint of beer, one tablespoon of brandy, and a teaspoon of sugar and ginger with a lemon peel.

Banks is an excellent local beer.

Da Costa Ltd. located in Bridgetown on Broad Street (Tel. 809-426-3451 carries an excellent selection of international liquors.

HANDICRAFTS

Many shops in Barbados carry an extensive array of gifts, souvenirs, and crafts featuring local designers and artisans. The designs of **Jill Walker** include superb color prints of Barbadian life and are available at many stores including De Costa's Mall. Crafts by **Rosslyn of Barbados** and **Tropical Weavers** as well as many of the straw works, jewelry, and pottery made by the local residents are available in many outlets.

Pelican Village is one of the best places to buy handicrafts in Barbados. It is located on the Princess Alice Highway about one mile out of Bridgetown. Souvenir hunting is excellent here. While you have to wander and search for quality, you can see the artists at work throughout this area. You can also find a good variety of mahogany carvings, rag dolls, basketwork, and rugs made from Khus Khus grass. Khus Khus grass is found in big clumps along the roadside as well as in cane fields where it creates "headrow" to prevent soil erosion. The grass is dried and crafted into different patterns and shapes. The end result is a beautiful dried grass rug that can be seen in many homes and hotels throughout this area. It being used in roofs, beach huts, and other crafts. The lily plant also provides pandanus used for many baskets and table mats.

The development of handicrafts in Barbados has been influence from several sources. Many are African designs from the Ibo, Ashanti, and Mandingo tribes that have been intertwined with designs from the Arawak Indians. These two, combined with subtle influences from the Dutch, Spanish, Portuguese, and English traders, make for a unique range of crafts found nowhere else in the world.

The **Barbados Handicraft Center** on Bridge Street displays many of these items. But local crafts can be found in small shops and stores all over the island. Don't be afraid to explore many out of the way places as well as larger stores for truly unique handicrafts.

Barbados has many fine artists and artisans, including pottery by Goldie Spiller and Susan Beale, limited edition prints by Heather Dawn Scott, watercolors by Jean Ellison, and original works of art and decorated pottery by Diane Butcher. One of the best sources for these items is the **Guardhouse Gallery** at the Grande Barbados Resort. Diane Butcher's works can be found at the **Waterfront Cafe**. The **Wents & Friends**, located in Christ Church, has paintings from local artists as well as hand painted clothing, pottery and wood carvings. The Skyway Plaza near the south shore hotels also has a selection of handicrafts, and the new duty-free terminal at Bridgetown Harbour has several local merchandise shops and push carts.

WHERE TO SHOP

Most major shopping in Barbados is found in Bridgetown. In fact, you won't need a map because the two main shopping streets are Broad Street and Swan Street. The major department stores, such as **De Costas, Harrisons**, and **Cave Shepherd** on Broad Street literally have everything you could possibly want. But some smaller stores located on Broad Street or Swan Street also have excellent selections. If you have limited time, we recommend that you concentrate your shopping along those two streets. You will find almost everything available in this area.

Some of the more delightful places to shop are found in what the Bajans call malls. While not large by U.S. standards, they are collections of stores under one roof. These areas offer one-stop shopping for both shopper and tradespeople. One of the newest and grandest shopping malls is **De Costas** on Broad Street in the heart of Bridgetown. The De Costas family has been in business in Barbados since the mid-19th Century when they founded the first De Costas store on Broad Street in 1868. This new De Costas store combines modern and traditional architecture into a pleasant area of 20 shops offering a good variety of merchandise. Here you will find the **Colonade Shop** for luxurious china and crystal; **World of Fabrics** for materials, notions, and patterns; **Paris Dreams Boutique** for Gnoff Gnoff and Tokefu fashions; **Baileys Watch and Jewelry Shop**; **Top**

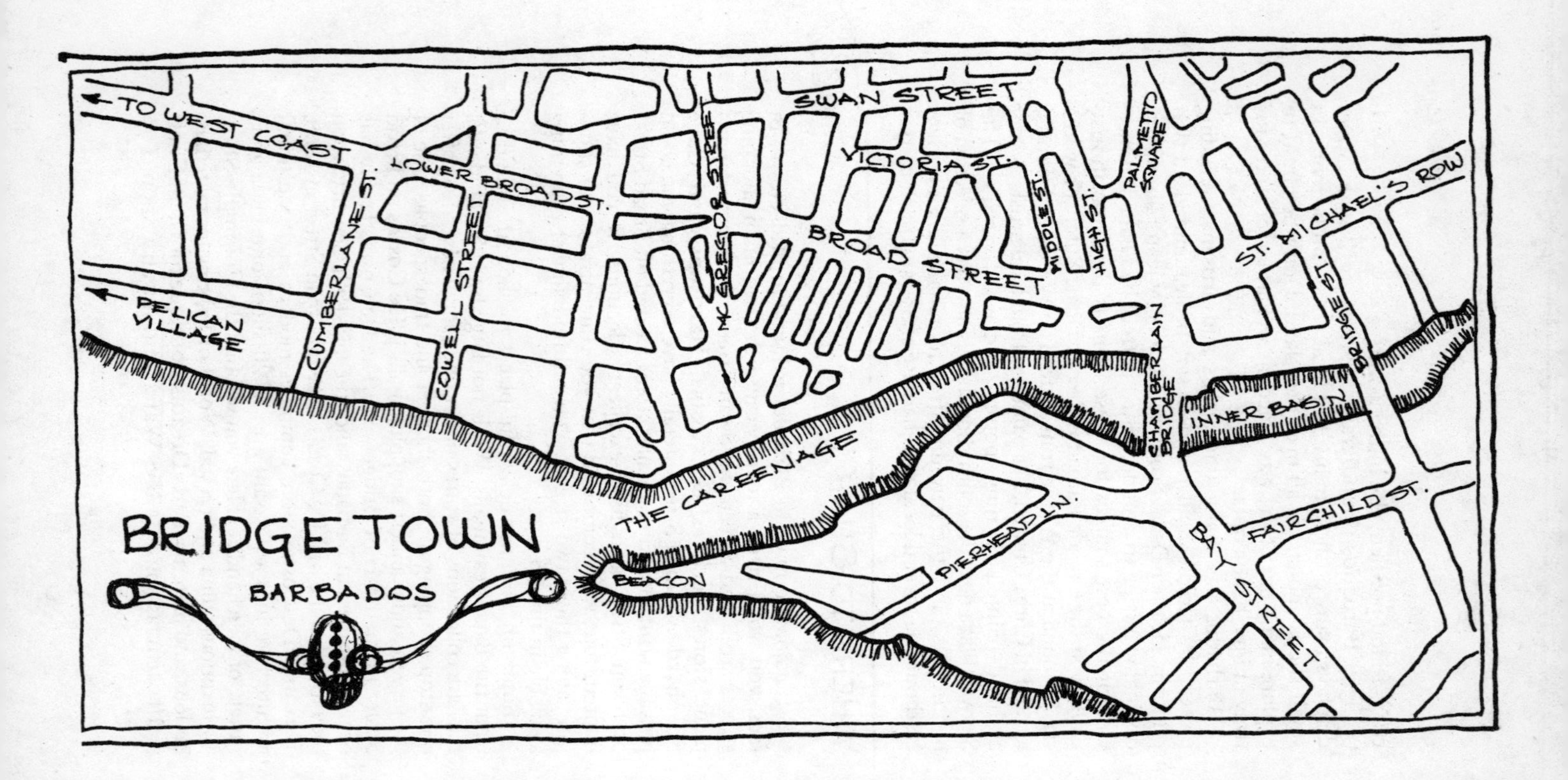
BRIDGETOWN
BARBADOS
TO WEST COAST
PELICAN VILLAGE
SWAN STREET
VICTORIA ST.
LOWER BROAD ST.
CUMBERLANE ST.
COWELL STREET
MC GREGOR STREET
BROAD STREET
MIDDLE ST.
HIGH ST.
PALMETTO SQUARE
ST. MICHAEL'S ROW
BRIDGE ST.
CHAMBERLAIN BRIDGE
INNER BASIN
THE CAREENAGE
PIERHEAD LN.
BEACON
FAIRCHILD ST.
BAY STREET

Mode for T-shirts; and **The Best of Barbados** for Jo Walker's prints and exclusive designs.

Nearby you will find a small mall called the **Galleria**. This is a fine example of the traditional Barbadian gingerbread made of local wood and coral stone. Recently opened, The Galleria's seven shops have proved to be an instant success. Here you will find **Mike Carma** which offers excellent gold and silver jewelry, Majorca pearls, watches, and gifts; **In Transit** and **In Transit Kids** with locally made fashions and casual wear and T-shirts for men; **Demars** specializing in gold by the inch, costume jewelry, and accessories; **XRTA Classy**, a boutique with women's fashions and accessories; **The Hyde** for leather shoes, bags and accessories; and **All Occasions** with gifts, novelties, and party items. Up stairs at the Galleria is the air-conditioned Rascals Restaurant which serves breakfast, lunch, and dinner.

Broad Street is also home for Barbados' first shopping complex—**Mall 34**. Developed in the early 1980's, it includes **Top Mode** for fashion wear; **Trend Setters** for female fashions (also found in the De Costas Mall); **Paris Dreams Boutique**; **Justin** for accessories, bags, belts, hats, and costume jewelry; **Flamboa** for casual clothes; and many other shops specializing in gifts and souvenirs.

The new duty-free shopping terminal at the Bridgetown Harbour has 33 shops in a tropical atmosphere. The inside recreates a Barbadian street scene right down to the store fronts resembling the chattel houses with their many colorful facades.

Quaside Center, located at Rockley Beach; and **Hastings Mall** at Hastings Christ Church just south of Bridgetown are two additional places to shop. Both house a number of unique stores as well as restaurants.

Several top hotels also have collections of quality shops worth visiting. At the **Royal Pavilion** (Porters, St. James) is the **Courtyard**. Here you will find the Cartier shop offering fabulous Cartier rings and Yves St. Laurent and Ferarri jewelry. Other shops in the Courtyard include **Valenti**, a high fashion boutique; **Jake**, a top quality men's boutique; **Taxco** featuring silver items from Mexico; and **Zone**, a general shop with books, gifts, and souvenirs.

At the **Companion Hotel**, next to Gooder Bay, you will find the **Emerald Boutique** for fashion wear and the **Dew Drop Inn** for menswear. The **Arcade at the Hilton** includes **Paris Dream**, which handles a variety of costume jewelry and jump suits by Tokefu. Also look for **Petals** for quality shoes and **Boutique Caribe** for original boutique fashions and fabrics. The arcade also has a Barclay's Bank that opens at 8:30am, Monday through Friday.

One shop worth visiting is **Lindsay Corbin's** boutique and workshop at Dover in Christ Church. The silk screens and hand prints of 100% cotton fabrics are designed here. Most prints are in bold colors and designs.

On Megragor Street, just off of Broad Street, look for two very popular boutiques—Java Flair and Rider. **Java Flair** sells European and North American imports as well as a 100% cotton Anotta Collection. Leather bags and shoes are available as well as accessories in belts and jewelry. **Rider** is a men's shop featuring famous labels such as Boxer, Second Image, Sirio and Bintom of Italy.

At the **Careenage**, where in recent years boutiques and restaurants have replaced old warehouses, you will find two excellent boutiques. Designer Carol Cadogan runs **Petticoat Lane** at the Bridgehouse complex. Carol is well known for her cotton dresses in pastels and earth tones as well as for leather wear, silks, and laces. She has an excellent collection of accessories and handmade bracelets, bangles, and other jewelry. Next to the Waterfront Cafe is **Origins** which features the fashions of Diane Butcher. Simplicity and elegance are her hallmarks. In addition to her wonderful and innovative fabric designs, Diane sells original works of art and decorated pottery.

Another important center outside Bridgetown for fashion is **Holetown**. This west coast area, where the first Colonialists settled, is rich in up-market hotels, restaurants, and fashionable boutiques. On First Street you will find two excellent shops, Dotto and Gaye Boutiques. Both shops have been in business for 15 years. Specializing in locally made fashions, they feature well-known designer labels as well as clothes from leading designers of France, Italy, and Britain. **Dotto** offers beach wear to elegant evening wear and includes the New York New Man label. **Gaye Boutique** carries fashionable resort wear for women, men, and children; swim wear, casual clothes, and evening attire; and a first class collection of shoes. At the Sandy Lane Hotel is **Gatsby's** which carries Carol Cottigan's one-of-a-kind creations among many other items of evening and resort wear imported from Europe and the United States.

The Discovery Bay Hotel includes **De-Ja-Vu**, with numerous fashions under such labels as Rosco, Surf 'n Sand, and Derrek Went.

South of Bridgetown, at the Grande Barbados Resort, you will find a branch of the **Buttercup Boutique** with its collection of beautiful casual and elegant wear from around the Caribbean.

West coast hotels are near The Sunset Crest Shopping Center. There is in-bond shopping at **Cave Shepherd**.

Small areas of shopping are all over Barbados. Sargeants Village in Christ Church has the Sheraton Center and Quayside Shopping Center is also in the vicinity. Chattle House Village is located at St. Lawrence Gap.

SPECIAL TIPS FOR CRUISE SHIP PASSENGERS

The primary shopping area of Bridgetown is accessible to you within minutes including the new nine million dollar duty-free shopping terminal at the Bridgetown Harbour. Since the city center is about one mile from the Deep Water Harbor where the ships tie up, we recommend that you take a taxi to Trafalger Square. If you have most of the day, or even half a day, the shops on Broad and Swan Streets will introduce you to Barbados' best shopping. An excellent place to start is the **Cave Shepherd** department store on Broad Street. A short walk beyond Trafalgar Square is Bridge Street where you can visit the **Barbados Handicraft Center**. If time permits, some hotel shops, such as those in the Hilton, are worth the taxi ride.

If you have only an hour or two, **Pelican Village** is within steps of the ship. Although not as fully stocked as the department stores and jewelry shops in town, you will find an excellent selection of gifts and local crafts here.

ENJOYING YOUR STAY

ACCOMMODATIONS

As a major resort destination oriented toward rest and relaxation, Barbados has many hotels of all types and price ranges: deluxe resorts, expensive hotels, small hotels, and even timesharing condominiums. The Board of Tourism has an updated list of cottage rentals. They can be contacted through Caribbean Home Rentals, P.O. Box 710, Palm Beach, FL 33480.

St. James:

- **The Royal Pavilion**: Tel. 809-422-4444. Fax 809-422-3940. Located on the west coast with all but three of it's 75 rooms facing the sea. The rooms are elegantly decorated with pastel fabrics, light pickled wood furniture, and exquisite marble baths. A nice feature is complimentary water sports and duty-free shopping. Expensive.

- **Glitter Bay**: Tel. 809-422-4111. Fax 809-422-3940. Shares facilities with the Royal Pavilion, but is more informal and family oriented. It's the former estate of Sir Edmund Cunard and overlooks the Caribbean coast. There are extensive gardens and trees. The pool has a waterfall. The hotel has a stretch Mercedes which you can hire for the round trip to the airport. Expensive.

- **The Colony Club**: Tel. 809-422-2335. Fax 809-422-1726 Offers excellent rooms for relaxing on your private patio or sitting next to the water on the terrace for a snack or breakfast and casually enjoying the beach all day. The Club is famous for barbecues and great calypso entertainment. Expensive.

- **Sandy Lane**: Tel. 809-432-1311. Fax 809-432-2954. Offers 380 acres of quiet luxury. Converted from a sugar plantation. Complete with a beach, golf course, and tennis courts. Excellent personal service. Includes lush gardens with birds and butterflies. Expensive.

- **Almond Beach Resorts**: Tel. 800-425-663. All-inclusive with amenities, but a very quiet approach with laid-back luxury.

St Michael:

- **The Barbados Hilton International**: Tel. 809-426-0200. Fax 809-436-8646. Located on Needham's Point with two beaches. About one mile from Bridgetown, it is in close proximity to the major shopping areas. Offers excellent duty-free shopping in the arcade located adjacent to the hotel, in case time is of the essence. Includes access to horseback riding, water sports and tennis. 182 rooms. Expensive.

- **Sandals Barbados**: Tel. 809-424-0888. All-Inclusive for couples only. Beautiful white sandy beach. 178 rooms with complete facilities. Expensive.

St Peter:

- **Cobblers Cove**: Tel. 809-422-1460. Located 11 miles from Bridgetown, it is on the northwest coast and one of the island's favorite honeymoon retreats. Its 38 suites are each located in a wooded tropical garden setting.

Informal elegance with some of the best cuisine on the island. Overlooking a gorgeous beach.

- **Almond Beach Village:** Tel. 800-425-6663 is the newest resort for Almond Beach Resorts. All-Inclusive designed for the easy going quiet vacation.

St. Philip:

- **Marriott's Sam Lord's Castle:** Tel. 809-423-7350. Fax 809-423-5918 or 800-228-9290. Located about 14 miles east of Bridgetown and named after it's original owner, who delighted in luring ships into the reefs and collecting loot from the wrecks. The Great House is still standing and is a museum as well as the check-in area for the hotel. Seven rooms have canopied beds. If you want to stay close to the beach, ask for a room by the sea. Some limited shopping available. Expensive.

- **Crane Beach Hotel:** Tel. 809-423-6220, Fax 809-423-5343. One of the island's most appealing properties located on a cliff overlooking the Atlantic. A beautiful Roman style pool with columns. The beach below can be reached by 200 steps. Four poster beds, suites and apartments—all with a scenic view.

RESTAURANTS

Barbados has gone to great lengths to secure the best trained chefs for their finest restaurants and hotels. The specialty of Barbados is **flying fish** which is considered the national dish. Served in a variety of ways, it is most delicate and moist when broiled. A favorite side dish is **coo coo** (corn meal and okra mixed). Local soups can be an entire meal in themselves, because they are thick and spicy. When you read that a hotel or restaurant is having a "cohoblopot," this refers to a buffet of good Bajan cooking. The **local hot sauce** needs only one drop to provide its full Scotch Bonnet pepper flavor. Don't forget to try **Banks**, the local beer. Remember when ordering **rum** to ask for "see through" to get white rum.

St James:

- **La Cage aux Folles:** Tel. 424-2424. A tiny and intimate restaurant located in the restored Summerland Great Houses. It is considered a true gourmet restaurant with frequent menu changes. Open for dinner only, reservations are a must with seating for only 21. Expensive. Major credit cards accepted.

- **Fathoms:** Tel. 432-6525. Both inside and outside dining by the ocean in this eatery. The restaurant is casual during the day, but reservations are necessary at night because of the "great desserts."

- **Raffles:**Tel. 432-6557. One of the most popular "top" restaurants on the island. Exotic and filled with atmosphere. Open for diner only and reservations are a must.

- **KoKos:** Tel. 424-4557. Adventurous foods, unusual combinations "new Bajan" dishes. Dinner only and reservations are important.

St. Michael:

- **Brown Sugar:** Tel. 426-7684. Located adjacent to the Island Inn at Aquatic Gap. Some of the tastiest Bajan dishes are prepared here. Serves dinner in a lovely candlelight garden setting. Also open for lunch, except weekends. Expensive and credit cards are accepted.

St. Lawrence:

- **Witch Doctor:** Tel. 435-6581. Located at St. Lawrence Gap, this restaurant decorated with African woodcarvings and combines both Bajan and African dishes. The Chicken pri-pri (marinated in lime) is from a Mozambique recipe. The pumpkin soup is especially tasty. Top it off with homemade raisin topping over ice cream for dessert. Open for dinner only. Very casual, but reservations are needed and credit cards are accepted.

- **David's Place:** Tel. 435-6550. Overlooks St. Lawrence Bay. Excellent bajan cooking, especially for local flying fish. Inexpensive.

St. Joseph:

- **Atlantis:**Tel. 433-9445. Known for its famous Sunday Brunch. Down home dishes island style Inexpensive—reservations necessary.

8

Bermuda

Greeted with at least as much enthusiasm as Bermudians feel for their beloved national sport of cricket, shopping on this small, semi-tropical island is a favorite pastime for travelers. Of course, visitors are also enthralled by Bermuda's legendary outdoor sites and activities. It is just that shopping—one of the most prized indoor activities here—draws just as many raves.

Imagine Fifth Avenue or Knightsbridge sophistication in the midst of a semi-tropical oasis. Think of elegant boutiques and department stores housed in handsome, old historic buildings. Envision not one but three major shopping areas, not to mention clusters of stores scattered throughout the rest of the island. Bargain hunting here is rather a contradiction in terms since there is no such thing as hunting for bargains. Savings are waiting for shoppers everywhere.

In many vacation spots, visitors take breaks from sunbathing and sightseeing to go shopping. In Bermuda, it is often the other way around. There is something addictive about spending and saving at the same time, especially when the choice of goods is as vast as it is here. The island may be small, but there is nothing small about the selection of excellent buys. Not every item in every store is a bargain. But no matter what you buy, you will be delighted with the high quality of merchandise, the

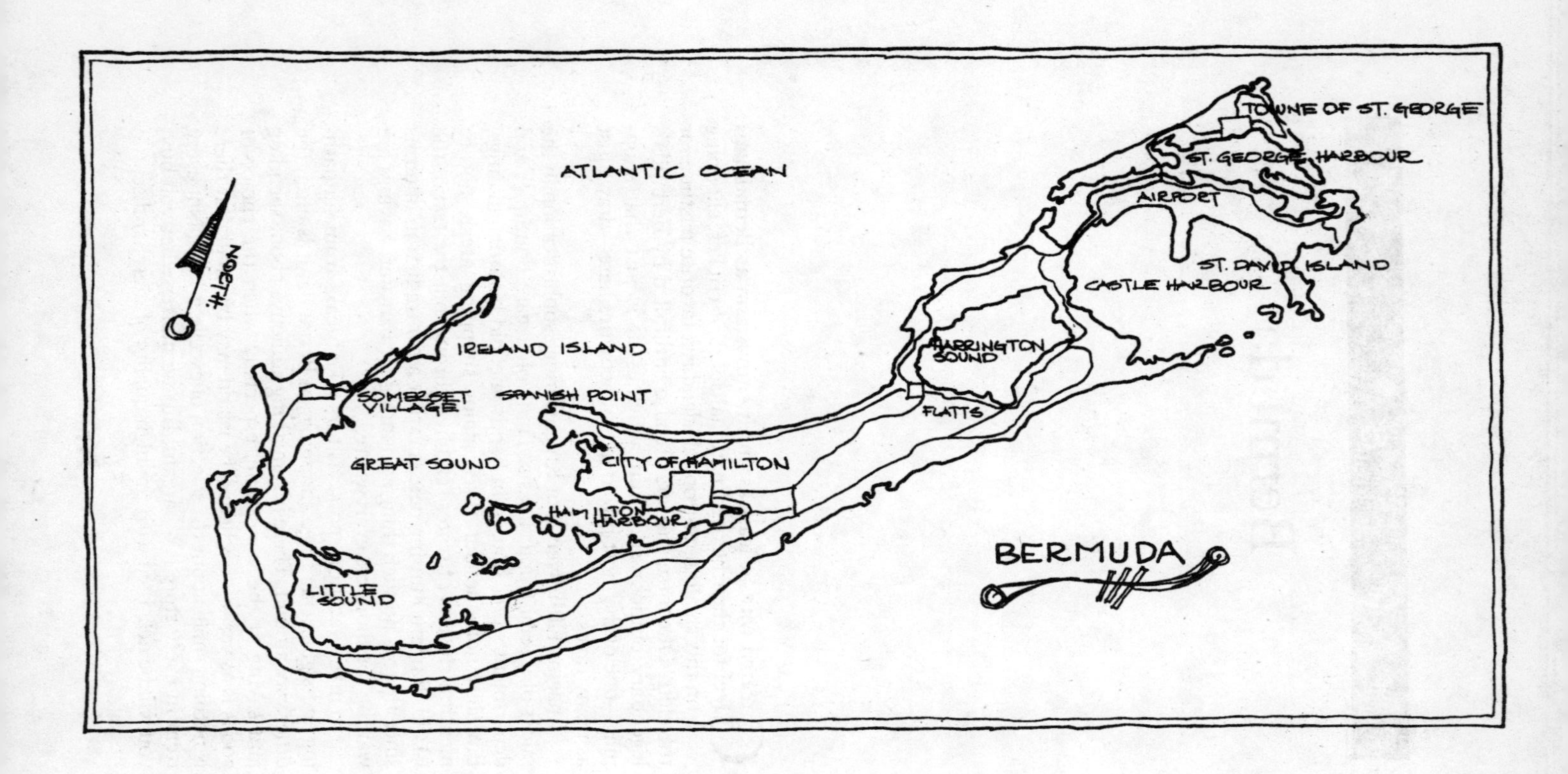

TOWNE OF ST. GEORGE
ST. GEORGE HARBOUR
ATLANTIC OCEAN
AIRPORT
ST. DAVID ISLAND
CASTLE HARBOUR
NORTH
IRELAND ISLAND
HARRINGTON SOUND
SOMERSET VILLAGE
SPANISH POINT
FLATTS
GREAT SOUND
CITY OF HAMILTON
HAMILTON HARBOUR
BERMUDA
LITTLE SOUND

friendliness of the shopkeepers, and the knowledge that your savings are anywhere from 20 to 50% over U.S. prices. Here you will find Wedgwood, Royal Copenhagen, Royal Crown Derby, and other fine china for 25% to 50% below the U.S. prices; 18K gold jewelry for up to 40% off; 20% savings on Tissot, Patek Philippe, Rolex and other fine time pieces; and distinctive Souleiado fabric for $16 a yard instead of the $30 a yard you pay in the U.S. In Bermuda you will find another paradise for shoppers.

GETTING TO KNOW YOU

The story of Bermuda began in the 16th Century. Spaniard Juan de Bermudez is normally credited with discovering the islands. He visited there in 1503, but failed to claim them for his country. It wasn't until 1609, more than a hundred years later, that the British Admiral Sir George Summers' flagship, the Sea Venture, became shipwrecked off the coast of Bermuda.

For more than three and a quarter centuries, Bermuda has remained under the flag of Great Britain and the Bermudians are proud they are the oldest former British colony with an elected House of Assembly.

There are three major areas in the nine Parishes on the islands that hold the metropolitan flavor for Bermuda. The city of Hamilton, the town of St. George and the village of Somerset. One hundred and eighty years after Sir George Somer's arrival in Bermuda, Hamilton (named after Governor Henry Hamilton, 1788-1794) was incorporated as a town. Though for many years it was a busy port and center of commerce for the Island, Hamilton did not become the capital of Bermuda until 1815, when the Legislature moved the seat of Government from St. George's. The city itself covers an area of 177 acres, has a resident population of around 2,000, and is one of the world's smallest and most attractive capitals.

- **Expect savings from 20 to 50% over U.S. prices.**
- **November and December are the best times to shop—no hoards of other travelers, and shopkeepers have more time to show their many treasures.**
- **While there are no drive yourself cars for hire by visitor in Bermuda, it is very easy to get around by taxi, bus, ferry, or motor assisted cycles (no driver's licence required).**
- **Bermuda is not really a duty-free island, but you can buy imported goods at very low dutied prices.**
- **A special logo differentiates genuine local items from those of foreign origin.**

Somerset, the largest of the islands in Bermuda, is rich in places of historical interest outstanding beauty and unique charm. There are old plantation houses and a beautiful nature reserve. Somerset Bridge, built in the early 1600's—reputed to be the world's smallest drawbridge—opens just wide enough to let the spar of a sailboat pass through. The tiny village of Somerset lies nestled around beautiful Mangrove Bay.

Arranged in the shape of a fish hook, the approximately 180 islands have a land area of approximately twenty-one square miles. Though situated far north of tropical latitudes, Bermuda, nonetheless, has a mild climate with an annual average temperature of about seventy degrees Fahrenheit. The average annual rainfall is approximately 50 inches and is evenly spread out over the 12 months. Bermuda's sunshine is an abundant commodity. There has never been a year with fewer than 340 days on which sunshine has been recorded—the average is 351 days.

Early residents long ago discovered the excellent building property of the limestone which lies beneath the sandy soil. Cut from hillside quarries, the stone is soft and porous and easily sawed into building block sizes. Exposed to the weather, the limestone of Bermuda's houses harden, and there are hundreds of homes on the island today that are more than a century old. Thin slabs of the limestone are laid in overlapping layers to form the distinctive terraced roofs on which rain water is collected and directed to storage tanks beneath or beside every home. The roof of every Bermuda building is limewashed or painted white.

The people of Bermuda have had an adventuresome past. Their fortunes have gone up and down in such ventures as whaling, ship building, pirateering, and until the early twentieth century, farming. In the last quarter of the 19th Century, farming flourished in the islands. The colony's soil and climate produced excellent vegetables, including onions for export to the U.S. market. Trade was so brisk that the capital of Hamilton was often called Onion Town. The onion market collapsed, however, when Texas farmers discovered how to simulate the growing conditions.

Today there are no agricultural exports from Bermuda. There is also no heavy industry of any kind on the islands, but soft drink concentrates, perfumes and pharmaceutical drugs are some of the island's exports from the light industrial companies operating as a free port in the former royal naval dock yard at the western end of the island. The turn to tourism came with the steamships in the early 1900's, and has been a rewarding one for Bermuda. In the last half century, Bermuda's tourist trade has grown by leaps and bounds and now accounts for 70% of the nation's economy. More than 100 resorts offer a wide variety of accommodations. Among them are large and small hotels, cottage colonies, housekeeping apartments, guest houses and time sharing resorts.

THE BASICS

LOCATION AND GEOGRAPHY

Bermuda is the second most isolated inhabited island in the world. It is not really one island but approximately 180 large and small islands encompassing about a 21 square mile area. In looking at Bermuda on the map, it appears to be nothing more than a tiny dot in the middle of the Atlantic Ocean.

Although made up of many islands, the seven largest of them are connected by bridges and causeways. From East to West, Bermuda is about 21 miles long with a maximum width of about two miles. According to geological records, the island is perched on the summit of a submarine mountain that rises about 15,000 feet from the bottom of the sea and was created approximately 100 million years ago by a volcano. It is a rolling, fertile land, with pink sand, blue water and a variety of colorful flowers. Although it is not one of the tropical islands of the West Indies, as is sometimes thought, palm trees and other tropical plants thrive. The islands may be small but they are diverse in landscape. Bermuda has no rivers or streams and is dependent upon rainfall for its water supply, which is caught on the white roofs of homes and stored below in underground tanks. The northern most point of mainland Bermuda is St. Catherine Point in St. George's; the most southerly point is Sinky Bay near the Sonnesta Beach Hotel in the St. Hampton Parish. The most easterly point is Greathead at St. David's; and the most westerly point is Reckhill in Sandys Parish.

CLIMATE, WHEN TO GO, WHAT TO WEAR

Bermuda is a semi-tropical island, and the Gulf Stream which flows between Bermuda and the North American Continent keeps the climate temperate—not too hot, not too cold. Bermuda's weather is interesting because it has two seasons—summer and spring. Bermuda has no rainy season and there is no time of the year when you will encounter an excess of rain. Showers may be heavy at times but the skies usually clear quickly. The weather does not often interfere with the enjoyment of outdoor sports and recreation. Summer temperatures prevail from May to mid-November, with the warmest weather in July, August and September.

The temperature rarely rises above 85 degrees Fahrenheit—perfect for shopping, sunning, swimming, or touring the islands There is normally a cool breeze at night, but most hotels and guest cottages are air conditioned. Spring-like weather provides cooler temperatures from mid-December to late March with an average daytime temperature of 70 degrees dropping to about 60 degrees in the evening. Very often the months of December and January are warm enough to allow you to sun and swim. The change of seasons comes during mid-November through December and from late March through April. Either spring or summer weather may occur during the change of seasons, and the visitors should be prepared for both.

Bermuda is extremely pleasant to visit any time of the year. In fact, many visitors from the U.S. have found the November and December time frames the most pleasant for shopping in that there are not hoards of other travelers, and the shopkeepers have much more time to show you their many treasures.

The atmosphere of a Bermuda hotel, guest house or cottage colony and indeed Bermuda itself, is one of British reserve and dignified formality. As a rule, you should dress conservatively. Bathing suits, abbreviated tops, and short shorts are not acceptable except at beaches and pools. In public (including public areas of hotels), beach wear must be covered. Bare feet are not acceptable anywhere in public. It is an offense to ride cycles or appear in public without a shirt or just wearing a bathing suit. Joggers, however, may wear standard running shorts and shirts. Casual sportswear is acceptable in restaurants at lunch time, but most of the larger restaurants and nightclubs in and out of hotels request gentlemen to wear a jacket and tie in the evenings. It is best to check on dress requirements when making dinner or nightclub reservations, since some do have evenings when a jacket is not necessary.

During the warmer months of May to mid-November, women should consider wearing summer weight sports clothes, cotton dresses, swimsuits, casuals of lightweight travel fabrics, a light dressy sweater or wrap for evening, cocktail type outfits for evenings, and a raincoat or a light-weight windbreaker. Men should consider summer weight sports clothes, swimsuits, a lightweight suit or sport jacket, a tie for evenings, and also a raincoat or a lightweight windbreaker. During the cooler months of December through late March, the dress for women will normally center around light-weight woolen or fall weight casuals, sweaters, skirts, slacks, dressier sweater or wrap and cocktail type outfits for the evening, and a raincoat or warmer jacket. For the men, lightweight woolens or fall weight casuals, sports jacket, slacks, sweaters, suit or sports jacket, a tie for evening and a raincoat or winter jacket.

During the change of seasons from mid-November to

December and late March through April, either Spring or Summer weather may occur, so a combination of clothing is normally ideal.

Of course, Bermuda shorts are acceptable year round; however, for the more dressy occasions, you will find that the famous Bermuda shorts, which stop just above the knee are normally worn with long socks. It is not uncommon to see many businessmen wearing Bermuda shorts with shirts and ties year round and occasionally as an evening dress in the summer.

GETTING THERE

Arriving by air in Bermuda is convenient from most cities on the East Coast of the United States. American Airlines, Continental, Delta, Kiwi, Air Canada and USAir all provide service to Bermuda from east coast cities. Air Canada offers non-stop service from Toronto four times weekly in the summer and five times weekly in the winter with connecting services from all of Canada as well as connections with the airlines through New York. British Airways flies daily from London.

Most airlines offer travel packages ranging from honeymoons to sports, to shopping programs. A few years ago the Bermuda government relaxed its policy on charter flights and now permits charters from many cities not offering scheduled service. This obviously allows many more visitors from the U.S. to enjoy the shopping delights of Bermuda.

You can, most certainly, reach Bermuda by sea. One of the most beautiful ways to arrive in Bermuda is aboard a cruise ship and, many of the cruise lines sail from New York to Bermuda during the summer and early fall. Other ships from Norfolk, Port Everglades, Miami and European ports also provide frequent service. Royal Caribbean's cruise ships, Celebrity Cruises Norwegian Cruise Line and Cunard Lines, normally schedule a weekly trip from New York to Bermuda and sail from May through October. Other ships often call on the island. The best way to arrange a cruise to Bermuda is to contact your travel agent or write to the Bermuda Department of Tourism. Their address is 310 Madison Avenue, Suite 201 New York, New York 10017-6083.

Another interesting way to arrive in Bermuda is by private vessel. Since Bermuda is so easily accessible from the east coast of the United States, sailing to the island has become popular during the past few years. There is really only one safe passage through the reefs into the main island area, so skilled sailing, good charts, and pre-arranged visiting rights are essential.

DOCUMENTS

All travelers arriving in Bermuda must carry with them proof of citizenship and personal identification relevant to return to their own country or for re-entry through another foreign country. Visitors from the U.S. are required by Bermuda Immigration authorities to have possession of any one of the following items: (1) passport, if expired should be sufficiently recent so that the photograph does resemble the bearer, (2) a birth certificate or a certified copy of the certificate, (3) a U.S. re-entry permit, (4) a U.S. voters registration card if it shows the bearers signature, (5) a U.S. naturalization certificate, or (6) a U.S. alien registration card. Please note that a driver's license is not acceptable as proof of citizenship. Visitors from Canada are required by the authorities to have in their possession either a valid passport, a Canadian certificate of citizenship, or a valid passport plus proof of their landed immigration status. U.S. and Canadian citizens not bearing one of the above documents may be refused entry into Bermuda.

A return or onward ticket is also required of all visitors. Most visitors with a confirmed return ticket and place of accommodation will have no difficulties with the Bermudian Immigration control. Passengers arriving with an open ticket may have a greater limitation placed on the length of their stay, however. Passengers arriving without return tickets or Bermuda Immigration authorization to land on a one-ticket basis, will not be admitted unless they have prior authorization from Bermuda Immigration Authorities.

ARRIVAL AND DEPARTURE

Arrival in Bermuda is extremely well organized at the airport and at the cruise ship terminals. At the airport your first stop will be at the Immigration counters. The first few booths of the Immigration area are visible from the door that you enter after departing the airplane. However, there are three or four more counters in the next room that normally are set aside for residents of Bermuda. We have found, on a number of occasions, that once the residents of Bermuda clear Immigration, those lines are available to other visitors. It is certainly worth a peek under the staircase to see if there is an open line rather than waiting for an hour in the three visible longer lines.

After clearing Immigration and retrieving your baggage, you will have to clear Customs. Visitors may bring into Bermuda duty-free all wearing apparel and articles for personal use, such as sporting equipment, cameras, and golf bags. In addition, 50 cigars, 200 cigarettes, one pound of tobacco and one quart of liquor and one liter of wine also may be brought in duty-free. Visitors are also permitted to bring in duty-free approximately 20 pounds of meat. Other food stuffs may be dutiable at between 5% and 25% of the value. All imports may be inspected upon arrival.

Air passengers departing Bermuda must pay a $35 departure tax at the time of their check-in; children under 12 years old pay $25 and children under two are free. There is also a port tax for ship passengers of $60 per person; however, if you are on a cruise ship this is normally collected in advance by the cruise company.

When returning home, the Customs regulations are set by your home country. Travelers are permitted to take back merchandise duty-free as follows: U.S. citizens, $400 after 48 hours out of the country and once every 30 days. For Canadian citizens, the limit is $100 after 48 hours and once every three calendar months or $300 after seven days once per calendar year. Plant materials which will propagate are not permitted without prior permission from either country. U.S. Customs pre-clearance is available in Bermuda for all scheduled flights, and all passengers departing to the U.S. must complete the written declaration forms before clearing U.S. customs in Bermuda. These forms are available at hotels, travel agencies and airlines on the island.

CURRENCY, TRAVELER'S CHECKS, CREDIT CARDS

The legal tender is the Bermuda dollar (BD$), which is divided into one hundred cents. Prior to July 31, 1972, the Bermuda dollar was pegged to the Pound Sterling; however, it is now pegged through gold to U.S. dollars on an equal basis—BD$1 to U.S.$1. U.S. currency is generally accepted everywhere—in shops, restaurants and in hotels. Other foreign currencies must be exchanged. U.S. travelers checks are accepted most everywhere on the island and most of the major credit cards such as VISA, Mastercard, American Express and Diner's Club are accepted in many shops and restaurants and in most hotels. Since all hotels do not accept all credit cards, it is wise to check before you leave home as to which cards are accepted or what other arrangements for payment can be made.

TIPPING

In cases where the gratuity is not included in the bill, 10% to 15% is generally an accepted amount for most services. A large number of hotels and guest houses add a percentage or set amount by person per day in lieu of tips to the bill for accommodations and other services. When in doubt, always ask as to whether a gratuity or service charge is added. If not clearly stated on the bill, you should ask; and if it is not included, you should follow your own rules for tipping.

LANGUAGE

All Bermudians speak English and are extremely friendly and courteous. You will have little encounter with any other language on the island so traveling and communicating poses no problem.

BUSINESS HOURS

Business hours for most of the shops are 9am to 5 or 5:30pm. Occasionally some may close for lunch, but in the main shopping areas of St. George's and Hamilton, this is rather rare. Some shops are open on Sunday if there is a cruise ship in port in either St. George's or Hamilton and most of the hotel shops do maintain some Sunday business hours.

TRANSPORTATION AND TOURS

There are no drive yourself cars for hire by visitors in Bermuda but you will find it very easy to get around by taxi, bus, ferry, or motor assisted cycles for which no driver's license is required. Public transportation is also excellent and the buses and the ferries offer convenient and inexpensive ways to get around. Bus passengers are required to have exact change in coin. You might want to ask about bus tokens or books of bus tickets at your hotel or bus terminal in the city of Hamilton. Bus passengers can also take advantage of multi-day passes available from the bus terminal and the Visitors Service Bureau in Hamilton. Children under 16 may not drive motor assisted cycles. All cycle drivers and passengers are required by law to wear a safety helmet, securely fastened at all times.

Driving in Bermuda is on the left hand side and the speed limit of twenty miles per hour is strictly enforced. All cars, including taxis, are restricted in size and may carry a maximum of four persons. The taxis with the blue flags belong to Bermuda's famous and outstanding qualified tour guides. These drivers can offer very good service in getting you around the island and locating many of the special shops that you may be seeking. You will find, however, that all taxi drivers are extremely courteous and their cabs must be inspected often for safety and appearance.

Cyclists should note that the gasoline stations are normally open from 7am to 7pm, Monday through Saturday with limited operating hours on Sundays and holidays. Most are closed on public holidays.

There are a number of cruise tours available from St. George or Hamilton and bus tours throughout the island are readily available. Information about the cruise tours or bus tours are available at most hotels and at various places around the cities of Hamilton and St. George.

RESOURCES

Like most tourism locations, Bermuda has a number of weekly and seasonal publications, such as ***Preview of Bermuda***, ***This Week in Bermuda***, and a larger tabloid size paper entitled ***Bermuda Dateline***, all of which are available at hotels. The most complete and informative information, however, is distributed by the Bermuda Department of Tourism. In addition to maps and small brochures outlining the historical sites, the Department has very detailed and specific guides. Magazine sized books with titles such as ***Bermuda Shopper's Guide***, ***Bermuda Sportsman's Guide***, ***Bermuda Golfer's Guide***, ***Bermuda Honeymoon Guide***, and ***Where to Stay in Bermuda*** proved to be invaluable to us. The Department does not make hotel or transportation reservations, but can provide you with a tremendous amount of useful literature. You may call them at 800-223-6106, Continental U.S.; 800-223-6107, New York; 416-923-9600, Canada; or 01-734-8813, England. You may also write to the Department at the following addresses:

Bermuda Department of Tourism

Global House
43 Church Street
Hamilton, HM12, Bermuda

P.O. Box HM 465
Hamilton, HM BX, Bermuda

Suite 1070
150 N. Wacker Drive
Chicago, IL 60606-1605

Suite 201
310 Madison Avenue
New York, NY 10017

Suite 2008
235 Peachtree Street NE
Atlanta, GA 30303-1223

Suite 1010
44 School Street
Boston, MA 02108-4201

Western Region
Representative
Tetley/Moyer & Assoc.

Suite 111
3151 Cahuenga Blvd. West
Los Angeles, CA 90068-1768

Suite 1004
1200 Bay Street
Toronto, Ontario M5R 2A5
Canada

European Representative
Bermuda Tourism
BCB Ld.
1 Battersea Church Rd.
London 11 3LY, UK
England

SHOPPING IN BERMUDA

Shopping in Bermuda is still a highlight of every trip to the island as it has been for decades. What you will find here is not just a hunt through shops for bargain after bargain, but a relaxed and enjoyable activity in which everyone takes part. The shopkeepers in Bermuda have for many years catered to shoppers who like quality and style. Their objective has been, therefore, to make shopping here a joy rather than merely a search for low prices. They will even recommend another shop if they do not have exactly the item you are seeking. Prices of choice imports are, of course, lower than you would pay at home and quality shopping abounds. Bermuda custom duties have been substantially lowered on items such as watches, cameras, cigars, antiques, ceramic figurines, many fabrics and jewelry, and the merchants actually pass the savings on to the shopper.

Fine china has long been one of Bermuda's strengths, and many stores in Hamilton and St. George carry hard to find items and even have stock in discontinued patterns, so you may even be able to find the piece or two for that set you thought you would never be able to complete. Crystal is also an excellent buy, whether you are looking for perfume bottles or paper weights in various shapes and sizes. You will also find a wide selection of woolens imported from England, Scotland and Iceland at very good prices.

Stores in Bermuda often specialize in the unusual. If you have been searching high and low for just the right brass nautical item to hang in your den, you are likely to find it in either Hamilton or St. George. Many stores throughout the island have become a haven for antique lovers. You might find a set of bone and silver fish servers, a copper tea kettle, an inlaid wooden box, a pair of crystal decanters, and a map yellowed with age or other intriguing remnants of the Bermudian and British days gone by.

WHAT TO BUY

Although virtually every free-port and in-bond product that is available in most of the Caribbean islands is found in Bermuda, there are some products that make shopping here a highlight. Included is the excellent art, the antiques and collectibles, china, crystal and linens, watches and jewelry, fine clothes, especially from Europe, and many other items that are original only to Bermuda, including cedar products.

Bermuda is not really a duty-free island, but you can buy imported goods at very low dutied prices. Also available in Bermuda is in-bond shopping. Buying in-bond goods such as liquor and cigarettes means that you are purchasing merchandise at a low price because this merchandise has technically not entered the country. If you buy two bottles of in-bond liquor for instance, it will be delivered to the airport or your ship when you depart. Be sure to order "in-bond" liquors several days before your departure. In-bond prices on liquor can be nearly 50% lower than elsewhere. Note that there is no "in-bond" liquor store at the airport. It should also be noted that Bermuda is a GSP country—a country with a Generalized System of Preference status. This means that certain goods may enter the U.S. completely duty-free. To qualify, at least 35% of the item must be crafted in Bermuda.

Bermuda did not become a world-class shopping center overnight. Trading ships have sailed into Hamilton Harbor for centuries and the merchant tradition is a long standing one. Many of the stores in Bermuda have been run by the same family for generations, building experience and international reputations for quality the shopper can trust. Many family businesses have developed long-term and close relationships with their suppliers. As a result, some of these stores carry a unique variety of a certain product. Bermuda shoppers can often find better selections here than in Paris, London or even New York. For instance, **A. S. Cooper & Sons** carries a wider selection of Wedgwood china than any retail store in the United States. There are collector's items, special pieces made by Wedgwood exclusively for Coopers. It is hardly surprising that the cedar doors to the store have Wedgwood Jasper handles, and that the Wedgwood plaque at Cooper's entrance was presented by the Chairman of the Board of Wedgwood.

Similarly, **H. S. & J. E. Crissen Limited**, operated for two generations by the Crissen family have a special relationship with Rolex watches, and their selection is one of the finest in the world. In fact, Crissen has collections of eight Swiss manufacturers.

Peniston-Brown Company Limited has been Bermuda's only perfume specialist since 1932. For over 40 years this company has been exclusive agents for the House of Guerlain. Their extensive range and variety of Guerlain perfume, cosmetics and beauty products can be equaled in only three stores in the whole of North America.

People love to shop in Bermuda, for the pleasures of finding super quality, rare or unusual objects or even the satisfaction of great savings. They come back again and again because shopping in Bermuda is an adventure found in few other places. It is the delight of shopping in one of the most picturesque cities in the world.

ART

Local art can be found throughout Bermuda. Of special note are the many painters specializing in water colors and oils depicting the landscapes of the island. Some of the more famous artists residing in Bermuda are Diana and Eric Amos, Carole Holding, Desmond Fountain, Alfred Birdsey, and Jo Bluck Waters.

Diana and Eric Amos reside and work on Old Road in the province of Warwick and are well known throughout the island. Diana studied painting in London and uses outside light to influence her paintings. Her husband, Eric, is known as the island's leading bird artist and he is about to publish a guide to the birds of Bermuda. One of his paintings is in the British Royal Collection; and his work has been featured in London's Tryon Gallery. There is a permanent display of their work, including limited edition prints at Stonington Beach Hotel. A selection of Diana's paintings is also displayed at the **Windjammer Gallery** in the New Crisson Hind Gallery in Hamilton. Both artists accept commissions, and guests are welcome by appointment.

Desmond Fountain is a sculptor and his most recent works include many life-size children as well as other smaller scaled bronzes. Some of his sculptures can be seen at the **Emporium Atrium** on Front Street and the Bank of Bermuda Courtyard on Par-la-ville Road in the city of Hamilton. His works can also be seen at the **Windjammer Gallery** on the corner of Reed and King Streets in Hamilton.

One of the most delightful Bermudians that we have met is Alfred Birdsey. Mr. Birdsey's work has been displayed internationally at shows and galleries in the U.S., Canada, the United Kingdom, Australia, and New Zealand. His art is prominently displayed throughout Bermuda, especially on the walls in the airport. Of special note are his many watercolors that adorn the walls in the departure lounge. Mr. Birdsey's water colors, oils, lithographs and prints, as well as whimsical animal pictures by Jo Birdsey and floral pictures by Antoinette Birdsey can be seen at the **Birdsey Studio**, 5 Stowhill in Pageant. The telephone number of the studio is 236-6658 and his studio is open from 9am to 4pm, Monday through Friday.

Carole Holding, a watercolor artist, was born in England and came to Bermuda in 1968. She has developed a well-known soft watercolor style that captures Bermuda's light and colors. She particularly enjoys painting flowers and scenes of the Bermuda countryside. She has won many awards and honors in Bermuda and elsewhere and her work can be found in many galleries in Bermuda, including in the **Windjammer Gallery** on the corner of Reed and King Streets in Hamilton.

Joy Bluck Waters is another world renowned painter who resides in Bermuda. Her works have been exhibited in London, Paris, and New York, including the Royal Institute of Oil Painters, the Paris Salon, Gallery Madison Ninety, Monti Carlo's International Arts Guild and the Carifpa Games in Jamaica. She specializes in landscapes and still life, and uses both oils and water colors. The seascapes of the south shore of Bermuda are one of her favorite subjects. Her studio is located in Spithead, 45 Harbor Road in Warwick, and visitors are welcomed by appointment.

The artists featured above as well as many others are found in a variety of galleries throughout Bermuda. In addition to the Windjammer Gallery in Hamilton and the **Crisson Hind Fine Art Gallery** on the second floor of the Crisson Building at 71 Front Street, Hamilton, the **Bermuda Art Center** located at the dockyard, directly opposite the Maritime Museum, is a must for every art lover. The Art Center, as its name implies, is dedicated to the visual arts, and although it was opened in 1984, it is already recognized and respected for its schedule of local and international exhibits. Besides hosting shows for resident artists, usually painters, there are other workshops, classes and events throughout the year and visitors are welcome. Information concerning current programs is available from the gallery assistant normally who is there from 10am to 4:30pm on Tuesday through Friday and from 1 to 5pm on Saturdays and Sundays. The gallery is closed on Mondays. In addition to the large, well appointed exhibition space, there are four studios rented to artists who can work on the premises. Frequently visitors can see and meet them at work on their various projects. Most exhibits feature work for sale and there is a small shop where you can find limited edition prints. Notepaper, books and cards, as well as a fine selection of jewelry designed and made in Bermuda make excellent take home gifts. The Bermuda Art Center is a non-profit organization and the arts and crafts produced locally are duty-free for those bringing them back to the U.S.

ANTIQUES AND COLLECTIBLES

Antique shopping in Bermuda is interesting and easy. Here you may find old books, unframed pictures, maps, porcelain, silver, brassware, copperware and furniture. Shops will handle the appropriate certificates so that items which qualify as antiques can be imported into the U.S. free of duty. Most shops will arrange shipping if necessary.

One of the leading antique specialists in Hamilton is the **Thistle Gallery** on Park Road. It offers an extensive selection of English period furniture, porcelain and silver, and an extensive array of small items. It is open Monday through Friday and Saturday by appointment.

Another excellent source of antiques is **William Bluck and Company, Ltd**. Bluck's is a local business that for over the past 140 years has dedicated itself to bringing to Bermuda some of the finest, most beautifully made items in the world. They are located on Front Street in Hamilton at the Southampton Princess and at the Sonnota Beach Hotel. In their collection, you will find anything from an 18th Century snuff box to a very grand piece of mahogany furniture. They also have excellent examples of brass and copper and some pieces of very old silver and a variety of maps and prints.

At the west end of Front Street at No. 2 in Hamilton, you will find the **Heritage House**. The collection at the Heritage House is a varied collection of antiques, paintings, and very unusual gifts. The owners have a connection with the leading galleries in the United Kingdom and are assured a wide variety of art as well as antiques from Europe.

If you collect antique maps and prints, you should visit **Pegasus Maps and Prints** located at No. 63 Pitts Bay Road across from the Hamilton Princess Hotel. They carry eighteenth and nineteenth century maps and have a large selection of inexpensive hand colored Bermuda map reproductions.

CHINA, CRYSTAL AND LINEN

China, crystal and linen can be found in many parts of Bermuda and is of the highest quality. **A. S. Coopers and Sons, Ltd.** on Front Street in Hamilton specializes in Wedgwood china and have some of the most unusual pieces to be found in the world. In addition to Wedgwood, you will also find Royal Copenhagen, Royal Doulton, Anysley, Belleek and Crown Stratforshire in the china gallery. The fine crystal such as Galway, Lalique and Baccarat, as well as Waterford, can be found in many of the fine shops throughout Bermuda. You will find the largest selections in Hamilton at **William Bluck and Company, Ltd.** and **Triminghams**, both of which are located on Front Street as well as at **Vera P. Card, Ltd.** in both Hamilton and St. George's.

Linen is available at many shops such as **H. A. & E. Smith, Ltd.**, and some of the smaller shops, but one of the finest collections of linen can be found at the **Irish Linen Shop** on the corner of Front and Queen Streets in Hamilton. There you will find some of the highest quality linens available as well as the wonderful French tablecloths and bolts of materials from Souleiado and Patrick Frye. Most of the prices on linen at the various shops will be approximately 20% to 30% below U.S. prices, and in the case of the fabrics from Souleiado, you will find prints in bolts as well as in ready-made articles unique to all the world. In addition to the normal linen items, you will also be able to find magnificent Madeira hand embroidered tablecloths, Irish damasks, hem stitched linen and some easy to care for linen blends from Ireland.

Bargaining for the many fine items of china and crystal is certainly not to be done in Bermuda. The prices quoted are set and the shopkeepers expect to sell the items at the marked price. However, we have found that discussion with the shopkeepers and clerks may result in some excellent bargains. For example, in looking at many of the Wedgwood items at A.S. Coopers, we were quoted a price for the current Christmas plate, which is part of the famous Wedgwood collection of plates issued for the holidays. The current edition of this particular plate has a set price and there will be no discounts or bargaining. However, with further inquiry as to back issues, we were advised that some of the previous years stock was available and the prices were significantly lower than the current edition. Also, upon further inquiry as to many of the antique Wedgwood plates in the Christmas collection which are certainly not available anywhere, we were advised that there were some customers of Coopers who had placed some of the older editions with them on consignment for possible sale. We were shown many of these beautiful items and were presented with the prices that were *requested*. Simply put, most of the merchandise in all of the stores is expected to be sold for the prices marked. However, many of the very special items, especially items that have been placed in the shops on consignment will sometimes be available at lower prices than that originally asked. We would not put this in the same category as the hard bargaining that is available to you on other islands such as Haiti or the Dominican Republic; but, when you are looking at exquisite items that are one of a kind, any discount is truly a bargain.

WATCHES AND JEWELRY

Since many of the shops in Bermuda have specific arrangements with various companies, you will find some items of jewelry and watches available in Bermuda that are unavailable elsewhere in the Caribbean. Some of the finest jewelry available can be found at such places as the **Crisson Jeweler** on Front, Reed and Queen Streets of Hamilton, as well as from **Astwood Dickinson** on Front Street in Hamilton.

The jewelry and watches that are available from the fine stores in both Hamilton and St. George's are certainly not the run of the mill items that are available in many of the tourist related outlets elsewhere in the Caribbean islands or in the U.S. Here, as is the case for china and crystal, you are looking at some of the highest quality merchandise available. You will not find a good deal of bargaining over the price. In fact, attempts to heartily bargain on these items will normally be rebuffed. You can, however, be assured that the quoted prices are some of the best that you will ever find. However, if you are purchasing several items, a discount may be possible.

CLOTHING

The items of clothing available in Bermuda are truly a find. You will find sweaters, tartans, and many other items from the British Isles, Scotland and Ireland, prominently displayed in many of the shops. Here again, although there is no bargaining as on individual items, the prices quoted on these high-quality items are approximately 20% to 30% less than you will pay in the U.S. Stores such as **Archie Brown & Son, Ltd.** on Front

Street in Hamilton, and **Triminghams** also on Front Street in Hamilton carry simply the finest woolens outside of England and Scotland. Many items are occasionally marked down for sales, especially during the off season (winter) months when they have very few, if any, cruise ships and the number of tourists drops off significantly. This is the time that many of the shops wish to move out some of their merchandise to get ready for the next year's shipment that will soon be arriving.

For specialty items of clothing, there are some well known designers available. Polly Hornberg is Bermuda's best known and most successful fashion designer and many of her works can be found at **Calypso** on Front Street in Hamilton and at the branches of the shop at the Princess Hotels and the Coral Beach Club.

For items of clothing such as rugby gear, sweaters and yachting items, Bermuda is also a gold mine. Many fabrics in cotton as well as in wools are available. Probably one of the most well known is **Davidsons of Bermuda**, which is not only located on Front Street but has outlets in many of the hotels.

In addition to wools, cottons and tartans from Europe, you will find cotton batik from Indonesia and islands in the Caribbean, as well as exquisite lace work from Hawaii and elsewhere. One of the most prevalent outlets for these types of items is **Frangipani** on Water Street in St. George's.

BERMUDA ORIGINALS

Genuine Bermuda-made products are clearly identified by a sticker which says Bermuda product and are growing in both quality and quantity. The Chamber of Commerce has designed a special logo to differentiate genuine local items from those of foreign origin. Fragrant Bermuda cedar items, such as candle holders, friendship goblets, lamps and bookends are just some of the things on display at the fine stores and gift shops throughout the island. Hand crafted Bermuda cedar handled button bags come in many delightful colors that are interchangeable and can be monogrammed at **H. A. & E. Smith, Ltd.** on Front Street in Hamilton. **A. S. Cooper & Son, Ltd.**, also on Front Street, has a selection in their store known as the Bermuda Shop devoted entirely to lovely gift items depicting local scenes, especially attractive for use in the kitchen and dining room.

In the fragrance line, you will find Bermuda Sovereign, a light masculine fragrance and three tropical perfumes, and colognes like Frangilique, Coralique and Lalique. Perfumes and toiletries produced locally by Royall Lyme are also attractively

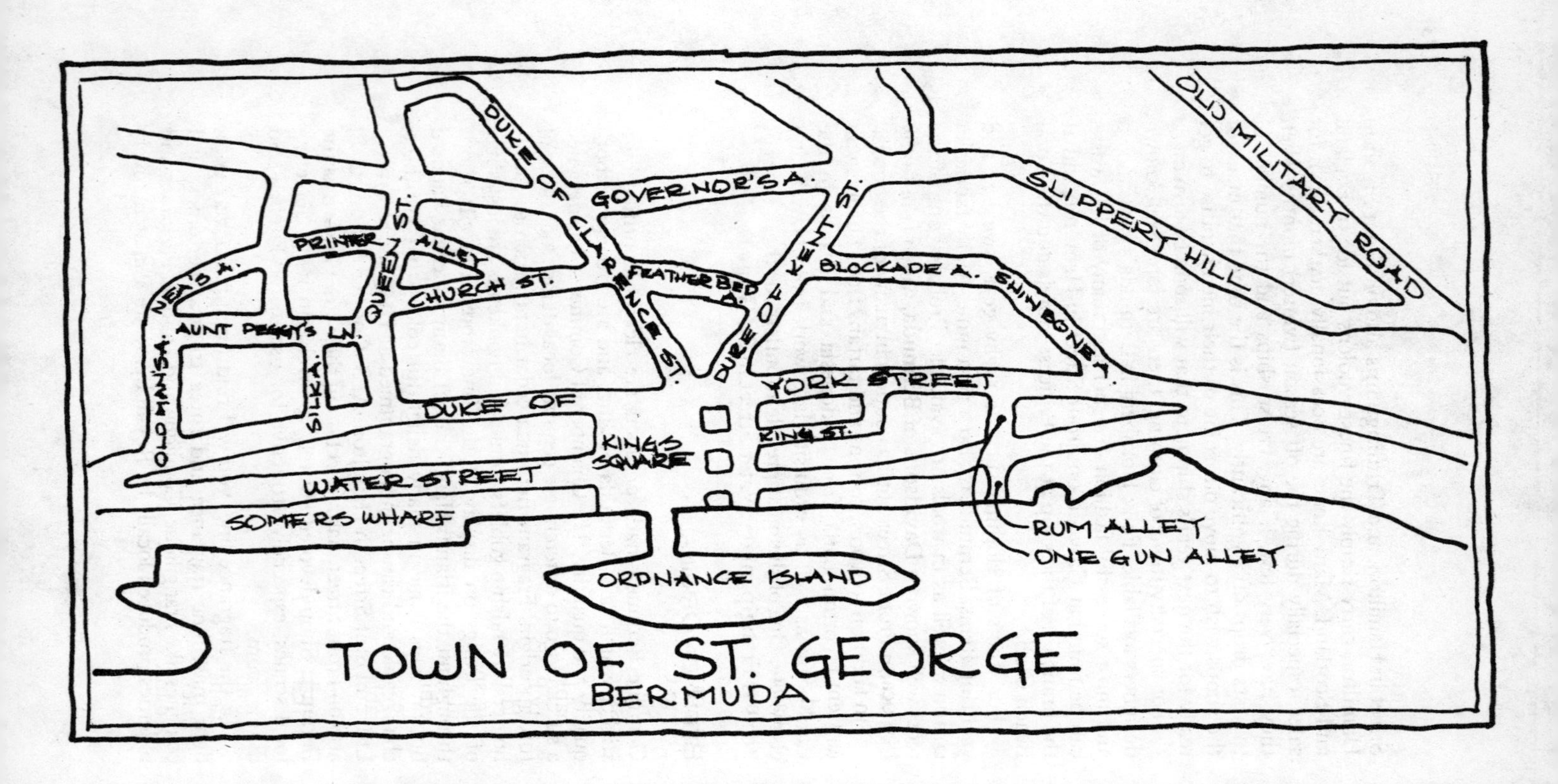

OLD MILITARY ROAD
SLIPPERY HILL
DUKE OF
GOVERNOR'S A.
KENT ST.
DUKE OF
CLARENCE ST.
BLOCKADE A.
SHINBONE A.
FEATHERBED A.
PRINTER
ALLEY
QUEEN ST.
CHURCH ST.
NEA'S A.
AUNT PEGGY'S LN.
OLD MAN'S A.
SILK A.
YORK STREET
DUKE OF
KING ST.
KINGS SQUARE
WATER STREET
SOMERS WHARF
RUM ALLEY
ONE GUN ALLEY
ORDNANCE ISLAND
TOWN OF ST. GEORGE
BERMUDA

packaged in bottles cast from the original clay mold. Royall Lyme, Royall Spyce, Royall Bay Rum, and Royall Muske are all to be found at perfume shops and gift shops island wide. The exquisite perfumes and colognes made from Bermuda's own flowers by Bermuda perfumeries are also available at fine stores such as **H. A. & E. Smith, Ltd**. in a perfume shop on Front Street as well as their main outlet in Baileys Bay.

Locally made liquors are produced by Somers Distillery, Ltd. Bermuda Gold Banana Liquor, Bermuda Triangle Rum Swizzle and cream cocktails are available at **Frith Liquors** and other liquor outlets throughout the island. **Gosling Brothers** produces the famous Black Seal Rum, original Rum Swizzle, and Silver Label Light Rum.

Many outlets also carry some of the locally handcrafted gold jewelry pieces depicting the graceful, long tailed bird, the Bermuda Fitted Dingy as well as the St. Davis Lighthouse and others. **Otto Wurz** in the Vallis Building on Front Street in Hamilton and the **Astwood Dickinson** stores all carry some of the locally made jewelry.

In the line of clothing, the ultimate Bermuda production is an item known as Tucker's Tees—imprinted sports wear with award winning Bermuda designs in many styles and colors available in stores throughout the island.

In addition to Bermuda stamps, there are also fine reproductions and originals of island maps and prints of local scenes. One of the largest stamp outlets is the **Bermuda Coin and Stamp Company**, located in Old Sellers Lane next to Walkers Arcade. **Pegasus**, best known for its maps and prints, is located across from the Princess Hotel in downtown Hamilton.

Of all the products made and produced in Bermuda, probably one of the most famous is Outerbridge's Original Sherry Pepper Sauce. The original recipe supposedly came from an old navy recipe and is a pleasant blend of peppers and 17 exotic spices and excellent sherry. It is used throughout the island in every restaurant in soups, seafood and just about everything else that is served. The Outerbridge's Sherry Pepper Sauce as well as many of the other Outerbridge's products are available at most shops in Bermuda.

WHERE TO SHOP

Most all the shopping in Bermuda is available in three main locations as well as many of the larger hotels. The shopping experience is made a lot easier by having everything concentrated in these areas. The three main shopping areas will be in

Somerset on the western end of the island, the town of St. George on the eastern end, and the main hub of shopping will be found in the city of Hamilton.

The shopping in Somerset is all located in a two block line of stores with **Triminghams** at the helm. The **Old Market**, once a meat market, carries jewelry, ceramics, scrimshaw and even a very good selection of Waterford crystal objects. On the way out there is a full selection of island perfumes. In addition to a small version of an English sport shop and **W. J. Bagel & Sons** at the east end of the street, there are some smaller souvenir and gift shops. Certainly one does not come to Somerset just to shop; however, the few shops there are certainly a delight and worth a stop on your way back from Somerset village, **Island Pottery** or **The Bermuda Art Center** at the dock yard.

Just beyond Somerset you will find the dock yard area and **Island Pottery Limited**. A visit to Island Pottery will be one of the most interesting and educational highlights of your visit. Located in the formal historical navy dock yard, Island Pottery manufactures ceramic items with a tradition in truly Bermudian flavor such as the famous long tail birds, the unique moon gates, Gibbs Hill Lighthouses and decal decorations of the Bermudian national flower, the hibiscus. The manufacturing facility extends over 4,000 square feet and the retail shop occupies an area of nearly 1,000 square feet. You can not only see some of the exquisite items that are produced here but at times you will be able to tour the factory to see the various manufacturing processes such as hand throwing, mold making, slip casting, glazing and firing. Some of the items that are produced are truly unique to the island, and in some cases have been produced specifically for a particular client.

At the eastern end of Bermuda is St. George. Most of the shopping in the St. George area will be confined to Water Street, a three to four block area near King Square in the middle of town. At the **Paradise Gift Shop** with entrances on King Square and York Street, you will find an interesting variety of attractive merchandise including brassware, copperware, English bone china, Irish knits, Italian and German porcelain, alabaster, and Spanish woodcarvings. Also available are locally made products such as Spanish perfumes, gold and silver jewelry, and traditional souvenir items such as straw goods, shell items and Bermuda T-shirts. The many shops of Water Street, however, will carry most of the items of the exquisite nature that Bermuda is known for. At **William Bluck & Company** on Water Street on Somers Wharf, you will find a complete array of quality china, porcelain, crystal, silver and antiques including Spode china, Herend porcelain and Baccarat, Lalique, and Daun crystal. Although this is a branch of one of Bermuda's oldest businesses, you will find the prices here as well as the other shops in St. George equal to those found in Hamilton. Also located in the immediate shopping area surrounding Somers Wharf is **Bananas**, at York and Bridge Streets which offers a large selection of Bermuda labeled merchandise. This ranges from mens, ladies and children's wear including the famous Banana's T-shirts, umbrellas, beach bags, and jackets. You can also find Bermuda sunglasses in fashion colors as well as many items made of straw. At the **Benetton** outlet on the western end of Somers Wharf on Water Street, you will find clothing that Benetton is internationally famous for at prices up to 50% less than you will find in the U.S. This store includes a complete line of children's wear. At **Crackerbox** on York Street you will find a full selection of gifts and memorabilia of Bermuda. There are shell and coral jewelry, much of it hand crafted locally. There is also a wide variety of the normal Bermuda theme clothing and beach towels as well as Outerbridge's Sherry Pepper Sauce and other food items.

If you are on a cruise ship and the ship is only stopping at St. George, do not feel cheated. The many shops along Water Street, especially the Somers Wharf area will carry a full range of items and in most cases the same items that are available in downtown Hamilton. Obviously the selection of china and crystal will not be as great nor will the larger jewelry stores be represented here; however, you will be able to enjoy the excellent prices and quality goods such as clothing from England, Scotland and Ireland.

For the widest range of shopping in Bermuda, however, you must visit downtown Hamilton, especially on Front Street and on Reid Street between Queen and Parliament Streets. The city of Hamilton is easily reached from any of the hotels by taxi or bus or motor driven cycle. The cruise ships also call at the city of Hamilton, and you may literally be able to see many of the shops from the ship. Shopping in Hamilton is very convenient in that virtually every shop could be visited in less than one half day.

In addition to those cruise ships which tie up only at Hamilton, there are some ships that will stop at St. George and then move around to the city of Hamilton. We have known many visitors to the island who have departed the cruise ship, and with permission, have shopped in St. George, taken a taxi from St. George over to Hamilton, continued shopping, and met the ship as it docked in Hamilton.

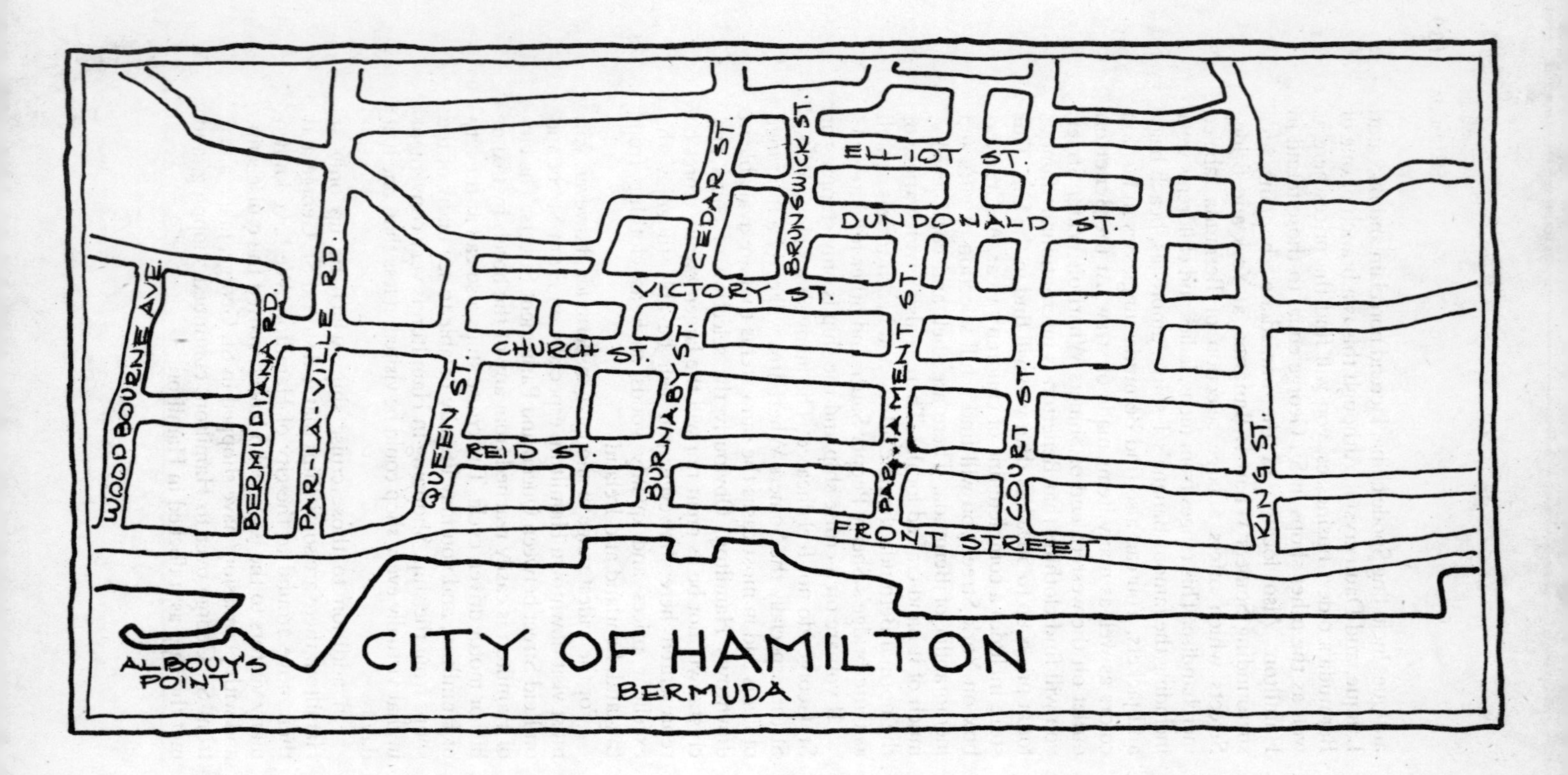
CITY OF HAMILTON
BERMUDA
ALBOUY'S POINT
FRONT STREET
WOODBOURNE AVE
BERMUDIANA RD.
PAR-LA-VILLE RD.
QUEEN ST.
BURNABY ST.
PARLIAMENT ST.
COURT ST.
KING ST.
REID ST.
CHURCH ST.
VICTORY ST.
CEDAR ST.
BRUNSWICK ST.
ELLIOT ST.
DUNDONALD ST.

On Front Street in Hamilton you will find the outlets of most of the famous shops that Bermuda is known for. **H. A. & E. Smith, Ltd.**, known for china and crystal to world class fashions and gifts is located at 35 Front Street. They also have branch stores at the Belmont Hotel and Southampton Princess. **Triminghams**, one of Bermuda's largest and most prestigious stores, is located at 37 Front Street. Triminghams has a reputation for offering fine quality European imports at up to 50% savings compared to U.S. prices. These buys are featured throughout the store in the form of sweaters, British woolens, fine china and crystal. French perfumes, mens wear, women's fashion, accessories, giftware, fine jewelry and more are found in every department. Fine china made by Royal Worcestershire, Anysley, Spode, and Meissen is side by side with Waterford, Galway and Atlantis crystal. The sweater selection at Triminghams is outstanding and contains styles made of cashmere, lambswool, cottons, specialty knits and Shetlands that are at prices well below the U.S. equivalent.

A. S. Cooper & Sons Ltd., is a must for any shopping trip and is located at 59 Front Street. This is Bermuda's oldest and largest china and glassware store. Wedgwood is exclusive with them and their display of bone china, dinnerware, giftware, oven to tableware, Jaspar, Prestige pieces and jewelry is extensive. Other popular names to be found at A. S. Cooper & Son, Ltd. are Coalport, Minten, Royal Doulton, Belleek and Royal Copenhagen. The collector's gallery at Coopers is renowned for limited edition of Bing and Grondahl, Boehm with their Lladro collection being one of the largest we have ever seen.

Astwood Dickinson, at 83 Front Street, offers some of the finest gemstone jewelry and internationally famous time pieces, all at excellent prices.

At 27 Front Street, you will find **Archie Brown & Son, Ltd**. which has become a landmark for the cruise ships and a must for those looking for the very best British woolens and craftsmanship. Many visitors come back year after year to stock up on sweaters and to visit some of their favorite salespeople. Here you will find cashmere from Pringle of Scotland, which is exclusive with Brown's, cashmere from Berry Scotland and McGeorge of Scotland. Paris tweed jackets for both men and women and many of the bulky hand-made Irish knits are all 20% to 40% below U.S. prices. Brown's is also one of the best known outlets for many of the tartan products and has virtually every design available.

These, some of the finest Bermuda has to offer can all be found within three to four blocks on Front Street or on Reid Street immediately behind it in the city of Hamilton. To list them all would be impossible and to list every possible high quality item would also be an impossible task.

Shopping in Hamilton will be an experience that you will long remember. You will not find a lot of the clutter of souvenir type items that are present in many other islands. Here you will find high quality merchandise at very reasonable prices and some of the most friendly, knowledgeable and courteous salespeople you have encountered.

SPECIAL TIPS FOR CRUISE SHIP PASSENGERS

If your time in Bermuda is limited, you will still have time to visit most all the shops in either St. George, or in Hamilton. You will probably not have time to go to Sommerset, **Island Pottery**, or the **Bermuda Art Center** in the west end at the dock yard, but all the shopping you will need is steps away from the ship.

In St. George, concentrate on the area near King's Square on Water Street and in Somers Wharf. Nearly all the shops that are in Hamilton are there, as well as a few specialty shops that are unique to St. George. The prices here are identical to Hamilton, so do not feel you are paying more because the area is smaller. The selection may not be as large in St. George, but the quality merchandise is there and excellent salespeople are waiting to assist you.

In Hamilton, concentrate your efforts on Front Street. If you start at the corner of Front Street and Queen Street—where the bird cage is in the middle of the intersection—work your way down Front to Parliament Street, turn left, go one block to Reid Street, turn left again on Reid, proceed on Reid back to Queen, then left again back to Front Street, you will have seen virtually every shop in town. There are a few additional shops worth visiting on Front across from the Ferry Terminal, Visitors' Service Bureau and head office of the Bank of Bermuda, if you have time. That sounds like a lot, but it can be done in one afternoon.

For a complete flavor of Bermuda, check to determine if your ship stops first at St. George and then moves around to Hamilton. If it does, you may be able to shop in both areas the same day. Keep in mind that the traffic speed laws are strictly enforced, so it will take a taxi about one-half hour to get from St. George to Hamilton at the very least. This is not New York, so even a determined, "Step on it, I'm late," is not going to get you there any faster.

If you have only an hour, we would suggest you visit one of the elegant stores that carry a variety of merchandise such as Trimingham's, A.S Cooper & Sons, Ltd., H. A. & E. Smith, Ltd., William Bluck & Co., Ltd., or Vera P. Card, Ltd. If you only have time for a sweater or rugby shirt, pick Archie Brown & Son, Ltd., Davidson's of Bermuda, the English Sports Shop, or Trimingham's.

ENJOYING YOUR STAY

THE SITES

One of the best ways to see either St. George or Hamilton is to take a walking tour of one or both. The Visitor Centers have excellent walking tour maps free of charge. Since both cities are small, a good tour will not take more than a few hours.

You should also consider doing some of the following things while in Bermuda:

- A ferry trip from Hamilton to Somerset or the Dock Yard. The Ferry Terminal in downtown Hamilton at Queen and Front Streets has all the information.
- A tour of the islands by taxi. Some of the most informative and nicest drivers in the world drive taxis in Bermuda. Look for the taxis with blue flags for the drivers who are expert tour guides.
- A visit to one of the forts—Fort Scaur, Gates Fort or Fort St. Catherine
- A visit to the museums and art galleries. All are listed in the guide books available in your hotel, especially one entitled ***This Week in Bermuda***.

ACCOMMODATIONS

Since Bermuda is dependant on tourism, you will find accommodations ranging from elegant resort type hotels to small guest cottages. Here are some of the most popular places:

- **The Belmont Hotel, Golf and County Club**: Tel. 800-225-5843. Fax 809-236-6867. A deluxe resort hotel situated on 110 acres overlooking Hamilton Harbour. P.O. Box WK 251, Warwick WK BX, Bermuda.

- **Elbow Beach Hotel, A Wyndham Resort**: Tel. 809-236-3535. Fax 809-236-8043 or 800-223-7434. Located on Bermuda's south shore overlooking a pink sand beach—the best beach in beach in Bermuda. The hotel is self-contained in 50 acres of botanical gardens. P.O. Box HM 455, Hamilton HM BX, Bermuda.

- **Marriott's Castle Harbour Resort**: Tel. 809-293-2040. Fax 809-293-8288 or 800-223-6388. One of Bermuda's classic resorts offering European elegance is located on a hilltop overlooking Castle Harbour and Harrington Sound. The hotel is located on 250 acres, has 450 rooms, and an 18-hole golf course. P.O. Box HM 841, Hamilton HM CX, Bermuda.

- **The Hamilton Princess:** Tel. 809-295-3000. Fax 809-295-1914 or 800-223-1818. Located on the edge of Hamilton Harbour. Guests have access of all of the facilities of the Southampton Princess—just 20 minutes away by private ferry. P.O. Box HM 837, Hamilton HM CX, Bermuda.

- **Southampton Princess**: Tel. 809-238-8000. 809-238-8968 or 800-223-1818. Stands on one of the highest points in Bermuda offering a panoramic view over the entire width of the island. The hotel has 600 rooms and suites. P.O. Box HM 1379, Hamilton HM FX, Bermuda.

You'll find many small hotels and cottage colonies. A comprehensive listing of these is in the Bermuda Department of Tourism's booklet, ***Where to Stay in Bermuda***. In addition, you may receive information in regard to smaller properties that are for rent from Bermuda's Small Properties, Ltd., P.O. Box PG300, Paget PG Bx, Bermuda, Tel. 809-236-1633, 1-800-637-4116, Fax 809-236-1662.

RESTAURANTS

There are literally hundreds of places to eat in Bermuda. A representative list of even the different kinds would be very difficult, but some of the more well-known are:

- **Fisherman's Reef:** Tel. 292-1609. Located on Burnaby Hill just off Front Street in Hamilton, and specializes in seafood.

- **Romanoff:**Tel. 295-0333. Located on Church Street in Hamilton is an award-winning restaurant serving a wide variety of international favorites. Prices are a little on the high side, and reservations are certainly recommended.

- **Tavern on the Green:** Tel. 236-7731 or 236-9260. Located in the middle of the Botanical Gardens and serves classic and local Bermudian dishes.

- **White Horse Restaurant and Bar:** Tel. 297-1839 or 297-1838. An old Bermudian style tavern located on King's Square in St. George. You may dine inside or out, weather permitting.

- **Black Horse Tavern:** Tel. 293-9742. Located on St. David's Island is one of our favorites. This small restaurant is patronized mainly by local residents and is a little out of the way from either St. George or Hamilton. It is, however, worth the trip for local Bermudian foods, especially fresh chowders and other seafood.

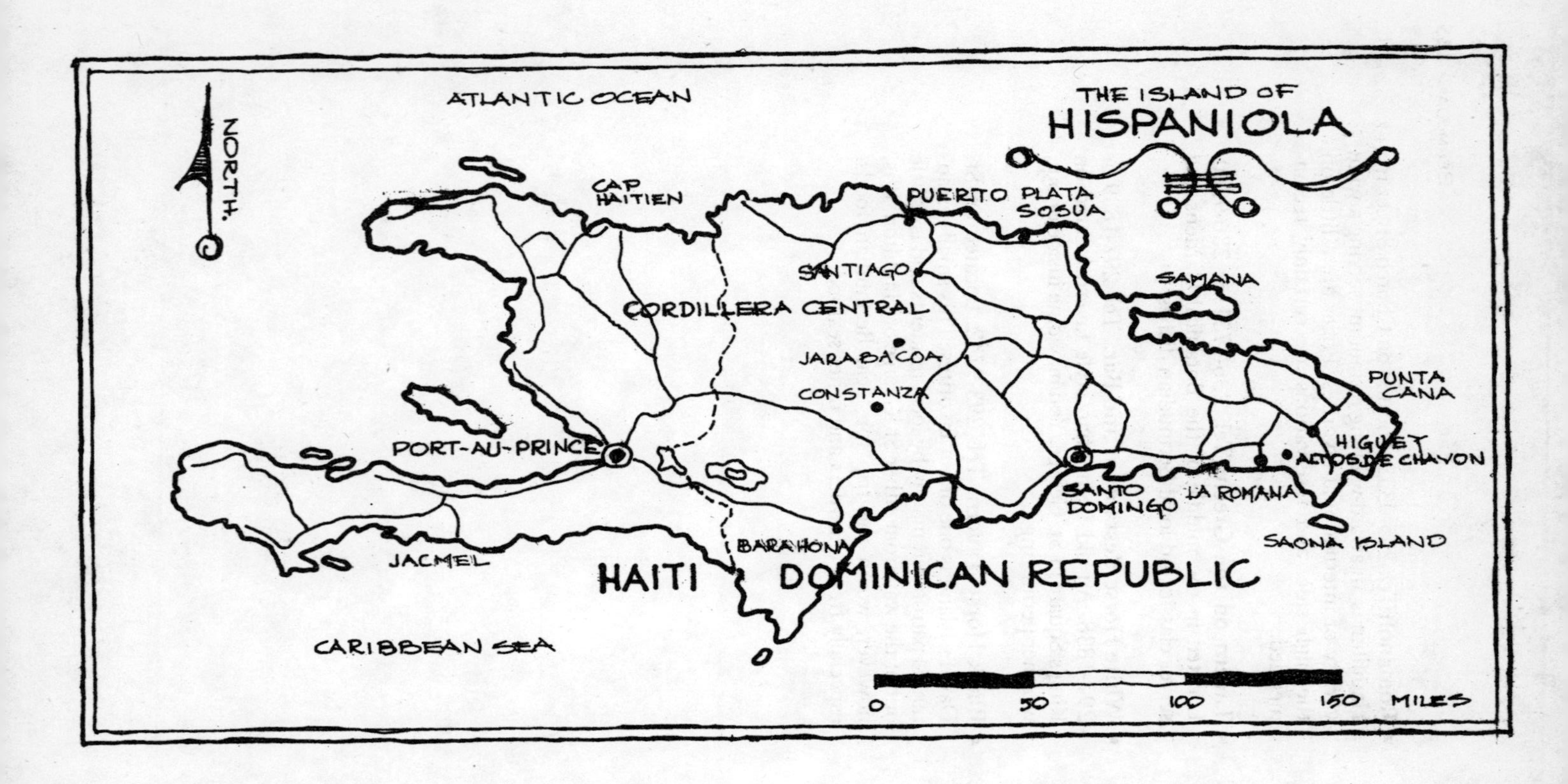
THE ISLAND OF
HISPANIOLA
ATLANTIC OCEAN
NORTH.
CAP HAITIEN
PUERTO PLATA
SOSUA
SANTIAGO
SAMANA
CORDILLERA CENTRAL
JARABACOA
CONSTANZA
PUNTA CANA
HIGUEY
ALTOS DE CHAVON
PORT-AU-PRINCE
SANTO DOMINGO
LA ROMANA
SAONA ISLAND
BARAHONA
JACMEL
HAITI
DOMINICAN REPUBLIC
CARIBBEAN SEA
0
50
100
150
MILES

9

Dominican Republic

Although Christopher Columbus discovered what is now the Dominican Republic in December of 1492, the country has only recently emerged as one of the more exotic shopping treasures of the Caribbean. Here you can find the beautiful faceless Lime statuettes, world renowned fashions such as those created by Oscar de la Renta, an emerging art industry that is beginning to rival that of any country in the Caribbean, and the semi-precious stones of larimar and amber.

Shopping in the Dominican Republic can run the full range of exquisite and expensive jewelry shops in Puerto Plata, Altos de Chavon, and many of the hotels to the popular market in the urban center which rivals any of the great bazaars of the world. Since the Dominican Republic is one of the largest countries in the Caribbean and its principal city of Santo Domingo is one of the largest cities in the region, shopping here can take on a little different flavor than exists on many other islands. The main shopping district in the old colonial city of Santo Domingo will enable you to walk to many of the shopping areas. However, there are many shopping centers located throughout the city which do require some time to get to. If you are in Santo Domingo and wish to explore the artisans of Altos de Chavon or the many shops in Puerto Plata, each will take an entire day.

Whether you are shopping for stylish fashions, the many varieties of unique Dominican art or some of the most beautiful precious stones in the world, the Dominican Republic is worth your time and effort.

GETTING TO KNOW YOU

At the time of discovery by Christopher Columbus in December 1492, the island of Hispaniola was inhabited by descendants of the Arawak Indians. The natives called the island Quisqueya, which means "greatness," or Haiti, which literally means "rugged or high mountains."

The lure of gold brought more ships to Santo Domingo, a settlement founded by Bartholomew, the brother of Christopher Columbus, became a major port on the southern side of the country. The country was visited many times by Columbus and other earlier explorers and entered a very long era of occupation and political development from the mid 1500's to the mid-1800's. The country became well known throughout the world, however, in the early 1900's when the Dominican Republic was occupied by the U.S. Marines to be followed by the government of Raphael Trujillo who ruled the country until his assassination in 1961. Since the first elections in 1962, however, the Dominican Republic has enjoyed a very stable democracy and is now on the verge of becoming a major tourist attraction and a country capable of self-support.

Prices in the Dominican Republic are still among some of the lowest in the major Caribbean shopping areas. A dinner at some of the finest restaurants can run as little as US $10, and many objects of art and some of the most unique jewelry available anywhere in the world can be had for very reasonable prices.

The Dominican Republic has started to attract investments from many foreign countries and that along with an expected 300% increase in cruise ship traffic during the next few years, will make the country one of the most visited in the Caribbean. The Minister of Tourism has also predicted that within the next few years, the Dominican Republic will offer the greatest number of hotel rooms (25,000 at this time) of any destination in the Caribbean.

Of the many cities and villages in the country, most visitors will be attracted to Santo Domingo, Puerto Plata or the La Romano area. Santo Domingo is a large city on the southern coast of the Dominican Republic and like most large cities is often noisy, has too much traffic, and too many people.

However, it is one of the safest cities in the world and it offers every sort of entertainment from discotheques to casinos and a variety of very fine restaurants. There are great shopping arcades, market places, boutiques and craft centers in virtually every part of the city. In addition, Santo Domingo is the cultural center of the country. There are many performances by symphony orchestras, ballet companies, chamber orchestras, and solo recitals. This Caribbean capital also has an unusual historical past and colonial landmarks to take you back to the 16th Century. Santo Domingo is supposedly the resting place for the remains of Christopher Columbus although there has been a controversy raging for many years as to whether Columbus is buried in Santo Domingo, Spain, or Cuba.

On the northern coast of the Dominican Republic is Puerto Plata, the main port of call for many cruise ships. The area surrounding Puerto Plata is blossoming with many resorts, especially in the Playa Dorada area. The city of Puerto Plata has also expanded the number of boutiques and shopping outlets and virtually every item available in the country can be purchased within walking distance from the cruise ships.

On the eastern side of the island you will find the city of La Romano, which was a thriving sugar port at the turn of the century but is now known primarily for its proximity to Casa de Campo, a resort known throughout the world. The Casa de Campo complex is comprised of about 7,000 acres of land with 14 swimming pools, 900 hotel rooms and villas, 17 tennis courts and some of the best golf in the Caribbean. Near the Casa de Campo is the recreation of a hillside village from the south of France known as Altos de Chavon. This village was totally recreated on a hillside overlooking the Chavon River and was primarily constructed as a potential artist village for both local and international artists. There is an active two-year college of art located here teaching sculpture, pottery, silk screening, painting, weaving, dance and music.

THE BASICS

LOCATION AND GEOGRAPHY

The Dominican Republic lies in the very center of the Caribbean. It occupies the Eastern two-thirds of the island of Hispaniola, which is the second largest island in the Caribbean. Only Cuba has more land mass than Hispaniola. The northern coast of the Dominican Republic faces the Atlantic Ocean while the Caribbean Sea is to the south. Haiti occupies the other one-third of the island and 70 miles to the east is the island of Puerto Rico. The Dominican Republic is slightly more than 19,000 square miles in size and has a population nearing 7 million. Its principal mountain range is the Cordillera Central which contains one of the highest peaks in the Caribbean. Pico Duarte rises a little more than 10,300 feet above sea level. Four other rugged mountain ranges or cordilleras run the length of the island, and between these lie rich fertile valleys. One of the depressions in the southwestern regions holds Lake Enriquillo, which is the lowest point of the Dominican terrain at 144 feet below sea level.

Almost one-third of the Dominican Republic coastline contains beaches. For tourists, especially those arriving by cruise ship, the most appealing area is the northern coast and the beaches near the city of Puerto Plata. Another spectacular beach is located at Punta Cana which is 20 miles long—one of the longest in the Caribbean. Along the southeastern coast are the beautiful beaches near Boca Chica and La Ramano.

CLIMATE, WHEN TO GO, WHAT TO WEAR

The Dominican Republic has a very pleasant climate. A tropical country, it is within the 70 to 80 degrees Fahrenheit range on the northern coast and slightly warmer in the Santo Domingo area in July and August. On the northern coast the trade winds and the mountains combine to give the air a fresh crystal clear quality. Although the temperature does not vary greatly from month to month, if you do go to the Dominican Republic between December and February, you will experience some slightly cooler temperatures in the evening. The daytime temperatures, however, remain fairly constant throughout the year. April to May and August to October are considered the rainy seasons, although it does not mean that it rains all the time. You might have a week of steady rain during this period; however, in this part of the world, the tropical showers are somewhat brief and there is a predictable pattern. It is not unusual to find it raining about the same time each day during the rainy season, but you will find many hours of sunshine during the day to enjoy shopping.

If you are vacationing at one of the beach resorts, the dress is casual. In most of these areas, a nice pair of slacks or a summer dress is considered formal. The resort hotels of Playa Dorada, Boca Chica and Casa de Campo sometimes have activities at night for which you may want to bring casual but somewhat dressy clothing. Many of the resort facilities have discotheques and one or two restaurants. Men may want to take a blazer; women might pack a nice dress or a pants outfit. Expected dress in the larger cities is more conservative. Business suits are the proper attire for business calls. Women planning to visit the Cathedral should wear dresses.

As with most of the Caribbean islands, ultra casual resort type clothing should be limited to the resort areas and shorts are not acceptable for in-town shopping and are simply not allowed in many restaurants and casinos. If you like to dress up, Dominican Republic is also a place where you feel very comfortable in a full suit and tie. Some of the dining rooms such as the Alcazar at the Santo Domingo Hotel are places where a jacket or suit and tie will be the norm rather than the exception.

GETTING THERE

The Dominican Republic is accessible from virtually every island in the Caribbean and from most major U.S. coast cities. The country is served by a number of international airlines such as American, Continental, Carnival, Dominicana and ALM. Charters include Transglobal from Minneapolis. There are two major international airport facilities. The recently expanded Las Americas International is near Santo Domingo and La Union International near Puerto Plata services the northern coast. Punta Cana also has an international airport facility with a very busy charter flight business. There are a number of smaller airfields located throughout the country which will facilitate domestic travel. The busiest of these is Herrera Airport near Santo Domingo. Although the Dominican Republic may not be known by all tourists and shoppers, there are many who do know it well. Especially around the holidays, we have found all flights from the U.S. as well as connections from Puerto Rico to be totally booked. So plan ahead and make reservations early.

In addition to the air travel to the Dominican Republic, arriving by sea is becoming a very popular option. Some of the cruise lines include Cunard and Costa. There are many cruise packages available which include the Dominican Republic on their itinerary and again the best source of this information will be the various individual cruise lines or your local travel agent. Keep in mind that arriving by ship in the Dominican Republic although certainly an exotic adventure in and of itself may somewhat limit your accessibility to all the shopping areas. The country is large and it may not be possible to drive from Puerto Plata to Santo Domingo and return if you have just a few short hours in port. If shopping is one of the main items on your itinerary and you do arrive at Puerto Plata, we recommend that you inquire about the charter flight service from Puerto Plata to

Harrera Airfield outside of Santo Domingo. Although many of the fashions, jewelry, and objects of art are available in Puerto Plata, the prices are normally 20% to 30% less in many of the areas in and around Santo Domingo.

Whatever your means of arrival, be prepared to pay $10 for a tourist card. This must be paid in non-Dominican currency.

DOCUMENTS

To enter the Dominican Republic, citizens of the United States and Canada need a tourist card, which may be purchased through the airline at your point of departure, through any diplomatic Consulate, Dominican Tourism office abroad, or upon arrival. The charge for the tourist card is US$10. The card is good for a maximum stay of approximately ninety days and either a valid passport or proof of citizenship, such as an original copy of a birth certificate is needed to obtain the card. A reproduced birth certificate, driver's license, or other form of identification are not acceptable. It is advisable to check with the nearest Consulate or Dominican Tourism Office for the most up-to-date regulations. Although you can enter the country with a birth certificate, it may be somewhat difficult to get back into the United States without a passport. For shoppers heading for the Dominican Republic and Haiti, we highly recommend using U.S. passport rather than other documents.

Be sure to keep the tourist card because upon departure, you must return it and pay a departure tax of US$10. The departure tax must be paid in US currency after you check in at the airline counter but before you go through Immigration.

ARRIVAL

Arrival in the Dominican Republic is fairly easy although the line at Immigration can be long. As in many islands, many employees are not in a great hurry to move large numbers of people through the booths and proceed to check all the documentation at their own speed. Once through Immigration, your luggage can be retrieved and you will proceed to customs. Customs is rather thorough and you should be prepared to have your baggage searched. One word of caution, punishment for the possession of any form of narcotic drug, even in small amounts, is severe and involves up to $50,000 dollars in fines and up to ten years in the prison. Diabetics or other individuals who require prescription drugs should travel with a doctor's prescription indicating that the medication is required. There are limitations on the amount of alcohol, cigarettes and gift items that are allowed into the country duty-free. Although no duty is levied on personal belongings, keep in mind that if you are traveling through the Dominican Republic from such places as St. Thomas, you may have a slight problem passing through Customs with larger amounts than one liter of alcohol, 200 cigarettes or 100 dollars worth of gift items.

Once through Customs, your baggage will normally be retrieved by porters who will help you find a cab to take you to your destination. Be careful, keep an eye on your luggage. There is a great deal of theft of luggage in this area. Although the official language is Spanish, English is spoken by most everyone at the airport. The taxi cabs are not metered and you should inquire as to what the normal charge will be from the airport to your hotel or other destination. Most of the fares are set and you will find most everyone in the country very honest with regard to those charges. Rental cars from most of the major rental car companies are also available; however, we highly recommend that you make arrangements prior to arrival. The number of automobiles that are available are not as plentiful as they are in other cities, and if you do not have reservations, it may be difficult to get one at the airport. Also, be prepared to pay slightly higher charges for rental vehicles in the Dominican Republic than you would in other parts of the world. There are no automobiles manufactured in the country and the import duties combined with the cost of operation are rather high. This results in the rental fees being much higher than you would normally find in the United States.

- **April to May and August to October are considered the rainy seasons.**
- **Taxi cabs are not metered. Agree on the cost of a ride before taking a cab.**
- **Avoid changing more money than you need as the banks and other exchange outlets are not permitted to convert pesos back into U.S. dollars.**
- **Few local residents outside the major shopping areas speak English. Many cab drivers do not speak English.**

CURRENCY, TRAVELER'S CHECKS, CREDIT CARDS

The Dominican peso, written RD$, is the official monetary unit of the Dominican Republic and fluctuates in value relative to the U.S. dollar. The peso symbol is the same as the dollar symbol, so if you are unsure—ask for further information. You will find most prices are quoted in Dominican pesos at an exchange rate of approximately RD$12.30 to US$1. You certainly do not want to end up paying in U.S. dollars when the price is quoted in the Dominican pesos. Although U.S. dollars are accepted in most places, it certainly is convenient to have pesos available for your purchases. You may exchange currency at the airport, commercial banks and at most large hotels and resorts. However, avoid changing more than you need as the banks and other exchange outlets are not permitted to convert pesos back into U.S. dollars. Since it is very difficult to change Dominican money back into any other currency, we suggest that you buy Dominican pesos only as you need them. Try to end your stay with almost no pesos if possible since whatever you have leftover will certainly become a souvenir and not something you can exchange. You should exchange currency only at approved designated places. There are people on the street who will offer to sell you pesos at what appears to be an extremely favorable rate. Most will take advantage of your limited knowledge of the monetary situation and you may actually get fewer pesos than you would at a bank. In addition, there have been many incidents of counterfeit bills exchanging hands during these particular transactions. The practice of exchanging pesos for U.S. dollars on the street is now illegal in the Dominican Republic and in addition to being the victim of a con game, you might also find yourself in difficulty with the legal authorities. The best advice—avoid all deals on the street for exchanging currency, no matter how good they may seem.

Traveler's checks are accepted by most gasoline stations and most of the tourists hotels and facilities. You will find that you will get a very fair exchange rate when exchanging traveler's checks for pesos at any of the banks and hotel exchange windows.

Most major credit cards are accepted in the Dominican Republic. This can prove more convenient than trying to exchange currency into pesos. It has been our experience that the exchange rates that are applied through the billing system are normally very fair. However, we found on more than one occasion that after bargaining for a particular object of art or jewelry that when we offered to pay for the purchase with a credit card we were told that a 10% charge would be added to the price that we had negotiated. You may still consider the use of a credit card if you are purchasing an expensive item of jewelry or art from any of the galleries in that if there is some difficulty later as to its authenticity, the credit card company may be of some assistance.

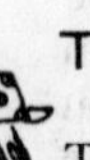

TIPPING

The government imposes a 15% tax on hotel rooms and 10% tax on food and beverages throughout the country. In addition, hotels, nightclubs and restaurants normally will include a 10% service charge on the bill. It is customary, however, for you to leave an extra 10% gratuity for good service. Porters, taxi drivers, beach attendants and housekeeping staff at the hotel should be tipped according to your usual custom and the quality of service offered.

Tipping or paying a commission to some of the teenage helpers or guides that you will certainly meet in any busy shopping area is a totally different matter. Some of these "helpers" will ask to be tipped at a rate of approximately ten percent of the purchases for which they have helped you bargain. Others will ask for a specific amount. We have found it quite helpful to have some of the helpers or guides available in certain circumstances, however, a clear understanding of what you are going to pay them should be made up front. On the other hand, there are helpers or guides who will not ask you for a commission or a tip, but there will be a commission added to your purchase by shopkeepers and the guides will be compensated later. The commission is normally about 10% of the price of your purchases. If you do not want the assistance of these helpers, you need to be firm in turning down offers of assistance and make it very clear to the shopkeepers or artists with whom you are dealing that no one has been employed by you and no commission is to be added to the price. We, however, found in some of the downtown shopping areas such as the Mercado Modelo that the use of a guide was most helpful. We found that even though most of the guides are teenagers, they do speak both Spanish and English and did in fact assist us in many cases where a particular shopkeeper could not speak English.

LANGUAGE

The official language of the Dominican Republic is Spanish, but English is spoken at most of the major hotels and resort areas. However, we experienced that once outside of the major shopping areas of Santo Domingo, Puerto Plata or the Altos de Chavon area near La Romano very few of the local residents understand English. This becomes a concern if you are traveling alone with a rental vehicle since many of the roads are not clearly marked and it is easy to get lost or turned around in many small villages that you pass through. In those situations, basic Spanish will normally get you back on the right track and on your way. We also experienced a need to use some basic Spanish to purchase gasoline in some of the small villages and in ordering at some of the smaller eating establishments. You will find that many of the taxi cab drivers do not speak English; however, this normally is not a problem, since the doorman at the hotel can convey your destination to the driver in Spanish. In addition, most of them will understand your destination if it is a major shopping area or hotel for your return even though you are conversing in English. The Santo Domingo Sheraton or Hotel Lina sound about the same no matter what language you are using.

BUSINESS HOURS

Most of the shops and shopping centers are open from 8am or 9am in the morning until 12 noon and again from 2pm to around 6pm. Most, however, are closed on Sundays and all Dominican holidays. We also experienced a number of shops in some areas closed on Saturday afternoons. If you do plan to try to shop on a weekend, inquire at your hotel as to what will be open.

TRANSPORTATION

Whether you are staying in Santo Domingo, Puerto Plata or one of the other resort areas, you will find taxi service readily available. Each of the hotels has a number of taxis on duty throughout the day and evening and the hotel doorman will summon a taxi driver from a nearby area. Many of the hotels have taxi services that can be called in case you wish to reserve a taxi for a particular time. We found that all hotels have a standard rate sheet indicating the various charges. This is important because in the Dominican Republic taxis are not metered and determining the cost of a trip in advance may be difficult if you do not speak Spanish. The taxis operating out of the major hotel areas tend to be larger cars and in many cases air conditioned. You will find, however, that some of the taxis that may be hailed from the streets may not be air conditioned nor in the best of repair. For a short trip this may not be a problem; however, we normally did inquire as to whether the taxi cab had shock absorbers or adequate springs if we intended to use a particular driver for a tour. Sitting in a cab without shock absorbers for two to three hours over bumpy roads may not be your idea of a good time.

By law, the taxi fares in the Dominican Republic are stated in Dominican pesos and pesos are accepted in payment of the fare. Tipping the driver is not required but is customary.

In Puerto Plata you may also find a great variety of public taxis or *publico* available. Be clear on the fare as you get in and be aware of the fact that most will not speak English at all. For the most part you will find that even though the fares are rather cheap, these particular cars are usually not in very good condition, and the driver tends to go at break neck speed. You may have a number of other passengers pile in on top of you since the drivers try to cram up to five or six passengers in the back seat. Generally speaking, we do not encourage or recommend that you experiment with the *publico* transportation unless you are very adventuresome and want to participate in some of the local culture.

One of the best ways to see the Dominican Republic is by private car and renting a vehicle in the Dominican Republic is not difficult. There are 40 to 50 registered car rental companies and most of the larger American rental companies such as Hertz, Avis, National and Budget can be found at the airport terminals and at offices throughout Santo Domingo and Puerto Plata. Although the rental prices are somewhat higher than in the United States and Canada, most of the automobiles are equipped with engines that get high mileage so the additional cost of gasoline will not add too much to the bill. You will find virtually every type arrangement available from a basic charge with a charge per mile as well as weekly rates with unlimited mileage.

If you do rent an automobile, you should definitely consider buying the additional collision insurance and be sure that you purchase a good map. Once outside the cities of Santo Domingo, Puerto Plata, and La Romana, you will find that very few roads are marked with signs, although the roads are generally in good condition. In addition to the lack of road signs, you will find that most Dominican drivers tend to speed. Although driving is on the right hand side, you should pay close attention to the vehicles around you since most of the drivers take great delight in exceeding the speed limit anytime they can. Be cognizant of your speed, because there may be numerous speed traps. In some cases, the existence of a speed trap is clearly marked, in other cases it may simply be a police car or motorcycle on the side of the road with a radar gun. Outside the major areas, virtually none of the policemen speak English so if you are pulled over for a traffic infraction, it can be a long drawn out confusing experience.

If you drive in Santo Domingo be prepared for the windshield cleaners at every street corner. Young boys will offer to wash your windshield or simply wash it without your okay and then expect to be paid. The going rate for this service is about one peso.

The hotels can arrange for specific tours to just about any place in the country. There are a number of tour operators in the major cities such as Santo Domingo, Puerto Plata or La

Romana and they can arrange anything from private automobiles to small buses to light airplanes.

In Santo Domingo there are a number of excellent city tours available which can be booked at most of the major hotels. One includes a day tour of the city which covers the colonial district, the cultural complex, shopping and residential areas. Most of the city day tours take three to four hours. Another tour available centers around shopping. This particular type of tour will enable you to visit the duty-free shops in town for bargains on perfumes, watches, sound equipment, cameras and liquor. The tour usually includes the main commercial area of El Conde Street for a quick look at the various shops and boutiques and then a trip to some of the Hendrick craft centers such as Plaza Criolla on the 27th of February Avenue. This type of tour could be extremely helpful if you have limited time and want to get a full flavor of virtually everything that is available in the city.

There are also four hour excursions in the evenings to night clubs, discotheques and to one or more of the cities excellent casinos. Most of these specific types of tours are conducted in mini buses seating approximately fifteen people or you can arrange to have a private drive made available through most of the travel agencies.

RESOURCES

There are a number of tourist type newspapers available at the various hotels; however, we found a particular publication called the ***Dominican Republic Guide Book*** available in Santo Domingo to be one of the most helpful. It is one of the more complete books on the entire country and covers virtually every area of the country for the traveler. It's available at most hotel book shops for approximately RD$95.

There are not many other specific guide books or maps available throughout the country. An inquiry at a car rental agency or the hotel will be the best opportunity to collect anything that is currently in print.

SHOPPING WELL

Until recently, the Dominican Republic was not considered to be a destination for those interested primarily in shopping. Although the rich variety of fruits and vegetables as well as the Dominican coffee had been well known for years, their magnificent art and jewelry is something rather new on the world

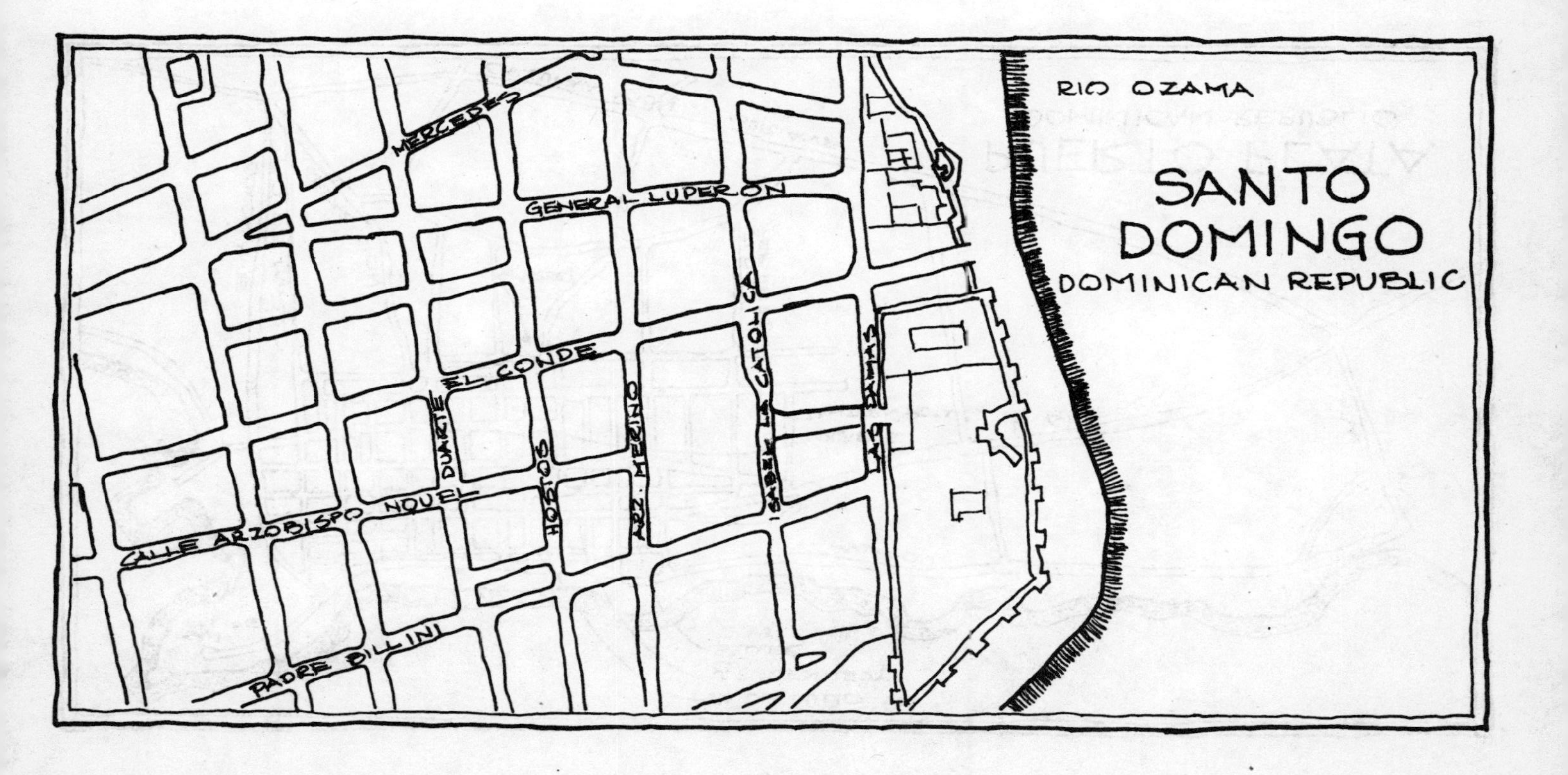
RIO OZAMA
SANTO DOMINGO
DOMINICAN REPUBLIC
MERCEDES
GENERAL LUPERON
ISABEL LA CATOLICA
LAS DAMAS
EL CONDE
ARZ. MERINO
HOSTOS
DUARTE
CALLE ARZOBISPO NOUEL
PADRE BILLINI

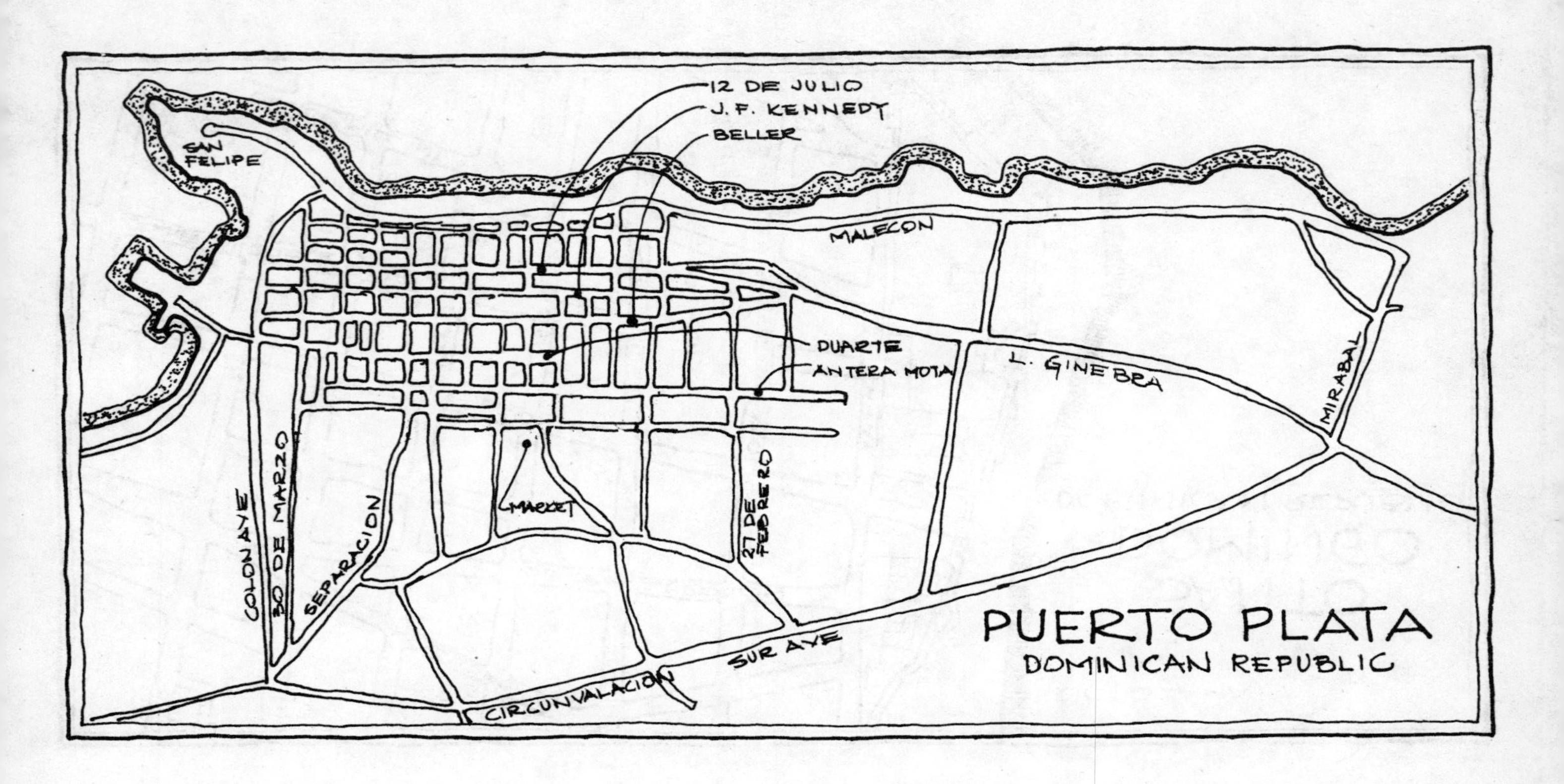
12 DE JULIO
J. F. KENNEDY
BELLER
SAN FELIPE
MALECON
DUARTE
ANTERA MOTA
L. GINEBRA
MIRABAL
27 DE FEDRERO
MARKET
COLON AYE
30 DE MARZO
SEPARACION
SUR AYE
CIRCUNVALACION
PUERTO PLATA
DOMINICAN REPUBLIC

market. The sale of Dominican art has been on the rise since 1974 when the U.S. Trading Act of that same year gave U.S. residents and citizens a great break on bringing home Dominican art: paintings, sculptures, and handicrafts are completely free of duty. The more recent policies with regard to developing countries of the Caribbean Basin also have remained extremely flexible. That very same year also brought a discovery which has affected the jewelry industry. It was in 1974 that the semi-precious stone larimar was introduced to the world.

WHAT TO BUY

The shops around the larger cities of the Dominican Republic offer merchandise from many parts of the world. You can certainly purchase your quota of watches, perfumes, and other imported articles. But there are some products that make the Dominican Republic truly an exotic shopping adventure. These include fashions, jewelry made from the semi-precious stones amber and larimar, furniture, art and handicrafts. These items can be purchased in many places in the country at prices that are a fraction of what you would expect to pay in the U.S. In addition, some of these items are very unique to the Dominican Republic and are literally not available elsewhere in the world. To really enjoy this shopping experience, however, you must know where to look, how to purchase, and how to make that very special find that may turn into a family heirloom.

FASHIONS

Although a good deal of the fabric found here is imported from the U.S., you will find an ample selection of fabrics brought in from both Europe and Asia as well as the linens and cottons produced locally. El Conde Street in Santo Domingo is a good place to browse for fabrics of every nature. The prices are reasonable and there seems to be a fabric store on every corner. You will see names like Flomar, Palcio, Gravia, Gonzalez Romas, and La Opera. **Navidad Villa** on Lope de Vega also offers a large selection of fine fabrics with many imported from Europe. Certainly one of the best wholesalers of fabric in the country who also sells directly to the public is **Almacenes Doble A**. They have a downtown store right off El Conde Street at 19 De Marzo Street and a less hectic branch store located at 103 Mexico Street. They carry a wonderful selection of fine fabrics at very fair prices. **Manikin** at the Gallerias Camerciales on 27th of February Avenue is a small fabric boutique; while the **Mundo Modas** fabric store at Plaza Lincoln carries a very select group of some of the more expensive fashions. Many of the boutiques in town have a selection of fabrics for those who want to have something custom made. For custom men's apparel, **La Coruna** at 804 Winston Churchill Avenue, just a few blocks from the 27th of February Avenue, is a high-quality, high-priced establishment. Here you will find some of the best tailors in town and the selection of fabrics includes fine English cashmere. As always, quality does cost, but it will still be much less expensive than custom made clothing in the United States, Canada or Europe.

Ciprian is more accessible and a fine establishment which is located on the second floor of Plaza Naco. Here you can order custom tailored dress shirts, blazers and suits, as well as sport shirts known as chacabanas which are worn out over trousers. They also have an ample selection of linens, cottons and cashmeres. A three-piece suit here can cost between $150 - $200 U.S. and is made to order in a choice of fabrics. Women might consider having a tailored suit made here in a variety of summer fabrics. **Cablieri** at 18 Lope de Vega Avenue is a rather new shop for men and handles all the range of clothing from formal dress wear to casual items. **Sunny**, another shop to consider for men's wear, has mostly off the rack modern styles. It is located one block from the Marengue Hotel. On your way to Plaza Maccou, take a left turn at Roberto Pastoriza Street and Sunny is located at Number 152. Almost their entire stock is made in their own workshop.

There are many outlets available for custom made and ready to wear women's apparel. Sometime ago, most of the ready to wear clothing available in the Dominican Republic was actually imported by the local boutiques primarily from the U.S. and consequently at very high prices. This is no longer the case. A great deal of clothing is being produced in the Dominican Republic at prices that are very reasonable. Almost every important boutique has its own seamstress producing most of the outfits in their own workshop. If you have enough time to have something custom made, you should have several fittings to be sure that you are getting what you want.

One of the up and coming Dominican designers is Marcy Jaquesez. She has her own boutique across from the Nacional on Abraham Lincoln Avenue. In addition to having many off the rack items available, this is one location where you can have things made to order. **Cashe Boutique** on the second level of Plaza Noccow is another that will handle custom orders in addition to their off the rack selections for both men and women. The Embassy Club in Hotel El Embahador is a little out of the way but well worth the trip. Vielka has a boutique line that is sold off the rack with much of it designed and made in their own shop. Her boutique and workshop are located at 101 Nicholos Urean Street at the corner of Charles Sumner Street in Los Protos. If you are looking for linen, you should visit the shop by the name of **Mimosa** at Plaza Noccow at 59 Fantina Alco Street. You will find most of the blouses here are literally works of art. You can also have something made to order in their fine selection of fabrics and designs.

Ready-made and designer clothing are available at many of the finer boutiques throughout the city. At Plaza Noccow for example you will find **Abraxas and Maria Christina Boutique** specializing in Casharelle, Charles Jordan, Raphael and Ressos. Also, **Potopoff** at Plaza Criolla is a unique shop for swim wear, Danskins, hand painted pareos and shorts, T-shirts and anything that looks tropical or that can be worn at the beach.

For larger sizes in women's clothes, **La Doma Elegante** is located at 47 A Manuel de Js. Troncoso Street and specializes in larger sizes as well as maternity clothes. We have found a shop by the name of **D'Sport** on the corner of Al Mater and 27th of February Avenue that has a large selection of sportswear. Another good and convenient place for ready to wear clothes and a nice selection of accessories and handicrafts is the **Jaez Boutique** in the Sheraton Hotel Shopping Arcade leading up to the main door.

For Oscar de la Renta fashions, probably the best line is carried at Altos de Chavon by **Freya**. There is also a **Freya Boutique** of Santo Domingo across the avenue from Plaza Noccow at 3 Tiradentes Avenue.

Some of the best buys in the Dominican Republic are on clothing for children. Generally speaking they are meticulously made and the prices are excellent. **Bebe Landia** on El Conde Street in Santo Domingo has a selection for infants and children in linen and cotton. **La Casa de Los Ninos** at 35 Gastovos Mejia Ricart Street is another store exclusively for children's wear and toys.

You will find dealing with the various boutiques and fashion outlets in the Dominican Republic to be a true delight. Here for the most part you do not have to worry about some of the scams that you might encounter somewhere else in the world such as switching goods for an inferior product, misrepresenting the quality of certain fabrics, or if you do order the item, having the item never reach you because it was never shipped. Although we certainly recommend that if you are going to have something custom made in the Dominican Republic that you take it with you, in the event that your time is short and you need to have something shipped, you will find most of the merchants extremely trustworthy.

JEWELRY AND SEMI-PRECIOUS STONES

There are a number of fine jewelers throughout the country such as **Di Carlo** on El Conde Street in Santo Domingo and **Everett Designs** at Altos de Chavon near La Romana. They both offer a wide variety of some of the finest stones set in Dominican gold or silver as well as silver pieces of eight salvaged from sunken galleons. They also work well with the native stones and coral. If you are interested in something very rustic and very special, the ceramic jewelry designed by Carlos Despradel Eduardo Fiallo can be found at many different galleries and gift shops. The **Centro de Arte Nouveau** on Independencia Avenue next door to the rear entrance to the parking lot of the Sheraton Hotel has a wide selection. In Puerto Plata you will find some of the finest jewelry and accessory shops in the entire country. **Harrison's** specializes in gold jewelry but you will find a large selection of work done in coral and antique crystal. The designs are original and the prices are realistic. The shop itself is located in an old building with an enormous staircase leading up to a very small gallery, three showrooms and a friendly bar where you can sample the local beer. **Harrison's** is located at 14 John F. Kennedy Street.

When you mention jewelry in the Dominican Republic, however, larimar and amber come to mind. Larimar is often called Dominican turquoise and tends to be a pale blue shade and has the strength of agate. The stone is found along the southern coast and in one of the mountain ranges. Its very distinctive light blue color is caused by the presence of cobalt oxide. The Dominican Republic is the only place in the world to date where larimar is found, and it has only been mined in the last decade. Its greatest promoter, Miguel Mendez, named the stone *lari* for his daughter Larisa and *mar* because it is the color of the sea. Larimar can be found in all major gift shops in Santo Domingo, Altos de Chavon, Puerto Plata, and other towns in the interior of the country. It is usually set in Dominican silver though we have occasionally seen it set in gold. Recently necklaces combining larimar with black coral have become a very popular and striking item. If you do not see a stone in the setting you like, most stores will be glad to set it according to your specifications.

You will find that most of the shops are reputable and the larimar is authentic. Beware, however, of stones available from various street vendors. The quality of the stone will be much lower, the workmanship of a lesser quality, and in some cases the stone may be fake. Unless you are an expert, purchase only from a reputable shop.

The other semi-precious stone that is very popular in the Dominican Republic is amber. Amber is actually a fossilized resin from trees. Thirty to forty million years ago as the sap ran down the trees, it trapped tiny insects and leaves and bits of flowers and ferns as it flowed. Many of the pieces of amber purchased today have small crystallized fossils embedded within.

Artisans have always used amber for decorative purposes in both jewelry and religious art. In the Dominican Republic it has traditionally been used to craft jewelry. Today it is also being used to shape everything from delicate figurines to chess sets. Many shops even prefer amber in rough form to use as paperweights or unusual conversation pieces. Amber deposits have been found elsewhere in the world, but the Dominican amber is considered to be the best by the artisan. It comes in a wide variety of color—clear, lemon, ruby red, blue and black, but the most popular color is the gold or caramel colored stone. Usually the presence of fossils makes the stone more valuable since only one stone in about every hundred has evidence of early life frozen in it. We found some exquisite examples of this in the form of entire insects such as bees or ants. A piece of amber that has an entire insect in it can cost from US$200 to US$300 prior to being placed in a setting.

As with larimar, you should purchase amber only from a reputable dealer. There are many stories of pieces of colored plastic being sold at very high prices. Amber can be authenticated by a number of different methods. One is the use of ultra violet light which shows the blue transparency of the stone; another is a practical experiment involving rubbing the stone and testing its magnetic properties. The most common test is to rub a piece of amber on a piece of wool or felt and see if it will pick up a very small piece of tissue. If the tissue sticks to the amber, it is the real thing. If it does not, the stone you are looking at is not amber.

Most of the gift shops along El Conde Street and at the Plaza Criolla as well as in the old market places will offer an abundant selection of amber in Santo Domingo. The gift shops in Puerto Plata, the International Airport gift shops, and all the resort hotels are normally well stocked with amber jewelry, particularly in the caramel shades. The rarer shades are normally available in the finer jewelry shops. The milky white shade is the rarest of all and is really a collector's item. To see the history of amber, a visit to the amber museum in Puerto

Plata at 61 Deuarte Street on the second floor of the Tourist Bazaar is truly a must.

FURNITURE

Craftsmanship in the Dominican Republic has now reached very high standards, especially in the production of wood, wicker and rattan furniture, most of which is currently exported. There are a number of fine furniture stores and workshops in Santo Domingo and Puerto Plata. **Alfonso's** at Plaza Noccow has its own craftsman producing the store's exquisite designs under their own trademark. The wicker and rattan furniture are especially well made in the Dominican Republic although you will find the prices extremely high. There seems to be a great emphasis on the Victorian style and although the quality is high, the prices are not going to be much lower than you will find in the states. **Artesania Rattan** located on the ground level of the San Carlos Building at Ramulo Benton Court Avenue has a definite oriental flavor in its designs. The store also offers many home accessories at fairly decent prices. Of particular interest are the woven place mats, baskets and chests. **Gonzalez Munebles** on 27th of February Avenue at the corner of 30 De Marzo Avenue has a huge selection of wicker and rattan furniture and accessories for the home. One of the major producers and exporters of wicker is **Delgados**. Their showroom is located at 58 Maximo Gomez Avenue which is right around the corner from the U.S. Consulate. There are many quality furniture companies and in addition to those that we have noted, the Santo Domingo and Puerto Plata phone books will also list many other dealers and companies specializing in a particular type of furniture.

One of the most popular items of furniture is the Dominican rocker that made a name for itself in the Kennedy years when the famous Kennedy rocking chair became a familiar sight. Many gift shops in both Santo Domingo and Puerto Plata offer a fine selection of rocking chairs and they come boxed for easy traveling. **Macaluso's** in Puerto Plata will take phone orders and deliver the rocker to your hotel. Many of the resort shops carry them as well, and they are also available at the old market place in downtown Puerto Plata. Dominicans seem to have a preoccupation with the Victorian design and a rocking chair known as the Marie Terresa. The Kennedy rocking chairs are very big sellers. Both are available in mahogany and both can be found in the Modello Market in Santo Domingo.

ART AND HANDICRAFTS

The Dominican Republic is becoming almost as well known as Haiti for its abundance of rich art. The Dominican Republic has a number of outstanding artists such as Balcacer, Guillo Perez, Leon Bosch, Bario Suro, Clara Ledesma, Condito Bedo, Justo Suzanna, and Azar among others. Works of all the great painters can be viewed at any number of the prestigious galleries throughout Santo Domingo. Many of the galleries are easily accessible from the major hotels in the city. **Gallery Nader** on La Atarazana is an essential shop to visit in the colonial city. The gallery is situated in a colonial landmark building complete with a Spanish patio. It holds a representative collection of some of the finest artists from the entire island. George Nader, who owns many galleries in Haiti, also has a gallery in Santo Domingo, located at 49 Gastovo Mejia Recart Street, an easy walk from Plaza Noccow. The **Centro de Arte Nouveau** is a progressive gallery located on Independencia Avenue just outside the rear parking lot of the Sheraton Hotel. This one is a favorite for the established masters as well as for work done by young artists new to the art scene. In addition to regular exhibits, they have an excellent framing business with a beautiful assortment of locally crafted frames. The **Arawak Gallery** is another accessible and well known establishment on Pasteur Street. In addition to paintings, they also have a selection of prints and lithographs.

Sometimes it is possible to go straight to the artist in cases where his gallery or taller (workshop) is open to the public. At 5 Dr. Baez Street is a lovely old Dominican house which houses the **Centro de Arte Candedo Bedo**. One of the most unique things about this center is that you will always see a lot of activity. The Bedo Blue has become his signature and he is one of the most acclaimed Dominican painters today. **Juillo Perez** at 302 Haunty Street just west of Winston Churchill Avenue also has a gallery and workshop.

In addition to the art that can be found at many of the finer galleries, Dominican art is found everywhere in the country. From the street along the waterfront in front of the many more popular hotels, to the Mercado Modello, to many of the very small gift shops, the Dominican art is vibrantly displayed. In the more primitive style, you will note that most of the figures, especially of women, do not have faces. This is a very popular style in the art of the Dominican Republic and is also evident in the lime porcelain statutes. It is based upon the fact that women in the Dominican Republic should be displayed as an "every woman" model and their faceless figures essentially make them all equal. It is sometimes difficult, especially in the open air market places to distinguish some of the Dominican art from the Haitian art. We were directed to a number of large open air stalls along the Mercado, which is the street along the waterfront in front of the Sheraton Hotel and Hotel Santo Domingo where the Haitian art supposedly hangs. Much of this is out in the open, day and night, rain or shine and is difficult to determine whether it is truly Haitian or a copy of Haitian art painted by a Dominican painter. Much of this art should sell for no more than $30-$50 U.S. If you are looking for quality art and want to assure that you know what you are buying, we highly recommend that you visit one of the more reputable galleries or gift shops in the hotels.

Your choice of arts and crafts abounds at every corner. One of the more popular items is the Dominican carnival masks in all shapes and sizes. They run from the whole size replicas to the small miniatures which certainly make good conversation pieces upon your return. The small ones sell for no more than US$1 to US$2 and are available in a great variety of colors. We found the largest selections in some of the gift shops surrounding the Cathedral in the colonial area of downtown Santo Domingo.

For other assorted arts and crafts, most of the shops are located in the colonial area of Santo Domingo and all are within walking distance of the cruise ships in Puerto Plata which have a wide variety of unusual items that are seen very few places elsewhere in the world.

WHERE TO SHOP

The old market places in the center of town have become increasingly popular for tourists who are trying to grasp some of the local atmosphere. On Santo Domingo's Mella Street, you will find the Mercado Modelo. Over the years this has evolved from a very drab dark two-story market to a much cleaner and more congenial market place full of handicrafts, woven baskets, straw hats, and woodcarvings. It also has many shops offering jewelry and accessories. It is very tourist oriented, and its vendors approach you from all sides with their wares. They all seem to have a boundless capacity for bargaining. This is one of the places in the Dominican Republic where true bargaining still exists. Upon our many visits there we have still found it very convenient to hire a guide to escort us through the endless isles and into the various shops. Of course, many of the guides will certainly take you to a relative's stall or a merchant whom they know will give them a better commission and this is one place where you should definitely determine before anything is purchased whether you are going to pay the guide or whether he receives a commission from one of the vendors. It is here that we found the use of credit cards virtually impossible. Many of the small vendors simply are not set up to accept any credit card, and those few that do would not accept any of the cards without adding an additional 10% onto the price.

Not far from the Mercado Modelo is Calle El Conde (El Conde Street). This is one of the largest shopping areas in Santo Domingo and probably the busiest. The street covers nine blocks from Independencia Park to the Plaza of Columbus. It was closed to traffic some years ago and is truly a street where you can find shop after shop of Dominican wares. The area is considered to be the major commercial center of the city and the shops and stores offer anything you may be looking for. Not counting the businesses on the side streets, El Conde has over 115 stores and shops. There are a variety of excellent clothing stores for all ages featuring many of the latest styles. Gifts and jewelry shops provide a wide selection to choose from whether you are in the market for souvenirs or expensive diamonds. Shoe stores are very well represented here with fourteen or more competing for your needs. Shoes and sandals are normally a very good buy in the Dominican Republic since leather is predominately used for footwear. Man-made items are extremely expensive to import into the Dominican Republic, and since leather is overly abundant, the quality is going to be very good and the prices very low. One of the nicest things about shopping along the street is that it has been closed to traffic for some years. This certainly makes browsing and shopping much easier.

In contrast to the crowded Mercado Modelo and the shopping streets around El Conde and El Conde itself are some of the shopping areas that are considered to be in the uptown area. One of the most popular is Plaza Criolla. The shopping center has a unique design, one where you feel that you are walking through a village market place. It is located on the 27th of February Avenue facing the Olympic Center. If you are staying at or near the Hotel Lina, you merely need to cross Maximo Gomez Avenue and walk along the intersecting avenue one block. You can also conceivably walk over from the Caribe I or the Continental Hotels. From all other locations, a short taxi ride will bring you to its entrance. The split level arcade of the plaza is designed in a village format centered around a clock tower. The central market offers a mini market of fruits and vegetables across from the ice cream shop. The village market handles a dozen shops with gift shops featuring fine items ranging from crushed shell picture frames, tortoise shell evening bags, horn, black coral and a number of amber and larimar shops. A word of caution here, since tortoise is an endangered species, U.S. Customs will not allow anything made of tortoise shell into the country.

Although the Plaza Criolla is convenient and does not contain all the hustle and bustle of the downtown shopping areas, prices tend to be a bit more expensive. Here you may find discounts given at the shop owner's discretion, especially if you are buying more than one item. Do not expect the shop owner to bargain on the price very much. Here, however, most of the boutiques and shops will accept major credit cards. Most of the shops here do close at lunch for an hour or two, but some have adopted the custom of staying open all day.

The **La Hortaliza** on Winston Churchill Avenue, about three blocks north of the intersection of 27th of February Avenue, is a miniature version of the Modello Market, but more sophisticated. Here you will find not only fresh produce but a large assortment of baskets, brass beds, pottery, glazed decorative tiles and other handicraft items. Because of its uptown location, the prices tend to be higher than the downtown market.

MODERN SHOPPING PLAZAS

In addition to the more traditional shopping areas, in Santo Domingo you may also find some shopping plazas that are more modern in design. One of the more well known is **Plaza Nokho** located on Tiradentes Avenue. Plaza Nokho offers two levels of department stores, housewares specialty shops, small boutiques, hair styling salons, jewelry stores and several casual restaurants. Many of the boutiques at Plaza Nokho also do custom orders and in many instances you will find the custom clothing not much more expensive than some of the off the rack items. In this particular shopping center you will see a lot of fine quality work in linen as well as a variety of excellent quality children's clothing.

At the intersection of Abraham Lincoln and the 27th of February Avenue is one of Santo Domingo's most modern and spacious supermarket facilities, **Centro Commercial Nationale**. It has a small commercial center which offers a few specialty shops, shoe stores and small department stores for women's, men's and children's apparel.

UNUSUAL ITEMS IN UNUSUAL PLACES

One shop you definitely do not want to miss while in Santo Domingo is **Tu Espacio**, which translates into "Your Space." It is located at 102 Cervantes Street, not far from the Sheraton Hotel. **Tu Espacio** offers antiques, arts, handicrafts and many other odds and ends. You will find that this old house has every room furnished with furniture and accessories, all of which are for sale. The selection is beautiful and the displays imaginative. You will find antiques mixed in with modern pieces, baskets, potteries, and ceramics. It is a fun place to visit and should definitely be included in your shopping itinerary. Also one of the most interesting areas to shop for many gift items are some of the local hardware stores. **La Ferreteria Americana** has plenty of pots and pans, garden hoses and paint brushes, but they also have one of the largest gift selections in the city. Here you will find Italian pewter trays, brass accessories from Taiwan, crystal, silver and many ceramics such as the traditional lime dolls.

On the second floor of Plaza Nokho you will find **Triana** which carries a large selection of hand painted ceramic plates, vases, coffee and tea services, candle sticks and fruit bowls. Some of the crafts are local but many are imported from Spain and Central America. If you are looking for hand-painted pottery and ceramic items that are 100% Dominican and original in design, then you should visit **Maria Lejos** downtown at 53 Nouel Street, which runs parallel to El Conde Street.

Cenadarte (Centro Nationale de Artesania) is a government sponsored and operated handicraft institute which exhibits and sells crafts of local students and artists. To get there follow Teradentez Avenue past Plaza Nokho to cross John F. Kennedy Avenue, after reaching the office of Public Works, make a left turn. **Cenadarte** is the second building at the corner of Calle San Cristobal. It is not one of the more accessible craft centers in town, but well worth the trouble. The workshops of the institute train artisans in the skills for leather crafts, macrame, weaving, ceramics, glazed clay pottery, furniture, jewelry and handbags. The prices in the shop on the premises are quite reasonable. The gift shops and workshops are open from 8am to 2pm daily.

"DUTY FREE" SHOPPING

Special note should be taken of duty-free shopping in the Dominican Republic. Although the country, like many of the other areas in the Caribbean is not entirely duty-free, there are outlets that are close to it. The shops at the airports may have better prices on some items since the goods are not available to the general public, hence the duties levied are not the same as on products sold elsewhere. In addition to the large selection of duty-free items at the principal international airports, Santo Domingo has shops located immediately behind the Atarazana and at the Centro Dellos Heros which have the same facilities and price list as the airport shops. Keep in mind that these purchases must be made in U.S. currency and they are delivered to you at the airport before boarding your flight. It is very much like the in-bond shopping on some of the other islands. There is a good selection of watches, cameras, fine silver, jewelry; but the biggest sellers are liquor, cigarettes, and perfume.

OUTSIDE SANTO DOMINGO

Outside of the city of Santo Domingo, the two main shopping areas will be Puerto Plata on the northern coast and Altos de Chavon in the far eastern portion of the country.

In downtown Puerto Plata, all the gift shops are open from 9am to 6pm Monday through Saturday. Supermarkets, hardware stores and pharmacies close at noon and reopen as late as 3pm, closing for the day at 6pm. Some small neighborhood markets in the Bario Reyes and 30 Day Marzo area are open after siesta until about 9pm.

At Altos de Chavon outside of La Ramano, most of the craft shops and art galleries are open during the day from 9am until 5pm or 6pm in the evening. Most are closed all day Sunday and all holidays. For unhurried shopping, some of these shops will certainly be the best although you will find the prices especially for amber and larimar to be at least 30% to 40% higher than in downtown Santo Domingo. There are two reasons for this: first, you will find some of the highest quality craftsmanship here and, second, it is also located near the very expensive posh resort of Casa de Campo. You will find in these shops that bargaining is simply not done although we did find that there were some discounts available on some items, especially if you were buying more than one item.

SPECIAL TIPS FOR CRUISE SHIP PASSENGERS

For most cruise ship passengers, time in the Dominican Republic is very limited and you will normally have only a portion of the day to shop. In most cases, you will be arriving at Puerto Plata and you should concentrate on the immediate shopping areas closest to the cruise ships. There are a number of small tourist oriented papers available which list many of the shops and what they carry, and all the shops are within easy walking distance of the cruise ships. In order to get a very good idea of what is available in some of the lines of semi-precious stones, a unique collection of Dominican amber is on display at the Amber Museum located at 61 Deuarte Street. This is located one block up from Central Park and the museum offers an English guide for tours from 9am to 5pm Monday through Saturday. One of the finest shops in all of the Dominican Republic is located in Puerto Plata—**Harrison's** at 14 Avenue of John F. Kennedy. Although there are numerous other gift shops within a short walking distance, if you had but one stop to make, we would certainly recommend **Harrison's**.

ENJOYING YOUR STAY

THE SITES

Since the Dominican Republic is steeped in history and many of the historic buildings built during the time of Columbus are still standing, revisiting history here is as easy as visiting some of the beautiful beaches and resort areas. You might enjoy doing several of the following things during your stay in the Dominican Republic:

- A walking tour of the Colonial District of Santo Domingo including Parque Colon (Columbus Park), Columbus's Alcazar, the Museum of the Royal Houses and the Cathedral of Santo Domingo.

- The resort complex of Playa Dorada will eventually house 15 or more projects. For a relaxing day or two of golf or sunning and swimming on the northern coast of the country about 5 minutes from Puerto Plata, checking into one of the many resorts already located there is a treat.

- A visit to Casa de Campo and Altos de Chavon on the eastern part of the island. The view of the Chavon river from the plaza at Altos de Chavon is breathtaking.

- For fun in the sun, try the beaches on the southern side of the island between Santo Domingo and La Romana.

- Another very popular one or two day trip is to fly on one of the many charters from the Puerto Plata International Airport to Port-au-Prince, Haiti for shopping at the Iron Market or at one of the many art galleries.

ACCOMMODATIONS

There are literally hundreds of hotels of various sizes throughout the country, but you must remember that many will not have the same standard of accommodations that many U.S. visitors are used to on a vacation. There are, however, many that are of the same standard as the best hotels on the other islands. An ambitious hotel expansion is underway, especially on the north cost. This has brought more top quality rooms to the area.

Santo Domingo:

- **Hotel Santo Domingo:** Tel. 809-535-1511 or 800-223-6620. Fax 809-535-4050. Independencia Avenue, has luxurious accommodations as well as the well-known El Alcazar Restaurant with interiors designed by Oscar de la Renta. Includes a Premier Club for perks. Close to the commercial section of town.

- **Gran Hotel Lina & Casino:** Tel. 809-686-5000 or 800-942-2461. Fax 809-686-5521. Maximo Gomez Avenue at the corner of Abraham Lincoln Avenue. This hotel has been refurbished in recent years and also has one of the favorite restaurants in Santo Domingo.

- **Hotel V. Centenario:** Tel: 809-221-0000. Fax 809-221-2020. Located on the Malecon, this new five star hotel has all of the up to date features, including Cable TV and a mimi bar in the rooms, pool, casino, restaurant, bar, tennis and squash courts, sauna, and gym.

- **Santo Domingo Sheraton:** Tel. 809-686-6666 or 800-325-3535. Fax 809-687-8150. Located at 365 George Washington Avenue.Eleven stories with a good view of the sea. Good hotel shops and restaurants and a large casino. One of the busiest hotels in Santo Domingo.

- **The Jaragua Hotel and Casino & Spa:** Tel. 809-221-2000 or 800-228-9898. Fax 809-686-0528. Located at 367 George Washington Avenue and next to the Sheraton. Waterfalls, gardens, and seven restaurants (including a New York type deli) as well as a European spa. This is where Robert Redford stayed while filming "Havana."

Puerto Plata and Playa Dorada:

- **Paradise Beach Resort and Club**: Tel. 809-56-3663 or 800-752-0836. Fax 809-320-4858. A cluster of low rise building thatfronts the beach. Open air restaurants and water sports.

- **Jack Tar Village**: Tel. 809-586-3800. Specializes in "package" stays with everything included. A lush setting it has all water sports, golf, tennis, horseback riding and sauna. The casino is open to the public.

- **Playa Dorada Hotel and Casino**: Tel. 809-320-3988 or 800-423-6902. Fax 809-320-4448. Located on the beach and has one of the largest swimming pools in Puerto Plata. Golf course was designed by Robert Trent Jones, Sr. Good restaurants and sports package.

Samana:

- **Hotel Gran Bahia**: Tel. 809-538-3111 or 800-372-1323. Fax 809-538-2764. Out of the way in the northeast corner on Samana Bay. A luxury resort in Vicorian style. Facing the sea with forest and mountains behind, this new hotel has rooms with verandas that view the sea so you can watch the whales during the winter months. Guest are met at the airport and transferred to the resort by private plane.

La Romana and Altos de Chavon:

- **Casa de Campo**: Tel. 809-523-3333 or 800-223-6620 FAX 809-523-8548. Offers 740 rooms in this luxurious resort with some interior designs by Oscar de la Renta, and is definitely one of the most complete resorts in the world. Very expensive, but worth whatever you pay for the experience and endless activities. Two 18-hole golf courses. Recently redecorated and expanded.

- **La Posada Inn**: Tel. 809-523-3333 (the same as for Casa de Campo). Located at Altos de Chavon. A friendly and romantic hotel located on the grounds of Altos de Chavon. Near the restaurants at Casa de Campo.

RESTAURANTS

Dining in the Dominican Republic is as exquisite and varied as any place in the Caribbean, and the range of cuisine is limitless. Many are as elegant as those restaurants found in New York or any other large city, but the prices are still reasonable in most cases. Normal dining hours start about 9:00 PM for Domenicans. Try some of the local foods as well, such as Paella, Soncocho (stew with several types of meat) Platonos (plantains) and Majarae (corn meal custard). Some of our favorites are:

Santo Domingo:

- **El Alcazar:** Tel. 221-1511, ext. 650. Located in the Hotel Santo Domingo. Recommended by *Travel and Leisure* magazine as one of the best restaurants in the Caribbean. The Moroccan palace motif designed by Oscar de la Renta is magnificent. A fairly expensive restaurant. Reservations are suggested during the heavy tourist season and for late night dining.

- **Lina:** Tel. 563-5000. In the Gran Hotel Lina. One of the most famous restaurants in town and normally very busy. Very classy decor and many seafood specialties. Lina at one time was the personal chef to Trujillo.

- **Meson de la Cava:** Tel. 533-2818. Located in a natural cave in the Mirador section of Santo Domingo. You must enter down a spiral staircase and is usually quite crowded because of the unusual setting. Certainly worth a visit for the exotic setting and good beef dishes.

Altos de Chavon:

- **Casa del Rio:** Tel. 523-3333, ext. 2345. Very romantic. The recreated 16th century building overlooks Rio Chavon, giving a post card view. Food is prepared French style with Caribbean touches. Jacket required.

Casa de Campo:

- **Tropican:** Tel. 523-3333, ext. 3000. A very elegant restaurant located within the Casa de Campo resort complex. Excellent seafood and reservations are necessary.

Puerto Plata:

- **De Armando:** Tel. 586-3418. Calle Separacion, features international cuisine and Dominican favorites.

- **Neptune:** Tel. 586-4243. Right on the beach close to the waves. Great for seafood.

- **Flamingo:** Tel. 320-2019. Famous for its medalions in three meats and three sauces.

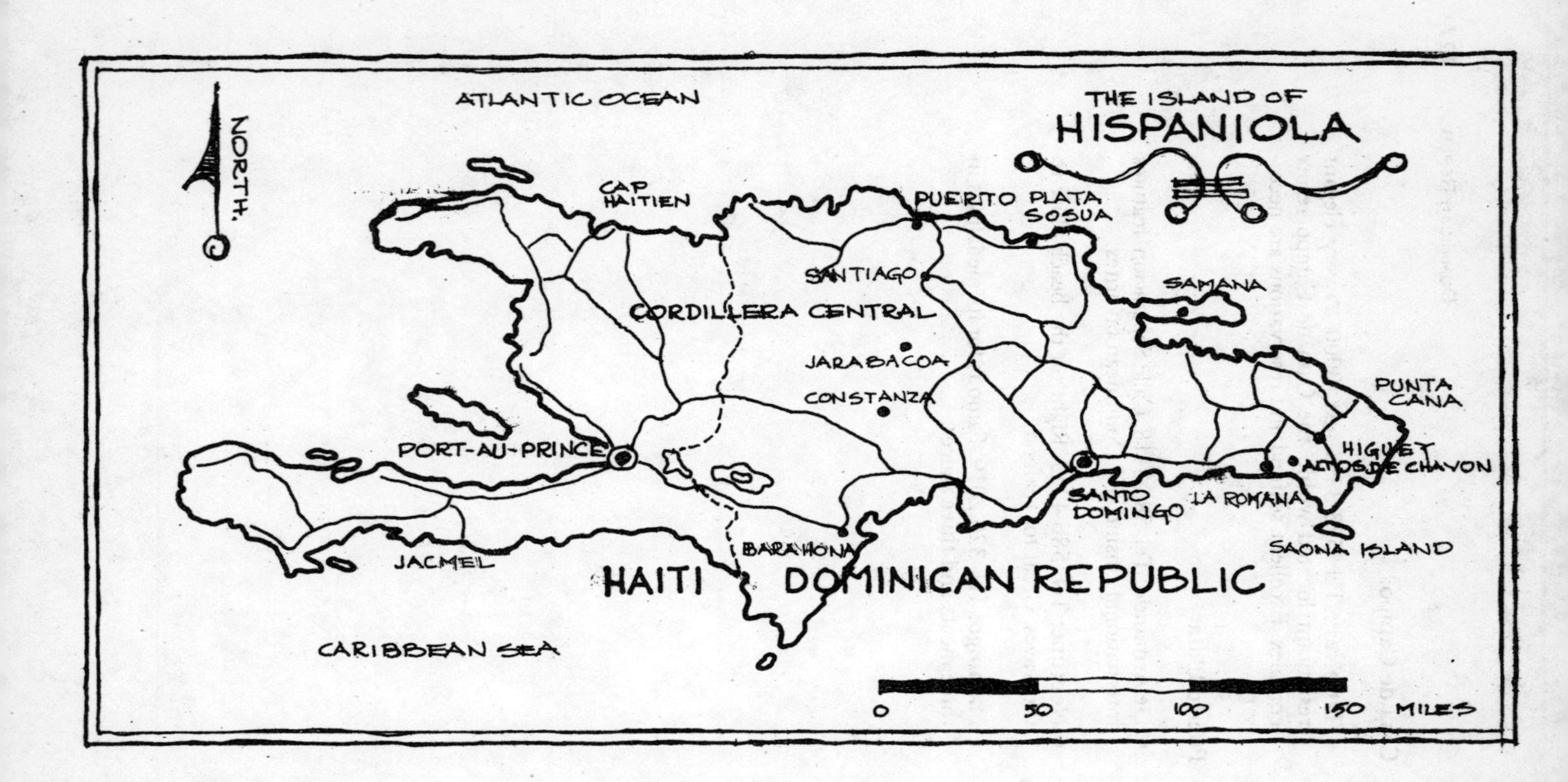
THE ISLAND OF
HISPANIOLA
NORTH.
ATLANTIC OCEAN
CAP HAITIEN
PUERTO PLATA
SOSUA
SANTIAGO
SAMANA
CORDILLERA CENTRAL
JARABACOA
CONSTANZA
PUNTA CANA
PORT-AU-PRINCE
HIGUEY
ALTOS DE CHAVON
SANTO DOMINGO
LA ROMANA
SAONA ISLAND
BARAHONA
JACMEL
HAITI
DOMINICAN REPUBLIC
CARIBBEAN SEA
0
50
100
150
MILES

10

Haiti

Of all the sunny paradises vying for your attention, there is no place quite like exotic Haiti (country map on page 148). Indeed, nowhere else in the Caribbean will you find such a rich display of diverse cultures. In Haiti, African and French cultures intermingle.

Haiti is called a country of contrasts—a place where the vibrant beat of the voodoo drums is wedded to a deep religious belief in Roman Catholicism. Here you will find wide open untraveled white sand beaches, black sand beaches and coral reefs. The Arawak Indians called it "land of high mountains," yet there are also wide open plains, lush vegetation and sun-baked beaches.

Despite encountering poverty common to many developing Third and Fourth World countries—Haiti has the lowest per capita income level in the Western Hemisphere—Haiti exhudes a definite *joie de vivre*, a sense of contentment, that simply does not exist in many other places in the world. Not only is Haiti different—the official slogan for the country is, in fact, *vive la difference*—its people are truly unique. Haitians are a warm, hard working, polite and genuinely friendly people.

If you are looking for plush resorts, quiet shopping malls and block after block of tourist shops, Haiti is not for you. But if you are looking for an exciting travel experience that will linger with you for many years to come, then Haiti may be your perfect destination. Haiti is an explosion of art and people, part French, part African, part Caribbean, and 100% unforgettable.

GETTING TO KNOW YOU

Haiti's population is approximately 6.3 million, with over 80% of the people living in rural areas. Port-au-Prince, the capital and largest city, has a population of 1.2 million. Cap Haitien, located on the northern coast, is the second largest city with a population of 65,000.

A TUMULTUOUS HISTORY

When Columbus discovered Haiti in 1492, it was inhabited by the Arawaks, a reputed tribe of gentle, peaceful Indians. They were killed by the thousands when Spanish armies came in search of gold. The Spanish were followed by the French, who brought slaves from Africa to work the plantations. In one of history's most glorious struggles for independence, Haitian slaves liberated themselves and ousted Napoleon's armies. This ended nearly two hundred years of French rule. The second-oldest republic in the Western Hemisphere, Haiti has been aptly described as American by geography, French by language, and African by tradition.

The history of Haiti from the mid-1800's to 1957 was one of constant seizures of power, assassinations and military occupation—even a 19-year period of occupation by the U.S. Marines from 1915-1934.

Recent history has been dominated by the dictatorships of Francois Duvalier, known as Papa Doc from 1957 to 1971, and his son, Jean-Claude (Baby Doc), from 1971 until his demise in 1986. Violence and political turmoil ensued and was followed by democratic elections, more violence, a military coup, U.S. military invasion and pacification, and another round of democratic elections. The aftermath of all this activity until recently has been to discourage tourism in Haiti.

The good news is that Haiti is open for business once again, and tourists should begin exploring this unique country in increasing numbers. The artists and craftspeople continue to produce unique and colorful Haitian treasures at reasonable prices. In the meantime, you are well advised to check with the U.S. State Department to make sure it's safe to travel to Haiti. While we expect the travel situation in Haiti will continue to improve in the forseeable future, be forewarned that the political winds in Haiti do change.

Cities and Sites

Port-au-Prince is the capital city. It's a large, vibrant, and crowded city that surprises many people who have not previously visited densely populated places. The Iron Market is a colorful downtown market where you can buy carved and polished mahogany, native art, baskets of all shapes and sizes, and brightly colored bags. The Cathedral of St. Trinity and the Museum of Haitian Art are "must" visits for art lovers.

Just above Port-au-Prince, the city of Petionville is a short taxi ride from downtown. This is a great place to wander through several art galleries and boutiques or dine at one of the fine restaurants in the area.

Haitian food will be one of the highlights of your trip. French cuisine, which many claim to be the finest in the Caribbean, has a distinctive Haitian character. Indeed, it tends to be combined with local spices. Tuesday morning is a good time to travel up the mountain (north) to the Kenscoff market. Here, hundreds of people sell fresh fruit and vegetables grown in the cool mountain region.

After the morning mist clears or at night, travel further up the mountain to Boutiliers for a magnificent view of Port-au-Prince. The castle-like Barbancourt Rum distillery is located in this area as well. There you may sample up to 20 liquors made from rum.

The north coast of Haiti boasts one of the most colorful cities in the Caribbean—Cap Haitien. This is where Columbus' ships first landed in the New World and celebrated Christmas Day in 1492. The wreck of the Santa Maria lies nearby. By 1670, "Le Cap" had become the wealthiest colonial capital in the new world, with abundant sugar, cocoa and coffee plantations. Today, many Haitian artists reside in the area. Cap Haitien is accessible by car from Port-au-Prince. A new highway, winding through the mountains, makes the four-hour trip one you will never forget as it winds over the mountains.

A few miles south of Cap Haitien are the stately ruins of Sans Souci Palace. One of the several palaces of King Henry Christophe, it had mountain streams flowing under the marble floor to cool the rooms, and in its day, the sweeping staircases and elegant banquet halls rivaled Versailles.

Towering over San Souci is the Citadelle, known as the eighth wonder of the world. It was built by Christophe in 1804 after the French were overthrown. It took 200,000 men 13 years to complete the structure which was big enough to house 10,000 soldiers and 365 bronze cannon. The excursion to its walls by jeep and horseback is unquestionably one of the grandest adventures in the Caribbean.

Jacmel, the sleepy little coffee city on the southern coast of Haiti is a story-book town with French Colonial homes dating back to the 17th century. A two hour horseback ride into the mountains will take you to the spectacular mountain pool known as Bassin Bleu.

THE BASICS

LOCATION AND GEOGRAPHY

Haiti is located within the stretch of islands known as the Greater Antilles—a 1½ hour flight from Miami, 3½ hours from New York and 4¼ hours from Montreal. Haiti is located in the western part of the island of Hispaniola, occupying 10,714 square miles (about the size of Maryland) of the second largest of the Caribbean Islands. The Dominican Republic occupies the eastern two-thirds of the same island. With the Atlantic to the north and the Caribbean Sea to the south, Haiti's two mountainous peninsulas stretch westward like pinchers of a giant crab partially enclosing the Gulf of Gonave. Three mountain ranges, rising 8,000 to 9,000 feet above sea level, dominate the landscape. Haiti means "high land" in Indian.

CLIMATE, WHEN TO GO, WHAT TO WEAR

Haiti has one of the most pleasant climates in the Caribbean. In general, it is warmer in the coastal areas, with never-ending summer temperatures ranging from 70-90 degrees fahrenheit. As the elevation in the mountain regions increases, the air becomes progressively cooler. An autumn like 50-75 degrees prevails in the high country where apples, peaches and strawberries grow, and the climate has been compared to that of San Francisco and Vancouver. Rain seldom lasts longer than an hour or two in the evenings. The driest months are December through March.

Dress in Haiti is casual, but conservative. As with most of the Caribbean countries, ultra casual resort type clothing should be limited to the beaches, resort areas and hotel pools. Shorts are not acceptable outside the resorts and hotels, and certainly not to be worn when visiting one of the cathedrals. Summer type dresses for the women or slacks and cotton shirts for either men or women will be most useful. We highly recommend loose fitting clothes made of natural fibers that breathe. A good pair of walking shoes should also be a high priority. This is one country in the Caribbean where a sport coat or suit is not seen often, but either certainly may be worn to one of the more elegant restaurants or casinos.

If you plan a side trip to the mountain areas, we recommend that you bring a sweater or light jacket, and blue jeans or other type of heavier slacks. It will make a horseback riding a lot more enjoyable.

Since the dusty streets in downtown Port-au-Prince takes a toll on clean clothes, plan to take a change of clothes for each day or locate a laundry near your hotel.

GETTING THERE

American Airlines flies directly from the U.S. Air Canada flies from Canada. Air France flies during the summer months between Martinique and France. Connecting service is also available from Haiti's neighboring destinations: Jamaica, Puerto Rico, Dominican Republic and Martinique. The connecting service is usually operated by small commuter-type carriers.

At the present time, the only cruise ships calling at Haiti are from the Royal Caribbean Cruise Line, and the only port of call is Labadee (or La Badie), Royal Caribbean's own private resort. Labadee is located on the northern coast near Cap Haitian, and has shopping, recreation and eating facilities that are constructed for the enjoyment of the passengers.

If you are plan to reach Haiti by private aircraft or private vessel, be sure to plan properly. Ports of entry by air are Port-au-Prince and Cap Haitien, both of which have macadam surfaces. You will need to notify the Director of Civil Aviation at the Ministry of Commerce in Port-au-Prince in advance of your arrival. Be sure to check the specific procedures before the trip. Unscheduled and unregistered flights over Haiti are not allowed, so do not decide at the last minute to just drop by Haiti to do a little shopping for art.

The only official ports of entry by private boat are again Port-au-Prince and Cap Haitien. You will need to notify the Director of Port Administration in Port-au-Prince if you are arriving by private vessel. Again, check ahead as there are specific procedures that **must** be followed.

If you do plan to sail to Haiti, the ***Yachtsmen's Guide to Haiti, Dominican Republic and Virgin Islands*** is a must. It is available at most marine supply stores in the United States.

DOCUMENTS

U.S. and Canadian tourists require proof of citizenship in the form of passport, birth certificate or naturalization papers. A drivers license will not be accepted. Visitors who have traveled in the U.S. or Canada within 14 days need no vaccination certificate. Entry visas are not required for citizens of Australia, Belgium, Canada, Denmark, Great Britain, Israel, Liechtenstein, Luxembourg, the Netherlands, Switzerland, U.S. and West Germany. You should be prepared to show a return or ongoing ticket, although we have not been asked to do so during our last two visits. An embarkation/disembarkation card will be issued on the plane if you arrive by commercial air. It will be valid for 90 days and should be kept with you at all times.

ARRIVAL AND DEPARTURE

Upon arriving by air in Port-au-Prince, you will be guided to the Immigration hall by the airlines personnel. We suggest you quickly go to a window marked "Visitor" to clear Immigration. As in most Caribbean countries, Immigration personnel are not noted for their speed in processing visitors. On our first trip, we followed everyone else and it took about an hour to get through both Immigration and Customs. On another trip, we got to the window first and were through Immigration, Customs, and in a taxi within five minutes!

After you receive the appropriate Immigration stamps on your passport and embarkation/disembarkation card, claim your bags and go directly to customs. The baggage claim area is small so you will not have any problem in finding the nearest Customs agent. There are also many porters to assist with your bags if you need help.

Customs clearance in Haiti is very thorough and drug laws are strictly enforced. You are allowed to import duty free one quart bottle of spirits, 200 cigarettes or 50 cigars. Fire arms must have prior clearance and written authorization, as do pets. There are no limitations on currency and there are no export limitations when leaving the country.

Unless you are being met at the airport, the best mode of transportation to your hotel is by taxi. Although rental cars are available, we recommend you get acclimated to the city first. Many streets are in need of repair, some are not marked and some may even appear to be impassable, especially nearer to downtown Port-au-Prince, due to heavy traffic—both on wheels and on foot. The taxis are not metered anywhere in Haiti, but rates are set and normally adhered to. The normal fare from the airport to your hotel will range from US$10 to US$15, but always inquire before you get into a taxi. There are many helpful attendants and porters when you leave the terminal who will assist you in finding a taxi, and most speak English.

There is a US$25 departure tax to leave the country, and it is paid at the airline counter. Either Haitian or U.S. currency is accepted, but be sure to have either the exact change or small bills. The airline counters normally do not have the cash to handle large bills or traveler's checks, especially if you are one of the first persons in line.

A special note in regard to departure at the airport. You will be met at the curb when you arrive by many porters who may each grab a bag and whisk it off to the security check point. If you have film that you do not wish to pass through an X-ray machine, carry them with you. All the porters will expect a tip, so we try to get out of the taxi before the bags disappear and designate how many porters we want. In that way you will only have to tip two or three people rather than eight. Also, keep track of whom you tip, as we have observed a few porters getting back in line for a second tip from a tired and unwary traveler. The normal tip is 50 cents to $1 per person. As your bags exit on the other side of the X-ray machine, they will again be attacked by porters. The same rules apply again.

After checking in at the airline counter and paying the departure tax, you will need to clear Immigration. Since there will be another security check at that time, keep your film handy until you are in the departure lounge. Be sure to leave enough time to shop in the many small stores upstairs from the departure lounge. There you will find art, coffee, papier-mache figures, perfumes, tobacco, crafts and a Barbancourt rum outlet.

Currency, Traveler's Checks, Credit Cards

The unit of currency in Haiti is the gourde. One gourde equals approximately 14 to 20 cents U.S. There is no charge for converting dollars to gourdes and vice versa anywhere in Haiti. U.S. dollars are readily accepted at the floating rate of 5 to 7 gourdes to the dollar. Be forewarned that black market conversions of dollars seems to be available at every street corner, and you will be offered anywhere from 20% to 40% more for your U.S. dollar. You will be given more gourdes which seems to be a good deal—but these good deals sometimes contain counterfeit bills, and you are very likely to be short-changed since you are not familiar with the local currency. We recommend exchanging money in banks and your hotel, and use gourdes for small expenditures such as taxis. This is not to say that you should never ask for a more favorable rate at a reputable location. But, unless you are known, do not expect to receive more than 5 to 7 gourdes for each dollar in most places.

Since the black market for U.S. money is ever present, we also recommend that if you are using U.S. currency for a purchase, that you get your change in U.S. dollars. If you are going to receive your change in gourdes, ask for a better price, since the vender will probably get from 20% to 40% more than the normal exchange rate for your U.S. cash. This is especially true in areas such as the Iron Market, small shops in Port-au-Prince, Jacmel and Cap Haitian, and vendors along the streets and roads. And, of course, remember, sometimes this works, sometimes it doesn't, but it certainly does not hurt to ask!

- **Dress in Haiti is casual, but conservative.**
- **Taxis are not metered, so establish the price before you enter the car.**
- **Take an ample supply of smaller U.S. bills—ones, fives, and tens. Smaller bills are difficult to find in Haiti.**
- **Credit cards are accepted at most hotels and larger restaurants but not in small shops or with street vendors and artists.**
- **Our personal checks were readily accepted in shops. So take a supply with you.**

We recommend that you arrive with an ample supply of smaller U.S. bills—ones, fives, and tens. Smaller bills are not always available, either in dollars or gourdes. We have found that even 20s are difficult to change other than at a bank. After you are there for a day or two, you will find that the five gourde bill is probably the most useful denomination of currency for everyday use. Most all larger shops, galleries and hotels will be able to take a traveler's check if it is not too large a denomination.

While credit cards can be used in most hotels and larger restaurants, they are not accepted in small shops, with street vendors or for art purchases directly from artists. We found, however, that our personal checks were readily accepted, and suggest that you take a supply with you. If the artist or shopkeeper has an arrangement with a bank, they seem to have no problem getting a check cashed.

Although incidents of crime are not great, we recommend that you take sensible precautions with your money, checks, and credit cards. There will be times when you will be in crowds of literally hundreds of people, and a loosely held purse, a large roll of bills, or a wallet in a back pants pocket invites trouble. If you are going to be in some of the more crowded market areas or galleries, we recommend a small wallet carried in the front trouser pocket for men, and a small bag that can be tucked up the arm or with a shoulder strap that can be worn bandolier style across the body for women.

Tipping

Most hotels and restaurants will add a service charge of about 10% to the bill, and this will be clearly marked. Additional tips are not expected, but we have found that appropriate tips to the hotel staff for special service, and to the chambermaid upon check-out is appreciated and noticed with a smile and a thank-you. Taxi and publique drivers do not normally expect to be tipped. Airport porters, upon arrival and departure, do expect a tip—normally about a US$1 per porter.

Tipping of the guides or helpers is something you must establish at the outset. Some of the guides at the Iron Market are taken care of by the vendors, but this is the exception. Usually the helper will expect a commission from you. In addition, a person who may introduce you to an artist or take you to a special shop owned by a friend may expect a commission of about 10% of your purchase. We have found this necessary to negotiate at times, depending on the circumstances, and how much we were actually helped.

Language

French and Creole are Haiti's official languages, most often blended into a pleasing colloquial dialect. Creole is rich in its numerous proverbs which have evolved from African dialects, the country's indigenous Indian tongue, the Norman French of the buccaneers and the language of the French colonists. In addition to French and Creole, English and Spanish are spoken. Most hotels, airline offices, restaurants and larger shops have English speaking personnel, but basic French certainly is useful in some of the smaller hotels, restaurants and shops. About the only time you will have any difficulty in communicating is if you are going outside the cities. In some of the rural areas basic French may be understood to a degree, but many of the people speak only Creole. If you do plan a trip to an out of the way place, consider taking a guide with you.

Business Hours

Most shops and galleries are open each day from about 9am to 6pm and on Saturday mornings until noon. Most are closed on Sunday, and the hours can vary slightly depending on the owner. Although you will find the hours for the art museums and related shops posted, these are frequently not adhered to. Before driving all the way across town or to Port-au-Prince from

Petionville to visit a museum, call ahead to ensure that it will be open that day and the hours of operation.

TRANSPORTATION AND TOURS

Taxis are available in most all locations. They are not metered, so be sure to establish the price before you enter the car. The fares to and from the airport are fairly standard, but there the standard ends. If you are going from Port-au-Prince to Petionville to shop, or vice versa, you should inquire at your hotel for guidance as to what the fare should be. If you need to have the use of a taxi for a number of trips, it will probably be better to consolidate your itinerary and hire a car for a day or half-day.

In addition to taxis, there are two very inexpensive ways to get around Port-au-Prince—publiques and the tap-taps. The **publiques** are small private autos with a red ribbon hanging from the rear view mirror. The fare for most any place in town will be about $.50 per person, but you may have to share the car with as many others as they can get in. Also, you have to find one going in the general direction you wish to go, and they reserve the right to pick up and discharge others along the way. Most of the drivers do not speak English, but do know most of the main places in town and the hotels by their English names. The drivers will normally be able to take you most everywhere, but we have had some refuse to go to the vicinity of the Iron Market and surrounding streets during the busy shopping hours.

The **tap-taps** are the colorfully painted trucks and small buses that you will see everywhere. These moving art galleries are constantly on the move, and although the fare is about the same or less than the publiques, many do run a preset route. In other words, you need to know where the tap-tap is going before you get in (some are enclosed) or on (some are not). Because you will joined by as many people as possible, we do not recommend the tap-tap for the first time visitor to Haiti. They are colorful to watch, but for the less adventuresome, may not be as comfortable as you would like.

Rental cars are available from Budget Rent-a-Car (Tel. 6-23240), Avis (Tel. 6-2333), and a few local companies. If you plan to rent a car, however, be sure to make reservations before you arrive. During our last trip, we arrived without reservations, and after two full days of trying, gave up on the possibility of finding a car of any size and price range. If you do make advance reservations or find a car after you arrive, your driver's license, and cash or a credit card is usually all that is necessary to complete the arrangements. Gasoline stations are few and far between, so plan to leave town with the full tank of gas if you are heading for a day in the outlying areas of Port-au-Prince.

Tours available in Port-au-Prince, from gingerbread house tours to major excursions to Jacmel, Cap Haitien, San Souci, and the Citadelle. Some of the major companies include:

Agence Citadelle, 34 Rue Bonne Foi, Tel. 22-5900.

Agence Martine, 4 Rue des Miracles, Tel. 22-2141

Southerland Tours, Cite de l'Exposition, Tel. 22-1500. (also Cockfight and Voodoo trips)

RESOURCES

Port-au-Prince can be somewhat disorienting for the first time visitor. The city has fallen into disrepair. Unfortunately, a good street map is almost impossible to find. There is a general map in a small brochure entitled ***Haiti: Visitor's Guide*** which we received from the Haitian Embassy in Washington DC. This brochure is also sometimes available at the information office to the left of customs at the airport. Other than a copy of a more detailed hand-dawn map we found at George Nader's art gallery near the main market area, that is the only map we have been able to find during recent trips. The Office of Tourism does not carry maps, and the only brochure available there is in French. Therefore, the secret to getting around until you are totally familiar with the city is to rely on a personal guide—and guides abound! On virtually every street corner, outside every hotel, art gallery and shop, near every park, you will find offers to be guided by everyone who is old enough to walk and talk. Some are experienced and can be of great assistance in finding art galleries, craft shops, furniture factories, and in some cases will be able to introduce you to one or more artists directly. Others are the experience, and will, for the same price, give you beautiful guided tours to nowhere.

- **Most shops are closed on Sunday.**
- **On virtually every street corner you will find guides who will solicit your business.**
- **Haitian craftsmen are particularly skilled in woodcarving, weaving, straw-work, and embroidery.**
- **Paintings sell for as low as $10 to $40 most everywhere.**

Here are a few tips on how you can best find and use a good guide during your stay in Haiti:

1. Ask at the hotel for a recommendation. Even though the hotels do not have staff personnel who can offer this service, the managers are normally aware of who in the local crowd is experienced enough to help you.

2. Whether a person was recommended by the hotel or found by you (or we should say who has found you!), determine if they have a car, or if you have to hire a cab in addition. We have not found one with a car, and although the taxi will be an additional expense, they usually have a friend who can provide the necessary transportation.

3. Come to an agreement up front as to the amount to be paid to both the guide and driver, and whether this will also cover any "commission" for having you buy from a friend, gasoline and other expenses.

4. Determine, in the event of a "commission" to be paid to the guide for some item purchased from a friend, whether you will be expected to pay the commission (normally about 10%) to the guide based on the amount of the purchase, or whether they will be "taken care" of by their friend.

5. Make it very clear from the outset that the purpose of the "guided" assistance is to accomplish what **you** want, not only what they want you to see.

6. Expect to pay about $30 per day each for the guide and driver. Of course, extraordinary service and the pesky commissions may add to that, but there is certainly no reason to overpay.

7. Unless there is a need to pay for some small item, such as gasoline or soft drinks, do not pay until the services are rendered and you have safely reached your hotel or other destination which is considered to be the final stop of the day. Of course, on the other hand, do not expect the guide or driver to pay for anything—even a telephone call. In a country where the annual wage for some is as low as $600 to $1000 per year, advances of even the smallest amount by a guide may be impossible. We have, on more than one occasion, advanced money for gasoline so we could get to our destination.

8. Although the guide is basically to serve your needs, they can also be of immense help in finding that *unknown* and up and coming artist, that small craft item that you had no idea existed, and introducing you to some fascinating people.

9. **Inside guides** at such places as the Iron Market—you will have them whether or not you want them and whether or not you bring someone with you—are usually paid a commission by the vendor. You are not expected to pay them if that is the case. Otherwise, they will ask you for a tip for helping. The exact arrangements should be established before you begin making purchases. The best known inside guides are Meka and Peter Paul at the Iron Market. They can be of great help. Indeed, shopping at the Iron Market may be difficult without the assistance of Meka.

10. If you are not satisfied with the services of a guide, do not feel obligated to use them again. There are hundreds of others to choose from. If you feel that you have been taken, mention it to the manager of the hotel. The word will spread quickly.

11. If you are satisfied with a particular guide or driver, most all others will respect your wishes and not try to spirit you away. On our last trip, we even had a competing taxi driver outside the Hotel Oloffson run two blocks to get Alex, a driver we have used on a number of occasions, out of bed to take us to a gallery simply because we mentioned we were looking for Alex.

12. If you rent a car, a good driver/guide can also be a great assistance in finding some obscure address in and around Port-au-Prince. If you are going outside the city, especially into the county, a Creole speaking guide/driver is almost a necessity.

WHAT TO BUY

Shopping in Port-au-Prince is not like that found in some of the other Caribbean shopping havens such as St. Thomas or San Juan, nor what it was five to ten years ago. Many of the shops that lined the downtown streets are now closed. The *petite*

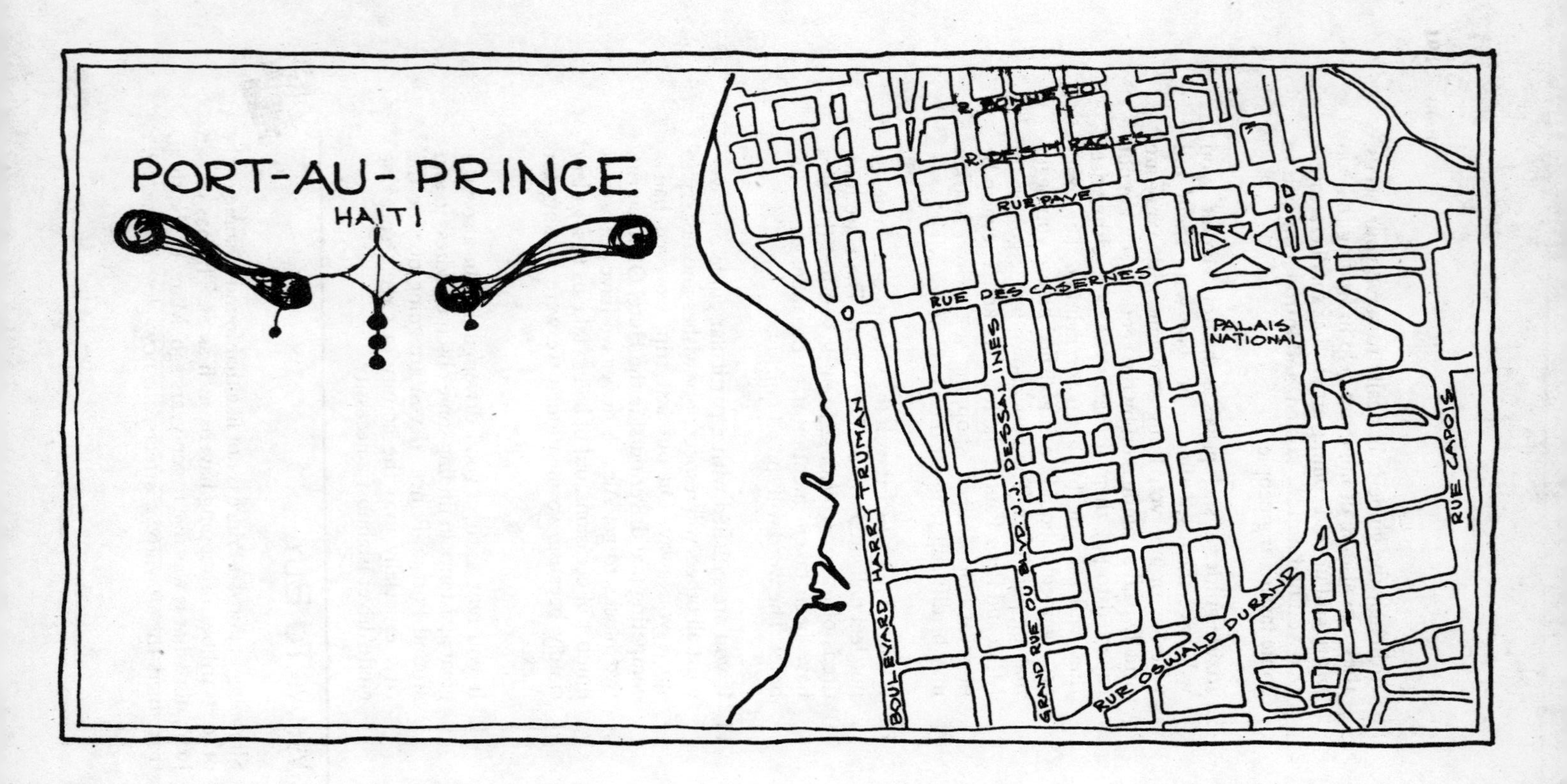
PORT-AU-PRINCE
HAITI
R. BONNE FOI
R. DES MIRACLES
RUE PAVE
RUE DES CASERNES
PALAIS NATIONAL
BOULEVARD HARRY TRUMAN
GRAND RUE OU BLVD. J.J. DESSALINES
RUE OSWALD DURAND
RUE CAPOIS

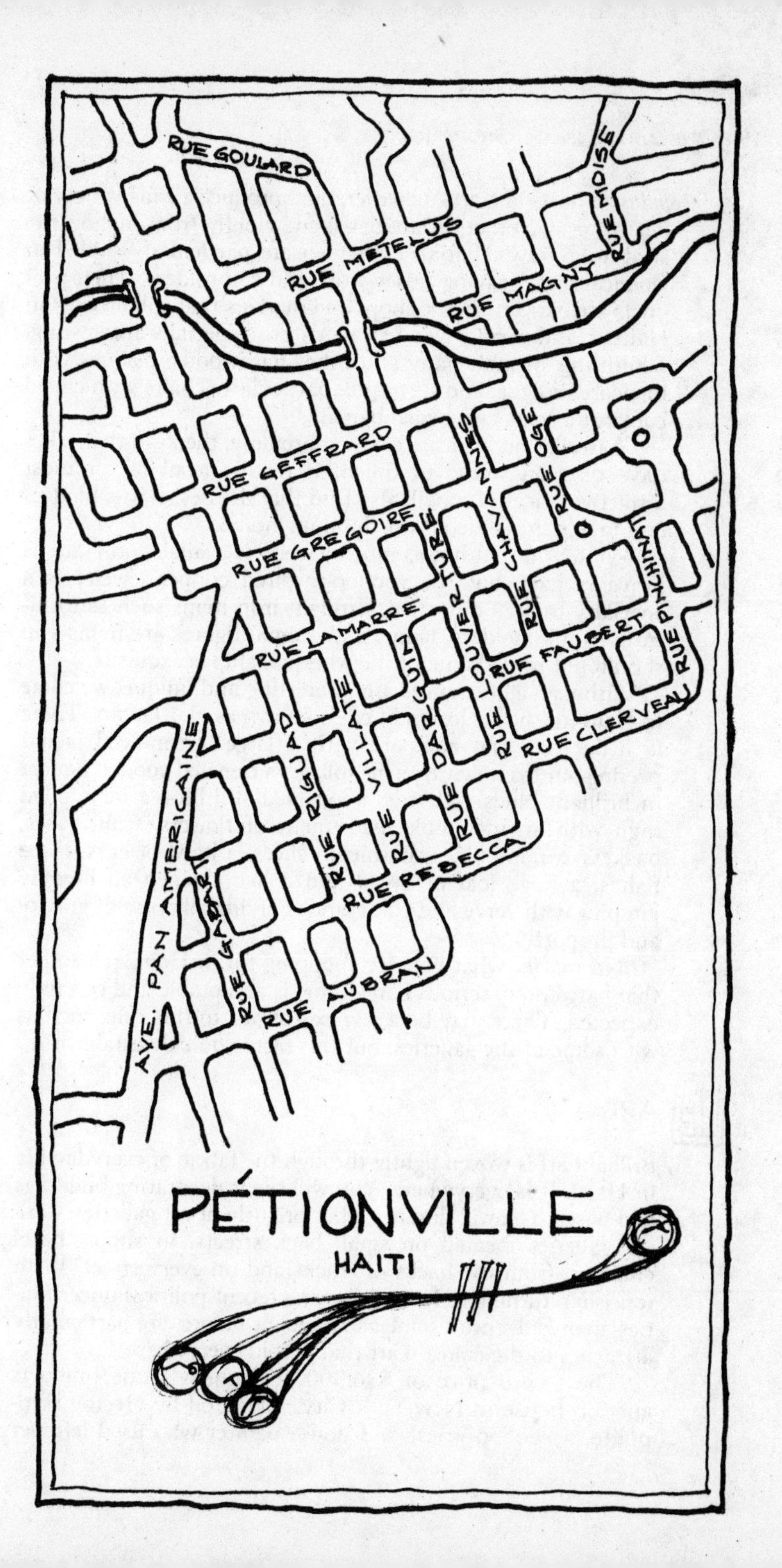
RUE GOULARD
RUE METELUS
RUE MAGNY
RUE MOISE
RUE GEFFRARD
RUE GREGOIRE
RUE LAMARRE
RUE CHAVANNES
RUE OGE
RUE LOUVERTURE
RUE FAUBERT
RUE PINCHINAT
RUE CLERVEAU
RUE DARGUIN
RUE VILLATE
RUE RIGAUD
RUE REBECCA
AVE. PAN AMERICAINE
RUE GABART
RUE AUBRAN
PÉTIONVILLE
HAITI

industrie of handicrafts, however, does produce a wide variety of beautiful and practical articles made chiefly from mahogany, sisal and straw. Haitian craftsmen are particularly skilled in woodcarving, weaving, straw-work and embroidery. Their products are bargains in the shops and markets that still do exist in Haiti. Hand-carved wooden goods are especially interesting. Sculptures of mahogany and other hardwoods, plaques with intricate designs, and furniture, particularly chairs with caned backs and seats are special bargains.

You will find intricate hand embroidery, the kind that takes days or even weeks to finish, is readily available at most attractive prices. You will also find that dresses, skirts, blouses and men's shirts are all worth taking home.

We found that not as much jewelry is available in Haiti as in years past, but the voodoo-inspired copper jewelry is a specialty to seek out. Also, wrought iron items such as furniture, candle holders, lamps and animal figures are items you should not miss. Some of the workmanship is exquisite.

Although all the crafts are interesting and unique, we come to Haiti for the explosion of color known as Haitian art. There is little than can compare with a large, green-eyed jaguar peering out from dense jungle foliage, a frenzied voodoo dancer in brilliant blues and reds, a lopsided still life—a table piled high with an incredible assortment of flowers, fruit, vases, baskets, a pumpkin, watermelon slices, a bowl of eggs, three fishes, a huge loaf of bread and a live chicken all literally jumping with verve and color while defying all sense of gravity and proportion.

No matter what you are shopping for in Haiti, remember that bargaining, serious bargaining, is acceptable and certainly expected. There may be a few exceptions to this rule, such as with some of the galleries, but this fact is quickly established.

ART

Brilliant art is woven tightly through the fabric of everyday life in Haiti. It is everywhere. You will see it decorating buildings and buses. You will find it sold in brightly lit art galleries, dark art galleries located on small back streets, in shops, hotel galleries, from the backs of trucks and on every street. With tourism returning to Haiti following recent political uncertainties, many adventuresome shoppers, as before, are particularly attracted to the colorful art that is sold everywhere

The record price of $36,300 at Sotheby's, the fine arts auction house in New York City, for an oil by Hector Hyppolite, a voodoo priest and house painter who used leftover housepaint, chicken feathers and his fingers to paint, has helped to solidify the Haitian art market as never before. A German collector privately paid $72,000 for a Hyppolite several years ago, and we saw a few in art galleries that will command like prices. Hyppolite, who died in 1948 at the age of 46, painted over 600 paintings in his short career, most of them being colorful renderings of voodoo deities and Christian images interposed in dramatic, moving configurations.

One of the long undisputed masters of Haitian art, however, was Philome Obin. who died in 1987 at the age of 95. He lived his entire life in Cap Haitien in the northern part of Haiti, where he painted mostly historical subjects, though departing now and then to paint a bouquet of flowers, a family gathering or the portrait of a friend.

Rarely will you find a Haitian painting of a landscape without people or animals. Haitian art mirrors the life and activity around it.

For the art shopper, Haiti offers not only paintings for the collector of expensive art, it offers everyone the opportunity to find that special explosion of color for very reasonable prices. Paintings are sold for as low as $10 to $40 most everywhere. Of course, the difference will be in the quality, the type of art, and will certainly be based on how well known the artist is. **Issa's Gallery** at 17 Ave du Chile near the Hotel Oloffson, **Galerie Nader**, 256-258 rue du Magasin de L'Etat, **Galerie Monnin**, 382 Blvd. J.J. Dessalines, all in Port-au-Prince, and **L'Atelier Galerie Nader**, 48 rue Gregoire, in Petionville can all be of great assistance for the first time Haitian art buyer. One special part of shopping for art in Haiti is not only being exposed to the wide range of what is available in the many galleries, but that chance or arranged meeting with one or more of the 800 plus artists currently producing works in the country. A highlight of our home is a six by ten foot colorful jungle scene which we helped design and commissioned to be done by an artist we were introduced to through a guide we met at our hotel. It is the culmination of a chance meeting that would take a full volume to relate, an experience we will certainly not forget, and a painting that is not soon forgotten by anyone who visits our home.

If you are a casual art shopper, some of the following "does" and "don'ts" may prove helpful in navigating Haiti's art community:

DO:

1. Take the time to visit as many art galleries as possible so that you are somewhat familiar with the style, names, price ranges and quality of the various artists.

2. Try to visit an artist at work—in his home or in a studio where more than one artist may be painting.

3. Remember that Haitian art can take the form of paintings on canvas, painting on hardboard, paintings on screens, and a wide array of sculptures of stone, metal and wood.

4. Realize that much Haitian art is a copy of some popular style of an artist who has become famous, or is on the way to becoming the subject of the serious collectors. Some is worth $300-400, but a similar scene may have a value of $10. It depends on the artist.

5. Take the art with you. It can be removed from the frame if it is an oil and rolled for carrying home with you or shipping.

6. Have the art wrapped completely at the gallery or studio for carrying or shipping. There are not many sources of packing materials—tape or cord—readily available.

7. Consider having the exterior decorative frame made for you in Haiti. The quality is superb, and the cost is a fraction of what it will cost when you get back home. In fact, it will not be unusual for you to find that a good frame for any painting will cost you more at home than you paid for the painting in Haiti!

DON'T:

1. Pay a lot for a painting from an artist you know nothing about. There are many more average paintings available than good ones—unless you really know where to look.

2. Be afraid to ask questions about paintings and artists.

3. Be reluctant to ask if you can meet the artist and if the artist sells directly or through a gallery. Some will sell

directly although the same artist may supply more than one gallery with paintings. Others have developed an excellent working relationship with one outlet, however, and will only sell through that source.

4. Buy art with the idea that you are going to bring it home and sell it for a fantastic profit. Even serious collectors in the U.S. and elsewhere are not going to pay inflated prices for something that does not have value.

5. Buy it if you do not like it. Nothing gathers dust faster than a large colorful market scene that you carried all the way home, but would never dream of hanging on a wall.

If you are a serious collector, or think you would like to begin to invest in art that seems to be about explode in the world marketplace, you may want to focus on those artists who have recently become known. Based on conversations with major gallery owners and collectors, we've been able to identify a few artists currently in Haiti who are selling in the $200-500 and $500-$1,000 ranges. Their art may appreciate significantly within the next few years.

PAINTERS:

Henri-Robert Bresil
Abner Dubic
Nelson Dubic
Raymond Dorleans
Prefete Duffant
Franklin Latortue
Ernst Louizar
Antilhomme
Levoy Exil
Prosper Pierre-Louis
Louisiane St-Fleurant
Denis Smith
Dieuseul Paul
Lafortune Felix
Claude Joachim
Ramphis Magloire
Stivenson Magloire
Camy Rocher

SCULPTORS:

Georges Liataud
Serge Jolimeau
Gabriel Bein-Aime
Nacius Joseph
Kersaint
Louis Decimus

Above all, the best way to buy art in Haiti is to experience it, shop around, ask a lot of questions, and only buy what appeals to you.

FASHIONS

A short trip up the side of the mountain above downtown Port-au-Prince is Petionville. There you will find many boutiques, such as **Bagaille**, 23 rue Panamericaine, **Bagatelle**, 84 rue Panamericaine, and **Helene Shop**, 67 rue Panamericaine, spread throughout this residential community. From fascinating originals, to made-to-order embroidered blouses, to mens shirts, to expertly tailored suits—all are there to be found.

Some of the prices at the boutiques may seem to you to be a trifle high. However, Haiti has some wealthy residents who are able and willing to pay for good quality, well tailored clothing.

There are no large shopping malls available for browsing, but we found that the telephone yellow pages, and asking questions of the local residents led us to many small shops in both Petionville and downtown Port-au-Prince. If you have limited time, a good guide will be invaluable to you in finding many of the out of the way places which specialize in high fashion, but may not have an address published anywhere.

Handbags, denim and muslin children's clothing and hand-crocheted items are not only excellent buys, but of high quality.

MAHOGANY

Handcrafted table items, such as large plates, napkin rings, salad bowls and candle holders; large and small carved figures and figurines; door panels and furniture are exquisitely crafted in Haiti. Since the country has an excellent supply of mahogany and other hardwoods, you will find the prices about one-fourth to one-half what you would expect to pay at home. You can see many of the items at **Mahotieres Industries, Parc Industriel, Meubles & Decors, Delmas**, and **Modern Furniture Design (MFD)**, Rlle Nazon. In addition, you will find these items available at small shops everywhere.

We especially like the large mahogany dinner plates we found at the Iron Market which can be used by themselves or as a base for a smaller china plate at the dinner table. The versatility of these type of items is almost endless. You will find items to add the perfect touch to an elegant dinner, or for use at a barbecue in the backyard. The most prevalent shape of the dinner plates is square, not round, and we were able to purchase eight at about US$3.25 each. These are normally finely crafted, with the wood grain adding to the unique flavor of each plate. We did find, however, that they are not always of exactly the same size and color. It is always a good idea to inspect each one carefully. In addition to the larger plates, you can compliment your table with small versions for butter, jams and relishes. You will probably notice these in use at most restaurants in the Port-au-Prince area.

One word of caution about wood products. Although most, especially the mahogany dinner-ware items, have been carved and finely finished, there is the possible chance that there are small worms or termites in the wood. Always visually check any wood items for small telltale holes. If many are clearly visible, you may want to look for another bowl, figure or napkin ring. Even if there are no visible signs, one way to correct the situation is to place the items in a freezer as soon as possible for about a day. We have always done this and have never had a problem. Whether we were lucky enough to never have purchased an item with small visitors, or we got rid of the problem upon arrival home, is hard to say.

In addition to the smaller items, Haiti offers some of the best crafted wooden furniture in the world. The various factories produce chairs, tables (large and small), chests and headboards for beds. Although some of these places are certainly not located in areas easily found, they are there and are worth finding if you are in the market for such items.

Metal and Wrought Iron

Haiti has long been known for the wrought iron railings on the ornate gingerbread houses, but has now become one of the best sources for wrought iron furniture. You will see this furniture not only displayed on virtually every main street in Port-au-Prince, but made right there on the street as well. We have seen everything from baker's racks, coffee tables, and headboards to complete dining room sets all for sale within one city block. Although this furniture is not made in a factory but is hand crafted as you watch, it is of excellent quality.

You may not always be able to take a large wrought iron piece with you, but shipping can be arranged. The number of freight forwarders is not as plentiful as in some other countries, but the telephone yellow pages are a good place to start. Also, check with Federal Express, DHL, and United Parcel as to their limitations on size. All three have offices in Port-au-Prince and have English speaking personnel to assist you.

Other metal items such as sculptures, figurines and bowls, are prominently displayed throughout the city. Most all of these are hand crafted and are normally available at very low prices—even before the bargaining begins. You will want to pay special attention to the sizes, especially of the large bowls and other kitchen type items. The unit of measure will not usually be what you will find at home, and although not critical in all cases, can be a little confusing if you are trying to measure something for a special recipe.

CRAFTS AND ANTIQUES

All kinds of crafts are available, and are all hand crafted in Haiti, with the exception of some items of jewelry. We did find small collections of metal Voodoo jewelry, but very little else is currently being made.

Of special interest and beauty are the textile wall hangings, rugs, bedspreads and other decorator items which are made in small factories and in individual shops and homes. Some of the most exquisite will be found at **Les Ateliers Taggart**, 52 Bois Verna, and their outlet upstairs at **Gingerbread**, 52 Ave. LaMarttiniere.

Antiques are displayed in many small shops, but there are few shops that specialize in antiques only. The **Maison Defly Antiquite**, rue Legitime, Port-au-Prince, has antique furniture of mahogany, and a complete collection of antiques can be seen at **Decoralys**, rues Oge & Faubert, and **Traditions**, rues Chavannes & Geffrard, in Petionville. Of course, many of the antiques, both large and small, date back centuries. The European influence is dominant, and a rare find is possible in many places. Be sure, however, that you know something about the reputation of the shop owner or individual who is trying to get a very high price for any item. Counterfeiting of antiques is certainly not a thriving business in Haiti, but it can happen here as in anywhere else in the world.

Local crafts are not only unique, but well made. Haitian crafts and selected imported items are displayed in many small shops throughout town, but **Ambiance**, 17 ave. M, and **Gingerbread**, 52, ave. LaMartiniere probably have the most extensive collection of quality items. The **Hotel Oloffson Gift Shop**, 60 Ave. Christophe at rue Capios has a diverse collection of art and crafts at reasonable prices. One of the most noteworthy shops, however, is **MarBeth Galerie and Gift Shoppe** located at the Kaliko Beach Club north of Port-au-Prince. MarBeth has many of her own works as well as original one-of-a-kind crafts, many of which cannot be purchased elsewhere in the country.

One craft item that is certainly unique to Haiti is the Voodoo flag. These are beautifully crafted square sequined pieces of art, not really flags, that are used in the Voodoo ceremonies. The flags depict symbols of the various Voodoo gods, or *loas*, and are not displayed in most shops. We have purchased a few directly from a mambo, a Voodoo priestess, but that has to be arranged through a guide and can take a few days to coordinate. One of the best sources available to the public is the Voodoo flag artist-in-residence at the Hotel Oloffson, 60 ave. Christophe at rue Capios in Port-au-Prince. The shop is open every day except Sunday. If the artist is not there, the Oloffson gift shop next door has a few on display most of the time.

Toys are another product we do not always connect with Haiti, but some are truly unique. You will find them made of both wood and metal, but remember there does not exist the stringent government consumer controls we are so used to in regard to the safety of the toys for very young children. If you are looking for gifts, be sure to test the item yourself for small loose parts that could be dislodged.

Where To Shop

Most shopping for visitors to Haiti will be found in Port-au-Prince, and just above the city in Petionville. There are small shops located at the beach resorts, such as **MarBeth Galerie and Gift Shoppe** at Kaliko Beach; small shops and art galleries in both Cap Haitien and Jacmel. These are areas to consider if you are going there for sightseeing, but not worth an hour or two drive just to visit one or two small shops.

For art, the possibilities in both Port-au-Prince and Petionville are endless. With artists and galleries spread throughout the area there will probably be one no more than a block away from you in any direction. For works of individual artists who are just getting started, the Iron Market in the middle of downtown Port-au-Prince is a good place to start. You will quickly learn, however, that merely asking around about individual artists is really the best. We found that almost everyone we spoke with is either an artist or knows one! Because of the profusion of art and the copying of styles, here are a few tips which will eliminate some of the confusion:

1. Start with a visit to the Cathedrale de la Sainte Trinite (an Episcopal Church), rue Pavee at rue Jean Marie Guillox. Haitian art covers the walls, with some being over 500 square feet in size. You will be able to see the result of a project that was started in the early 1950's and works of the Haitian masters.

2. Works of these and other artists can be found in a number of galleries throughout Port-au-Prince, including the Centre d'Art at 56 rue Roy. The center is located in a gracious eighteenth-century residence. Its lower level contains the serigraph studio, a sales gallery, where selected works by undiscovered artists are sold at modest prices. The center's conservatory which flows onto a shaded veranda is also on the lower level. The main floor contains a spacious gallery, with changing exhibits, as well as smaller galleries that display modern paintings and metal sculptures. On the second level is the collector's room. Open by appointment only, this is one place where work by many of Haiti's early primitive painters can be purchased.

3. The National Museum of Art, in the central park area of downtown Port-au-Prince houses a shop where souvenirs and original paintings of up-and-coming artists can be purchased.

4. Some of the best buys in paintings can be found at COHAN (Cooperation Haitian-Netherlands), a non-profit art cooperative where paintings by lesser known artists sell for prices substantially below the various galleries. Representing the work of 100 young painters, COHAN is located on the second floor of a modest walk-up in the downtown area.

5. Visit some of the private collections on display at hotels. Our favorite one is in the Hotel Oloffson, a nineteenth century three-story gingerbread house located at end of rue Capios on ave. Christophe (about a half mile from the center of town). The collection there is owned by Dr. and Mrs. Carlos Jara and features the works of about 15 avant-garde artists. It is only a small part of Collection Flamboyant, which is displayed in its own gallery. These are some of the artists whose paintings are currently being sold in the $300 to $1,000 range, but will probably (according to some of the more serious collectors) be increasing in value four to five fold in the next few years. Richard Morse, the proprietor of the hotel, will be very happy to assist you. All the paintings displayed are for sale, as are others by the same artists that can be seen by appointment.

6. Visit as many galleries as time permits. One of Haiti's best known private galleries is **Galerie Issa**, located on the top of a hill near the Hotel Oloffson at 17 ave. du Chile. Not only does Issa El Saieh represent many wonderful artists, he is well known for the help he has given to many artists (some of whom you will find working on the lower level of his gallery/home), and to the charitable donations of art for auction he has given to many worthy causes both in Haiti and the United States. To spend some time with Issa is a delight, and you will leave richer in knowledge of the art world and in Haiti itself. Be sure to take the time to look at the many inexpensive craft items in addition to the thousands of paintings and sculptures.

   Aubelin Jolicoeur, a well known Haitian journalist, has turned his home, also near the Oloffson at No. 9 rue 3, into an art gallery named **Claire's**. In addition to an eclectic selection of art, **Claire's** is known for the compelling personality of its owner, who, if not at home, can often be found at the Oloffson. In addition to the hundreds of paintings and other works of art to be found at the **Damballa Art Gallery**, 141-247 rue du Magasin de L'Etat, **Galerie Monnin**, 382 Blvd. J.J. Dessallines, and the many other galleries, special note should be taken of **L'Haitian Nader Galerie**, 256-258 rue du Magasin de L'Etat, and **L'Atelier Galerie Nader**, 48 rue Gregoire in Petionville. Both of the latter (as well as two galleries in the Dominican Republic) are owned by George Nader. At Nader's you will find one of the most extensive displays of art in all price ranges, many books on Haitian art, and probably one of the best street maps of both Port-au-Prince and Petionville. The two shops in Port-au-Prince, which are located right next to each other, and the one in Petionville are not places that can be seen in limited time because of the vast selection. George and his son, George Jr., have been especially helpful to us in learning more about Haitian art, and we can definitely say that a visit to Nader's is a must before you buy anything.

In shopping for arts and crafts, antiques, jewelry and other Haitian artifacts, the streets of Port-au-Prince abound with an endless array of vendors. One of the first places we recommend is a delightful collection of all those items in a shop with the name of **Gingerbread**. **Gingerbread**, located at 52 ave.

LaMartiniere, is owned and operated by Axelle Liautaud. The merchandise here is of the highest quality and all Haitian with the exception of most of the jewelry. We found the collection of paper-mache animals to be the best we had seen, as were the handcrafted clothing, and decorator items. Upstairs at the same address is **Les Ateliers Taggart** featuring the textile wall hangings of Ginette Taggart. These are exquisitely woven and can be had in any design to fit any decor.

In looking for interesting fashions, there are two boutiques in Petionville worth visiting. One is **Bagatelle**, 84 rue Panamericaine, and the other is **Bagaille**, 23 rue Panamericaine. Both of these shops are within walking distance of both the El Rancho and Villa Creole hotels.

For an all around shopping experience, you must not miss the **Iron Market**. Located in downtown Port-au-Prince, the Iron Market is a fascinating collection of every conceivable item from produce to jewelry on sale at unbelievably low prices. If you have never been in the crowded market places in other parts of the world where even the slightest hint of interest in an item will bring five to ten other merchants to your side all offering the same thing you should prepare yourself for the pressure. But remember, as oppressive as it may seem on your first visit, a second or third trip back will open the door to some of the best bargaining and bargains found anywhere. Be prepared to be "helped" by guides, which in this particular setting is a must. Here is where you will meet Meka, Peter Paul and a whole host of others like them who will try to help you buy anything and everything in sight. The guides will help you bargain, but remember that the bargaining will not go below a price that includes a commission for the guide. The bargaining is intense, to say the least and can get rather nasty. This is all part of the game, however, and is expected. You need not tip those offering help, or offer a commission, if it is all covered by the vendors. It is always a good idea to determine the "rules" before you begin.

On the streets surrounding the Iron Market is a massive market, one of the biggest you will find anywhere in the Caribbean. Every conceivable item is for sale here. However, many everyday items such as foods, drinks, and clothing are of primary interest to locals. It is always fun to see what truck load or boat load of contraband just arrived. We have witnessed some days where everyone in sight was selling the same brand name chewing gum or the same brand of fruit drink, and other days when everyone seemed to be selling the same color, size and shape of can opener, flashlights and scotch whiskey. Although many of the items are made available through legitimate sources, many things will be available as the result of a contraband shipment from the Dominican Republic or other islands. It's a colorful sight not to be missed.

Wood items are available virtually everywhere, but if you are interested in some of the larger pieces of furniture, a trip to one of the mahogany factories is a must. Again, this is usually best arranged through a guide who will not only provide for transportation, but interpretation.

For a shopping experience without the hassles of bargaining, a short trip out of town to **Fermathe** is in order. There you will find the **Mountain Maid Self Help Outlet** run by Baptist missionaries. The Turnbulls, whose parents started the mission many years ago, help many local Haitians who would not otherwise have an outlet for their crafts. The Outlet will also sell by mail, so do not forget to inquire as to how to order that special craft after you return home.

Although Haiti has no shopping malls similar to ones found in the U.S. and Canada, shopping in Port-au-Prince is just as exciting as anywhere else for adventuresome shoppers. Shopping here may take more time and effort than just walking down to the hotel gift shop, but you will find numerous unique treasures in Haiti.

Enjoying Your Stay

Haiti has experienced a major drop in tourism since the Duvalier dictatorship departed in February of 1986 as well as the subsequent U.S. invasion in 1994. Because of the political unrest that resulted, most hotels and restaurants closed at that time. Unfortunately, not all have reopened and getting around the town of Port-au-Prince and to Cap Haitian or Jacmel by rental car on your own is something that should be tried only after you have become familiar with the country and its people. The businesses that have reopened, and the natural beauty of Haiti, however, are a delight.

The Sites

If you have an extra day, a trip to the northern part of Haiti to see **Cap Haitien, Sans Souci and the Citadelle** is well worth the effort. Tours can be arranged through your hotel or one of the tour companies in Port-au-Prince. The trip will normally take two days if you plan to go by horseback to the Citadelle.

Jacmel and the many small paper-mache outlets will encompass a full day trip, but the trip through the mountains and small villages on the way is worth it.

Haiti has a variety of **beaches** near Jacmel and north of Port-au-Prince on the way to Cap Haitian. Although most of the beaches are accessible by car, most all the beach resorts are closed. It is a very good idea not only to hire a driver to get to the beaches, it is also a very good idea to bring your own food, soft drinks and bottled water. Haiti has been referred to as the "sleeping giant of diving." Divers from all around the world are just beginning to discover reefs, wrecks and walls along the eastern and northern coast line. There are a few diving centers, but it is recommended that you bring your own equipment.

Voodoo temples are of interest to many visitors. Derived from the word *vaudou* meaning spirits, voodoo has often been confused with black magic. This is a misconception. Essentially, voodoo is a religion dealing with *loas* (gods) and the complex rituals that keep the individual in harmony with them. An ancient tradition, voodoo represents the determination of the Haitians to maintain their African heritage. Many sacred dances, to this day, are similar to those practiced by the inhabitants of the forest and coastal regions of Africa. Some of the hotels have *voodoo* shows, but they are really representative of the modern folk dances of the country. A visit to a voodoo temple can be arranged through your hotel or through one of the tour companies. Some of the better known voodoo temples and their locations are:

Max Beauvoir, Mariani
Alexander Abraham, Carrefour Route Cric
Crac Cine Drive, Cote Plage 22
Paul Sainvil, Arcachon 32
Jacques Godvin, Bizoton (derriere le marche)
Cesar Lange, Bizoton (derriere le marche)
Marabeau Murat, Bizoton (Societe Dereal)
Stecker Louis Jean, Bizoton (Societe Souvenance)
Francois Carelus, Diquini
Doudoune, La Belle Étoile, Bizoton
Gesner, Martissant
Satela, Route des Dalles
Sauveur, Marche Salomon
Israel Cantave, Croix de Missions

ACCOMMODATIONS

At present some of Haiti's leading hotels remain closed. However, many of the following hotels express the personality of this adventurous country:

- **El Rancho Hotel and Casino:** Tel. 57-2080. vue Panamericaine, Petionville. Located in a former private mansion in a quiet residential setting it contains 115 rooms and a casino.

- **Villa Creole:** Tel. 57-1570 or 57-1571. 95 Bourdon, Petionville. Another very friendly hotel in a quiet residential area near the El Rancho, restored with air conditioned rooms and TV sets.

- **Kinam Hotel:** Tel. 57-0462. Rues Moise & Lamarre, Petionville. A family type hotel located within walking distance of many restaurants, shops and galleries.

- **Plaza Holiday Inn:** Tel. 23-9800 or 23-8494. Rue Capios at rue du Champs de Mars, Port-au-Prince. Located in the downtown area near the National Palace.

- **Hotel Oloffson:** Tel. 23-4000 or 23-4101. Fax 23-4101. Located at 60 ave. Christophe at rue Capios. Not far from downtown, the Oloffson is a three-story gingerbread house which served as the settings for Graham Green's, The Comedians. The hotel still caters to authors and journalists and has a folk show each week. The bar and restaurant is also the gathering place for many of the embassies' employees. Many of the guests have stayed there several times before and always return for the relaxed atmosphere. The hotel has an excellent private collection of art that is worth the visit even it you are not staying there.

- **La Jacmelienne Beach Hotel:** Tel. 88-3451 Located on Jacmel Bay in Jacmel. On the water with an excellent downtown location. Near shopping and the market. Excellent outdoor dining area for lunch.

- **Kaliko Beach and Scuba Club:** Tel. 22-8040 or 22-6530. La Gonave Bay, north of Port-au-Prince. Excellent quiet beach hotel with small separate cottages. The Kaliko Dive Shop is adjacent. Also horseback riding and tennis are part of the package.

RESTAURANTS

Expect to find excellent French dishes in Haiti. Creole foods, which include varied spices and meats, including goat, are well worth trying. You'll find many open air restaurants with awnings. Depending on where you dine, you may want your taxi driver to wait for you. Some of Haiti's best restaurants include:

- **Chez Gerard:** Tel. 57-1949. Located at 17 rue Pinchinat, Petionville. Excellent French restaurant, one of the best in Haiti.
- **La Souvenance:** Tel. 57-7688. Located at rue Lamert, Petionville. Another excellent French restaurant.
- **Le Recif:** Tel. 46-2605. Located at rue Lamert, Pentionville. A variety of seafood from giant shrimp to octopus.
- **Le Steak Inn:** Tel. 57-2153. Located at rue Magny, Petionville, Charbroiled steaks served in the garden or inside dining room.
- **The front porch of the Hotel Oloffson:** Tel. 23-4000 or 23-4101. Christophe at rue Capios. Our favorite restaurant for local creole cooking. Best cheeseburgers and other sandwiches for lunch in Port-au-Prince.

11

Jamaica

Jamaica is a world class playground in the Greater Antilles Islands. It's a wonderful choice for first-time visitors to the Caribbean. It offers tropical forests, beautiful flowers, long beaches, and palm trees as well as excellent water sports, glass-bottom boats, golf, and tennis. Its many and varied accommodations include large resorts, villas, supper clubs, and small private cottages. But Jamaica also offers shoppers a wide variety of choices—from exquisite boutiques and quaint antique shops to the ever-present street vendors.

Jamaica has duty-free shopping available in every major tourist area. All packages except liquor, cigarettes and cigars (which must be picked up at the pier or airport) can be taken with you if you pay with U.S. or Canadian dollars or credit cards and have identification showing your non-Jamaican status. Expect to shop for French perfumes, watches, electronics, jewelry, crystal, and cameras at prices nearly 40% lower than retail prices in the U.S. You'll find many shopping areas, including local markets, all over the island selling Jamaican art, sculpture, woodcarvings, batik fabrics, Bay Rum cologne, furniture, ceramics, hand-made jewelry, Blue Mountain coffee, and Jamaican rum.

Jamaica's more than 4,000 square miles of beautiful moun-

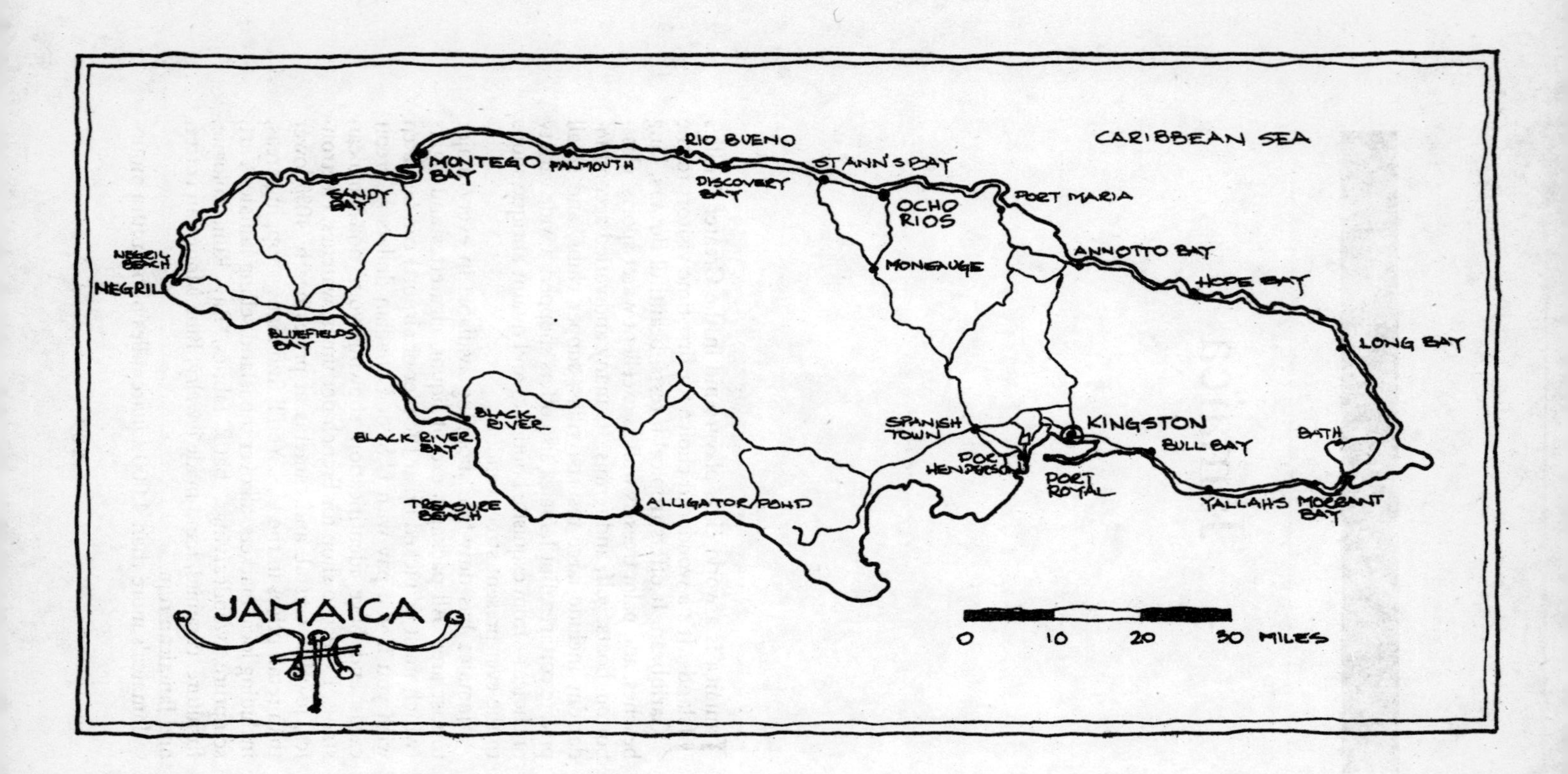
CARIBBEAN SEA
RIO BUENO
MONTEGO BAY
FALMOUTH
DISCOVERY BAY
ST ANN'S BAY
OCHO RIOS
PORT MARIA
ANNOTTO BAY
HOPE BAY
LONG BAY
SANDY BAY
NEGRIL BEACH
NEGRIL
MONEAGUE
BLUEFIELDS BAY
BLACK RIVER
BLACK RIVER BAY
TREASURE BEACH
ALLIGATOR POND
SPANISH TOWN
PORT HENDERSON
KINGSTON
PORT ROYAL
BULL BAY
BATH
YALLAHS
MORANT BAY
JAMAICA
0
10
20
30 MILES

tains rolling hills, rivers, and long sweeping beaches capture the attention of visitors. Its laid back atmosphere and "no problem —everything is fine" attitude personify an easy going and tranquil island. And it's a great place to shop.

GETTING TO KNOW YOU

The Arawak Indians called this island Xaymaca—land of wood and water. For five centuries they hunted, farmed, and celebrated their festivals. In 1494 Christopher Columbus arrived on the north shore. Within 100 years the Indian tribe was nearly extinct, having been pushed into hard labor and slavery. Failing to discover rich metals or establish strong settlements, the Spanish struggled with Jamaica for about 161 years. In 1655 Oliver Cromwell sent over 6,000 men to establish a hold in the Caribbean. Having failed to expel the Spaniards from Hispaniola, the British went on to Jamaica to accomplish this mission. British set up headquarters in Port Royal with one eye on colonization and the other on raiding Spanish ships carrying gold. The notorious buccaneer, Henry Morgan, was later rewarded with the Lieutenant Governorship for pirating raids and sacking of Spanish ships and Colonies in the area. One half of Port Royal sank into the sea in 1692 due to an earthquake, and this brought an end to what many considered to be the wickedest city on earth. Pirating continued to plague the surrounding waters until the late eighteenth century creating legends of men like Blackbeard and Calico Jack.

Jamaica's more than 430 sugar plantations brought stronger colonialism and the importation of 800,000 African slaves. The island produced more sugar than any other Caribbean island until the abolition of slavery. Rioting took place between freed slaves (offspring of white men and slave women) and Maroons (descendants from slaves freed by the Spaniards). In 1739 the Maroons agreed to a treaty that gave them land in central Jamaica which they still use today. After to the Morant Bay Rebellion in 1865, much of the power ended up in a new Governor's hands and a revamped constitution made Jamaica a Crown Colony until 1962 when the island became an independent nation within the British Commonwealth. As political and economic problems developed in the 1970's, tourism declined accordingly. Although the government took strong measures to return stability and visitors to the island, politics created a yo-yo effect until the mid-1980's when foreign investors built more resorts. Demonstrations today tend to be limited to Kingston's ghetto area rather than spill into tourist areas. Jamaican's now consider tourism to be their number one industry. Severely damaged by the 150 mile per hour winds of hurricane Gilbert in 1988, the island has recovered and now welcomes over 1 million visitors a year to new and refurbished resorts, hotels, supper clubs, and villas.

It is easy to get around and enjoy Jamaica. Your transportation choices include car rentals, taxis (the drivers also serve as guides), motor tours, and an historic train trip into the mountains beyond Montego Bay. You can go rafting through canyons, horseback riding along the beaches or in the mountains, or parasailing to get a good look at the north coast beaches.

On the still unspoiled northeast coast lies Port Antonio. Bright colored parrots chatter from high perches in the lush tropical forest above the village that encompasses twin harbors and Navy Island—a hideaway for the famous 1940's film star Errol Flynn. The coastline glides along to the north coast where you find the fine sandy beaches of Ocho Rios, Runaway Bay, and Montego Bay. The "garden" of Jamaica, this area abounds with orchids and flowers. Enjoy this area by exploring caves and climbing waterfalls at Dunn River. Polo is popular here along with six championship golf courses. History comes alive at the haunted Rose Hall Great House. Reggae music sways along with the discos and other night life.

Negril is the westerly beach area with seven miles of sparkling soft sandy beaches and constantly developing resorts, supper clubs, and cottages for those looking for the natural quiet life among the coves and inlets. Mandeville, located near the quiet south coast, is found at 2,000 feet elevation in the mountains. This is Jamaica's most English town and where over 256 species of birds congregate. Nearby is Williamsfield, home of High Mountain Coffee, Pioneer Chocolate, Shooter's Hill, and the world famous piquant sauce called Pickapeppa. The South coast of Jamaica seems endless. You can walk along the beaches for miles without seeing a soul. Kingston, the capital, considers itself to be the cultural center of the Caribbean. Reggae music was born here and still thrives. Art and theater are well represented here. Kingston is the island's main business center with a population of over 500,000.

THE BASICS

LOCATION AND GEOGRAPHY

Jamaica is part of the Greater Antilles Island chain in the Caribbean. It lies 90 miles south of Cuba. Only two other Caribbean islands—Cuba and Hispaniola—are larger than Jamaica. It is primarily volcanic in origin with its longest point being 146 miles and its widest point 51 miles. Blue Mountain Peak is the highest point on the island at 7,402 feet and the majority of the island is 1,000 feet above sea level. The island is surrounded by white sandy beaches and clear waters.

CLIMATE, WHEN TO GO, WHAT TO WEAR

In the winter season the average temperature is 75 degrees and in the summer about 80 degrees, with the mountains usually five to ten degrees cooler. The spring rainy season occurs in May and June, and it can rain frequently in September and October. As with most Caribbean islands that are lush with foliage, it can rain almost any day, but the rain comes in short bursts. Larger cities such as Kingston can be very hot during the day—sometimes in the 90's—but the trade winds from the northeast and breezes from the mountains keep the coastal areas very comfortable. Port Antonio receives more showers, because it is on the most tropical side of the island, but the rain usually comes in the morning and the sun shines by noon.

The Jamaican Tourist Board has an excellent record in attracting visitors to their country—over 1 million each year. While a visit to Jamaica is excellent any time of the year, do make reservations in advance, especially if your plans include the winter season between December 15 and April 15. Christmas is an especially difficult time to find a room, and it is essential to have a confirmed reservation (preferably in writing).

Where you plan to visit in Jamaica can make a difference in your choice of clothing. While attire in Jamaica is generally very casual, Kingston is a business and commerce center where men and women wear business attire (long pants for men—dresses for women). Many restaurants serving dinner in the resort areas of Port Antonio, Ocho Rios, and Montego Bay require a jacket and tie in winter (in summer a tie is optional) for men and evening pants or dresses for women. Negril has many beaches and clubs that allow topless bathing—but be sure to check before disrobing in public since topless bathing is only permitted in certain areas where you see a sign saying "Swimsuits

Optional." While casual dress is acceptable on the beach in Negril, short shorts and swimsuits are not proper attire for shopping and dining in town. In the evening most women select pants and dresses. Take at least one evening outfit during the winter so your dining and entertainment selections will not be too limited. However, should you come unprepared, you can always find a boutique right around the corner that offers colorful evening attire. Kareebas (Jamaican shirt-jack suits for men) are accepted everywhere. Take a jacket or sweater for the mountains, especially for wear in the evening, and remember to take a beach cover-up to protect your skin.

Be cautious in the sun even if you have a good start toward a tan, and keep plenty of sunscreen handy. If sailing or rafting on the river, be sure to have a hat and a long sleeved cover-up.

Jamaica has everything you need for an enjoyable stay, but remember staple items such as film, disposable baby diapers, formula, headache remedies, or suntan lotion are more expensive to purchase at resorts and local drugstores than in the U.S.

GETTING THERE

It's easy to get to Jamaica. The Island has its own airline, Air Jamaica, that flies from the U.S. cities of Atlanta, Baltimore, Los Angeles, Miami, New York, Philadelphia, and Tampa to Montego Bay and Kingston. It also departs from Toronto, Canada and London. Several American carriers such as American Airlines (New York City), Continental (Newark), and Northwest (Memphis) fly daily into the island. Trans Jamaica Airlines provides service within Jamaica. Air Canada provides service from Montreal and Toronto. Many charter services also fly from both the U.S. and Canada. British Airways has service from London.

Several cruise lines service Jamaica's three ports of Kingston, Montego Bay and Ocho Rios. Some cruise ships have "ship'n shore" holiday packages that can extend the cruise with a stay at a hotel or resort.

DOCUMENTS

Passports are not required for U.S. and Canadian citizens. However, proof of citizenship can be verified with a birth certificate, voter's registration card, or valid photo ID. A current passport will quickly get you through Customs and Immigration. The Jamaican government also requires a return or ongoing ticket. With proper documentation, visitors can stay for six months before further documentation is required.

ARRIVAL AND DEPARTURE

Kingston—Norman Manley International Airport

Since this is Jamaica's capital and business center, don't expect many resort services here. Keep your hand luggage light since the walk from your plane to Immigration is long. Be sure to fill out your Immigration card and have it ready. Hand this along with your on-going or return ticket and proof of citizenship to the Immigration official. Put your carbon copy receipt in a safe spot since you'll need it for departure. Customs allows items for personal use to come into the country duty-free. However, raw meats, pets, firearms, and flowers are prohibited. As soon as you pass through Customs, you will see the Tourist Board desk with general information to quickly acclimate you to Kingston. Be sure to stop by the airport exchange bureau to convert some money for the long ride into town. The bureaus are open for the arrival of every flight. Taxis and buses are found immediately outside. This is the airport to use if your destination is Port Antonio. If you have a transfer coupon for your hotel, present it to the driver if he is there. If not, it will be collected just before departure. If you are not traveling with a transfer coupon for one of the hotels or resorts, always have a clear understanding of the fare before you get into a taxi.

Montego Bay—The Donald Sangster Airport

You really feel you've arrived in the Caribbean here. Flights are generally greeted with Jamaican music, and rum is offered as you linger in the Immigration lines. This is another airport with a lengthy walk before reaching Immigration—the first stop. Jamaican laws are strict, and you will see that reflected in the attitudes of Immigration officials who are pleasant, but serious; they fully expect to see all appropriate documentation. The airport can be confusing with several flights arriving at the same time and lots of activity. Your prearranged rental car will be off to the right of Customs. If you have a transportation transfer from your travel agency, go outside and you will be guided to the appropriate hotel van or shuttle. A porter can be helpful here, because transportation is also going to Ocho Rios, Runnaway Bay, and Negril. These destinations are out of your way if you are headed into Montego Bay. There is no need to rush through all of this since no van will leave until all seats are filled and this can take several minutes.

You'll find two currency exchange bureaus—one immediately past Immigration and the other near the luggage claim area.

Cruise ships arrive in the heart of Port Antonio, Kingston, Montego Bay, and Ocho Rios, and it is easy to get to shopping via walking or taxi.

All passengers departing from Jamaica are required to pay a departure tax of J$200 per person (approximately $7 US, depending on the exchange rate). Be sure to save enough Jamaican dollars.

The beautiful tropical fresh flowers at the airport duty-free store can only be purchased with foreign currency. These may be confiscated when you arrive back home.

Currency, Traveler's Checks, Credit Cards

The Jamaican currency is the Jamaican Dollar. The exchange rate is no longer fixed and traded publicly, so it fluctuates daily. US$1 usually equals about J$30.00. Jamaican currency includes J$1, J$2, J$5, J$10, and J$20 bills. Coins are in denominations of 1, 5, 10, 20, 25 and 50 cents. Whenever you exchange money, be sure to get a currency receipt as this will be required when you reconvert your surplus Jamaican dollars at the end of your stay. Even though most prices in tourist areas are quoted in U.S. dollars, the Jamaican government now requires visitors to pay all bills in local currency. Be sure to exchange some money at the airport if you need to pay the taxi driver to the hotel, although some drivers will, in fact, accept U.S. dollars. You should have little difficulty in exchanging money since banks are plentiful and are open 9am to 2pm, Monday through Thursday, and from 9am to noon and 2:30pm to 5pm on Fridays. They are closed on weekends and holidays except at the airport, however. Hotels can exchange money, and cruise ship piers also have bureaus that are open. It is against the law to take Jamaican currency in or out of the country, and it is against the law to convert money on the street.

Traveler's checks are widely used and most hotels, shops and restaurants encourage their use. This is a major convenience for the visitor and prevents the constant exchange of money.

Tipping

Most hotels will add a General Consumption Tax 12.5% and restaurants will add a 10% service charge to your bill. Always check to see if it is included. If not, the general rule is 10% to 15% for waiters; one dollar a day for chambermaids; 50 cents per bag for porters and bellboys; and 15% for taxi drivers. If you stay at an all inclusive resort—tipping is not permitted.

LANGUAGE

It is very easy to get around Jamaica. There are no language problems since all Jamaicans are schooled in English. Because Jamaica was populated by slaves from various African tribes, their language was derived primarily from West African Twi and Ashanti. They created their own unique dialect called Jamaican Patois. They learned English in the fields from their overseers, thus combining many words from each language. Over 400 years of colonialism has brought more creative expressions such as "walk good" which is equated to "have a good day." The Rasta influence further enriches the language. For example "hail" is a rasta greeting from "haile" of Haile Selassie fame.

- **Even though most prices in tourist areas are quoted in U.S. dollars, all bills must be paid in local currency.**
- **Since taxis are not metered, be sure to agree on the fare before getting in.**
- **Car rentals are very expensive in Jamaica.**
- **The basic rule for shopping in Jamaica is to buy something when you see it—especially crafts—as you are likely not to see it again.**

BUSINESS HOURS

Shops in Kingston and Montego Bay are open from 8:30am to 5pm weekdays. Hours for rest of the island vary. Some shops close at 4:30pm and some are open until noon on Saturday.

TRANSPORTATION AND TOURS

Buses are inexpensive and colorful ways to get around Montego Bay and Kingston; however, their schedules are unpredictable and they can be crowded. In the country, you may be sitting beside someone carrying fresh produce and live chickens to market.

There are also many unscheduled **minibuses and jitneys**, but most seem to arrive frequently and service the same routes.

Most visitors, however, take **taxis** in Kingston or Montego Bay. Since taxis are not metered, be sure to agree on the fare before getting in. If you want to stop off the beaten path or in the country, ask the driver to return for you and give a time. All taxis have a 25% surcharge after midnight, although this charge is sometimes negotiable. They are easy to find and are identified with the letters "PPV" next to the number on the license plates. You can call for a taxi or hail one on the street or outside a hotel. You can also hire a taxi driver to take a guided tour or cross country trip.

It is also very easy to **rent a car** for the day. There are many rentals on the Island. Some companies have representatives at the hotels, but the greatest choice is at the airports. It is important to reserve in advance if you need a car for your entire stay, and we found it necessary to have a written confirmation in hand. Car rentals are very expensive in Jamaica with prices appearing to be fixed amongst the various companies. You will find that gasoline is about $2 an Imperial gallon—one-fifth more than the U.S. gallon. Jamaican roads are in good condition but sparse with markings. Rental agencies provide good maps, however, which makes finding your way around possible. A U.S. or Canadian driver's license is all that is necessary to rent a car, but be sure to use a credit card to avoid paying a huge deposit. Speed limits are 30 mph in town and 50 mph in the country. Be forewarned that Jamaican drivers know the roads well and take advantage of passing on curves and hills. Driving is on the left, and you need to constantly look out for goats, pedestrians, and bicyclers. If you are not be used to this kind of driving, you may feel more comfortable hiring both a car and driver.

Hotels and rental agencies have **mopeds** as well as **motor scooters** that can be rented by the day. A deposit is required.

Trains run daily between Montego Bay and Kingston. The one-way trip takes about five hours.

A quick and reasonable way to get from one point on the island to another is to fly. **Trans Jamaican Airlines** connects Kingston to Port Antonio, Ocho Rios, Montego Bay, and Negril. Book through your hotel or a travel agency.

Tours are wide and varied. Sightseeing tours are run by Jamaica Tours and several other operators. Some specialty tours such as "Up, Up, & Buffet" incorporate a hot air balloon ride.

Glass bottom boat rides are available, especially in Ocho Rios and Montego Bay. Many other excursions are also available including river rafting. Arrangements for these can also be made at your hotel.

There are several **train tours**, including the Governors Coach Tour using a private railway car that takes visitors into the mountains from Montego Bay. The Mandeville Rail Tour departs at 7:45am on Thursdays with a stop at Balvelava for shopping and continues to Williamsfield and Mandeville for a bus tour. At each station peddlers leap onto the train with their wares. This is a time for a quick "higgle," but look very carefully at your bargain before you part with your J$'s.

This is the place you can do your "higgling" (the word combines haggling and giggling) as Jamaican's call it. Be sure that when you conduct this transaction not to expect big discounts. Start by offering about 50% of the asking price and bargain until you reach a compromise which is generally about 25% off the original asking price. The best we accomplished was 30% off a product. However, there is usually a bonus here for participating in a good "higgle"—a "brawta"—a small free trinket or an additional placemat that the vendor will choose for you.

Meet The People is a special program sponsored by the Jamaica Tourist Board for visitors who want to meet Jamaican families, spend some time together, and share interests. It allows tourists to see how the locals live and to make friends. While this is a free service, it's nice to take a small gift to the host. You can inquire about this program and apply at any Tourist Board. The Tourism Center, 21 Dominica Drive, Kingston 5 (809-929-9200) can give you the local number for other cities if you are not in Kingston.

RESOURCES

When you arrive on the island, you should pick up a copy of ***The Visitor*** at the airport, your hotel, or at one of the Tourist Board Offices. It is published weekly. Another free guide is the ***Daily Gleaner***, published bi-monthly which keeps you in tune with shopping specials, the latest discos, and dining. Both publications keep you informed on what is happening and where it is happening. In Montego Bay, ***The Vacationer*** is available at hotels, shops, and restaurants. It has the latest on sales and nightspots and is also free. Each of these offer a slightly different view on what to do in Jamaica, so pick them all up along the way.

The Jamaican Record is the Kingston newspaper. In addition, most major hotels carry the ***New York Times*** the same day it is published.

The Jamaican Tourist Board has several locations throughout the island and in the U.S. and Canada. They have maps, booklets, and information on local events and they will happily answer any questions. The Tourist Board will assist you in signing up for the **Meet The People** program. The Jamaican Tourist Board locations are as follows:

Tourism Center
2 St. Lucia Ave.
Kingston 5, Jamaica
Tel. 809-929-9200
Fax. 809-929-9375

Cornwall Beach
P.O. Box 67
Montego Bay, Jamaica
Tel. 809-952-4425
Fax. 809-952-3857

Ocean Village Shopping
Center
P.O. Box 240
Ocho Rios, Jamaica
Tel. 809-974-2570

City Center Plaza
P.O. Box 151
Port Antonio, Jamaica
Tel. 809-993-3051
Fax. 809-933-2587

Adrija Plaza
Shop No. 9
Negril, Jamaica
1G9
Tel. 809-957-4243
Fax. 809-957-4489

801 Second Avenue
20th Floor
New York, NY 10017
Tel. 212-688-7650
Fax. 212-688-9730

Mezzanine Level
1110 Sherbourne Street
W. Montreal, Quebec H3A
Tel. 514-849-6386

3440 Wilshire Blvd.
Suite 1207
Los Angeles, CA 90010
Tel. 213-384-1123

1320 South Dixie Hwy.
Suite 1100
Coral Gables, FL 33146
Tel. 305-665-0557

1 Eglinton Ave.
Suite 616
Toronto, Ontario M4P 3A1
Tel. 416-482-7850

Mezzanine Level
1110 Sherbourne St.
W. Montreal, Quebec H3A
Tel. 514-849-6386

8411 Preston Road
Dallas, TX
Tel. 214-361-8778

SHOPPING IN JAMAICA

Shopping in Jamaica is everywhere. From the moment you step off the plane or cruise ship, you'll find something to buy. Crafts are sold alongside roads, in hotel shops, down the street at arcades, and around the corner at shopping centers. Numerous items are also sold on the street by an endless array of hustlers. When your train stops, Jamaicans jump on board to quickly sell T-shirts and straw goods. And just when you close your eyes on the beach, along comes another vendor selling more shell and coral necklaces. You should have no problem finding places to shop!

Although Jamaica is not a free port, in-bond shopping is offered on international items such as bone china and woolens from Great Britain, Swiss watches, French perfumes and crystal,

Japanese pearls and cameras, German cameras, and a host of other items from all over the world. Prices are especially good on items imported from England, since Jamaica belongs to the Commonwealth and is not subject to import tax. Visitors with identification showing visitor status can pay in Jamaican, U.S., or Canadian dollars as well as traveler's checks or credit cards. You can take any in-bond item with you, except liquor or consumables. If you purchase liquor outside the airport duty-free shop for consumption back home, leave ample time to have it conveyed to the airport or cruise ship—usually a half day in advance of departure.

Shopping for arts and crafts can be fun. Each part of the island offers some new twist on an item. You'll find original jewelry and one-of-a-kind art, straw works, clothing and woodcarvings, quilts, and figurines. The works of such Jamaican artists as Edna Manley and Albert Huie are considered museum pieces and are priced accordingly; however, many other artists are still reasonably priced. Batik is widely available and can be tailored into clothing at low prices compared to prices in the U.S. Remember that art, fashions, crafts, Blue Mountain coffee, Jamaican rums, spices, and sauces all fall under a U.S. Customs rule that permits an item to enter the U.S. duty-free if 65% of it is made in Jamaica.

WHAT TO BUY

Jamaica has a large and varied assortment of shopping choices. Art can be distinctive and expensive as well as inexpensive. Jewelry includes imported Mikimoto pearls available at the **India House** in Montego Bay at in-bond prices to the black coral collected from the river beds of the Blue Mountains. Here you will find original designs from one of Ruth Clarage's bright fabrics, Jamaica's famed Blue Mountain coffee, rum liqueur, Pickapeppa sauce, or even a Cuban cigar.

In-bond prices are about 20% to 40% lower than retail prices in the U.S. Arts and craft prices are reasonably priced but not necessarily inexpensive, with the best bargains found at the straw markets, road side areas, and beaches. The shopping centers have sales and discounts, and jewelers will negotiate on some quality pieces. The jellies, spices, sauces, liqueurs, and herbs found all over the island are wonderful items to take home to friends. One memorable way to do this is to shop at the factories where many items are made. Factory shopping is available at various locations such as the **High Mountain Coffee Factory** in Williamsfield where the famous Blue

Mountain Coffee is created, or at Shooter's Hill at the **Pickapeppa Factory** where Jamaica's world famous piquant sauce is made. Williamsfield also is the home of **Pioneer Chocolate Company**. Generally you can book the tour through your hotel during the week.

Jamaica imports a wide selection of **embroidered linens** from The Peoples Republic of China which are available in many stores, and substantial savings are found on French **perfumes**. Most famous brand names, such as Anais-Anais, Chloe, and Joy, are available here as well as the Jamaican Khus Khus scent. Others with names like White Witch or Forget-Me-Not are also reasonably priced. **Watches** remain one of the best purchases with prices as much as 40% below those in the U.S.

The basic rule for shopping in Jamaica is to buy something when you see it—especially crafts—as you are likely not to see it again. There are items unique to each area and the quality of straw items has improved through the years. Resort clothes have always been an excellent buy since local seamstresses are talented in making good quality copies from top fashion designers. The shopping centers and arcades are the major areas for shops selling in-bond goods and resort fashions.

ART AND ARTISTS

Jamaica is rapidly becoming a major art center. Unusual and eclectic as well as politically motivated art is now being produced on the island. Many contemporary artists reflect individuality in their work and quality is very good. Prices are high, but not exorbitant, especially if you find a young artist you like. The 1930's spurned names such as John Dunkley and Henry Daley. The late Edna Manley, who founded the Jamaican School of Art, is famous for her sculptures. She also founded the Jamaican School of Art. Other renowned artists are Carl Abrahams, Albert Huie, Ralph Campbell and Gloria Escoffery. You can find their works and those of artists of more recent fame at the **Harmony Hall Gallery** near Ocho Rios (809-974-4222). Harmony Hall is a nineteenth century great house that has been restored; it is a center for quality crafts of Jamaica as well as the noted artists referred to above.

Mutual Life Gallery located at the Mutual Life Centre, 2 Oxford Road, Kingston (809-926-9025) is in the corporate headquarters of an insurance company. You must pass a security check to reach the mezzanine level to see the works of these well known and new artists, and the exhibit changes monthly. The gallery is open from 10am to 6pm during the week and from 11am to 3pm on Saturdays.

For a historical perspective on Jamaican artists, visit Kingston's National Gallery which is located at 12 Ocean Boulevard in the Kingston Mall. Here you will find the works of primitive painter and sculptor Kapo. Paintings and sculptures trace the development of Jamaican art from the 1920's through today. You will also find the works of the intuitive masters: John Dunkley and both David Miller Sr. and Jr.

The **Frame Gallery** at 10 Tangerine Place, Kingston (809-926-4644) has been open since the early 1970's. Edna Manley's works are on display here plus over 400 other works of art. The gallery is open from 8:30am to 5pm during the week and on Saturday mornings.

In Montego Bay you will find both Jamaican and Haitian primitives and sculptures as well as carvings and antique maps at the **Gallery of West Indian Arts** (1 Orange Lane).

Five miles outside of Montego Bay, along the road to Negril, **Neville Budhai Paintings** (Reading Main Road) is a well known gallery that sells original paintings by Puerto Rican as well as Jamaican artists. Here you will also see lithographs, woodcuts, and batiks. The gallery is open from 8:30am until dusk.

Musical artist Bob Marley made Reggae music world famous. The big red gold and green gates at 56 Hope Road in Kingston provide the entrance to his typical Caribbean home which has pastel colors throughout. His music can be found throughout Jamaica and the world. While his recordings may be hard to find back home, they are plentiful here. Bob Marley's home is now a museum and is open from 9am to 4:30pm Mondays, Tuesdays, Thursdays, and Fridays. The entrance fee is J$10.

ANTIQUES AND COLLECTIBLES

Most antiques in Jamaica are old English items. All sorts of antiques, including maps, can be found at the **Montego Bay Gallery of West Indian Arts** and at the **Things Jamaican Ltd.** shops that line the garden area of the Devon House in Kingston. These shops offer a wide selection of excellent quality items that can be authenticated.

Devon House is located at the intersection of Waterloo and Hope Roads. Built in 1881, this house was furnished by its owner George Stieble with the elegance of the day. In 1983, it was completely restored to its original splendor for a visit from Queen Elizabeth; it is well worth the J$1 admission fee. As you depart, at the back in the enclosed court yard, you can browse through the seven shops of **Things Jamaican Ltd**. You'll find everything from a four poster bed to Lion Rampant antique spoons. They also have a collection of pewter knives and forks based on the original designs from items discovered in an archaeological dig from the Port Royal area in the mid-1960's. Also, look for items with the Tudor Rose Seal. These reproductions even show imperfections and, of course, are leadless. **Things Jamaican Ltd**. also has shops at both airports.

WATCHES AND JEWELRY

Watches are a very popular shopping item in Jamaica. You'll find excellent prices—up to 40% below U.S. prices. Most major international brands are represented here. At the **Swiss Stores** in Kingston and Montego Bay look for Patek-Philippe, Rado, Rolex, Tissot and Omega watches. In Ocho Rios, **Casa de Oro** at Pineapple Place carries Cartier, Concorde, Corum, Movado and Seiko. The **India House** in Montego Bay offers Citi and Raymond Weil among others. The **Hemisphere** at Wyndham Rose Hall Beach Club in Montego Bay also stocks Ebel, Girard-Perregaux. Be sure to have proof of your visitor status to take advantage of in-bond prices.

Jewelry is fashioned around Jamaican gemstones like black coral and coral agate. **Blue Mountain Gem Workshop** displays a Mike O'Hara collection of black coral from the Blue Mountain area. It's interesting to watch the polishing and casting of the stones here. Ceramic jewelry from **Ruth Clarage Ltd**, Ocean Village Shopping Center, is made to match the hand-silk screen print clothing, and she has shops throughout the island. **Ital Craft** located at Twin Gates Plaza in Kingston, specializes in shell necklaces and other one-of-a-kind jewelry made out of natural products from Jamaica. We also found some of Ital Craft jewelry in many of the fine boutiques. Keep in mind these are original items and therefore may not be the bargain price you are expecting. But they are unique and well worth buying if you like them.

You will also find many handmade necklaces that are sold on the beaches and at all the craft areas as well. Unlike shops with set prices, you can really bargain with the beach vendors.

In Montego Bay the **India House**, located at 51 St. James Street, is where you can find beautiful stones and pearls along with 18K gold jewelry. Know the prices of the more expensive items, even though it is very difficult to compare. Even experts vary over 40% in valuing items. If you are purchasing a high ticket item, be sure to negotiate. You can expect some reduction on the expensive items, even 18K gold jewelry. Mikimoto pearls, however, have set prices, and you will not be too successful trying to bargain the price down.

PERFUME

You'll find good buys on perfumes but most stores maintain inadequate stocks of international perfumes. If you search many shops, you are likely to find what you want. Christian Dior, Oscar de la Renta, Joy, Anais-Anais, Opium, and Chloe are some of the many famous brands sold alongside Jamaica's own fragrances. **Benjamins of Jamaica** is famous for their scent of Khus Khus which is made from the local grasses bearing the same name, and you can get it in perfume and cologne strengths. They also carry the earthy musk Cacique for men. White Witch is found at **Parfums Jamaica** and has a floral fragrance. Royall Jamaica Lyme is widely available and is a refreshing cologne or aftershave. It is manufactured at the **Royall Jamaica Lyme Factory** in Bogue near Montego Bay.

FASHIONS

Unlike most Caribbean Islands, Jamaica produces well made resort clothing. Numerous boutiques offer the most sophisticated clothing for daytime or evening wear. An outstanding shop is **Ruth Clarage Ltd.** (in seven locations). The silk-screened fabrics of bright clear colors are produced on the island in everything from swimwear to dresses. They are very tropical, yet can be brought home to wear as well. Matching original ceramic jewelry and accessories can be purchased for outfits. Hats are also plentiful on the beach as well as at craft areas—where you can have fun practicing your bargaining skills —and at the many hotel gift shops. **Pineapple Shop** has numerous island prints available in ready-to-wear or custom-made (within a few days), both at reasonable prices. Here, you can also purchase fabrics by the yard. **Pineapple Shop** is located at the Holiday Inn at Montego Bay as well as at Montego Freeport near Casa Montego, a small building near the pier that houses a few craft shops. **Daphne Logan Hewitt** specializes in very romantic evening wear and exquisite sports clothes. One shop is at the **Pegasus** in Kingston, and branch shops are found in resort areas.

Caribatik near Falmouth offers both men and women's resort wear in unique designs. **Lenny Harris** in Kingston is an excellent choice for menswear. Most hotels at the resort areas have good selections as well. If you need custom tailoring, **George Washington Hewitt**, 8 St. James Street in Montego Bay, is a good choice.

LINENS

It is difficult to compare prices on linens. Since Jamaicans embroider and use quality linen, prices are not cheaper than imports. There are also many excellent high quality buys from China. The **Devon House** in Kingston and **Things Jamaican Ltd.** in Montego Bay have wide selections of Jamaican items. Imported linens are available at **Casa de Oro's** locations in Montego Bay, Ocho Rios, and at **China Craft** in Rose Hall.

FOOD

While many islands in the Caribbean produce sauces, jellies, or spices, Jamaicans are very creative with these and other food items. The world famous **Pickapeppa** sauce holds no less than 21 Jamaican spices along with onions, raisins, tomatoes, tamarind, vinegar, mangoes, and small red Jamaican peppers. This sauce has been a success through word-of-mouth and is distributed in over 50 countries. We always stock up and find it a wonderful gift to take home for friends. If your travels take you to Mandeville, be sure to visit the factory in nearby Shooter's Hill. At the end of the factory tour, you receive a free bottle of this unique sauce.

You'll find many special **spices** in Jamaica. Jamaican ginger is of superior quality. Allspice, a combination of cinnamon, cloves and juniper, also has a medicinal meaning for Jamaicans in treating an upset stomach. Pepper elder is an important ingredient in jerk pork, a barbecue dish that is slowly cooked over green pimento wood and highly spiced. Port Antonio's Boston Beach is the most noted for jerk pork, but you can get it from beach side vendors all over the island. You can also get jerk chicken and jerk fish as well. It was created by the runaway Maroons who tried to survive by eating wild hog during their years of warfare against the English settlers. The **Devon House** and **Things Jamaican Ltd.** (at the Montego Bay Airport) have these spices among the variety of sauces they sell.

The **cassava bammy** is a local version of an English muffin that is easy to find. It has a distinctive taste and is usually available in most restaurants.

Ackee is a fruit peculiar to Jamaica and grows on huge trees. When cooked, it tastes like scrambled eggs or chestnuts, depending on whom you talk to. It is a staple dish and is generally served with codfish.

Blue mountain coffee is grown in its name sake mountains at an elevation of 7,000 feet. It is a gourmet's delight. Demand exceeds growth ability and the price reflects this at approximately $30 a pound. The Japanese have access to one half of each year's crop. The seal of the Jamaican Coffee Board is on every package to ensure that these deep red berries were grown, dried naturally, and roasted under strict government supervision. It is harvested by hand by expert pickers who select only the most ripened berries. There are 20 varieties from which to select. You are right at the source if you travel to **Pine Grove Coffee Plantation** in the Blue Mountains. However, the coffee is sold all over the island and at the airports. You may prefer buying it at the airport since the price is the same as elsewhere, and it is easy to pick up there rather than carry it around while shopping. The price in Jamaica is about half of what you will pay in U.S. gourmet shops.

Many well traveled visitors rate Jamaican food as the best in the entire Caribbean. The abundance of spices, vegetables, and fruits along with numerous varieties of fish and the creative cooking makes Jamaican dishes outstanding.

CIGARS

When political turmoil erupted in Cuba during the early 1960's, some of Cuba's most noted cigar makers immigrated to Jamaica. Tobacco was already an established crop in Jamaica. By combining Cuban expertise in producing handmade cigars with Jamaican tobacco, *Royal Jamaica* was born among other outstanding brands. When purchasing cigars, remember this is an in-bond item that must be picked up at your departure gate.

SPIRITS

A local beer called Red Stripe is available everywhere, and Jamaica is especially famous for producing fine rum. Using a special process, some Jamaican rum is aged 20 years while others are blended from various casks. **Appleton Rum** has been in operation for over 150 years. **Long Pond Sugar Factory and Distillery** produces Gold Label Rum. Both distilleries can be visited by making appointments through your hotel. **Tia Maria** is a famous coffee liqueur. **Rumona** is another famous coffee liqueur that is particularly delicious.

WHERE TO SHOP

While shopping is available all over this island, it is primarily concentrated in Kingston and in the resort areas of Montego Bay and Ocho Rios.

Jamaica is a large island with Kingston and Montego Bay being its largest cities. Be sure to take your common sense with you. If you make arrangements for guided tours, set the price before you go. The old come-on line "Let me show you at a good price" will primarily be a good price for the tour guide if you don't establish the price before you set out. If you set out on your own, be sure to lock your rented car, and don't leave items in view even in a locked car. Use safety deposit boxes in your hotel, and carry travelers checks and credit cards rather than large amounts of cash.

Two important "don'ts" apply here. Do not change money at bargain rates (it is against the law and it is enforced). Do not get involved in conversations that mention "ganja"—that's marijuana—or any other illegal drugs such as cocaine. Indeed, Jamaica is very strict about drugs. You may get a jail cell if you are caught with ganja, a locally grown marijuana. At the very least you will be deported. Make no attempts to mail it out of the country. There are strong controls at sea, and sniffer dogs are used for inspections at both airports.

Kingston, the capital of Jamaica, is the largest English speaking city in the Caribbean with a population of well over 500,000. It has everything from shacks to ultra modern buildings. Shopping is widespread, and the city is a very busy hubbub of traffic and people. Many visitors prefer to shop near their hotel or in New Kingston at the shopping center, **Devon House**, and the **Kingston Craft Market**. In downtown Kingston, the old part of town surrounds Victoria Park (now named Sir William Grant Park). Several arcades lead off King Street, with a wide variety of boutiques and shops. This is a very busy area and where you will most likely encounter "higglers" or people who approach you with phrases such as "hot stuff Mon" or "de best deal" and other hucksters trying to sell you inferior products at high prices. Usually a firm, but polite "no" sends them looking for their next victim. Don't inquire or engage in conversation with these people or you may find yourself the new owner of a freshly dipped "gold" brass chain!

The **Kingston Craft Market** is located downtown at the west end of Harbour Street near Kingston Cruise Pier. This is a government sponsored craft market in a huge covered area with individually owned stalls. You can also reach it from Straw Avenue and Cheapside. There are craft markets all over the island, but this is the largest with the widest selections, many of which not available elsewhere. Lignum vitae and Mahoe are woods of the island and they are carved into wooden plates, pepperpots, trays, bowls, and masks—you name it. All types of straw products from gaudy to refined hats, baskets, and mats to tortoise shell items are available at many stalls. Since tortoise shell products cannot legally be brought into the U.S., it's best to avoid these items. The **Craft Market** is the place you can do your higgling, but be forewarned that here, more than in any other market, you will be pushed, shoved, and hassled near the entrances and exits.

Devon House, located at 26 Hope Road (809-929-6602), is the showcase of Jamaican crafts. It has seven **Things Jamaican Ltd**. shops to explore. Here you will discover a fine collection of handmade embroidered linens and cotton batiks, straw goods of high quality, woodcarvings, and delectable items from famous Blue Mountain Coffee to spicy sauces, jams, jellies and honey. Furniture, sculpture, appliqued quilts, Jamaican rum, and replicas of spoons from Port Royal and other pewter items are also found here.

The **New Kingston Shopping Center** in New Kingston is the most modern of all centers and features a replica of a Mayan Pyramid in the middle with water cascading among beautiful plants. It has a pleasant atmosphere for shopping. Here you'll find many smart boutiques and shops operating at a quieter pace than downtown. It also includes several fast food establishments. Look for good prices and quality products, but there's no bargaining here. Our favorite shop is **Ruth Clarage Lt.**, especially for evening wear and accessories.

Nearby the New Kingston Shopping Center is **Sangster's Old Jamaica Spirits** at 17 Holborn Road (809-926-8888). While they have hundreds of bottles of rum on display, which may disorient you at first, once you enter the showroom someone will help you select from all the tempting flavors. Remember, rum is not just rum and liqueur is not just liqueur; each island has specialties. Just as Puerto Rico has their famous Bacardi rums and Sint Maarten has its unique guava berry liqueurs, Jamaica has their 100% Gold Rum Cream and Blue Mountain Coffee Liqueurs. There are all sorts of flavors from wild orange to coconut cream. What's nice about this factory outlet is that prices are based on the size of the bottle rather than its contents.

Ital Craft at Twin Gates Plaza (809-926-8291) specializes in accessories that are made from natural products on the island. It is a favorite shop for creative jewelry. The name in Rastafarian means "something good" and is definitely worth a visit.

At the airport the **Swiss Stores** carries an excellent selection of watches and original jewelry. You'll also find a branch of **Things Jamaican Ltd.** here.

A quick check with the tourist office will get you the latest list of Jamaican designers since new names emerge frequently for fashions and jewelry. Our two favorite boutiques for designer labels are **Ital Craft** and **Ruth Clarage, Ltd.**, but you will find many other good boutiques and new discoveries.

MONTEGO BAY

Montego Bay, or Mo Bay as locals call it, has several small shopping areas, such as Montego Freeport near the pier, The City Centre Building with good in-bond shopping, Holiday Village Shopping Center, Westgate Shopping Center, and Rose Hall.

The **Crafts Market** by the wharves on Harbour Street is where you will find a large selection of straw hats. You'll get lots of assistance here to help you choose just the right color ribbon to complement the outfit of the day. It can be fun browsing among the 150 stalls, but the slightest hesitation invites assistance and pressure to make a purchase. Amongst all the woodcarvings and straw items you'll find children's toys and games carved from wood as well as musical instruments. Visitors can even get their hair platted here, and you simply can't miss the large quantity of large wall hangings on display.

Things Jamaican Ltd. at 44 Fort Street (809-952-5605) has food and drink to sample while shopping among all of the Jamaican made arts and crafts. Look for jerk seasoning and jellies as well as the locally famous Busha Browne's sauces with a recipe that has been used for over 100 years. Along with these delicious chutney and spicy sauces are bowls and sculptures carved from wood and pewter reproductions of the Port Royal Collection based on items recovered from the 1692 earthquake. **Things Jamaican Ltd.** also carries the Port Royal Bristol-Delft Ceramic Collection based on the ceramic pieces also found from the 1692 earthquake. Most of these reproduced items had originally come from the Netherlands and Great Britain.

The **City Centre Building** has the **Presita Shop** with good cameras and stereos. **Chulani Ltd.**, another nearby shop, also has electronic equipment.

Sam Sharpe's Square is where you'll find the largest selection of in-bond shops. You can find Swiss watches, Irish crystal, English china and cashmere, and liqueurs.

The **Holiday Village Shopping Center** houses the **Blue Mountain Gems** shop (809-953-2338) which gives demonstrations of how rough stones are processed and become exquisitely polished end products. Most jewelry is fashioned around Jamaican gemstones. You can bargain to some degree here for

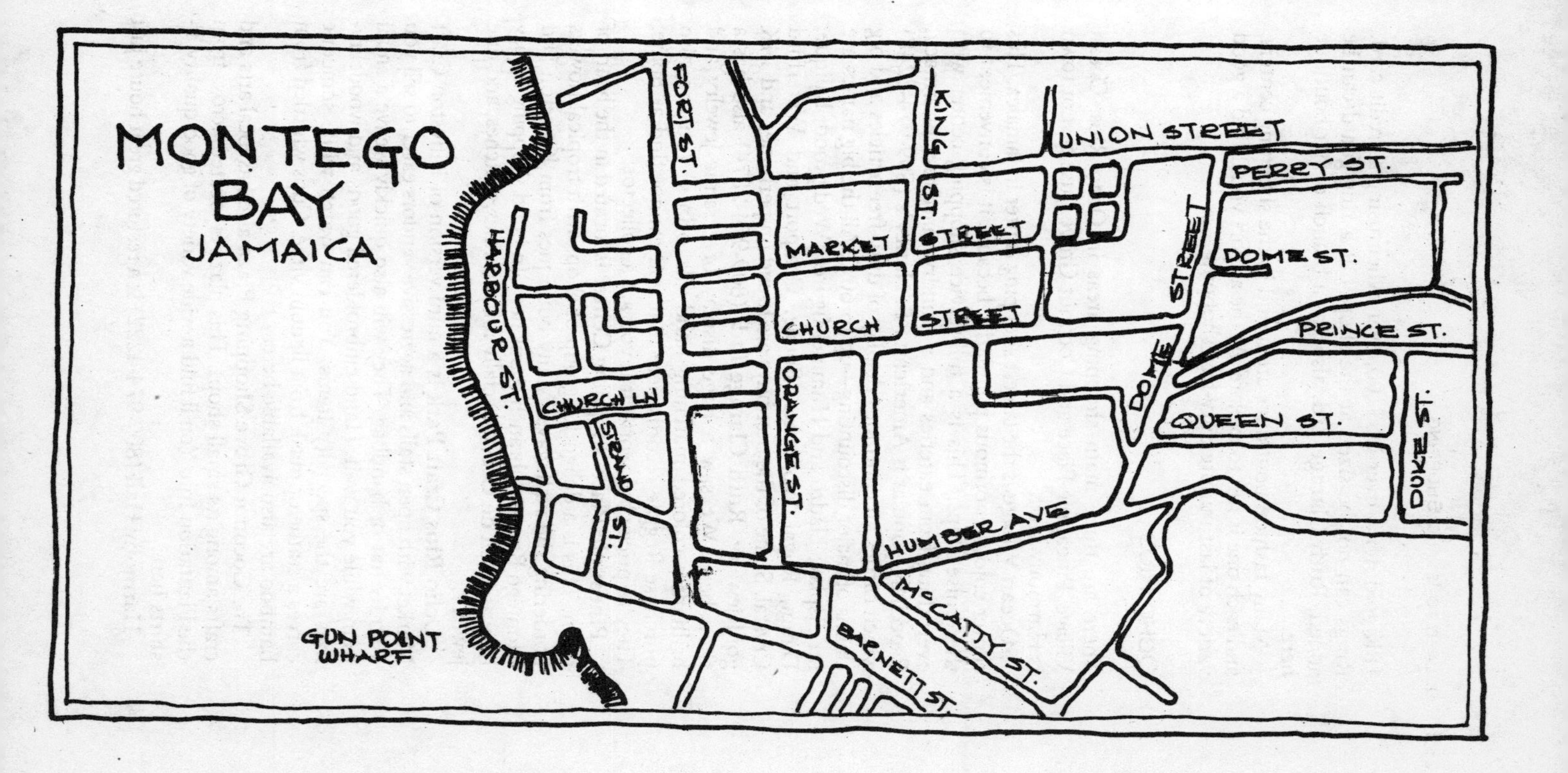
MONTEGO BAY
JAMAICA
UNION STREET
PERRY ST.
KING ST.
DOME ST.
MARKET STREET
CHURCH STREET
DOME STREET
PRINCE ST.
FORT ST.
QUEEN ST.
DUKE ST.
HARBOUR ST.
CHURCH LN
STRAND ST.
ORANGE ST.
HUMBER AVE
McCATTY ST.
BARNETT ST.
GUN POINT WHARF

18K gold items over US$100, even when using a credit card. Rings can not be sized at the shop, but a ring guard can be added. **Ruth Clarage Ltd.** also has a branch of her boutique here.

Many fashion boutiques are found in the shopping centers, and each one is fun to explore. At the airport you'll find a good variety of last minute duty-free shopping.

OCHO RIOS

There are three main shopping areas in Ocho Rios: Ocean Village, Pineapple Place and Coconut Grove. Just east of town is Harmony Hall.

Ocean Village is the largest shopping center in Jamaica. This center enjoys enormous popularity because it is convenient to the cruise ships. This is a full-service shopping center with everything from eateries and a laundry mart to a pharmacy. Especially popular is **Americana & Nancy's** (809-974-2248) which carries an enormous display of duty-free articles and big claims of major discounting—up to 60%. All the big names are on display: Lladro and Hummel figures, Wedgwood, Lalique, Daum, Royal Worcester, Spode, Coalport and Waterford Crystal. Some of the best buys are found on perfumes and 14K gold jewelry. **Ruth Clarage Ltd.** (809-974-2874) also has a shop here. We saw a large display of ceramic jewelry and brilliantly colored matching hand silk prints. You can also purchase Reggae records here that you cannot find at home. They're pricey but worth it if you are a collector.

Pineapple Place Shopping Center is located in the heart of town. This is a delightful group of shops with tropical flowers bordering the walkways. Many boutiques from Kingston and Montego Bay have branch shops here. In-bond shopping is easy here at **Casa de Oro**, especially for perfumes, watches, and fine jewelry.

Ocho Rios Craft Park is a mini version of Kingston Craft Market with open stalls and aggressive vendors eager to sell you a straw hat or handbag. They will also quickly weave a small item while you wait. Hand embroidered goods and woodcarvings are the specialty items. You can watch while someone carves a statue or mask from lignum vitae. Cups whittled from bamboo are also available here.

The **Coconut Grove Shopping Plaza** also has local arts and crafts among its small shops. This plaza is located across from the Plantation Inn. You'll find a wide variety of good quality T-shirts here.

Harmony Hall (809-974-4222) is a restored great house just east of Ocho Rios. Here you will find the works of Jamaican contemporary artists, original jewelry made from natural products, and a gift shop offering a variety of items.

FALMOUTH

On the north coast two miles east of Falmouth is **Caribatik** (809-954-3314). It is only open from November 15 to May 15 for the high tourist season. This is the studio/shop started by Muriel Chandler who introduced batik to Jamaica many years ago. Since her death a few years ago, Caribatik continues to be operated as a gallery, clothing factory, and shop. You will find brightly colored shirts, ties and dresses. Fabric can be purchased by the yard. The colors are lively and bright and very stylish.

PORT ANTONIO

Port Antonio is very quiet. **Sang Hing Giftland** in the City Centre Plaza downtown has a good variety of crystal, jewelry and bone china. East of town is the Trident Villas and Hotel (809-933-3311). It houses a small boutique run by Patricia Wymore Flynn, widow of movie star Errol Flynn.

NEGRIL

Negril, located on the western side of Jamaica, is the newest resort area. Shopping is limited since some exclusive resorts are closed to the general public. However, the local market near the Plaza de Negril has roadside vendors and it's fun to higgle here. One invitation you can easily turn down is to drink Mushroom Tea. After it rains, psylicybin mushrooms are picked, smoked, and brewed in tea. They can produce hallucinations and long term problems. We only found this in Negril.

SPECIAL TIPS FOR CRUISE SHIP PASSENGERS

Being a large island, cruise ships stop at four major ports: Kingston, Port Antonio, Ocho Rios, and Montego Bay. Unless you have a lot of time, it is best to stay near the port. For example, Ocho Rios is a two hour drive from Kingston and Port Antonio is a three hour drive.

In **Kingston** the dock is near the Straw Market. Shopping here alone can take up your entire time in port. It's a vast complex holding a cross section of items from all over the world as well as Jamaica. It is the largest market on the island and very busy. Be sure to bargain on everything.

Port Antonio is very quiet, but it is fun to go to the town market on West Street where you can buy crafts alongside locals who are buying their staples. Errol Flynn's Widow, Patricia Wymore Flynn, owns a very charming shop located in the Trident Villas and Hotel a few miles out of town. Farther east is the 2,000 acre Flynn ranch where tours can be arranged while cruise ships are in port.

Ocho Rios is a shopping haven with the Ocean Village Shopping Center located near the cruise ship docks. Open daily except Sunday from 9am to 5pm, it is a discount and in-bond paradise. **Americana & Nancy's** outlet claims discount items up to 60%.

Montego Bay has convenient shopping for cruise ship passengers. Within walking distance of the pier you will find Montego Freeport and Sam Sharpe's Square where in-bond shopping is plentiful. You can get a cab to **Neville Budhai Paintings**, only five miles west of the city on the road to Negril and see original paintings by Jamaican artists. Remember, you can take in-bond items with you if you show proof that you are visiting. Since cigars and liquor cannot be taken with you, be sure to allow enough time for these purchases to be delivered to your ship. These items are usually available near the dock so that departure times can be met with no problem.

A special **Meet the People** program can be arranged for the entire day or shorter. The Jamaican Tourist Board arranges family visits. You can be with a family for a day and really get an idea of what it is like to be a Jamaican.

ENJOYING YOUR STAY

There's an abundance of things to do in Jamaica. Since the sun is strong, grab that jippa jappa hat you picked up at the craft market and get out to see this beautiful island. All types of water sports are available. You can take boat cruises or train trips to the mountains and even go river rafting. Intra-island air taxis will take you sightseeing from Kingston to Montego Bay for as little as $28. Many visitors come just for the wonderful golf courses. Tennis is also readily available. True to its advertising, Jamaica has horseback riding along the beaches and into the back country. The hills along the north coast and Dunn River Falls are good places for hiking.

THE SITES

Although **Kingston** is the government seat and commerce center for Jamaica, there is still much to explore here. From the West Beach Dock in Kingston, a one-half hour ferry ride will take you to Port Royal. You can also drive on the Palisadoes Road.

Port Royal was the early capital and largest trading center in the New World and visited by several famous pirates such as Blackbeard.

While **Montego Bay** is excellent for shopping, it also is the departure point for the Governor's Coach Tour. Its very popular train ride takes you 40 miles into the picturesque interior. Here you can stop for a picnic lunch by the river. There are also tours of the Great Houses as well as boat cruises.

Falmouth is only 23 from Montego Bay. Arrangements can be made to go rafting the Martha Brae, a one-half day excursion including a dip in the pool and lunch. Two person rafts rent for $30.

Ocho Rios is close to Dunn River Falls, a 600 stair stepped cascade where you can walk up through the water holding hands as water tumbles down to a beautiful white beach where you can swim. A yacht tour is another way to arrive at Dunn River Falls. They are arranged by Water Sports Enterprises (809-974-2185). Ocho Rios also has glass bottom boat tours.

Port Antonio is a small quiet picturesque port with two harbors. It is famous for deep sea fishing. In addition, it became the home of Errol Flynn when he suffered damage to his yacht and had to put in for repairs. At Somerset Falls, in the gorge of the Daniels River, you can take a gondola ride to the hidden falls. A trip to the Blue Lagoon, about five miles east of Port Antonio, is an interesting excursion. It is known as the blue hole for the color of the waters. You can snorkel here or have dinner at the Blue Lagoon Restaurant which is open every day.

Negril, located 50 miles from Montego Bay, is still a quiet sleepy area with a seven mile beach. It is emerging as Jamaica's newest resort. You can still stake out an area and enjoy lots of privacy here. Spot Valley Farm offers a walking tour of a working pineapple and coconut farm.

Water sports are available everywhere, but you may want to try the **Negril Scuba Centre** which is located at Negril Beach Club Hotel (Tel. 809-957-4425 or 800-JAMAICA). Karen McCarthy has a staff of PADI instructors and dive masters who teach courses from beginners to full certification. It has a very informal atmosphere.

ACCOMMODATIONS

A major destination for visitors over the years, Jamaica offers a wide variety of accommodations. From quiet small hotels and secluded garden settings to all inclusive resorts, you'll find accommodations catering to couples only or to families. Take your choice—it is all here.

Kingston:

- **Ivor:** Tel. 809-977-0033 or Fax 809-926-7061. Located just outside of Kingston high on Jack's Hill with a view of the Blue Mountains and Kingston. The three guest rooms are furnished in antiques. Travelers love a home away from home and that is what is provided here. Lunch and dinner are open to the public. Reservations need to be made directly with the hotel. Arrangements can be made to be met at the airport.

- **The Jamaica Pegasus:** Tel. 809-926-3690 or 800-223-5672 from the U.S. Located at 81 Knutsford Blvd, Kingston 5, Jamaica, W.I. This is a convention hotel in the heart of Kingston with English furnishings and a daily 4pm Tea Service. It has a health club, tennis courts, and an outdoor pool. There are 350 rooms and each contains a satellite color TV. There are suites available on several floors with executive services. Expensive to moderate.

Montego Bay:

- **Half Moon Golf, Tennis & Beach Club:** Tel. 809-953-2211 or Fax 809-953-2731. In existence since the 1950's a major renovation took place after Hurricane Gilbert. It is filled with beautiful gardens from end to end against a long white beach. Two hundred guest rooms, suites and villas plantation style create an intimate atmosphere. Suites are roomy and many have their own small pools. The Sugar Mill restaurant is a wonderful spot for a romantic dinner and one of Jamaica's very best restaurants. All facilities are available, golf, tennis, squash, sailing swimming, water sports and some private pools with villas. The suites in the main house are very elegant. Expensive.

- **Round Hill Hotels and Villas:** Tel. 809-952-5150. P.O. Box 64, Montego Bay, Jamaica, W.I. This is where every famous person who visits Jamaica seems to stay. Situated on a 98 acre peninsula, this complex has all facilities (it is preferred that you wear all white on the tennis courts) and lively entertainment in the Disco. Dinner and dancing in the Pineapple House (jacket and tie or even black tie) in winter season. No singles or children in February. Villas are owned and rented in the owner's absence. Round Hill can handle up to 200 guests. There are 27 private villas on the hillside. Pineapple House is open from November 15 to April 15. Offers a private beach and swimming pool. Very expensive.

- **Holiday Inn**: Tel. 809-973-3404 or 800-527-9299 from the U.S. Located at 480 Rose Hall, Montego Bay, Jamaica, W.I. Its 560 rooms were completely refurbished after Hurricane Gilbert. Offers three restaurants, a swimming pool around a bar, four tennis courts, and a disco. Moderate.

Falmouth:

- **Trelawny Beach Club**: Tel. 809-954-2450. Located at Falmouth (about 40 minutes from Montego Bay), P.O. Box 54, Falmouth, Jamaica, W.I. Family oriented, but also includes honeymoon facilities. The total Jamaican flavor is here with local fabrics used for decorating and wicker furniture. Expensive.

Ocho Rios:

- **Charlie's Spa**: Tel. 809-666-3456 or 800-237-3237 from the U.S. Has it's own mineral spring and pool. This is a fully equipped health spa on the same level as a good European health spa. Offers a six-day his and hers program for a sharing experience. Includes a special croquet lawn and all water sports as well as an 18-hole golf course at Upton Country Club. Polo matches can be seen at St. Ann Polo Club. Book through Elegant Resorts of Jamaica. Expensive.

- **Couples**: Tel. 809-974-4271. P.O. Box 330, Ocho Rios, St Ann, Jamaica, W.I. This is an all-inclusive resort where everything is in pairs. All facilities are available for one set price. Each room has a patio on the beach or the sea. The booked stay must be at least eight days. Different entertainment is featured each evening, and there is the terrace. Also offers a private island for nude bathing. Expensive.

Port Antonio:

- **Trident Villas & Hotel**: Tel. 809-993-2602 or Fax 809-993-2590.Very chic with a country house atmosphere including peacocks that roam the property. There are guest rooms in the main building, but the most pleasing are in the villas along the shore with gazebos attached. Tennis, boating, hiking, horseback riding and deep sea fishing. Very exclusive, jacket and tie for dinner. Expensive.

- **Admiralty Club**: Tel. 809-993-2667. Navy Island, P.O. Box 188, Port Antonio, Jamaica, W.I. This is a private island paradise won in a poker game, so say some, by Errol Flynn the movie star. Villas and cottages are off the main clubhouse and the breezes and ceiling fans keep them comfortable. Complete with mosquito netting over the beds. Moderate.

Negril:

- **Negril Gardens**: Tel. 809-957-4408. Westmoreland, Negril, Jamaica, W.I. Located right on the beach with 54 rooms. Moderate to expensive.

- **Hedonism II**: Tel. 809-957-2400. Negril, Jamaica, W.I. This is exclusive and closed to the public. There are 280 rooms and guests must be above 16 years of age. There is a minimum stay of one week. Even though this is not a couples resort, all rooms are doubles. One section of the beach is reserved for optional clothing. There is the full schedule of sports activities and nightly entertainment.

- **Swept Away**: Tel. 809-947-4061 or Fax 809-947-4060. All Inclusive for the fitness set. Clinics, Tournaments, classes and a vegie bar are included in this package. The marvelous sport facilities are the focus, and it has been a big hit since opening in 1990.

RESTAURANTS

Jamaican dishes are a must to try while visiting the island. Pumpkin, red pea or pepperpot soups are a staple and delicious.

"Jerk" a highly seasoned pork or chicken or "spicy patties" that are pastry shells filled with beef or vegetables. Suckling pig is another favorite dish as is Ackee and Saltfish. Of course, wonderful continental cuisine is served in the finest restaurants. World wide tastes are accommodated by the fine chefs in Jamaica. Cost can be very expensive to extremely cheap. Some restaurants will provide transportation—especially in the tourist areas.

Kingston:

Kingston has such a wide variety of excellent international dining spots—Indian, Korean, Cantonese, British, German. Some of our favorites include:

- **Blue Mountain Inn**: Tel. 927-7400. Located outside of town on Newcastle Road but well worth the 25 minute drive. The French Provincial atmosphere and service is equally impressive as is the continental menu. It is rumored to have the finest selections of wines in the country. Once an eighteenth century coffee plantation, it sits 1,000 feet high in the mountains with lush foliage down to the river bank. It is especially elegant on cool nights with the fire glowing from the fireplace. Reservations are a must. Jackets (but not ties) required. Expensive. Accepts major credit cards.

- **Port Royal Grogg Shoppe**: Tel. 926-3580. Located in Devon House at 26 Hope Road. It is delightful eating on the patio. Jerk pork is served here along with over a dozen different rum drinks. Other Jamaican dishes are served at both lunch and dinner. A great place to sample the many flavored ice creams and Blue Mountain Coffee. Moderate.

- **Surry Tavern:** Tel. 926-3690. 81 Knutsford Boulevard. Located just off the lobby of the Pegasus Hotel, this is a typical British pub serving a buffet daily throughout the week. Have a draft of Jamaican Red Stripe beer and listen to a jazz jam session. Inexpensive—closed Saturday and Sunday.

- **Ivor Guest House:** Tel. 977-0033. Hellen Aitken, the owner is the hostess and services mainly Jamaican cuisine in this lovely and elegant restaurant overlooking Kingston's sparkling lights from Jack's Hill (about 20 minutes outside of town).

Montego Bay:

Montego Bay is a resort area offering many dining choices. Jerk pork, cooked shrimp, and other fun foods are sold right on the street. You can dine on a terrace overlooking the water or enjoy an exquisite dinner at an old plantation house. The restaurants we have enjoyed include:

- **Sugar Mill Restaurant:** Tel. 953-2314. One of Jamaica's best restaurants. Located across the road from the Half Moon Club (page 236) and overlooking the golf course, this elegant and romantic restaurant has terrific ambience and serves excellent seafood and steaks. We prefer dining outside. Expensive.

- **Diplomat:** Tel. 952-3353. 9 Queens's Drive. Provides a formal elegant evening in an old mansion with a beautiful view. You can retire to the drawing room with a choice of liqueurs or simply enjoy the beautiful sunset. International cuisine. Open only for dinner but closed on Sundays. Jackets are not required, but preferred. Expensive.

- **Marguerite's by the Sea:** Tel. 952-4777. Gloucester Avenue. Very popular with Jamaicans as well as visitors. The fresh catch of the day along with grilled lobster are both excellent and the setting is romantic. You'll need reservations in winter to get a table. Open for lunch and dinner. Expensive. Major credit cards.

- **The Calabash Restaurant:** Tel. 952-3891. 5 Queens Drive. Offers an excellent Jamaican menu that includes curried goat. Many celebrities have enjoyed the view of the sea from 500 feet above the sea while dining on the restaurant's famous Jamaican Christmas cake that is served year round. Moderate. Major credit cards accepted.

- **Pork Pit:** Located off Gloucester Avenue. Highly recommended for the best jerk pork and ribs in Montego Bay. If you like spicy foods, you'll enjoy this treat. Inexpensive.

Ocho Rios:

In Ocho Rios you can have inexpensive grilled lobster, dine by a waterfall or swing in a chair while sipping a rum.

- **Little Pub Restaurant:** Tel. 974-2324. 59 Main Street. Very tropical with a thatched roof. Serves lobster several different ways. Inexpensive. No credit cards accepted here.

- **Ruins Restaurant at Turtle River**: Tel. 974-2789. Redefines atmosphere when you sit at the base of a cascade of waterfalls amid a garden setting. Serves international dishes. Reservations are a must in winter season. Moderate prices. Major credit cards accepted. Closed Sunday.

- **Almond Tree Restaurant**: Tel. 974-2813. Located in the Hibiscus Lodge Hotel. A highlight of the bar is you can sit in swings. We've returned time and again for drinks. A tree grows through the roof, and you can see the Caribbean from the dining area. The bouillabaisse is recommended because it includes conch. Moderate in price with major credit cards accepted. A popular tourist area, reservations are necessary during the winter season.

Port Antonio:

A very quiet little port, this is the famous home for jerk pork. Other island specialties are easy to find, such as pepperpot soup and even rum raisin ice cream. All hotel restaurants are open to the public.

- **Triden Hotel and Restaurant**: Tel. 993-2602. Route A4, East of Port Antonio. Offers gourmet cuisine served by waiters in tuxedos on antique tables with Port Royal Pewter. Very expensive and dinner reservations are required year round. Men must wear jackets after 7pm.

- **DeMontevin Lodge Restaurant**: Tel. 993-2604. Located at 21 Fort George Street. Serves true Jamaican dishes in a gingerbread setting. The pumpkin and pepperpot soups and main dishes are cooked by Mrs. Mullings. She used to be Errol Flynn's cook and is considered the best by Port Antonio fans. This is more than a reservation—it's an appointment that must be made at least one day in advance.

Negril:

Some all inclusive resorts are closed to the public in Negril. However, you may want to head for the legendary **Rick's Cafe**, located at the end of Lighthouse Road, Tel. 957-4335. A popular gathering spot with a casual crowd, a visit is not complete here without viewing a sunset with a fresh daiquiri in hand. Lobster, red snapper, and grouper are among the dishes served here. Open daily. Accepts major credit cards. **The Hungry Lion** added a juice bar to its already vegetarian dishes. Tel. 957-4886. As more resorts move into this tranquil casual area—so will more eateries.

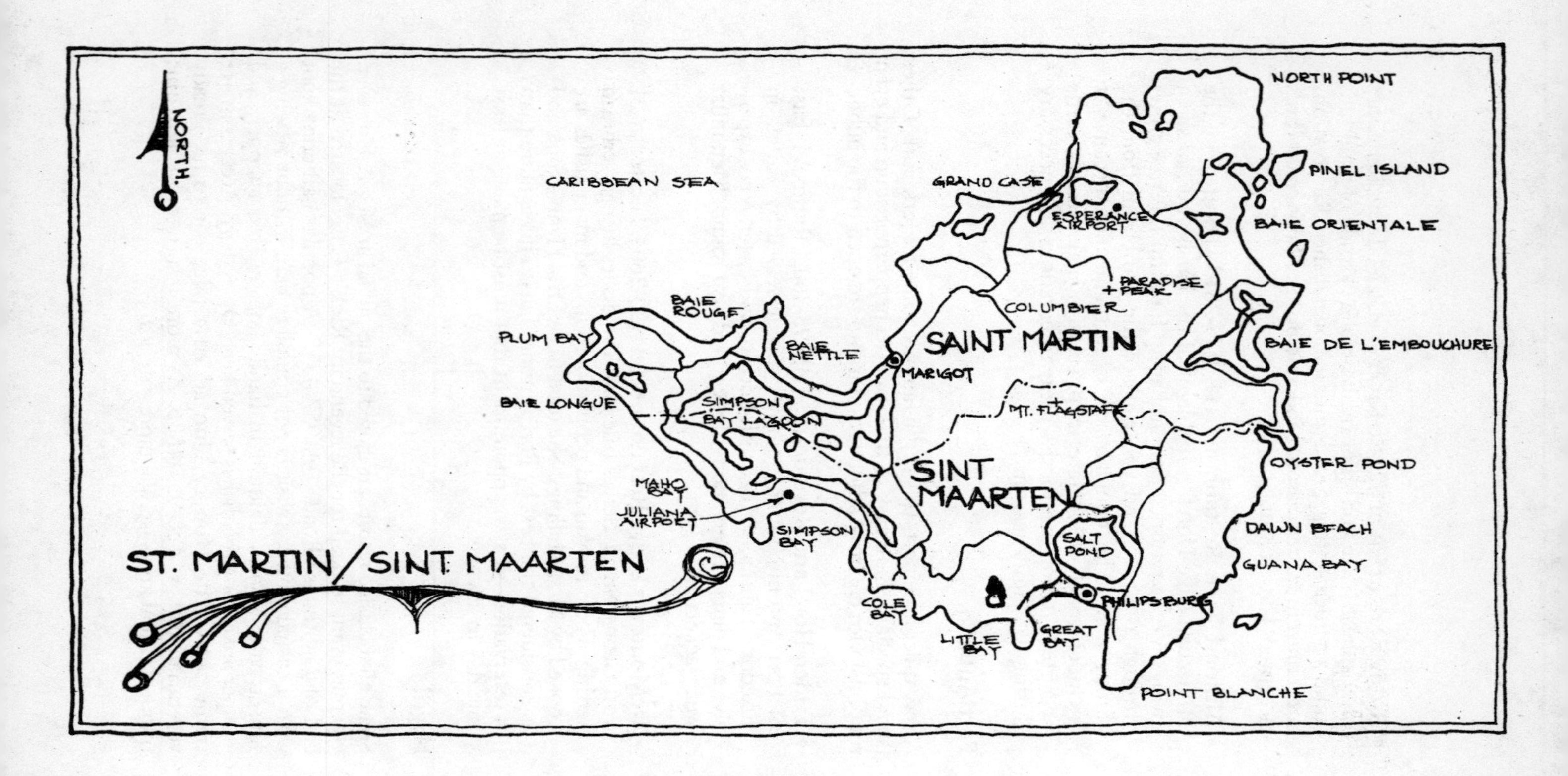
NORTH.
CARIBBEAN SEA
NORTH POINT
PINEL ISLAND
GRAND CASE
ESPERANCE AIRPORT
BAIE ORIENTALE
PARADISE PEAK
COLUMBIER
BAIE ROUGE
PLUM BAY
BAIE NETTLE
SAINT MARTIN
BAIE DE L'EMBOUCHURE
MARIGOT
BAIE LONGUE
SIMPSON BAY LAGOON
MT. FLAGSTAFF
SINT MAARTEN
OYSTER POND
MAHO BAY
JULIANA AIRPORT
SIMPSON BAY
SALT POND
DAWN BEACH
GUANA BAY
ST. MARTIN/SINT. MAARTEN
COLE BAY
PHILIPSBURG
GREAT BAY
LITTLE BAY
POINT BLANCHE

12

St. Martin/ Sint Maarten

Shopping in St. Martin/Sint Maarten is not just a pastime—it's a business. Shared by two separate countries, this small island in the middle of the Caribbean is a shopper's paradise. Indeed, there are few places left in the world where you can get such a fabulous array of goods at such remarkable prices. A duty-free port, the island has no purchase or luxury taxes whatsoever. This means that imported French perfumes, wines, Swiss watches, German and Japanese cameras, fine Italian fashions, and exquisite jewelry are bargains that will delight and amaze you. Although St. Martin/Sint Maarten is a tourist haven for relaxation and casino gambling, one of its major attractions is shopping. In fact, many people living in other parts of the Caribbean make special day trips to St. Martin/Sint Maarten just to shop.

You can expect two different cultures on this tropical island—Dutch and French. The southern Dutch side (Sint Maarten) is where the main airport is located; the French portion (St. Martin) occupies the northeastern side. This is an island with over 30 white sandy beaches, 200 restaurants, and hundreds of shops. The weather is usually in the 80's. Here the term "free port" truly has meaning. Although the goods are certainly not free, they can be purchased for up to 50% less than in the U.S.

or other countries. Free of import taxes, shopkeepers, merchants, and residents can bring into the country any amount of goods duty-free. As a result, goods purchased in St. Martin/Sint Maarten reflect these tax savings.

GETTING TO KNOW YOU

Inhabitants of this small half-Dutch, half-French West Indian island point proudly to more than 300 years of peaceful coexistence. The islanders delight in describing their 37 square mile island as "the smallest bit of real estate in the world shared by two countries," and they are quick to add "and probably the friendliest partnership in the world."

The first visitor to St. Martin/Sint Maarten was Christopher Columbus who sighted the land on November 11, 1493, the Holy Day of St. Martin of Tours. Prior to his arrival, the island was inhabited by both the Caribe and Arawak Indians.

In the 17th century, the French and the Dutch arrived and occasionally fought for the island's territory. They were, however, pushed off the island by the Spaniards. In 1648, the Spaniards finally left St. Martin/Sint Maarten, having found no further use for this island. Soon the Dutch and the French returned. After some armed struggles, both parties sat down and negotiated an agreement called the Mont des Accords. The accord divided the island in half and laid the foundation for present day St. Martin/Sint Maarten. According to legend, a Dutchman and a Frenchman stood back to back and started walking in opposite directions around the shoreline. Where they met, the line was drawn across the island to mark the boundary. In reality, the line was drawn through a mutual accord.

Despite the agreement, turbulence occurred in the area during the next 100 years. The island changed hands many times, from the French to the Dutch and occasionally to the British from Anguilla. This situation became more structured when Philipsburg became the capital of Dutch Sint Maarten in 1763 and Marigot was established as a center for French activity on the island.

During the 17th century, trade in salt, cotton, and tobacco became the main source of income for the settlers. Real affluence reached the island with the advent of sugar plantations which also changed the course of history in the entire Caribbean. Sugar plantations also brought slaves which, in turn, profoundly altered the racial and social structure of the region. A new breed of people came into existence, the Creole.

created their own languages and colorful customs. By mid-19th century, slavery was abolished and the sugar industry came to an end. The island slid into a period of oblivion only to be rediscovered in the 20th Century. Today the great discoverer is called the tourist industry.

On the Dutch half of the island, blue and white Delft china and French porcelain gleam in many shop windows. Food shops are ripe with red and yellow gouda and edam cheeses and aromatic with brie and camembert. Shops selling Dutch beers, liquors, chocolates, brandies, and perfume line the streets of bustling Philipsburg. Several restaurants in Sint Maarten also feature the savory pea soups and sausages served in Holland as well as bouillabaisse and pates, such as those found in the Bistros of Paris and Marseille. You'll also experience the calypso sound and the spicy flavors of the local West Indian culture everywhere. Blending smoothly with the Dutch influences, these elements add a unique international ambiance to Sint Maarten.

On the French side you will find an atmosphere reminiscent of a small city in France or even portions of side streets off the Champs Elysee. Even more surprising might be the sight of a French gendarme cap on the street corner. However, this is all combined with a bustling array of restaurants and shops that are there for one purpose—to delight the tourist and the shopper.

THE BASICS

LOCATION AND GEOGRAPHY

Located near the eastern most portion of the Leeward Islands in the Caribbean chain, St. Martin/Sint Maarten is the smallest plot of land in the world that houses two separate countries. Its 37 square miles encompass a 21 square mile French northern side called St. Martin and a 16 square mile Dutch southern side called Sint Maarten. With more than 30 beaches, the coastline is made up of crescent shaped bays and coves and the interior has rolling hills. Marigot, the French capital, is located between Marigot Bay and Simpson Bay lagoon, a very large body of beautiful blue water. Philipsburg, the Dutch capital, is located on the Great Salt Pond and on Great Bay Harbor. St. Martin is considered part of the French West Indies while Sint Maarten is considered part of the Netherlands's Antilles.

The closest islands to St. Martin/Sint Maarten are Anguilla, which is located nine miles off the coast near Marigot, and Saba and St. Eustatius, which are located to the southwest. The island is approximately 145 miles east of the U.S. Virgin Islands and approximately the same distance from Puerto Rico. Miami, 1,250 miles to the west, is about two and a half to three hours flying time away. The 1,500 mile flight from New York takes about three and one-half hours. The island services many small surrounding islands. Indeed, the Julianna Airport is now the second busiest in the Caribbean, second only to San Juan.

CLIMATE, WHEN TO GO, WHAT TO WEAR

With constant trade winds, the island is sunny and warm throughout the year. The average daytime temperature is 80 degrees fahrenheit. While it occasionally rains from September to November, the showers are brief and very spotty. Since the temperature varies little throughout the year, St. Martin/Sint Maarten is an ideal place to visit at any time.

Daytime dress for both men and women should be casual but conservative. Take clothing made primarily of cotton or no-iron cotton blends. On many tennis courts, white tennis attire is recommended. As in many other islands, wearing swimsuits on the streets and in hotel lobbies and restaurants is improper. Since you will want to enjoy the many beaches, be sure to bring at least one swimsuit and perhaps buy another fashionable one available on either the Dutch or French sides.

While evenings in most hotels and restaurants are informal, men should consider taking a jacket for one of the nicer casinos and plusher hotel restaurants. It's not required, but you may feel more comfortable doing so.

Unlike other islands which primarily offer locally produced fashions, shops in St. Martin/Sint Maarten stock an incredible collection of clothing from around the world. You may find the fashions here irresistible.

GETTING THERE

The island of St. Martin/Sint Maarten is easy to get to by air. American Airlines and ALM fly non-stop from New York with connections from most other cities through San Juan. Continental has recently begun non-stop service from Newark, New Jersey. All flights land at the Julianna Airport, as do most smaller commuter flights from the surrounding islands. Air Guadeloupe flies from San Juan and Guadeloupe; LAIT from St. Thomas/St. Kits and most of the southern Caribbean islands; ALM connects from San Juan, Aruba, Curacao, and Santo Domingo; BWIA flies in from Antigua and Trinidad; and

Windward Island Airways (WINAIR) flies between St. Martin/Sint Maarten and St. Kits, Nevus, St. Thomas, Saba, St. Eustatius, St. Barts and Anguilla. While there is a small airport for private planes and small commuters on the French side of the island near Grande Case, you will find most connections are most convenient at the Julianna Airport.

Numerous cruise ships schedule stops at St. Martin/Sint Maarten where passengers have the opportunity to enjoy the sites and shop the island. Most cruise ships dock off the coast near Philipsburg and then ferry passengers into town by launch. This procedure takes time, and heavy traffic during certain times of the day may limit shopping primarily to Philipsburg. If the seas get rough, this port may be eliminated from the ships itinerary and substituted with another island. A few cruise ships now call at Marigot in French St. Martin because of its improved pier facilities; however, most actually tie up near the Dutch side.

- **This is an island with over 300 white sandy beaches, 200 restaurants, hundreds of shops, and casinos.**
- **Since the temperature varies little throughout the year (averages 80), St. Martin/Sint Maarten is an ideal place to visit at any time.**
- **If you've arranged to rent a car, you will not be able to pick it up at the airport. The agency will deliver it to where you are staying.**
- **Taxis are not metered, but drivers do carry a government issued rate sheet. Ask about the rate before starting out.**
- **While bargaining is not normally done in shops, ask for any discounts. Traveler's checks may result in an additional discount of up to 10%.**

DOCUMENTS

Most visitors enter St. Martin/Sint Maarten at Julianna International Airport on the Dutch side. Dutch Immigration provides clearance for both sides of the island. U.S. citizens or residents can stay up to three months with valid proof of citizenship, a room reservation confirmed in advance, and a round trip airline ticket. Proof of citizenship includes a valid passport or one that has expired within the last five years, an original birth certificate or notarized photocopy, voter registration card, or a green card.

No papers are needed to cross from one side of the island to the other. If you enter the French St. Martin side at the smaller airport near Grand Case, you will need the same proof of citizenship, plus an official I.D. with a photo (if using identification other than a passport) as well as a return ticket. U.S. alien residents need a valid passport, and residents from other countries may be required to obtain a visa. If you plan to arrive on the French side, you should check with the French Consulate in the city of your departure for any specific requirements.

Upon arrival, you must complete an Immigration card. A

copy must be returned to Immigration upon departure. If you fly into another island or arrive by ship, the formalities may be slightly different. For example, we have on many occasions flown from San Juan to Anguilla, where we received an Anguilla Immigration card. When we departed Anguilla for Marigot in St. Martin by motor launch, no one in Anguilla asked for the card. Upon arriving at the water taxi dock near Marigot, no Immigration formalities took place. In fact, the Immigration card we received in Anguilla was accepted by the Dutch Immigration officers when we later departed from Julianna International Airport.

When departing, you must surrender your Immigration card and pay a $5 departure tax for destinations within the Netherlands Anitlles, and $10.00 to all other destinations. This is done quickly.

ARRIVAL AND DEPARTURE

Arrival, especially through Julianna International Airport, is relatively easy. While long lines may develop at the Immigration desks, the officers are very professional and try to get all visitors through as soon as possible. If a large number of flights arrive at the same time, retrieving your bags may take longer than normal since the baggage handling system may become overloaded. But once you receive your bags, you're on your way. Unlike entry in many other countries, clearing Customs in St. Martin/St. Maarten is all but automatic.

You'll find many taxis outside the terminal. If you've arranged to rent an automobile, the car may not be available for you at the airport. The taxis and some rental car companies have an arrangement whereby you must take a taxi from the airport. The car rental agencies will then deliver the car to wherever you are staying. A few will have cars at the airport.

If you arrive through Anguilla, you will clear Immigration and Customs there rather than in Marigot. If you arrive by water taxi at the pier in Marigot, walk down the pier to the first street to find a taxi. If taxis are not lined up here, it won't take long before one comes cruising by. If you arrive at the small airport near Grand Case on the French side, you should have no problem finding a taxi.

CURRENCY, TRAVELER'S CHECKS, CREDIT CARDS

The French St. Martin currency is tied to the U.S. dollar at a rate of about 5.5 French francs to US$1. The Netherlands Antilles florin or guilder, the official currency on the Dutch Sint

Maarten side, is tied to the U.S. dollar at the rate of Fl 1.8 to US$1. U.S. currency is accepted most everywhere on the island as are traveler's checks and most major credit cards. Store prices are normally quoted in U.S. dollars. Bargaining is not normally done in shops on either the French or Dutch sides, but traveler's checks can produce a discount. After determining if there are any discounts available, do not be afraid to ask if there is a further discount if you pay by traveler's checks. Sometimes you will receive an additional 10% discount for paying with U.S. traveler's checks.

Businesses normally do not charge a fee for using a credit card. If you make a substantial purchase, such as jewelry, china, crystal, or a very expensive item of clothing, use your credit card to handle such purchases. We have found that the major credit cards (VISA, Mastercard, American Express, and Diners Club) are accepted by most major hotels, restaurants, shops, and rental car agencies. You may, however, find that some small merchants do not accept credit cards.

TIPPING

Most hotels add a 10% to 15% service charge to all bills. You might consider leaving a small amount for the room maids and also tipping waiters at hotel restaurants slightly more for exceptional service. Most restaurants on the French side will include at least a 10% service charge in the check; however, the Dutch side of the island is less consistent. If you are unclear if a service charge is included in your bill or whether you should tip, always ask so you don't leave a double tip. If paying a restaurant bill by credit card, it is not uncommon for the restaurant to add the service charge in the box marked "Tax." Since there are no taxes on the island, keep in mind that this is actually the service charge or tip being added; don't leave an additional amount unless you wish to do so for extraordinary service.

It's customary to tip taxi drivers in St. Martin/Sint Maarten. Tipping 50 cents to $1 above the fare is sufficient. If you have, however, hired a taxi cab for a tour, a tip of 10% to 15% of the fare is normally expected. Porters and others who help you with your bags should be tipped about one dollar or fifty cents per bag.

LANGUAGE

Although the official language on the French side is French and the official language on the Dutch side is Dutch, English is spoken everywhere. You may occasionally find a small shop, restaurant, or cafe on the French side where the proprietor or waiters cannot or do not want to speak English; however, this is extremely rare.

BUSINESS HOURS

The shops in French St. Martin are normally open from 9am until 12 noon and again from 2pm until 6pm or 7pm, Monday through Friday. In Dutch St. Maarten, stores are open Monday through Friday from 8am until 12 noon and again from 2pm to 6pm. Shops on both sides of the island are normally open Saturday mornings but are generally closed on Sunday. However, when a cruise ship docks near Philipsburg on Sundays, many shops will open for a few hours to accommodate the cruise ship passengers.

Although the normal stated hours for shops include closing at lunch, many shops, especially along Front Street in Philipsburg, are open all day long and do not close for the noon hour.

TRANSPORTATION AND TOURS

Since the island is small, the best way to see it is to rent a car if you are going to be there for more than one day. Most major rental car companies are represented on both the French and the Dutch side of the island, but you should make arrangements prior to your arrival. Several companies rent cars, and arrangements with local firms can be made through your hotel. Most rental cars cost $30 to $50 a day with unlimited mileage. To rent a car, you need a valid U.S. or Canadian driver's license and a major credit card or a cash deposit of between $350 and $600. Driving is on the right side of the road. The main road completely encircles the island making it virtually impossible to get lost. Since there is no formal border between the French and Dutch sides, you can go back and forth with no difficulty.

Taxis on St. Martin/Sint Maarten are not metered. They are available most any time of the day. Drivers carry a standard rate sheet. You should inquire about the rate before embarking on a journey. The rates are determined by the government and are based upon carrying two passengers per trip and calculated by distance. An additional fee of $1 will be added for each additional passenger. Your driver will expect a 10% to 15% tip. Taxi stations are located at Wathey Square on the Dutch side of the island and near the Tourist Information Bureau on the French side.

Public buses run regularly between the island's two capital

cities for a very modest fee. Other buses travel hourly between Mullet Bay, Simpson Bay, Cole Bay, and Grande Case.

Ferries or water taxis are available from Philipsburg and leave about every 30 minutes. The trip to Anguilla, which only takes a few minutes, leaves from the pier at Marigot and departs normally on the hour. Since more than one company operates these water taxi services, there may be a water taxi available more frequently than the stated hourly schedule.

If you rent a car, keep in mind that parking in town can be a problem. During the day, traffic on Front Street and Back Street in Philipsburg is literally at a standstill, and there are seldom parking spots within blocks of most of the stores. The same goes for downtown Marigot—parking is virtually impossible. The most expedient way to get around is by taxi. But in order to keep the charges down, make arrangements to be picked up at specific times. For example, on our last trip, we left our bags at our hotel in Philipsburg and took a taxi to Marigot. Upon leaving our driver, we indicated that we would need to return to Philipsburg later in the day and made arrangements to be picked up at a particular corner at a particular time. With these arrangements you do not pay for the taxi cab to wait. We've done this on several occasions and have never been disappointed—the driver always returns as scheduled.

ACCOMMODATIONS

Since one of the main industries on St. Martin/Sint Maarten is tourism, you will find accommodations available in every shape, size, and expense category. From the exquisite accommodations of L'Habitation and Le Belle Creole in Marigot to very small hotels located above the shops on Front Street in Philipsburg, there is normally a room available.

If you are vacationing on the island and combining some fun in the sun with your shopping adventures, we highly recommend one of the larger resort areas near Simpson Bay or Mullet Bay. If, however, your main objective is to shop, some hotels in downtown Marigot, such as La Residence, offer the best of both worlds. You will stay in an exquisite small hotel, but you will be literally steps away from most shops and restaurants. On the Dutch side in Philipsburg, hotels such as the Sint Maarten Beach Club and the Holland House are located right in the middle of the shopping area. If your main objective is to shop, stay at a hotel near the main shopping areas.

RESOURCES

Some of the most helpful up-to-date information on St. Martin/Sint Maarten is available upon arrival. The small newspaper ***Sint Maarten Holiday***, along with two small books entitled ***Sint Maarten Nights*** and ***Focus on Sint Maarten and St. Martin***, are available free of charge at the airport and most hotels. They provide the latest information on shops and activities as well as contain maps of both Philipsburg and Marigot. The Sint Maarten Tourist Bureau (Tel. 22337), located at the Little Pier near where cruise ship passengers arrive, is open most weekdays from 8am to 5pm. The tourist office on the French side is located near the harbor (Tel. 87.53.26). It is usually open from 8:30am to 5:30pm weekdays.

The Dutch Sint Maarten Tourist Office provides the following free information: ***St. Maarten Holiday; St. Maarten Nights***; Sint Maarten hotel, villa, and guesthouse rates and descriptions; hotel brochures; package information; and specialized information on water sports, honeymoons, rental cars, and restaurants. For additional information, contact: Sint Maarten Tourist Office, 275 Seventh Ave., New York, NY 10001-6788, Tel. 212-989-0000; in Canada, 243 Ellerslie Ave., Willowdale, Ontario M2N 1Y5, Tel. 416-223-3501.

The French West Indies Tourist Board distributes hotel rate sheets, the ***French West Indies Travel and Sports Guide***, and other tour information. For information on the French side, write to the French West Indies Tourist Board, 610 Fifth Ave., New York, NY 10020, Tel. 212-757-1125, or contact them at one of the following addresses:

9401 Wilshire Blvd., Beverly Hills, CA 90212
Tel. 213-271-6665

645 N. Michigan Ave., Suite 430, Chicago, IL 60611
Tel. 312-337-6301

2050 Stemmons Fwy., Dallas, TX 75258
Tel. 214-742-7011

1 Hallidie Plaza, Suite 250, San Francisco, CA 94102
Tel. 415-986-4161

1981 Ave. McGill College, Suite 490, Montreal, Quebec
H3A 2W9, Tel. 514-288-4264

1 Dundas St.W., Suite 240, Toronto, Ontario M5G 1Z3
Tel. 416-593-4717

DUTY-FREE SHOPPING

Shopping here is not just a pastime—it's a major activity on the island. Just about anything imaginable can be purchased in the shops. Very demanding and price conscious, many shoppers return here because of the wide variety of high-quality merchandise available at low prices. Many goods sold in St. Martin/Sint Maarten are 50% below U.S. prices, because they are both duty-free and tax-free.

The main shopping area on the Dutch Sint Maarten side is in Philipsburg, along both Front Street and Back Street. The main commercial streets in St. Martin are in Marigot. They are Rue de la Republique and Rue de le Liberte and are criss-crossed by many side streets and arcades. Stores on both sides of the island are filled with the latest in high fashion clothing from France and Italy, plus electronic equipment, jewelry, leather goods, fine crystal, linens, and straw goods as well as liquor and cigarettes.

The island has hundreds of shops that accept U.S. currency or credit cards. The shop known for the largest diamond inventory in the Caribbean is **The Gold Mine**, and it is the sole agent for Carrera y Carrera and Vacheron Constatin watches. For all around quality shopping, one of the best shops is **La Romana**. This is the island's equivalent to Bloomingdales or Neiman Marcus. La Romana features designers such as Armani, Botaga, Veneta, Fendi, Ferre, Krizia, Trasarde, Valentino, and Versace. On the French side, St. Martin's boutiques include **Benetton, Boutique Soyna Rykiel, Stephanie Kelian**, and **Rodier.Little Switzerland** is highly regarded for china, crystal, jewelry, and **Oro de Sol** is known for such brand watches as Ebel and Cartier.

The arcades and shopping centers on the island are lined with small, quaint, and stylish shops. Many are set in small courtyards and covered by small canopies and shutters that frame the entrance ways.

Bargaining, or bartering, is not part of the island shopping culture on either the Dutch or French sides. Here you find high quality merchandise at deep discounted prices. While you need not waste time bargaining, you should inquire about discounts for traveler's checks. However, some bargaining is possible on The Little Pier in Philipsburg amongst vendors who sell hand-made wooden and straw items.

Some shops not only have several stores, but each outlet may have a specialty. One of the best examples is **La Romana**. While they have many shops, all are not alike. All do carry a full range of a particular kind of merchandise, but at one outlet you may find only jewelry, at another only leather goods, and at still another only fashions. Keep this in mind when rushing to make last minute purchases before the launch leaves for your cruise ship or on your way to the airport.

WHAT TO BUY

JEWELRY AND WATCHES

Many unique gems and gold designs can be found in the exquisite jewelry shops on both the Dutch and French sides. Prices many be 30% below what you pay back home. Much of the gold jewelry is sold by weight, except for ornately designed necklaces and bracelets containing diamonds or other precious stones. The best sales seem to take place during the summer months when 50% discounts are offered by many shops along Front Street in Philipsburg.

Superb watches, such as those made by Chopard, Rolex, Cartier, Baume et Mercier, Audemars-Piqet, Bertolucci, Ebel, Heur, Jean d'Eve, Rady, Raymond Weil, Vacheron et Constantin, Patek Philippe, Piaget, Corum and Omega, are available at the larger jewelry stores. Prices on some watches may not be as low as prices you might find elsewhere, including the U.S. However, prices on very expensive watches—those in the $1,000 plus range—may be 50% less than U.S. prices.

You will find the best selection of jewelry and gold at the better known shops such as **Oro de Sol**, which is located on Rue de la Republique in Marigot near the waterfront, and at the Piazza Cupecoy Casino; **Little Switzerland** on Front Street in Philipsburg and in Marigot; **La Romana** and the **New Amsterdam Store** on Front Street; and the **Gold Mine**—considered by some shoppers to be one of the most distinctive jewelers in the world. These shops offer some of the highest quality jewelry and gold available anywhere in the Caribbean. While they do not bargain, you can rest assured you are getting the best for your money.

For a wider selection of fine 14K jewelry, try **Caribbean Gems** (St. Maarten Beach Club on Front Street) and **The Gold Mine** (Front Street). While these are two of the best, you'll also find numerous other shops offering similar jewelry.

H. Stern Jewelers, Columbia Emeralds, Diamond Mine,

Caribbean Gems and **Gold Mine** are also excellent sources for diamonds, emeralds, rubies, sapphires, aquamarine, pearls, amethysts, topaz, opal, and onyx in all shapes and sizes. Keep in mind that unset stones may be taken into the U.S. duty-free despite their value.

Watches are available at most of the finer shops such as **Little Switzerland**, **Oro de Sol**, **Gold Mine**, and **New Amsterdam**. These shops carry top of the line brands and designs. If you are interested in the less expensive brands, many shops such as **Caribbean Gems**, and most shops carrying cameras and electronic items have a wide selection. Remember to do comparison shopping on the less expensive watches since prices here may be the same as back home.

CRYSTAL AND CHINA

Names such as Royal Doulton, Royal Copenhagen, Rosenthal Studio Line, Aynsley, Hummel, Lladro, Baccarat, Val St. Lambert, Waterford, Lalique, and Daum can be found in both Marigot and Philipsburg at prices 30% to 40% below U.S. prices. For a complete line of such items, be sure to visit **Little Europe** and **Little Switzerland** on Front Street in Philipsburg and **Oro de Sol** in Marigot.

Even after paying U.S. duties, you can still save 20% to 30% on crystal and china purchases. Since many pieces are one of a kind, consider paying by credit card and having the items shipped. Should items get broken, your credit card company may help you recover your expense. Having a shop ship your purchases is especially convenient if you are on a cruise ship. Cabin space is often limited and you have little control over luggage handling once the ship returns to home port. If you plan to carry any breakables with you, ask the shop clerk to pack your purchases well.

PERFUMES AND COSMETICS

Excellent prices on perfumes and cosmetics attract many shoppers to the island. At **Lipstick** on Rue de la Republique in Marigot, you will find good buys on fragrances from Fendi, Liz Claiborne, Alfred Sung, Eternity, Deneuve, and Anne Klein for women; and Francesco Smalto, Polo, Xeryus, and Giorgio for men. In addition, you will be able to purchase cosmetics and skin treatments from Clarins, Montana, Elizabeth Arden, Christian Dior, Lancome and Guerlain at savings ranging from 25% to 40% below U.S. prices. You will also find a complete selection of exclusive perfumes and fragrances from houses such as Halston, Paloma Picasso, and Maxim's at **d'Orsy's** on Marina la Royale in Marigot and at d'Orsy's two other locations on Front Street in Philipsburg. Although shops on the French side may have a better selection of one particular name than shops on the Dutch side, shops like **Penha** (near The Little Pier on Front Street and at the Royal Palm Plaza) and **The Yellow House** (just off Front Street to the left of the Post Office) also carry a complete line. In fact, based on our comparison shopping of the same products in both Marigot and Philipsburg, we found prices on the Dutch side to be slightly lower on some products. This is not true across the whole perfume and cosmetic line and thus you cannot go wrong shopping for these products in either place. But, if you find yourself only able to shop in Philipsburg, you will still be able to get the French product lines and at excellent prices.

LINENS

Another very good buy in St. Martin/Sint Maarten is linens. You'll find exquisite bath sheets, tablecloths, place settings, and other similar items. Frequently advertised sales offer 50% savings on linens. Look for sales at many shops along Front Street in Philipsburg, such as **Caribbean Palm** and **New Amsterdam**. On the French side in Marigot, you'll find excellent linens at good prices in many shops. Some of the best are found at **Oro de Sol** near the harbor and **Primavera** on Rue General de Gaulle.

Some of the best buys are found at the smaller shops that line Front Street. Their frequent sales can save you 40% to 50% over U.S. prices any time of the year.

FASHIONS AND LEATHER

One of the major reasons many people come to the island to shop is to take advantage of the latest imported fashions from France and Italy at savings of 40% to 50% over U.S. or European prices.

La Romana's outlet at the Royal Palm Plaza on Front Street in Philipsburg, as well as their shop on Rue de la Republique in Marigot, is one of the best boutiques on the island. They carry an excellent selection of items from Fendi, Giorgio Armani, Bottage Veneta, Versace, and Gianfranco Ferre.

For a complete sampling of French designer and chic casual clothes, try the many small boutiques near the Port la Royale in Marigot. Shops such as **Havane** at Port la Royale specialize in exclusive lines of both high fashion and sports designs for both men and women. You will find another large number of boutiques in the Galerie Perigourdine, a shopping complex located across from the Post Office in Marigot.

You will also find some excellent high fashion items in shops outside downtown Philipsburg and Marigot. European styles by Mistero, Pancaldi and Alma; sportswear from New Man, Valantino, Fila, Spazio, and Naf-Naf; and swimwear by La Peria and Anna Club can be found at many larger resorts. The **Aquarius (Alma) Boutique** at the Mullet Bay Beach Resort, for example, has an excellent selection of fashions and accessories. If you're staying are at a resort and don't have time to go shopping in town, you can still take advantage of duty-free prices and shop for bargains. While prices are higher at resort shops than at shops in Marigot or Philipsburg, they're still good buys compared to prices back home.

Beachwear fashions are everywhere. Specialty shops such as **Sandrine Boutique** on Rue de la Liberte in Galerie Perigourdine carry an exclusive line. **New Amsterdam** in Philipsburg probably has the largest selection anywhere.

Better known clothing lines such as **Benetton**, with its internationally known all natural fiber Italian sportswear, are well represented here. Their shops are found in Philipsburg and the Maho Beach Hotel Shopping Center.

Philipsburg is an excellent place to purchase fine Italian-crafted leather items such as belts, shoes and handbags. One of the largest selections is found at **Maximoflorence** in the Promenade Arcade. The **La Romana** outlet on Front Street also carries a complete line, including leather desk accessories. Leather prices at these and other smaller shops are some of the best you will find anywhere. Expect to save up to 40% over U.S. prices on such leather purchases.

Island Crafts and Fashions

Unique Caribbean crafts and fashions are available in many shops on the island. **Pierre Lapin** in Grand Case on the French side carries an excellent line of fashions and silk-screened fabrics from artists who reside all over the Caribbean. A favorite shop for many visitors and residents is the **Shipwreck Shop** on Front Street in Philipsburg. Here you can find the full line of Lord & Hunter spices, a Caribbean favorite. At **Caribelle Batik** look for handmade jewelry, hammocks, plates, bowls, basket-ware, pareos, T-shirts, and many other items. The **Shipwreck Shop** also has outlets at the Mullet Bay Beach Resort, Great Bay Beach Hotel, Divi Little Bay Hotel, and the Juliana Airport.

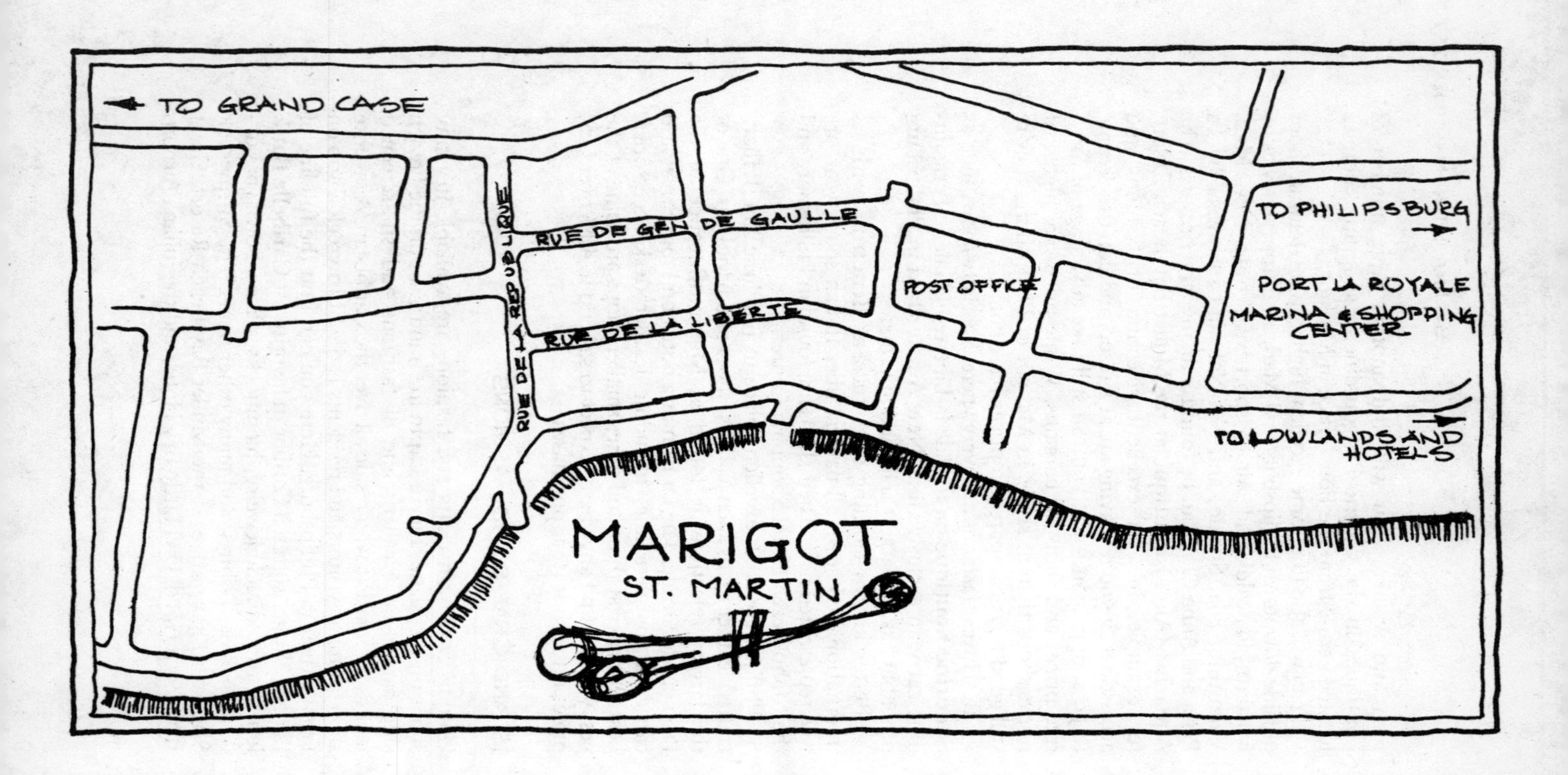
TO GRAND CASE
TO PHILIPSBURG
PORT LA ROYALE
MARINA & SHOPPING CENTER
TO LOWLANDS AND HOTELS
RUE DE GEN DE GAULLE
POST OFFICE
RUE DE LA LIBERTE
RUE DE LA REPUBLIQUE
MARIGOT
ST. MARTIN

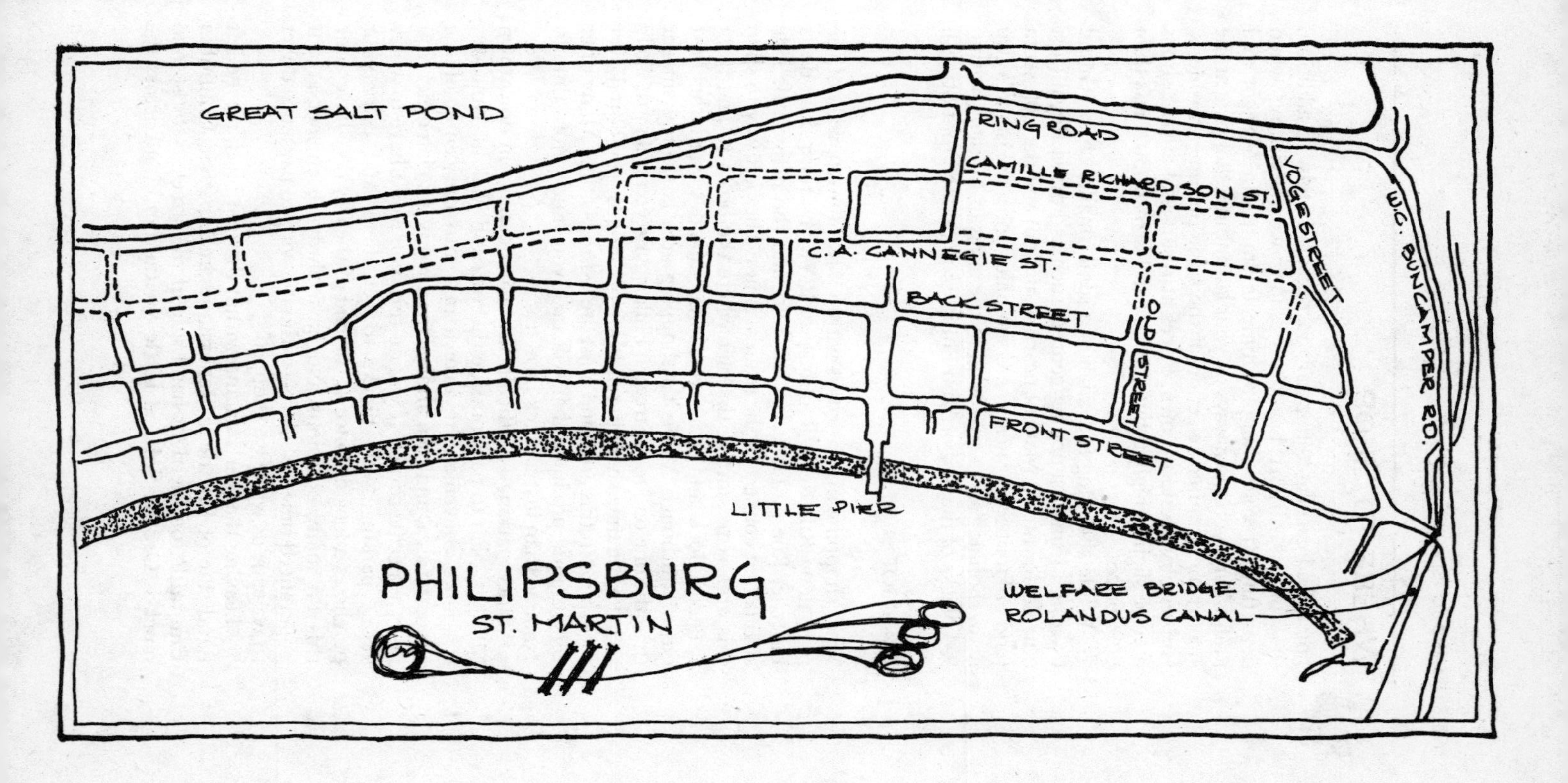
GREAT SALT POND
RING ROAD
CAMILLE RICHARDSON ST.
VOGESTREET
W.C. BUNCAMPER RD.
C.A. CANNEGIE ST.
BACK STREET
OLD STREET
FRONT STREET
LITTLE PIER
WELFARE BRIDGE
ROLANDUS CANAL
PHILIPSBURG
ST. MARTIN

WHERE TO SHOP

You'll find excellent shops at most resort hotels. In addition, the Juliana Airport has many shops worth visiting when departing. If your shopping time is limited in Marigot and Philipsburg, you can always do your last minute shopping at the airport for a limited selection of the same perfumes, fashions, and jewelry found in town. Prices at resort and airport shops may be slightly higher, but they are still 20% to 30% less than U.S. prices.

While shopping is available in some smaller cities (Grand Case) and small shopping centers such as Port la Royal (just outside downtown Marigot near the marina) and the Colisseum (end of Front Street near the Great Salt Pond), the island's two main shopping areas are found in the cities of Marigot (within 3-4 blocks of the harbor) and Philipsburg (along Front Street).

MARIGOT

Most shopping in Marigot is within a five minute walk of the pier along Rue de la Republique, R.V. Mauresse, Rue de la Libertie, Rue de General DeGaulle, and the many little side streets that connect to the main avenues. The best way to shop this area is to start at the pier where the boats to and from Anguilla dock and work your way inland toward the Post Office. Although Marigot's shopping area is slightly smaller than the one on Front Street in Philipsburg, you will most likely spend more time shopping in Marigot. Indeed, you'll find over 100 shops in this area, and most are worth visiting. Many offer very unique products that will take you much more time to examine than just a quick browse.

Since parking is difficult, if not impossible, in downtown Marigot, plan to park outside the area and walk in. However, it's more convenient to take a taxi into the center of the shopping area, and then arrange for the driver to later pick you up at a specific corner. If you do this, you won't have to worry about parking, walk blocks to get there, and carry your purchases a long distance at the end of the day. We have done this on many occasions and have always been met at our prearranged time and place—without having to pay a taxi driver to wait for us while we shopped.

Leaving the pier area and within the first block on the left hand side of Rue de la Republique are **Lipstick**, **Columbia Emeralds**; on the right hand side of the street in the second block is **Oro de Sol** and **Little Switzerland**; and across the street is **La Romana Jewelers**. Virtually everything you could dream of in the way of gold jewelry, watches, gems, and perfumes are found here at excellent prices.

Both Rue de la Liberte and Rue de General DeGaulle intersect with Rue de la Republique and run parallel with each other for the next four blocks. Here you will find numerous boutiques carrying European fashions, but with special emphasis on Parisian fashions. Two blocks off Rue de la Republique, across from the Post Office on Rue de la Liberte, is Gallerie Perigourdine. This is where you will find many fine boutiques for men and women, such as **Sandrine Boutique**.

PHILIPSBURG

Some of the Caribbean's best shopping is found on both sides of one street—Front Street—in downtown Philipsburg. The best way to shop this area is to start from The Little Pier; turn left onto Front Street and then walk down the street closest to the water for about four blocks; next, cross over and come back on the other side, continue beyond where you started for about four blocks, cross over, and come back to The Little Pier. If you follow this plan, beginning at Front Street after leaving the pier and with Burger King on your right, you will find the following shops:

- **The St. Maarten Tourist Office:** at the corner and the source of the weekly guide books and other information on hotels, restaurants, and sightseeing.
- **The Cellar:** excellent buys in fine 14K and 18K jewelry, perfumes, liquor, linens, and souvenirs.
- **Diamond Mine:** has everything that The Cellar carries.
- **Lil's Shoppe:** ladies fashions, swimwear, perfumes and linens.
- **Mulders Jewelers:** exclusive jewelry of every design.
- **Sonovision:** electronics, cameras and gifts.
- **Colombian Emeralds:** the largest emerald specialists in the Caribbean.
- **The Jewel Box:** a wide variety of jewelry.

- **La Romana Jewelers:** one of the many La Romana shops on the island, this one specializing in jewelry.
- **Rams:** cameras, gift, and electronics.
- **The Windmill:** porcelains, crystal, and Delft china.
- **Ramchand's:** electronics, cameras, and gifts.
- **Gucci:** all the finest Gucci items.
- **Zhaveri Jewelers:** exclusive jewelry.

At this point you need to continue on down Front Street until you see the sign for The Red Snapper Restaurant, cross the street and head back the other side toward The Little Pier. Here you will find:

- **Arts & Gems:** all kinds of gift and jewelry items.
- **Leda of Venice:** some of the finest in Italian fashions.

After passing along a block or two of very small shops, houses, and a few small restaurants, you'll come to:

- **La Romana:** international boutique items.
- **Cards & Such:** cards, jewelry, and gifts.
- **Ashoka:** electronics, cameras, and gifts.
- **Little Europe:** a wide variety of jewelry and gifts.
- **Taj Mahal:** cameras, linens, and gifts.
- **Boolchands:** cameras, linens and gifts.
- **H. Stern Jewelers:** a wide array of exquisite and designer jewelry. One of the finest jewelers in the Caribbean, if not the world.
- **New Amsterdam Store:** linens, embroidery, jewelry, and gifts.

At this point you are across the street from The Little Pier. Continuing down the street, you will find:

- **Treasure Trove**: jewelry, watches, and gifts.
- **Little Switzerland**: one of the premier jewelers in the Caribbean. Also carries exquisite china and crystal.
- **Kohinoor**: cameras, linens, and gifts.
- **Benetton**: colorful Italian sportswear.
- **Batik Caribe**: very exquisite batik.
- **Maximoflorence**: excellent selection of fine Italian leather goods.
- **Deviation**: latest fashions and excellent prices.
- **Shipwreck Shop**: one of the most popular shops on the island for a wide variety of island crafts, books, magazines, and batik.
- **Caribbean Gems**: excellent source for 14K and 18K gold, watches, shell, and coral items.
- **Gold Mine**: one, if not the best selection of diamonds in the world, exquisite watches, fine 14K and 18K gold, gold chains by the inch, emeralds, and other gems.
- **Olde Street Mall**: a small side street with about 15 excellent shops.

As you exit the Olde Street Mall, cross Front Street and head for The Little Pier. As soon as you cross the street, you will see:

- **Desmo**: fine Italian leather goods.
- **Shopper's Paradise**: an excellent shop for good buys on T-shirts, 14K jewelry, and inexpensive watches.
- **Solid Gold**: exquisite jewelry and watches.
- **Optique Caribe**: wide variety of optical items. Excellent collection of sunglasses and other eyewear.
- **Roy's Jewelers**: exquisite jewelry and watches.

- **Penha**: one of the best choices for perfumes and cosmetics. Excellent prices.

At this point you are back at the Burger King at The Little Pier. On the pier itself you will find a wide variety of handmade wooden and straw items. This is the one place on the island where you can try your bargaining skills. You should not expect to find high quality goods but you'll find plenty of souvenir wooden bowls, vases, and straw hats.

Given the wide variety of quality products available in Philipsburg and Marigot, it's safe to say that if you cannot find it here, it simply does not exist in the Caribbean. Here you will experience the ultimate shoppers' paradise—quality items at the lowest prices. You'll also learn that while both St. Martin and Sint Maarten offer some of the most beautiful scenery in the Caribbean, its main attraction for many people is the shopping.

SPECIAL TIPS FOR CRUISE SHIP PASSENGERS

Most cruise ship passengers arrive in St. Martin/Sint Maarten by small launch. If you have a least a day, you can shop in both Philipsburg and Marigot. It takes about 20-30 minutes to get between the two cities by taxi, depending on the traffic. However, at times Philipsburg has tremendous traffic jams which can substantially delay your journey to this city. If you have less than a day, pick the city closest to your ship, either Phillipsburg or Marigot, and spend most of your time shopping rather than fighting the traffic. Don't worry about getting a better deal in the other city since duty-free prices are relatively uniform throughout the island.

If you have only an hour or so in Marigot, concentrate on the shops located within the first two blocks from the pier on Rue de la Republique. You'll have time to visit **Lipstick**, **La Romana**, **Columbian Emeralds**, and **Oro de Sol**. Not only will you be able to see the best merchandise the Caribbean has to offer, you might also meet someone who has flown all the way from the U.S. just to shop here.

If you have only an hour or two in Philipsburg, you will be able to visit five or six excellent shops just to the left of The Little Pier, including two **La Romana** outlets—one for jewelry and the other for fashions. To the right of The Little Pier, you can quickly walk to **Little Europe**, **Little Switzerland**, **Caribbean Gems**, **Gold Mine**, and **Penha**. Again, you will experience some of the best quality shopping in the Caribbean.

ENJOYING YOUR STAY

THE SITES

One of the best ways to see the entire island is to rent a car. You can spend an afternoon driving to one of the 30 plus beaches or visiting delightful smaller cities such as Grand Case. In addition, you might want to make a trip to nearby Anguilla. You can get a water taxi at the pier in Marigot and be in Anguilla within 20 minutes; or Tyden Air and LIAT have scheduled flights from Sint Maarten's Juliana Airport.

SIDE TRIP TO ANGUILLA

Our personal favorite island in the entire Caribbean, Anguilla has long, uncrowded beautiful beaches; excellent restaurants such as Blanchard's, KoalKeel, Le Fish Trap, Riviera, and the Cinnamon Reef Palm Court; exquisite luxury resorts such as the Cinnamon Reef Beach Club, Cap Juluca, Coccoloba Plantation, Cavecastle, and the Malliouhana; and a very relaxed atmosphere found in few other places. Try to go on Sunday. Have the taxi driver take you from the pier at Blowing Point to Johnno's Beach Bar at Sandy Ground for lunch. Just about everyone on the island seems to end up here sometime on the weekend, but Sunday lunch is the best time to meet many of the locals. Many people also sail over from St. Martin or Sint Maarten just for the day. You may even meet some people like us who stop by Johnno's for lunch on our way to St. Martin/Sint Maarten from Washington, DC!

Anguilla is the perfect Caribbean island for travelers looking for endless miles of untouched white sand beaches, and a quiet, low-key ambiance free of casinos, high-rise buildings and heavy traffic. It is an independent nation that withdrew from a long association with St. Kitts and Nevis in the late 1960's to become a British dependent territory. English is the language of the island, and the Eastern Caribbean dollar the official currency. The US dollar is accepted everywhere on Anguilla, so be sure to ask in which currency the price is stated (the exchange rate is about 2.70 EC to $1.00 US).

Although some of the more popular restaurants are listed above, most all the resort hotels have excellent dining. The Cinnamon Reef's Palm Court is one the best restaurants in all the Caribbean, and is alone worth the boat trip from Marigot.

Boat racing is a local past time, with highlight being the August Carnival. The unique sail boats can be seen all year, but are displayed in profusion during the first week in August.

If you have the time to spend a day on this 16 by 3 mile island, one of the best ways to get around is to rent a car. Conner's Car Rental (Tel. 6433) has the largest selection available. Visitors must obtain an Anguillian driver's license at the time of rental, driving is on the left, and the speed limit (usually 30 miles per hour) is strictly enforced.

In addition to the beauty found at the beaches, you must take the time to visit some of the luxurious resorts on the island. Cap Juluca, Malliouhana and Covecastles are not to be missed. You may find the roads leading to them not well marked, since one of the drawing features for the movie stars, etc, who have found Aguilla, is the privacy that the island offers.

The Anguillians are very conservative, and this is reflected in their mode of dress when appearing in public. Swin-wear is not suitable for wearing in the shopping or commercial areas.

With some the best beaches in the world, exquisite dining and unbelievable resorts, the only problem we have ever experienced in Anguilla is having to leave.

ACCOMMODATIONS

Since St. Martin/Sint Maarten is such a popular island, you will find accommodations available in virtually every price range and size.

St. Martin:

- **Mont Vernon**: Tel. 599-87-42-00. One of our favorites for views and location. Overlooks Orient Bay, with restaurant and free minibus service to Marigot, Philipsburg and casinos. Wonderful views and a great place to relax. Beautiful beach with watersports. Moderate.

- **Hotel La Samanna:** Tel. 590-87-51-22. A luxury hotel with a very intimate setting. It has a beach over a mile long. Expensive.

- **La Belle Creole**: Tel. 590-87-58-66. Just outside Marigot not far from the airport. Very large rooms, suites, and a gourmet restaurant. Very expensive.

- **Le Meridian L'Habitation:** Tel. 590-87-57-91. A resort located about 10 miles outside Marigot. Many rooms have kitchenettes. Expensive.

- **La Residence:** Tel. 409-87-80-37. Rue de la General de Gaulle in the middle of downtown Marigot. A small hotel in the middle of the shopping district. Very comfortable and close to everything. Moderate.

Sint Maarten:

- **Mullet Bay Resort & Casino:** Tel. 509-5-42801. One of our long-time favorites. Near the airport and almost a city in itself. Offers a large variety of rooms, includes suites, bungalows, and condos. Excellent restaurants. Offers a full sports program, including golf course. Recently renovated. A choice location. Expensive.

- **Maho Beach Hotel & Casino:** Tel. 509-5-42388. On Maho Bay about one-half mile from the airport. Expensive.

- **Great Bay Beach Hotel & Casino:** Tel. 509-5-22446. On Front Street in downtown Philipsburg. Shopping and many restaurants are within easy walking distance. Expensive.

- **Sint Maarten Beach Club Hotel & Casino** (Tel. 509-5-23434) and **Holland House** (Tel. 509-5 22572): Located in the middle of the shopping area on Front Street and near many good restaurants. Moderate.

- **Pasanggrahan Royal Inn:** Tel. 599-5-23588. Formerly the Governor's home, a VIP guesthouse and Royal residence, it is an authentic colonial style inn. Located on Front Street in Philipsburg within blocks of shopping and many restaurants. The restaurant and the Inn is one of the best in Philipsburg. Moderate.

RESTAURANTS

Since St. Martin/Sint Maarten has over 200 restaurants, you will find one within steps of wherever you may be. These are a few of our favorites:

St. Martin:

Le Nadaillac: Tel. 87-53-77. Gallerie Perigourdine, Rue de la Liberte in Marigot. Expensive, but excellent restaurant, with a truly French flavor.

- **La Vie en Rose:** Tel. 87-54-42. Boulevard France, Marigot. A French gourmet restaurant located on the second floor overlooking the harbor. Expensive.

- **La Maison sur le Port:** Tel. 87-56-38. Located at the harborfront in Marigot. Moderate priced excellent restaurant for lunch or dinner.

- **Captain Oliver Restaurant:** Tel. 87-30-00. Located in the Hotel Captain Oliver at Oyster Pond. Excellent for seafood. Moderate.

Grand Case:

- **L'Esacpe:** Tel. 87-75-04. 94, Boulevard de Grand Case. Authentic Creole house on a terrace by the sea.

- **Fish Pot:** Tel. 87-50-88. 82, Boulevard de Grand Case. Seafood restaurant with a beautiful view of the Bay.

- **Heva:** Tel. 87-56-85. 163, Boulevard de Grand Case. Located in a completely restored Creole mansion. One of the best restaurants on the island.

- **Chez Martine:** Tel. 87-51-59. 140, Boulevard de Grand Case. Friendly Creole beach house overlooking the Bay.

- **Il Nettuno:** Tel. 87-77-38. 70, Boulevard de Grand Case. Italian cuisine with homemade pasta and seafood.

- **Le Tastevin:** Tel. 87 55-45. 86, Boulevard de Grand Case. Beautiful terrace restaurant overlooking the water.

Sint Maarten:

- **L'Escargot:** Tel. 22483. 84 Front Street, Philipsburg. Good, moderate French restaurant.

- **The Red Snapper:** Tel. 23834. 93 Front Street, opposite the Caribbean Hotel in Philipsburg. Excellent ala carte menu featuring local seafood.

- **West Indian Tavern:** Tel. 22965. 8 Front Street, Philipsburg. An island tradition in a truly tropical setting. Has five gingerbread balconies on an old house that was built about 1830. Specializes in local dishes.

13

The U.S. Virgin Islands: St. Thomas, St. Croix and St. John

Included among the more beautiful islands of the Caribbean are the three that make up the US Virgin Islands—St. Thomas, St. Croix and St. John. They share the body of water, and have very similar histories, but all three are quite different

St. Thomas is the Caribbean's capital for exotic shopping. You'll find many bargains here amongst its more than 100 shops which offer international products up to 60% below U.S. prices. In addition to its almost perfect weather, U.S. Customs has made St. Thomas the perfect place to shop. The $1,200 duty-free allowance makes every purchase a double bargain. St. Thomas also offers a combination unparalleled in the Caribbean. In addition to being a shopper's paradise, this is home to Megan Bay, one of the world's ten most beautiful beaches. Its palm trees and clear aquamarine water, adjacent to lush forests and mountains, attracts people from all over the world. Its tepid climate is perfect for unending varieties of tropical flowers that are everywhere, from its 1,500 foot mountain tops to the depths of Charlotte Amalie's port.

St. Croix, the largest of the three islands, is 43 miles south of St. Thomas, much more laid back, and more diverse. From what seems to be a dessert with cactus scrub brush at one end,

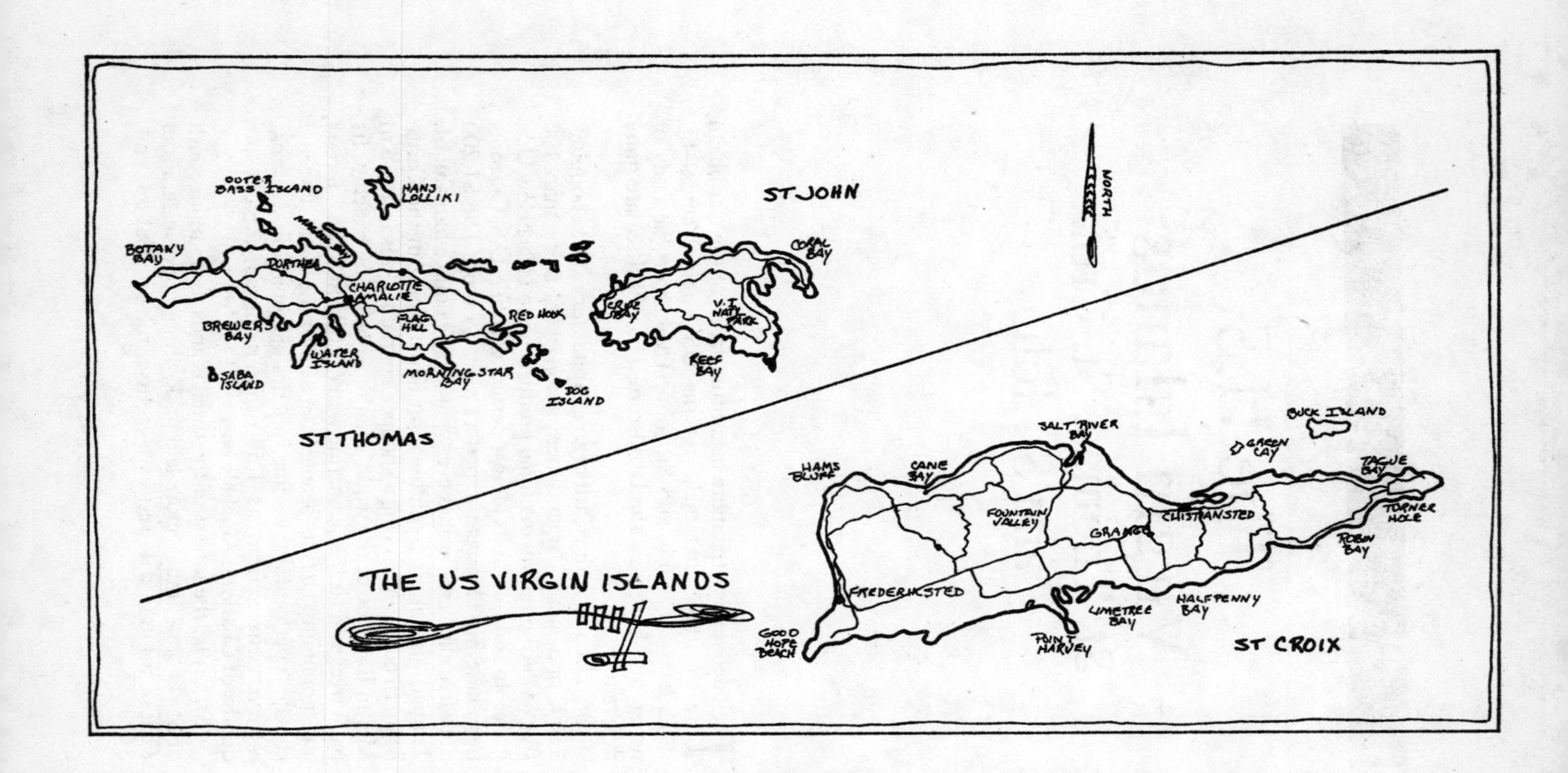

THE US VIRGIN ISLANDS
NORTH
ST THOMAS
ST JOHN
ST CROIX
OUTER BASS ISLAND
HANS LOLLIKI
MAGENS BAY
BOTANY BAY
DORTHEA
CHARLOTTE AMALIE
FLAG HILL
RED HOOK
BREWERS BAY
WATER ISLAND
SABA ISLAND
MORNING STAR BAY
DOG ISLAND
CRUZ BAY
V.I. NAT'L PARK
CORAL BAY
REEF BAY
BUCK ISLAND
SALT RIVER BAY
GREEN CAY
TAGUE BAY
HAMS BLUFF
CANE BAY
FOUNTAIN VALLEY
GRANGE
CHISTIANSTED
TURNER HOLE
ROBIN BAY
FREDERIKSTED
HALFPENNY BAY
LIMETREE BAY
POINT HARVEY
GOOD HOPE BEACH

to the rain forest near the middle, to beautiful vistas of the Caribbean from the Eastern most point in the U.S., St. Croix still retains the Danish sugar plantation atmosphere. Its two main cities, Christiansted and Frederiksted, are favorites of travelers who like to walk through unhurried shopping areas and parks, and are lovers of distinctive, gracious Danish architecture. Both have covered walkways, or galleries, and seem to be more cosmopolitan than many of the other island cities. With Buck Island just off the coast, St. Croix is a paradise for snorkeling.

St. John, about 5 miles east of St. Thomas is the smallest and least populated of the three islands, and nearly two-thirds of its land is set aside as the Virgin Islands National Park under the control of the U.S. Park Service. It is a non-commercial, low-key treasure island with beautiful beaches and ringed by many coves that are favorites of the boating set.

GETTING TO KNOW YOU

Christopher Columbus drew the world's attention to the Virgin Islands in 1493 while trying to find fresh water during his second trip to the West Indies. Since the Caribbe Indians prevented any further exploration of the nearby island of St. Croix, he left St. Croix, went north, and discovered St. Thomas, St. John, and the islands which are now known as the British Virgin Islands. Columbus named the entire chain in memory of the 11,000 virgins who supposedly followed Saint Ursela who had been martyred by the Huns in the Middle Ages. After leaving St. Thomas and St. John, Columbus sailed on to find Puerto Rico.

The Virgin Islands settled into a period of peacefulness until the late 1500's when Sir Francis Drake stopped in St. Thomas and St. John on his way to Puerto Rico to attack the Spanish in San Juan. Many flags have flown over St. Thomas since that time. The Dutch and French established colonies in the islands as well as the British. On St. Thomas, the Danes founded the town of Charlotte Amalie. By the late 1600's, there were over 50 sugar estates on the island and at the height of its sugar producing days, St. Thomas had 170 plantations. But the terrain proved too rugged for agriculture and the number eventually dwindled.

St. Thomas' economic focus shifted from agriculture to trade. In the mid-1700's, it became a free port where landed goods were exempt from customs duties and regulations. This atmosphere made it a favorite stopping point for many pirates, especially the infamous Blackbeard and Captain Kid.

Planters began to abandon the estates on St. Thomas after the Danish abolished slavery in the mid-1800's. The island's economy declined gravely during that period. The United States became interested in protecting its shores following World War I and bought St. Thomas, St. Croix and St. John from the Danes in 1917 for 25 million dollars. The U.S. Navy administered the islands until 1931 when the Department of Interior took jurisdiction. U.S. citizens first came in 1927, but the residents still do not vote in national elections even to this day.

Major tourism came to the islands, especially St. Thomas, only after World War II and has been building to the point where the islands now accommodate more than 1 million visitors a year. Although St. Thomas , St. Croix and St. John offer everything that any vacationer would want in the way of swimming, sailing, wind surfing and beautiful beaches, the island's biggest attraction is the shopping at Charlotte Amalie.

THE BASICS

LOCATION AND GEOGRAPHY

Clustered among the U.S. Virgin Islands, St. Thomas is one of the major islands settled within 100 or so islands, inlets and cays that are 1,600 miles southeast of New York City, 1,100 east southeast of Miami, and 70 miles directly east of San Juan. This island has an area of 32 square miles, 3 miles wide and 13 miles long. St. Thomas lies 18 degrees north latitude and 64 degrees west longitude. It is close enough to the equator to create brilliant sunsets. The Atlantic lies to the north and the Caribbean to the south. St. Thomas presents a picture of a mount jetting out of the Caribbean Sea with unforgettable scenery surrounded by powdery beaches, bays, and a natural deep port at the steps of Charlotte Amalie.

St. Croix is located south of St. Thomas, and St. John slightly to the east.

The 100 or so other islands, inlets and cays are mostly uninhabited. The U.S. Virgin Islands are part of the Leeward Islands and the Lesser Antilles and have a total population of over 100,000.

CLIMATE, WHEN TO GO, WHAT TO WEAR

The U.S. Virgin Islands are sunny all year with temperatures ranging from the 80's during the day and in the 70's most nights. The humidity is low due to the gentle easterly trade winds. Rain is not as plentiful as one might think on any of the three islands—about 50 inches a year. The tropical showers are usually over in just a few minutes. While there is no particular rainy season, less rain falls in the summer months. Since wells are few and far between, rain is collected from rooftops and channeled to household cisterns. Although salt water distillation plants help, water is considered very scarce by the residents. It is not unusual to see signs requesting the sparing use of water.

Because of their almost perfect climate, the U.S.Virgin Islands are wonderful to visit any time of year. However, with the crush of cruise ship passengers and high season tourists over by late spring, the summer months are more pleasant for those who may prefer shopping in Charlotte Amalie on St. Thomas.

Given the mild climate and casual resort atmosphere, it is best to take light weight clothing appropriate for any Caribbean island resort. Shorts, slacks, shirts and sun dresses will be ideal items for your wardrobe. Try to pack only clothes with a high cotton fiber content since other fabrics may become uncomfortable. As in the other islands in the Caribbean, you should avoid wearing bathing suits and short shorts in public markets and stores.

GETTING THERE

The U.S. Virgin Islands are some of the one of the easiest islands to get to from the United States. American Airlines, Continental, Delta and USAir have non-stop flights for many different cities. The smaller air carriers such as American Eagle and LIAT have service from other islands as well as from San Juan.

Since San Juan is now a major hub for many airlines, you might want to compare the cost of flying non-stop from one of the U.S. cities or connecting through San Juan. We have found the stop through San Juan can cost significantly less than going non-stop. Your travel agent should be able to provide you with routing and cost comparisons to the islands.

All the cruise ships that call on St. Thomas sail into the beautiful harbor surrounded by Charlotte Amalie. The West Indian Company dock is over 2,000 feet long and all ships may tie up there or at the Crown Bay west of town. Ships and small crafts can drop anchor in the Rhodestead and arrive at the town waterfront by launches also. As many as seven large cruise ships can anchor in the bay at the same time. Over 21 cruise lines arrive in St. Thomas throughout the year from New York, Norfolk, Virginia, Florida and Puerto Rico.

The cruise ships that call on St. Croix will arrive at either Christiansted or Frederiksted. Although still not as popular as St. Thomas, St. Croix is steadily growing as a cruise ship destination for those who prefer a more quiet atmosphere.

St. John is most accessible by ferry from St. Thomas or by private boat. There is now ferry service available from St. Thomas to St. Croix, with the trip taking about one and one-half hours.

DOCUMENTS

The entry requirements for any of the U.S. Virgin Islands are very simple. No passports or visas are required of U.S. or Canadian citizens. For other nationalities, the U.S. Virgin Islands requirements are the same as those for entering any other part of the United States since the Virgin Islands are considered part of the U.S. However, you should consider bringing proof of citizenship such as a birth certificate or passport if you are contemplating side trips to any of the islands surrounding the Virgin Islands. A short day trip over to the British Virgin Islands will be impossible without the proper documentation. Since the U.S. Virgin Islands are considered part of the U.S., there is no arrival fee nor departure tax.

ARRIVAL AND DEPARTURE

The airport arrival procedure is very quick and simple. The airport is a World War II hanger converted for commercial air use. Generally all flights are greeted by someone from the Tourist Bureau who distributes documents of the week's events in St. Thomas and St. Croix. You'll also find a booth where you can sample rum punch while waiting for your bags. After collecting your baggage and going through customs, which is very efficient, you should be quickly on your way.

Taxis are available immediately outside the door with the various drivers calling out the names of the hotels as their destination. It is somewhat difficult to get individual taxis, and it is normal to have a group transported to the hotel. The taxi cabs are not metered and rates are quoted per passenger. The rates are doubled if you wish a van to be private and the charge for suitcases are 50 cents each. The cost of getting from the airport to downtown Charlotte Amalie is about $3.50. The taxis carry a surcharge between midnight and six in the morning of $1 into town and $1.50 for an out-of-town fare. When traveling between any other point, be sure to determine the fare in advance with the driver.

Since this is a U.S. territory, there are no departure taxes for U.S. citizens. In addition, you will clear Customs in St. Thomas on St. Croix before boarding your aircraft. Departure is, therefore, very easy, and you will not have to wait in long lines. You should, however, arrive at the airport 30 minutes early so that you have plenty of time to clear Customs.

CURRENCY, TRAVELER'S CHECKS, CREDIT CARDS

Since the U.S. dollar is the basic currency of the U.S. Virgin Islands there is no difficulty determining the cost of the item you wish to purchase. Traveler's checks are readily accepted at most shops.

Major credit cards (Visa, Mastercard, American Express, Diners Club) are accepted by most major hotels, restaurants, shops, rental car agencies, tours, cruises and travel agents.

TIPPING

As a general rule, St. Thomas, St. Croix and St. John all follow the tipping procedures that you would find in the U.S. It is customary to tip 15% in most all situations. Be aware of the fact, however, that some hotels do add a 10% to 15% surcharge to cover the service. If it is not clearly stated on your bill, do not hesitate to ask so that you are not tipping at a double rate.

LANGUAGE AND EXPRESSION

The Virgin Islanders are a very friendly people who speak English or a lilting version known as creole or calypso. This form of English is spoken throughout the islands. A wide smile and "okay" is a very common expression used in greetings.

BUSINESS HOURS

Following the pattern of most islands, the shops in St. Thomas and St. Croix are open from 9am to 5pm, except on Sundays and major holidays. The shops located in the arcades of some large resorts may also be open on Sunday for limited hours.

TRANSPORTATION AND TOURS

A variety of rental cars are available from many different rental companies. St. Thomas and St. Croix are serviced by all of the major companies such as Avis, Hertz and Thrifty. However, the rental prices here are not inexpensive. Rates run from $20 to $75 a day and usually include unlimited mileage. Weekly rates are available, and if you are thinking about renting a car, you should definitely inquire about a weekly rate. If you do not have a major credit card, you will be asked to leave a deposit with the rental company which ranges anywhere from $100 to $150. Temporary licenses can be obtained at the Public Safety Office, and some hotels also have special packages available for jeeps. If you are thinking about renting, it is always wise to reserve a car in advance. On our last trip to the islands, we picked up the last rental at the airport on St. Thomas, and had to wait two days for a car to become available on St. Croix.

Parking can be challenging in St. Thomas, but you'll usually find spots at the municipal parking lot across from the court and next to the shopping area. The charge is 50 cents an hour or $4 for the entire day. In Christiansted on St. Croix, parking is very limited. We found it more expedient to take a taxi to town and leave the rental car at the hotel. Remember that driving in St. Thomas and St. Croix is a surprise to many in that you must drive on the left. Also, speed laws are strictly enforced. The general speed limit is 35 mph outside of town and 20 mph in town.

Taxis are plentiful on all three islands, and are relatively inexpensive. The taxis are not metered and the rates are determined by your destination rather than actual mileage. You will find that the general fee runs from $3 to $8-9 for most trips. The special fares can be arranged for any tour with a driver, and it is not unusual for a driver to collect for a round trip especially from hotels for shopping. We have done this several times and have never been disappointed as our driver has always been where and when we requested. This certainly makes it convenient by eliminating the big search for taxis back to the hotel when you are ready to return. Most taxi drivers will not cruise the main street or back street because of the tremendous traffic. If you have not arranged for a return trip to your hotel, you will probably have much more success in getting a cab near the waterfront than any other place.

RESOURCES

You'll find an endless number of travel books and information on St. Thomas. You will find overall information regarding the island, shopping, tours, and other vacation activities in virtually every travel guide.

When you arrive in St. Thomas, one of the most useful

resources you will find is called ***St. Thomas This Week.*** It's an 8 ½ by 11 yellow magazine that is published every week and has virtually everything you need to know about the island including the latest information on shopping. **St. Croix This Week** is the counterpart on St. Croix and is usually pink in color.

The Division of Tourism has a number of Visitor's Information Bureaus on the islands: the airports, Havensight Mall near the cruise ship pier on St. Thomas, and the docks at Charlotte Amalie. The Grand Hotel in Charlotte Amalie maintains a visitors' lounge where you can check your shopping bags while you rest and return to find more "goodies."

Information on the Virgin Islands in the U.S. and Canada can be obtained by contacting the U.S. Virgin Islands Division of Tourism at:

1270 Avenue of the Americas
New York City, NY 10020
212-582-4520

343 S. Dearborn Street
Suite 1003
Chicago, IL 60604
312-461-0180

3460 Wilshire Blvd.
Suite 915
Los Angeles, CA 90010
213-739-0138

900 17th Street, NW
Washington, DC 20006
202-293-3707

235 Peachtree Street
Suite 1420
Gaslight Tower
Atlanta, GA 30303
404-688-0906

2655 Lejeune Road
Suite 907
Coral Gables, FL
305-442-7200

234 Eglinton Ave. E.
Suite 306
Toronto, Ontario M4P 1K5
416-488-4374

SHOPPING IN ST. THOMAS

Shops displaying goods from all over the world make St. Thomas a shopper's paradise. The main shopping is along the harbor at Charlotte Amalie. An area several blocks wide and over a half mile long, it is comprised of numerous shops located in old warehouses that have been attractively converted to stores. Charming old alleyways and narrow streets still use the old world terms such as Raadet's Gade, something leftover from the days of the Danish settlers. Everywhere there are courtyards with restaurants providing shaded tables and cool drinks.

While shopping here can be overwhelming, planning can help you reap your share of the bargains. A little homework goes a long way in shopping St. Thomas. The best savings at this time are on crystal and fine china (up to 50 percent off U.S. prices), jewelry, and perfume. Imported beauty products are also excellent buys. Many of the latest fragrances arrive in St. Thomas before they reach the U.S. mainland. Electronic and photography items, however, seem to be priced equal to many of the discount shopping outlets in the U.S. However, liquor and cigarettes are real bargains at 50% to 75% below stateside prices.

- ❑ Because of almost perfect climate, the U.S. Virgin Islands are wonderful to visit any time of year.
- ❑ Taxis are plentiful and relatively inexpensive on all three islands. Taxis are not metered. Rates are determined by your destination.
- ❑ The best savings are on crystal and fine china, jewelry, and perfume.
- ❑ The best clothing buys in St. Thomas are in woolen specialties.
- ❑ Most shops sell jewelry than any other item in St. Thomas.

Why are prices so much lower in St. Thomas than in the U.S.? The answer is that merchants have learned to stock their shops for tourists. They carry the most wanted merchandise and they carry the latest and lightest selections. They do not have to pay more than 6% tax on imported goods, and over 1 million visitors per year keep the selections fresh. With its excellent reputation, we have found many people from nearby islands hopping over just to shop for the day.

WHAT TO BUY

Although shops in St. Thomas offer many famous name brand goods at low prices, some shops and buys are better than others. In St. Thomas you can find a large sampling of china, crystal, perfumes, electronic items as well as Indonesian batik prints and Haitian art. Most prices are 20% below U.S. retail prices. Since prices are fairly uniform throughout the island, you need not visit every store to discover the best buys. The best buys in St. Thomas are found on fine china, jewelry and crystal, followed by perfumes and art. Buys on cameras and electronic items may not result in great savings.

CAMERAS AND ELECTRONIC ITEMS

You will find virtually every major brand of camera and photographic accessory available at excellent prices. However, you will find that these prices are comparable to the discount prices that you may find in the outlets in New York City and elsewhere in the U.S. You will find the staff of some stores, such as **Royal Caribbean** and **Boolchand's**, are friendly and quite knowledgeable. Some of the values are worth considering, especially regarding complete camera outfits consisting of camera, lens, flash and various accessories. The staffs are also knowledgeable in regard to the proper type of film to be used in the islands and many places offer film processing.

Other electronic items, coming mostly from Japan, are also well represented in St. Thomas. Discounts of up to 40% are common, although the smart shopper will know the model numbers and prices back home and mentally add any duty to the price—if you will be over the amount you can take home duty-free. If you do purchase here, make certain that the item has a valid warranty and service network for repairs. Stereos, video games, compact disc players and even computers can be found here.

FASHIONS

The best clothing buys in St. Thomas are in woolen specialties. Since a variety of sweaters can be found at prices well below U.S. prices, you should consider looking at these particular items very carefully, especially those made of cashmere. Fashions from China can also be found at low prices, especially those made of silk. European and American designers are well represented, too, with better discounts off the trendy European labels. Locally crafted resort wear is colorful and makes an excellent remembrance. Keep in mind that clothing made in the U.S. Virgin Islands carries no tax and does not count towards your duty free exemption.

Dilly D'Alley's fashions range from casual to dressy with just about everything in between. Resort wear is highlighted here with the emphasis on good looking hand painted and decorative tops. At the **Beach House**, swimwear and accessories come in sizes to please just about everyone. Next door you will find custom printed t-shirts, children's swimwear and sports wear. For a glimpse at the ever changing fashion scene from the top designers in France, Italy, London and Japan, **Lion In the Sun**, near the waterfront, carries a complete line of covers sportswear, day and evening styles, shoes and accessories.

PERFUMES

Another fine buy throughout St. Thomas is imported perfumes. Many of the same brands that are well-known in the U.S. can be found here at as much as 40% to 50% less than the prices at home. One of the unique aspects of shopping for perfumes in St. Thomas is that many of the latest items from Europe are here one to two months before they are sold in the major cities in the U.S. **Tropicana Perfume Shoppes**, one of the world's largest, offers extraordinary prices on fabulous perfumes. They carry cosmetics by Princess Marcella Bourgese, Yves St. Laurent, Beaupe and La Prarrie. Their select lines of the very latest designer cosmetics also include Estee Lauder, Clinique, Chanel, and Lancome. Their prices on Calvin Klein, Chanel, London, Hermis, and others are approximately 20% below the U.S. prices.

JEWELRY

It may be spelled "jewelry" but it still comes out "savings." Gold and gem stones, especially emeralds, are excellent buys in St. Thomas for the knowledgeable shopper. Remember that the European gold markings are different from those in North America. About 24K means solid gold in the U.S. and Canada. You are likely to find it marked 999 here. It is the percentage, minus any decimal points: 99.9 percent pure. If you are shopping for 18K gold, look for the marking 750; if it's 14K gold, the number will be 585. The more exclusive St. Thomas shops, such as **A.H. Riise Gifts, Blue Caribbe, Columbia Emeralds,** and **H. Stern** offer return privileges. And some even have branch shops in the U.S. and Canada.

You will find more shops selling jewelry than any other item in St. Thomas. Some shops have their own jewelers and repair facilities. Others handle repairs for the best shops. In the latter category, one example is **One Carat**, on the waterfront near **Down Island Traders**, who does repair for H. Stern. This shop will also hand fabricate a setting in gold for as little as $300. St. Thomas is a great place to bring an unset stone and to have a special setting made. **Hermella Jewel Studio** in the historic Grande Hotel at the head of Main Street, has a large selection of unset gemstones. If you have a standard cut stone, we found that **George Jenser's** and **Blue Diamond** have precast settings for rings and pendants starting as low as $15. **Jenser's Jewelry** store specializes in selling gold chains by the inch, some beginning as low as 55 cents, and it has a golden opportunity room where everything is under $100. The family has been in business in St. Thomas for over 25 years.

At **Blue Diamond**, fresh water and cultured pearls are sold by the inch and a setting can be created in one day. There are also shops such as **Circe**, a tiny shop in Pom Passage, displaying unusual items such as twin opals for $75,000 as well as six outlets of **H. Stern** which carry jewelry in virtually every price range. If you need to compare quality and clarity of any stone, we suggest that you make your decision after visiting H. Stern. St. Thomas has jewelry at every price level, and no matter where you turn there is another shop or branch of one that you were just in.

St. Thomas has many jewelers who will set diamonds for you. But ensure that you know what you are buying. You can find inexpensive precast settings as well as hand made settings. Most retailers of the quality items have set prices. But if you are willing to spend the time, generally there is some room for negotiation, especially on the higher priced items.

Most street vendors will discount jewelry prices by at least 20% during the off season.

PORCELAIN AND CRYSTAL

Some of the best sources for bargains on porcelain in the world are found in St. Thomas. Shops carry the most popular patterns of the finest manufacturers. **A.H. Riise Gifts, Little Switzerland**, and the **Crystal Shop**, for example, offer excellent European selections at good prices. But even U.S. brands and patterns can be purchased for as much as 30% less than prices back home. Since most shops normally ship direct, you don't have to worry about carrying delicate items on the plane with you.

WATCHES

St. Thomas is a mecca for name brand watches. Whether you are looking for inexpensive watches for daily use, rugged sport watches, diving or elegant dress models costing thousands of dollars, St. Thomas has it. **A.H. Riise Gifts, Boolchand's, H. Stern, La Romana, G. Jenser's**, and **Little Switzerland** all carry complete lines.

ART

It is easy to find virtually every type of art from the Caribbean as well as from other parts of the world in St. Thomas. Indeed, art abounds in the shops of St. Thomas, and galleries seem to be everywhere. On **Crystal Gade**, Jonna White has a gallery displaying her own etchings, calligraphy and paper casts. **Haversite Mall**, next to the cruise ships handles many local artists with a wide selection available and also offers framing services. The **Artworks Gallery** at Zoris in the Sandalmaker on Norre Gade also displays the works of seven or eight local artists. Haitian art and art from many of the other islands of the Caribbean can be found at the **Down Island Trader Shop** on the waterfront. Here, the works of better known Haitian artists include primitives, metal works and statues having a distinct voodoo flavor. Older prints of the Caribbean are on display at the entrance to **Riise's Alley**. The **Fort Christian Museum** has a gallery featuring a different artist each month.

It is best to deal with reputable galleries or merchants who have reputations for value and honesty. Remember, if you see a "hot find," where the price seems just too good to be true, it generally is. Most shops will wrap your purchases and deliver them to your hotel or cruise ship.

Jim Tillett's Complex at Estate 22 incorporates an art gallery, workshops and restaurant in a tropical garden east of town. At the art gallery you will find works by many local artists as well as Jim Tillett's own paintings, graphics and maps. Nearby in **Kilnworks Pottery**, Peggy Stewart designs many things in pottery, there is an enamel ware workshop and a handicraft jeweler. Tillett fabrics, sold by the yard, are designed and hand screened on the premises and watchers are welcomed. Three times a year a popular and colorful event takes place in the gardens when island artists and craftsmen will gather to display and sell their wares.

One of the most popular island artists is **Jonna White** who has a gallery exclusively for her own work on the corner of Crystal and Nye Gade, two short blocks up from Main Street in Charlotte Amalie. She works in several mediums, but in her own unique style, often using handmade paper and paper casts. Her creations range from tropical to ancient symbolism.

At the mountain top overlooking Magen's Bay you can find several crafts people at work on island products. **Linda Stanton** produces jewelry, copper boxes, and dishes; Casey of **Kalee's Creations** produces hand painted woodcarvings.

Bakery Square Shopping Mall on Back Street in Charlotte Amalie, once an old bakery, is an attractive complex housing island artisans.

ISLAND PRODUCTS

Island products, being duty-free, are doubly attractive as take home gifts. Local artisans and resident manufacturers turn out a variety of things to buy, all of them capturing the sunny style that has become St. Thomas' trademark.

Designing unusual jewelry began for Alan O'Hara in 1952. A businessman/tourist, O'Hara spotted an agate embedded in the pavement on a street in Jamaica. That started a 10 year search for gems and most of the time you may find him at **Blue Carib Gems** in Bakery Square cutting, polishing and creating settings for Caribbean gems.

Shell wind chimes gently sway in the breeze at the **Sand Dollar**, also in Baker's Square. Island leaves and sand dollars or shells are covered in 24K gold as pendants.

A glimpse of the arched doorways of the **Cloth Horse** reveals tapestries from Haiti, straw furniture from Santa Domingo, and a few charming antiques from that same island.

Down Island Traders with two shops, one in Baker's Square, the other on the waterfront, specializes in unique Caribbean products. In stock are native seasonings and cookbooks, tropical fruit jellies, coffees and teas available individually or packaged in baskets as gift assortments. Both stores feature Caribbean art work, handicrafts, and exclusively designed T-shirts. On the second floor of their waterfront shop, they maintain an excellent gallery of Haitian art—many of the paintings by Haiti's more prominent artists.

The **Straw Factory** is the place to go for anything in straw. They are a short walk up Garden Street in Bakery Square and only short blocks from Main Street. Here you will find hats, bags, rugs, placemats, and mini baskets.

Several of the more than 25 styles in leather sandals, hand made at **Zora**, the sandal maker, on Narre Gade can be worn right out of the shop, others take a 20-minute wait, still others are fitted and mailed to you duty free. Another popular buy are fished-shaped bags in great colors.

At the **Crafts Co-op** on Back Street, you will find paintings, gift cards in tropical colors, island dolls, and clothing, prints and local scenes, and people. Small acrylic paintings here begin at a mere twelve dollars.

Another group of artisans work on St. John at Mongoose Junction in Clues Bay. Here, in a variety of attractive shops, look for pottery, contemporary hand made fashions and boutique canvas bags. **Goldsmiths R. & I. Patton** produce lovely gold pieces with island designs. This is just a short ferry ride out of Charlotte Amalie.

Flavors of the Virgin Islands last a long time when you go home with a Caribbean cookbook. There are several available that are filled with native recipes for favorites like coconut bread, fish (in fungi), cock chowder and rum drinks.

Another favorite take-home gift is the local music—steel bands, schratchi bands, reggae and calypso.

THE MORE YOU LOOK

If you browse the downtown streets of Charlotte Amalie and the arcades located within the various hotels, you will discover many other shopping opportunities. The ever changing variety of products from all around the world make shopping here an unbelievable experience. The streets running between the waterfront highway and Main Street are filled with a vast array of jewelry, perfumes and fashions not yet available in the U.S.

WHERE TO SHOP

Imports from around the world make shopping part of the fun of a trip to St. Thomas. Charlotte Amalie stores line either side of Main Street and border historic walkways in model buildings once used as Danish warehouses. They are open from 9am to 5pm, except Sundays and major holidays. Another shopping mecca can be found at Haversite Mall, an attractive oasis near the West Indian Company Dock. More than 26 shops, many branches of prominent Main Street stores, are open when cruise ships come to call, which is almost everyday. The largest hotels offer a bonus—their shops remain open in the evenings. At the Frenchman's Reef you can wander among 24 stores in a two-story arcade.

If you have limited time in St. Thomas and wish to see most everything that is available, we suggest that you concentrate on the shopping area in Charlotte Amalie near the waterfront and work your way along Main Street. Beginning at the corner of Waterfront Highway and Post Office Alley, you will find one of the two shops of **Down Island Traders**, the other is located near Bakery Square. Both of these shops are brimming with island-made jellies, candies, Caribbean teas and coffees, herbs and spices and other island gifts. Above the waterfront store, in the gallery, you will find Haitian art and other folk art presented. Both stores are worth a visit, but the location at Post Office Alley and Waterfront Highway has the most extensive collection of all goods.

Next to Down Island Traders on Post Office Alley is **Peach Bloom**, which specializes in distinctive one-of-a-kind antique jewelry pieces, most from the era of 1930 to 1940. Here you can find bracelets, cameos, charms, lockets, pins, pendants, rings, stick pins, watches and some baby jewelry. This particular shop will deliver to your hotel or ship.

On Tolbod Gade, around the corner from Down Island Traders, half way up the block towards Main Street, you will

FAVORITE ISLAND SHOPS

Camera and Electronic Items

Royal Caribbean Boolchand's

Fashions

Dilly D'Alley's
Lion in the Sun
Beach House

Perfumes

Tropicana Perfume Shoppes

Jewelry

A.H. Riise Gifts
Columbia Emeralds
Down Island Traders
George Jenser's
Circe
Blue Caribbe
One Carat
Hermella Jewel Studio
Blue Diamond
H. Stern

Porcelain and Crystal

A H. Riise Gifts
Crystal Shop
Little Switzerland

Watches

A.H. Riise Gifts
H. Stern
G. Jenser's
Boolchand's
La Romana
Little Switzerland

Art

Crystal Gade
Artworks Gallery
Riise's Alley
Jim Tillett's Complex
Kalee's Creations
Haversite Mall
Down Island Trader Shop
Fort Christian Museum
Kilnworks Pottery

Island Products

Blue Carib Gems
Cloth Horse
Straw Factory
Crafts Co-op
Sand Dollar
Down Island Traders
Zora
Goldsmith's R & I Patton

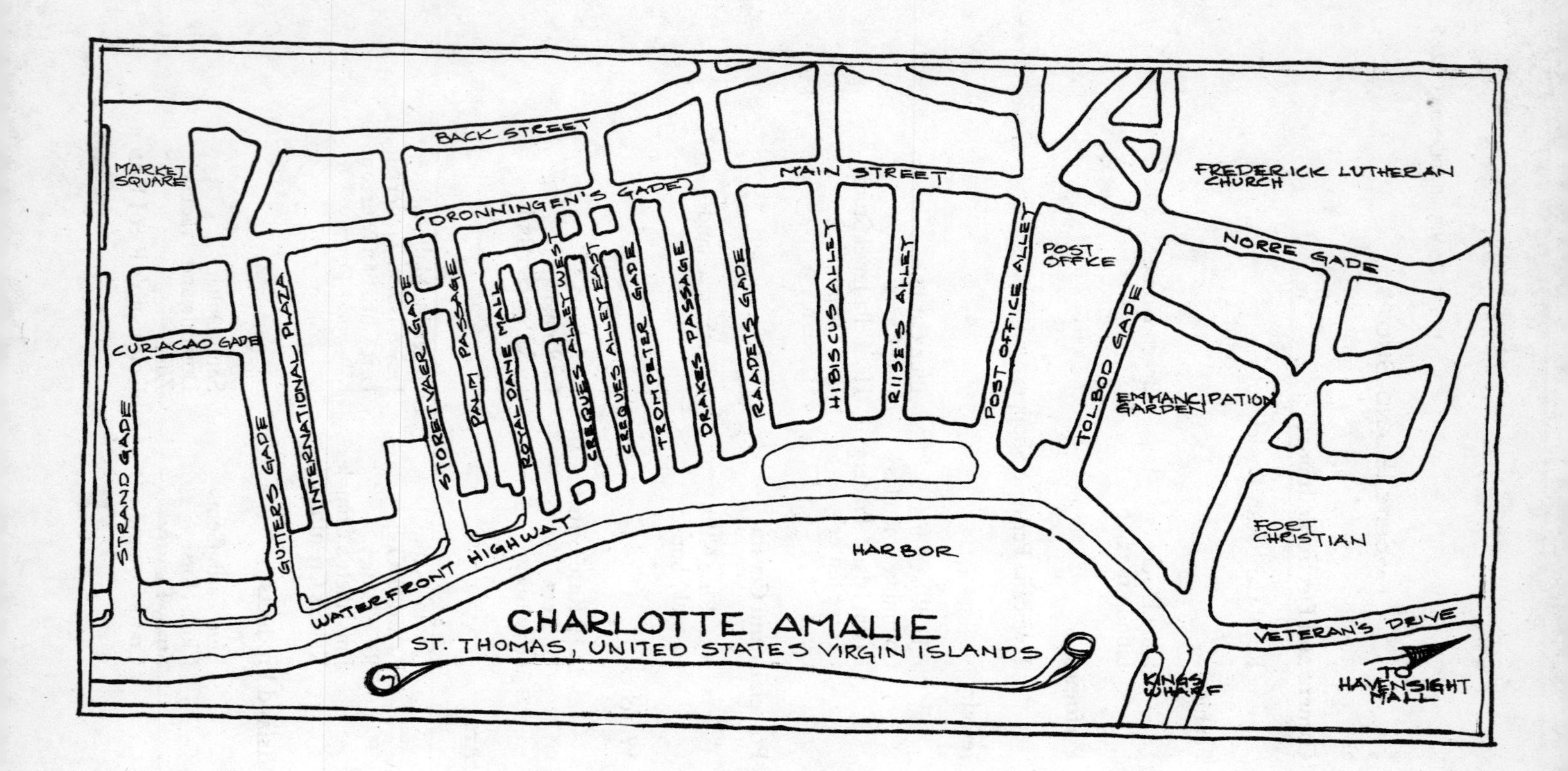
CHARLOTTE AMALIE
ST. THOMAS, UNITED STATES VIRGIN ISLANDS
BACK STREET
MARKET SQUARE
MAIN STREET
FREDERICK LUTHERAN CHURCH
DRONNINGEN'S GADE
NORRE GADE
POST OFFICE
CURACAO GADE
STRAND GADE
GUTTERS GADE
INTERNATIONAL PLAZA
STORETVAER GADE
PALM PASSAGE
ROYAL DANE MALL
CREQUES ALLEY WEST
CREQUES ALLEY EAST
TROMPETER GADE
DRAKES PASSAGE
RAADETS GADE
HIBISCUS ALLEY
RIISE'S ALLEY
POST OFFICE ALLEY
TOLBOD GADE
EMMANCIPATION GARDEN
FORT CHRISTIAN
WATERFRONT HIGHWAY
HARBOR
VETERAN'S DRIVE
KINGS WHARF
TO HAVENSIGHT MALL

find the first of Little Switzerland's shops in St. Thomas. **Little Switzerland** specializes in jewelry, especially Rolex watches and many other beautiful items of gold and silver. They also handle Waterford and Baccarrat crystal, Wedgwood and Herene china and Lladro figures. Many of the prices here are about 50% less than you would pay in the U.S.

On the corner of Tolbod Gade and Main Street is **Hermella's Jewel Studio** where you will find hundreds of elegant clasps and catches. The island residents come here to buy their fine jewelry. Unset diamonds and gem stones are also their specialty. If you walk three blocks on Norre Gade, you will find **Zorz of St. Thomas**. She has been famous for years for leather sandals, handicraft belts and a variety of canvas bags, carryalls, and purses. Her sideline is imported hand-knotted oriental rugs.

Returning past the Post Office on Main Street, and turning up Garden Street, you will find the Straw Factory on the left. Here you will find handcrafted items from over 50 countries and the Caribbean Islands including St. Thomas. You will find many varieties of hats, handbags, wood carvings, West Indian dolls, and unique decorator items such as placemats and wooden table wear. Around the corner to the left on Nayne Gade, you will find the **Jonna White Art Gallery**. The gallery contains her own recognizable style of paper casts, etchings on handmade paper, often inspired by tropical birds, flowers, people and ancient symbols presented in a contemporary manner. The prices in this galley will range from $90 to approximately $1,000.

Off of Back Street on the way down to Main Street is Bakery Square. This used to be a main area for breads, cookies and cakes but is now a small conclave of shops housing several local artisans. It is worth a visit to see the variety of the local art. Next to Bakery Square is the **Blue Carib Gems and Rocks Factory**. This particular outlet is family owned and operated and you can watch Caribbean amber and larimer, black coral, agate, and many other stones being polished and fashioned into gold and silver jewelry. Since this is a factory, the prices here are going to be somewhat lower than in many of the other shops.

Continuing to Main Street, you will arrive at the corner of Main Street and Post Office Alley and find two **Cardow** jewelry shops directly across the street from each other. Cardow has another shop on the waterfront; all three specialize in many different items of jewelry, especially gold bars. Next to Cardow is a Little Switzerland outlet called **Rosenthal Studio**. Here you will find a Rosenthal Studio line of contemporary designs in china, crystal, and flatware that is 45% to 50% lower than

U.S. prices. Here you can also buy Bjorn windblown art pieces and other crystal figurines as well as crystal candle holders. Next to Little Switzerland is **Linen House** where you will find decorative tablecloths and placemats in all sizes, shapes, colors, and bargains. Across the street is the first of the two **Tropicana Perfume Shops** which have wall to wall perfume displays. It carries a wide range of brand perfumes and cosmetic products from around the world. Adjacent to Tropicana is one of two **Columbia Emerald** outlets. In addition to a fine selection of set and unset emeralds, this shop carries watches made by Seiko, Citizen, Raymond Weil, Jean LaSalt, Tesalt and Omega.

Continuing down the street, you will find **A.H. Riise Precious Time Boutique** which is noted for its Swiss watches. Virtually every make imaginable is handled by this shop as well as German clocks. You will find prices approximately 30% off U.S. prices. In addition to the famous makes found in the U.S., you'll find Swiss styles made by Alfex, Swatch, and Orbit. Tucked in the archway leading to the Riise Alley is the **A.H. Riise Art Gallery**, which is famous for its collection of historic contemporary prints, posters, maps and cards depicting aspects of West Indian life from lush settings to local market scenes. Next to it, you will find the **A.H. Riise Gift Shop**, which is one of the loveliest shops in St. Thomas. There is a very extensive array and display of china, crystal, jewelry, perfumes, cosmetics, sweaters, and rugs. Conveniently located on the Mezzanine of the Riise Gift Shop is **Rugs by Terbenian**, an importer of fine oriental rugs. Prices here are lower than in the U.S. and they ship anywhere in the world. If you continue along Riise's Alley, near the waterfront end of the alley, you will come to **Lion in the Sun**. Here you will find an ever changing fashion scene from the top designers of France, Italy, London, and Japan; they always seem to have a new collection of sportswear, day and evening wear, shoes, and accessories. Next to it, and across the street, is **Gucci**. Here you will find handbags, luggage, jewelry, scarves, belts, and assorted leather goods. And, of course, it is here you will find the distinctive Gucci watches.

When you return to Main Street, the next stop you come to is **La Romana**. The shop is filled with fashions, jewelry, handbags, and accessories. Among the fashion names are La Pierra, Burberry's, Zigna for Men, La Romana's private collection, and Diane Freis. You will also find watches by Porche, Hooblot, Blank Pane, and Breitling.

After leaving La Romana, take a left and go down Hybiscus Alley to the Waterfront Highway where you will find two noteworthy stores. At Raadets Gade is the **Shane Company**, direct diamond importers who display hundreds of diamonds in every shape and carat weight. These and other gems can be found at tremendous savings over stateside prices. Here you can buy gems already mounted or choose a stone and setting separately and have them mounted at no extra charge. A short walk up the Waterfront and a right turn onto Greg's Passage will lead you to **Opals of Australia**. Here you will find opals in all colors, sizes and prices. We found mosaic pendants in sterling silver starting at $9, and rings priced from $85 to $18,000.

Heading up Greg's Passage back to Main Street and turning left, go down a few blocks and you will find one of the six **H. Stern** jewelry shops. There are two on Main Street and one each at Haversite Mall, Frenchman's Reef, Stouffer's Grande Beach, and Bluebeard's castle. These shops are filled with beautiful jewelry in every price range. In the block containing H. Stern, on both Trumpeter Gade and Royal Drakc Mall, you will find many shops with unusual fashions. **Chi Chi's** specializes in Italian leather and another **Dilly D'Alley** handles fashions ranging from casual to dressy and everything in between. Around the corner, off of Royal Dane Mall, are many shops in three narrow alleys. Housed in this small mall are stores such as **Purse Strings**, which specializes in straw, canvas, and leather selections and the **Ship Wreck Shop**, which overflows with Caribbean handicrafts. A short walk back up the Main Street near Palm Passage, you will find two more exquisite jewelry stores. Most of the jewelry at Blue Diamond is custom made and is either 14K or 18K gold using precious stones from their gem collection. **Blue Diamond** will create a special setting for you or you can choose one of their already designed pieces. Here, fresh water and cultured pearls are sold by the inch, and there's a jewelry repair shop on the premises. On the other side of Main Street is **G. Jenser's** jewelry store which has been in business for 25 years and specializes in selling gold chains by the inch, some as low as 55 cents.

If you turn onto Palm Passage, again heading toward the waterfront, you'll find two boutiques that are worth visiting. **Janine's Boutique** carries a tremendous collection from Paris at prices substantially less than in the U.S. Men will find blazers from Valentino, St. Laurent, Pierre Cardin, Casherelle and Christian Dior. Very close by is **Louisa Boutique** which offers Italian fashions. Look for luxurious cotton, linen, and silk evening gowns as well as stunning Italian leather shoes, sandals, leather bags and belts and some dazzling costume jewelry.

If you're looking for china and crystal, go back to Main Street, turn left, and walk to Old Market Square. The **English Shop** has shelves filled with china and crystal from Spode,

Colport, Royal Dalton, Minten, Wedgwood and Royal Worchester. The china comes from Europe and Japan at savings of 30% to 50%. The English Shop also has a second shop at Haversite Mall. You may also want to stop at **Universal Liquor and Gift Shop**, located across from Market Square, for many bargains. Among them are 14K gold jewelry with diamonds, emeralds, rubies, sapphires; tablecloths from China; Seiko, Citizen, Cassio, and Orbit watches; and liquor service that is fast, courteous, and with a guaranteed delivery to the airport or ship.

Near the downtown shopping area is Haversite Mall with more than two dozen shops offering a variety of attractive wares in a garden like setting. It includes specialty shops as well as branches of shops found downtown.

SPECIAL TIPS FOR CRUISE SHIP PASSENGERS

If you only have a few hours in port, you can still do a great deal of shopping in St. Thomas. By concentrating on shops located in an area bounded by the waterfront, Strand Gade, Main Street, and Tolbod Gade, you can see most of what St. Thomas has to offer within a matter of hours. The secret is to get a copy of ***St. Thomas This Week*** or any other free guides for island visitors that contain a detailed map listing all of the shops. One guide includes a two-page map which outlines 130-150 shops by name and address located within this area. Keep in mind that your space aboard ship may be limited, and most shops in St. Thomas are willing to ship the merchandise to the U.S. for you. If you plan to continue on to other islands where you also plan to shop, such as St. Martin or the Dominican Republic, we strongly suggest you to ship your larger merchandise home from St. Thomas.

SHOPPING ON ST. CROIX

Shopping on St. Croix is on a much smaller scale than St. Thomas, and much more casual. The shops themselves will be much smaller, and there will be fewer shoppers to contend with. This provides the opportunity for the shopkeepers, however, to provide much more personal service.

The prices here will be 30-50% below U.S. prices, and of course, there is no tax.

WHAT TO BUY

Most of the same products available in St. Thomas can be found here, but there are fewer shops. Most will be located in downtown Christiansted, with more and more opening in Frederiksted as the cruise ship traffic increases. Here you will find numerous shops offering antiques, art, china, crafts, crystal, jewelry, perfume, and watches. For arts and crafts, look for **American West India Company, Designworks, Folk Art Traders, Karavan West Indies**, and **Le Shoppe**. For jewelry and watches, you'll find **Columbia Emeralds, House of Vizia, Little Switzerland**, and **The Natural Jewel**.

SHOPPING ON ST. JOHN

Since St. John is not of the same mold as the other shopping havens of the Caribbean, the more traditional shopping is going to be confined to the hotels and resorts, However, there is a Santa Fe-like art scene emerging all over St. John.

WHAT TO BUY

Art is the main attraction on St. John and is available at a number of studios and galleries. Other items of interest include handmade pottery, sculpture and blown glass from the **Donald Schnell Studio**, at Mongroose Junction, island-designed jewelry, canvas products and hand-painted clothing.

WHERE TO SHOP

Most of the shopping is going to be located in the shops at Mongoose Junction, near the ferry dock, and in the shops at Cruz Bay.

The art galleries, however, are located in various locations. **The Coconut Coast Studios** on Frank Bay is a few minutes walk from Cruz Bay. It specializes in the work of Elaine Estern and Lucinda Schutt, and features watercolors. **Coral Bay Fold Art Gallery** in Warfside Village in Cruz Bay displays the oil, graphite and pastel art of Karen Samuel. **Bajo El Sol/Under the Sun Art Gallery Art Studio** is a co-op located at Mongoose Junction with a number of artists featured. Two other shops which feature local artists are **Frames of Mind** located at the Lumberyard Complex in Criz Bay, and **Wicker, Wood & Shells**, at Mongoose Junction.

ENJOYING YOUR STAY

THE SITES

St. Thomas

St. Thomas has a lot more to offer than shopping, idyllic tropical scenery, and beaches. While this mountainous island is one of the most beautiful stretches of land in the Caribbean, it also has an exotic history, making it a fascinating place for sightseeing. Because it is small, it can be explored in a day. The former pirate haunts, Danish relics, lovely old buildings, and even street names are all reminders of a past influenced by foreigners and filled with good fortune as well as tragedy.

Some of the most interesting sightseeing tours in St. Thomas include the following:

- **Tour of Charlotte Amalie:** A leisurely walking tour of historic Charlotte Amalie is perhaps the best way to learn about the island, city, and its people. The best starting point is the main post office building. Just across the street, east of the post office, is the Grande Hotel. Built in 1841, it is an excellent example of 19th Century architecture. Today, it is the home of the St. Thomas Visitor's Center. Here you can pick up additional information on what to see and do. Be sure you get a free copy of ***What To Do/Best Buys in St. Thomas***.

- **Exploring the Island:** Should you decide to take a trip around the island of St. Thomas, you will come across some of the loveliest beaches in the world. But there is more to this tropical island than stretches of white sand, palm trees, and warm breezes. Following Veteran's Drive out of town, you will come to the West Indian Company, where you can enjoy a view of the harbor. Next, turn on to Frenchman's Bay Road and begin to climb up the mountain side. Frenchman's Bay Road will eventually become Bovoni Road and turn away from the coast. Bovoni leads into Red Hook Road, which takes you past National Parks Dock, where you can catch the ferry to St. John.

- **Megan's Bay:** If you continue around the island, follow Smith Bay Road and you will pass Mandahl Beach in the Mahogany Run Golf—one of the world's most scenic golf courses. Mahogany Road becomes Megan's Road which will lead you to a dead end at the fabulous Megan's Bay Beach. National Geographic named it one of the 10 most beautiful in the world. On the weekends the beach can get a bit crowded, but during the week you will have no problem claiming your own plot of sand.

- **Drakes Seat:** Continue on the road from Megan's Bay, and follow the road as it climbs up the mountain. Here, overlooking more than 100 Virgin Islands sprawled out in a turquoise sea, where the Atlantic meets the Caribbean, is Drakes Seat. Photographers are sure to find a friendly island resident with his burro available for pictures. Be prepared, however, to pay a small fee.

- **Blackbeards Tower and Bluebeards Castle:** Heading over the hill and back down towards Mafoli, you will pass Blackbeards Tower when you return to Charlotte Amalie. On your way down the mountain, you are sure to catch a glimpse of Bluebeards Castle, perched on the left above the town. In the earliest days of Danish settlement on St. Thomas, the castle was the center of military and government island life. The central tower was built by Bluebeard for one of his true loves, Mecredita. When the pirate discovered she had been unfaithful, the story goes, he killed her and sailed away never to return. In fact the stone fortress was built as a watch tower to supplement the defenses of Port Christian.

- **Coral World Marine Park:** This unusual marine attraction is located in the northeast shore of St. Thomas, an easy taxi ride from Charlotte Amalie. Alternatively inexpensive tours can be arranged at most hotels. Coral World covers a four acre peninsula that spreads into the blue green ocean like a finger.

- **Water Sports:** St. Thomas is a water sports enthusiast's dream; the weather is usually flawless, the beaches gorgeous, and the water is warm and gentle. Boating, swimming, sailing, wind surfing, water skiing, deep sea fishing, snorkeling and scuba diving are all options. Boating is enjoyed for its own sake as a means for fishing and diving. From wind surfing to outboarding to catamaraning, to yachting, the places and challenges are many for the novice seafarer as well as the seasoned skipper.

St. Croix

A trip to St. Croix would not be complete without a visit to the **Buck Island Reef National Monument.** It is a protected national park and consists of 700 acres of Caribbean Sea and 180 acres of land. **The Barrier Reef** is the single, most outstanding feature of the park. It surrounds much of the island as a submerged fortress-like wall rising over 30 feet from the sea floor. There is colorful lagoon, patch reefs of elkhorn coral and sea grass beds. The underwater trail has signs that identify the coral reef ecology. The island itself rises about 300 feet above the sea; is covered with thorny bushes and organ pipe cactus; and has a beautiful coral sand beach.

Another excursion worth exploring is a trip to the **St. Croix Life & Environmental Arts Project (St. Croix LEAP).** The LEAP is a non-profit educational alternative located at the west end of the island about two miles up Mahogancy Road from the beach north of Frederiksted. Emphasizes the wood arts such as tables, counters, headboards and wall-hangings.

St. John

The main diversions on St. John are exploring the endless miles of park land and enjoying the sailing and bathing opportunities. A walk though the small town of Cruz Bay is also a pleasant way to spend part of a day.

ACCOMMODATIONS

Like many islands in the Caribbean, the U.S. Virgin Islands offer excellent accommodations. You'll find resorts, hotels, inns, and condominiums as well as cottages available in a wide range of prices. Some of the best quality hotels include:

St. Thomas

- **Stouffer Grande Beach Resort:** Tel. 809-775-1510. P.O.Box 8267, Smith Bay Road. Located seven miles northeast of Charlotte Amalie, it is perched on a steep hillside above a thousand square foot white sandy beach beside the Caribbean. Here you can enjoy beachfront breakfast, lunch, and dinner at Bay Winds, which features continental and authentic Caribbean cuisine. On the premises is one of the most innovative swimming pools on the island, with zig zag edges that provide a high tech vision of an Aztec ritual bath, plus an additional pool. You'll find a collection of boutiques and all kinds of water sport rentals here. Expensive.

- **Frenchman's Reef:** Tel. 809-776-8500 or 800-524-2000 from the U.S. P.O. Box 7100. Located in Charlotte Amalie just 10 minutes from the main shopping area. Has 250 rooms, two huge swimming pools, nine bars, and all types of water sports. Known as "The Reef," it contains some of the best dining facilities on the island. If you wish to stay self-contained, you'll even find 24 hour duty-free shops that can satisfy every browsing need. Includes a sightseeing helicopter service. You can also opt for the water taxi to the harbor area for more extensive shopping. Very expensive.

- **Sapphire Beach Resort and Marina:** Tel. 809-775-6100. P.O.Box 8099. A large complex with its own marina, where you can rent a sailboat and go snorkeling near St. John for the day. Located on the east end, it is almost a private retreat. The condominiums and two story villas include kitchen facilities. Very casual, but elegant. Very Expensive.

- **Pavilions & Pools:** Tel. 809-775-6110. Rt. 6. Make a reservation for your own private pool outside a villa. Floor to ceiling glass walls and tropical garden baths are just part of this intriguing privacy that is self-contained. Located next to Sapphire Bay, the beach is also at your disposal. Very Expensive.

St. Croix

- **Buccaneer**: Tel. 8O9-773-2100. On a hillside not far from Christiansted, it is one of the largest facilities on the island. Three beaches, a beautiful 18-hole golf course, tennis courts and a spa. Most of the rooms have private terraces. Four restaurants and a view of Christiansted. Very Expensive.

- **Hotel on the Cay:** Tel. 809-773-2035. On a island in the harbor near downtown Christiansted. Its own beach and pool. Ferry service available for the pier. Expensive.

- **Hibiscus Beach Hotel:** Tel. 809-773-4042. Very comfortable hotel on the water. Excellent staff and open-air restaurant serving exceptional continental fare.

- **Radisson Carambola:** Tel. 809-778-3800. A stunning hotel on 46 acres overlooking the water. Three dining rooms with excellent sport facilities, including access to the famed Carambola Golf Course. Very Expensive.

- **Cormorant Beach Club:** Tel. 809-778-8920. On a 1,600-foot beach with 34 rooms and four suites. Pool, tennis and restaurant. Expensive.

- **Cottages By the Sea:** Tel. 809-772-0495. Located on the western end of the island one half mile from Frederiksted. All cottages are completely furnished with kitchenette and maid service, and mere feet from the beach. Moderate.

- **King Christian Hotel:** Tel. 809-773-2285. Very charming hotel located on the harbor in downtown Christiansted. Very near all the downtown shops, Moderate.

St. John

- **Cannel Bay:** Tel. 809-776-6111. The premier resort in the U.S. Virgin Islands. Built into the ruins of on old sugar plantation, it has 171 rooms on 170 acres. Seven beaches are protected by coral reefs. Dinner is served in three locations. Very Expensive.

- **Hyatt Regency St. John:** Tel. 809-776-7171. The thirteen guest-room buildings are terraced on a hillside overlooking Cruz Bay. Many restaurants and all sports. Very Expensive.

RESTAURANTS

You'll find a wonderful mixture of restaurants in the U.S. Virgin Islands. It is a challenge to find original island cuisine here because of the intercontinental tourism. Red snapper, conch, grouper are all fresh and fit in with the kallaloo soupy stew along with onions and garlic. Goat water is highly spiced and fun to try. Also try the fresh fruit pies and tarts. Some of our favorite restaurants include:

St. Thomas

- **Au Bon Vivant:** Tel. 774-2158. Located on Government Hill. Offers a superb view of Charlotte Amalie and the harbor lights. Known for its classic French food. French champagne can be ordered by the glass here. The tables on the terrace are the best. Expensive.

- **Victor's Hide Out**: Tel. 776-9379. 32A Sub Base off Route 30. Definitely take a taxi since it is hard to find on your own. Located high on the hilltop and serves the best ribs on the island as well as native dishes. Closed Sundays, but open for lunch and dinner the rest of the week. Moderate.

- **Daddy's**: Tel. 775-6590. Located on the east end. Has native food. Moderate.

- **Eunice's**: Tel. 775-3975. 67 Smith Bay. We've been enjoying the food here for years. The servings are generous, making it a popular place. Reservations are needed for dinner. Open every day.

St. Croix

- **Cafe Du Soleil**: Tel. 772-5400. Located on Prince passage on Strand Street in downtown Frederiksted. Lunch and dinner overlooking the sea. Reservations suggested. Moderate

- **Cormorant Beach Club**: Tel. 778-8920. One of the finest restaurants on the island overlooking the sea. Excellent choice of fresh seafood. Sunday brunch. Reservations suggested. Expensive.

- **Amalie's Terrace**: Tel. 773-2035. Located at Hotel on the Cay in the Christainsted harbor. Excellent selection of lobster and fresh seafood. Expensive.

- **Duggan's Reef**: Tel. 773-9800. An excellent open-air restaurant on the east end of the island. Local favorite. Moderate.

St. John

- **Chow Bella**: Tel. 776-7171. Located at the Hyatt regency, serving Italian and Oriental cuisine. Excellent open-air restaurant with music nightly. Reservations strongly recommended. Very Expensive.

- **Caneel Bay Beach:** Tel. 776-6111. Terrace Dining Room: Elegant open-air tables overlooking the beach. Excellent lunch buffet. Jackets required at dinner during the season. Reservations required. Very Expensive.

- **Paradiso:** Tel. 776-8806. Great array of pastas, salads and seafood located at Mongoose Junction. Reservation recommended. Expensive.

- **Pusser's:** Tel. 774-5489. Specializing in English dinner pies and located at Wharfside Village, Cruz Bay. Expensive.

14

Puerto Rico

Puerto Rico is big enough to spend days driving around from San Juan to "out on the island" as the locals say. Most visitors never get beyond the resorts and casinos or Old San Juan to the quieter life of the mountains and countryside.

Although Puerto Rico, especially San Juan, is noted as the home port of numerous cruise ships, and is the vacation land for many Americans and travelers from around the world, it is also a shopper's Mecca. Although not a duty-free port—and unable to offer fashions, jewelry, and electronic goods at prices that compete with St. Martin/Sint Maarten or St. Thomas—the sheer number of shops available from Old San Juan to the largest shopping centers near San Juan and in Ponce can be overwhelming. From the hundreds of small and elegant shops in Old San Juan to the more than 200 outlets available in the Plaza Los Americas, to the new shopping areas in Ponce, you will be able to find every type of fashion, beautiful jewelry, elegant gold and silver pieces, and an abundance of crafts.

Of particular note in San Juan are the traditional Puerto Rican crafts such as the **Santos**, a small wooden figure depicting a religious scene or representing a saint. The techniques and styles used by the local artists are passed on for generations

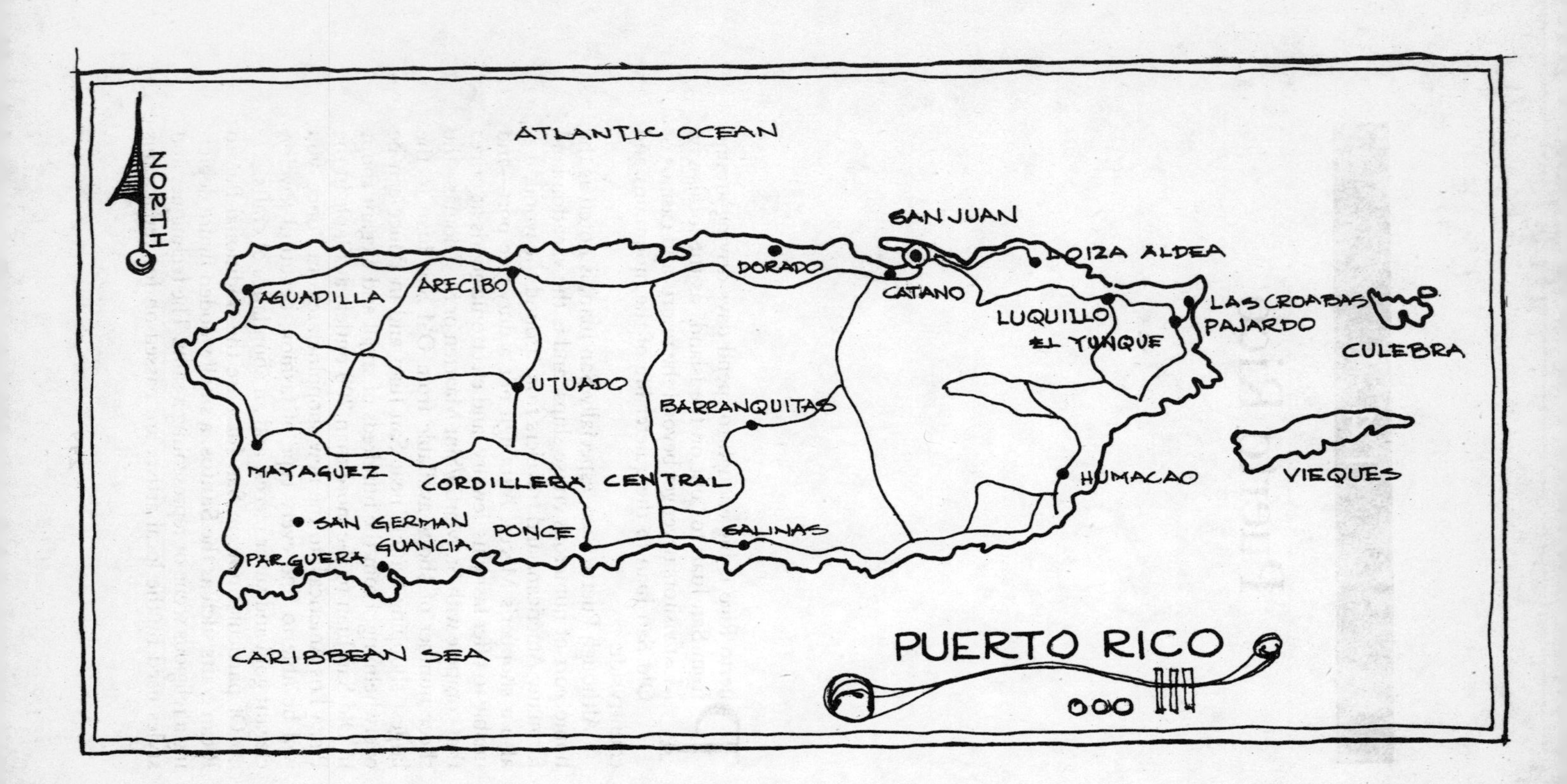
NORTH
ATLANTIC OCEAN
SAN JUAN
DORADO
LOIZA ALDEA
CATANO
LAS CROABAS
LUQUILLO
PAJARDO
EL YUNQUE
CULEBRA
AGUADILLA
ARECIBO
UTUADO
BARRANQUITAS
VIEQUES
MAYAGUEZ
CORDILLERA CENTRAL
HUMACAO
SAN GERMAN
PONCE
SALINAS
GUANCIA
PARGUERA
CARIBBEAN SEA
PUERTO RICO

generations within the same family, a factor which explains the very personalized nature of the figures.

Shopping in San Juan also takes on a rare special flavor. Though the older part of the city, known as Old San Juan, covers barely a quarter of a square mile, it was built in the tradition of many old Spanish cities. The city is full of small parks and plazas where you can rest. Strolling the streets of Old San Juan invites shopping discoveries around every corner.

GETTING TO KNOW YOU

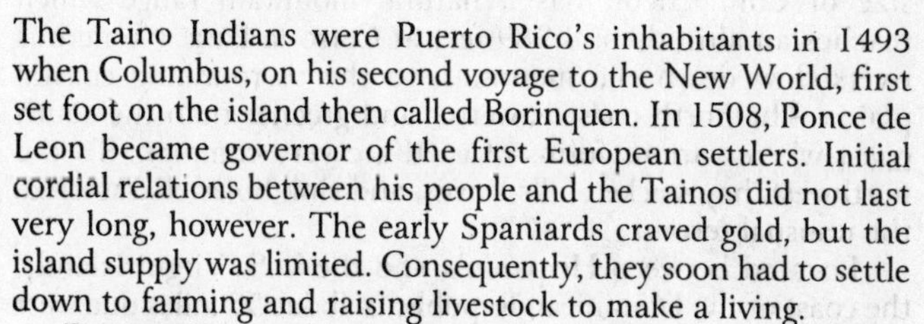

The Taino Indians were Puerto Rico's inhabitants in 1493 when Columbus, on his second voyage to the New World, first set foot on the island then called Borinquen. In 1508, Ponce de Leon became governor of the first European settlers. Initial cordial relations between his people and the Tainos did not last very long, however. The early Spaniards craved gold, but the island supply was limited. Consequently, they soon had to settle down to farming and raising livestock to make a living.

During the next three centuries, settlers spent much time defending Puerto Rico from the Spanish empire's traditional enemies—principally the Dutch in 1625, and the English in 1595, 1598 and 1797—and the fortresses in Old San Juan grew more and more massive as a consequence. At the same time, islanders struggled to develop an internal economy based primarily on the production of cattle, sugar cane, tobacco and coffee. By the end of the 1880's, Puerto Rico had succeeded in maturing socially, economically, and politically. The 1815 Cedula de Gracias offered many advantages to immigrants from Spain and the new Latin America republics. The Spanish, in turn, were instrumental in making Puerto Rico a top sugar exporting colony.

Following the Spanish-American War in 1898, Spain ceded the island to the U.S. Puerto Ricans became U.S. citizens in 1917 and adopted common law status in 1952. After World War II, the island began an intensive industrialization program, and today is a major producer and exporter of manufactured goods, high technology equipment, and pharmaceuticals.

Today's Puerto Rico is a blend of Spanish, African, Indian, and American cultures. The island is among the most highly developed and modernized in the Caribbean, preserving its ethnic heritage while successfully adapting to the rapidly changing world.

The biggest attraction for shopping in Puerto Rico, of course, will be San Juan, especially Old San Juan. The capital city of now bustling Puerto Rico is actually located on a small island.

THE BASICS

LOCATION AND GEOGRAPHY

Lying between the Atlantic Ocean and the Caribbean Sea, Puerto Rico is the eastern most and smallest of the islands in the Greater Antilles. The 110 by 35 mile island, roughly the size of Connecticut, has a natural mountain range which reaches an altitude of 4,389 feet at Cerro la Pata. Numerous rivers flow down the mountain to the surrounding coastal plains. The north coast is wetter and greener than the south coast where various forms of cacti are very common. To the northwest, hay stacked hills, caves, and sink holes characterize the unusual terrain.

Located between Hispaniola and the U.S. Virgin Islands, the coast of the Dominican Republic is about 55 miles due west across the Mona Passage, and St. Thomas is about 40 miles to the east.

The island is accessible from many U.S. cities and the three and one half hour, 1,600 mile trip from New York, or the two and one half hour trip from Miami make the island very accessible. According to the U.S. government's last census, nearly 3.2 million people live on the island and approximately 1.1 million of those people live in the San Juan area.

Puerto Rico actually lies within the Atlantic Standard Time Zone, and it is one hour later than Eastern Standard Time on the U.S. east coast. For example, if it is 9am in San Juan, the time is 8am in New York and Miami. However, when the Eastern Time Zone changes to Eastern Daylight Savings Time, the time in Puerto Rico and the eastern U.S. are exactly the same.

POLITICAL FLAVOR OF PUERTO RICO

Neither a state nor a territory, Puerto Rico enjoys a unique relationship with the United States under its current common law status. Puerto Ricans are citizens of the U.S. and have most of the rights, privileges and obligations of other citizens.

In practice, Puerto Rico functions much as a state. In national U.S. elections, Puerto Ricans may vote in presidential party primaries, but not in the elections themselves. However, Puerto Rico does have a voice, although not a vote, in the U.S.

Congress through a resident commissioner who is elected by the people to a four year term. He or she has all the privileges of a member of Congress but without a right to vote except in House Committees to which he or she belongs.

In keeping with the U.S. principle of "no taxation without representation," Puerto Ricans are not subject to U.S. Federal taxes. Puerto Ricans pay comparable taxes, however. This allows for fiscal autonomy and a Customs union that allows free trade anywhere in the world and duty-free trade with all other parts of the U.S. The Federal government does retain control of Customs, interstate trade, and the postal service, coast guard, lighthouse service, and licensing of radio and television stations. Federal courts are maintained to adjudicate civil and criminal matters that fall under the jurisdiction of the U.S. government.

CLIMATE, WHEN TO GO, WHAT TO WEAR

While Puerto Rico's climate is definitely tropical, it is made pleasant by the almost constant trade winds. Seasonal temperature changes are slight, ranging from an average winter temperature of 73 degrees Fahrenheit to an average of 82 degrees Fahrenheit during the warmest month of August. Because the terrain rises from sea level to nearly 4,000 feet at some points, the temperatures and rainfall vary considerably across the island. The coldest temperature ever recorded in Puerto Rico was 40 degrees Fahrenheit in 1911 and more recently a 39 degree temperature was recorded in the Toro Negro Preserve.

While there is no true rainy season in Puerto Rico, more rain falls in June, August, September, and October than any other months. Because of the mountains, there are odd pockets of heavy rainfall; however, San Juan's average is only 60 inches per year. Daily weather reports are available throughout Puerto Rico in both Spanish and English by calling 254-5488.

The general mode of dress in and around San Juan and other parts of Puerto Rico is not much different than in the other tropical islands. Men generally wear suits and ties for business occasions. However, the "guayabera," an embroidered loosely worn shirt, is cool and considered perfectly acceptable in most areas. For women, work dress depends on their occupation. Women in executive positions usually wear suits, dresses, or stylish separates. Pants are generally accepted. Blazers are especially popular because of air-conditioning in most offices, cars, and public buildings.

Evening wear, especially at the hotels and the Performing Arts Center, is quite formal with a covered look because of the air-conditioning. Dresses of all lengths are acceptable. Depending on the occasion, men wear suits, tuxedos, blazers, or long-sleeved guayaberas.

For shopping, we recommend casual dress. However, as in most cities throughout the Caribbean, bathing suits and short shorts are not acceptable in the main shopping areas, hotel lobbies, or shops nor in most restaurants. Since many of the shopping areas in Old San Juan will require some walking, we strongly recommend a pair of very comfortable walking shoes rather than loose fitting sandals. Remember, this is a very old city where you will encounter some cobblestone streets as well as pavement that is not always perfectly smooth.

For the young, almost anything seems acceptable today, although the style in Puerto Rico tends to be a bit dressier than in the United States. High heels and mini skirts are the rage for teenage girls as well as cropped jackets and virtually anything with bright colors. For young men, black turtlenecks with jeans or baggy trousers are extremely popular.

For many residents of San Juan, designer jeans and stylish T-shirts are everyday wear and have become almost a daily uniform. Because of the number of outlet shops such as Hathaway and Ralph Lauren, it is very easy to become an accomplished brand name shopper.

GETTING THERE

Puerto Rico is one of the most accessible islands in the Caribbean and some airlines such as American have made San Juan their *hub* for that part of the world. Even if you are not planning to go to San Juan, you will pass through the airport to most other islands in the Caribbean. In addition to being accessible to the U.S. mainland, San Juan is readily accessible from virtually every other Caribbean island and is represented by a list of airline carriers too numerous to mention here. From the U.S., however, American, Delta, U.S. Air and TWA have frequent service to the island, primarily from New York, Newark, Washington, DC, Raleigh-Durham, and Miami.

International carriers flying into San Juan's airport include British Airways from London, Lufthansa from Frankfurt, Iberia from Madrid, and Air France from Paris.

Seven airlines, Aero Virgin Islands, American Eagle, Sunaire Express, Air Jamica, Dominicean Airlines, and LAIT offer regional services connecting San Juan with the surrounding islands.

For cruise ships, the San Juan port is the busiest ocean terminal in the Caribbean. Fifty percent of all trade in the region, totaling some $1.4 billion passes, through this port. It is also the life blood of Puerto Rico's economy. Large container ships, carrying everything from consumer goods to construction materials, link San Juan with cities around the world. The harbor sits inside San Juan Bay and almost is a land locked body of water some three miles long with an average width of one mile. The long bay protects vessels even when the Atlantic Ocean is at its roughest.

The Bay also shelters large cruise ships that call at the port. Last year, cruise ships pulled along side San Juan's piers some 500 times and more than 420,000 passengers disembarked. A special walkway connects the piers and leads to the cobblestone streets in historic Old San Juan. While visitors explore the city and other points of interest, the residents of San Juan admire the ships themselves. The following ships stop in San Juan. Carnival, Celebrity, Costa, Crystal, Cunard, Diamond, Holland America, Norwegian Princess, Regency, Royal, Royal Caribbean, Seabourn and Sun.

Other ships do visit San Juan on a periodic basis. You should check with your particular cruise line to see if and when they do call at this port. Ponce is also becoming another port of call for Puerto Rico.

DOCUMENTS

U.S. citizens do not need documents to enter the airport or the cruise ship terminal in San Juan since Puerto Rico is governmentally part of the United States. However, residents of other countries should check before leaving home as to exactly what types of documents are necessary. As in most all cases, a valid passport is always acceptable; however, other proof of citizenship might be acceptable in certain cases.

ARRIVAL AND DEPARTURE

Arriving at Luis Munoz Marin International Airport can be an experience in and of itself. Most airlines arrive at the main terminal. Since this is one of the region's largest and busiest airports, you will encounter the normal airport crowd. Adding to the crowds is the Puerto Rican custom of friends, relatives, and even occasional onlookers meeting incoming and departing flights. The crowds at the gates make arrival and departure somewhat difficult. Indeed, you'll have to press through crowds who are there only for the purpose of watching. Some of the walkways within the airport can be rather long. If you do have heavy carry-on baggage, use a small cart or have someone carry the bags for you. After you retrieve your luggage and pass through security, transportation is readily available outside the terminal.

If you arrive by a small inter-island carrier or American Eagle, the arrival gate will be further away from the main terminate. However, the walkways are clearly marked, and you should have no difficulty finding the baggage claim area.

If you connect in San Juan for flights to other islands, carefully follow the transfer procedures. If your next flight is on a larger aircraft, your connection will probably be in the same area you arrived. Since you need not pass through Immigration or security, your transfer should be relatively easy. If however, you are connecting to a flight on one of the smaller inter-island airlines, you must exit through security and Immigration and go to a different departure terminal. If you are only connecting, do not make the mistake of getting in the long lines at the ticket counters to check on your seating arrangements. Just proceed directly to the departure gate and arrange to have your seat checked there—especially if your connection time is short. In the departure area at Luis Munoz Marin International Airport you should pay close attention to the departure procedures. Departure announcements for smaller aircraft are sometimes made by the person at the door checking boarding passes rather than over a loudspeaker. Some passengers get left behind because they fail to pay close attention.

Be forewarned that some smaller aircraft have limited baggage capacity. If you travel to other islands by small aircraft, all of your baggage may not accompany you. Consequently, you may want to keep smaller, valuable items with you as well as an extra change of casual clothing or a bathing suit so you can at least enjoy your stay at your final destination until your bags arrive.

If you arrive by small, private aircraft, the Isla Grande Airport off the Avenida Fernandez Juncos in San Juan is the most complete aviation center in the Caribbean. Permission to land at private or military airports must be obtained from the proper authorities, and there is a moderate landing fee for small aircraft using either the Luis Munuos Marin International or Isla Grande Airports.

Puerto Rico has no departure tax nor Customs to clear. However, given the airport congestion, you should leave a little additional time for airport procedures. The lines going through the Immigration check point and at the airline counters are usually long. An hour should be enough; however, if you want to browse through the airport shops, you should allow additional time.

There are no Customs duties on purchases from Puerto

Rico. The U.S. Department of Agriculture does, however, inspect all luggage returning to the U.S. mainland for prohibited food products. Check with your hotel regarding which items you can carry with you. A few of the more popular and permissible items are pineapples, avocados, coconuts, papayas, oranges, lemons, and limes. If you are planing to take a topical plant home, keep in mind that it must be entirely free of soil. Peat moss is permitted as growing medium, however. If you have a question regarding permissible items, contact USDA APHIS PPQ, Luis Munoz Marin International Airport, Isla Verde, Tel. 753-4666 or 753-3715.

CURRENCY, TRAVELER'S CHECKS, CREDIT CARDS

Puerto Rico's currency is the U.S. dollar. Traveler's checks and credit cards are accepted by hotels, restaurants, and most gift shops in and around San Juan. In fact, shopping here is similar to shopping anywhere in the U.S.

TIPPING

Since fixed service charges are not normally added to bills in San Juan and other parts of Puerto Rico, tipping here is very much like any city in the U.S. Airport porters are normally tipped 50 cents to $1 per bag; taxi drivers 15% of the fare; chamber maids $1-2 per room per day; and hotel doormen 50 cents to $1 for any special attention. The standard tip in a hotel dining room or any restaurant is 15% of the bill. If you travel on a special tour package, check to see if gratuities are included. In many cases the meal coupons do not cover tips. In that case, it is customary to leave the tip in an amount that would equal 15% of the bill had you actually paid for the meal.

LANGUAGE

Although Spanish is spoken throughout Puerto Rico, English is understood and spoken in all major hotels, shopping areas, and restaurants. Puerto Ricans do welcome efforts by travelers to speak Spanish. If you want to learn more about Puerto Rican Spanish, ask the sales people you encounter how to speak this version of Spanish; they will be more than happy to assist you with their language.

BUSINESS HOURS

Most shops in Old San Juan, Condado, and Isla Verde are open from 9am until 5pm or 6pm. Many stay open later in the evening. If you have a particular shop you want to visit, check with them directly about their hours. Some shops are closed on Sunday. However, since San Juan is such a busy port for the cruise ships, you will find most shops in the Old San Juan area open on both Saturday and Sunday. Most shopping centers are open during normal business hours—9am to 6pm—and in many cases until 9pm.

- ❑ **Puerto Rico has no departure tax nor Customs to clear.**
- ❑ **Fixed service charges are not normally added to bills.**
- ❑ **Most shops in the Old San Juan area are open on both Saturday and Sunday.**
- ❑ **Taxis are metered in the city, but be sure the meter flag is in the "up" position when starting out.**
- ❑ **Since traffic jams in and around Old San Juan can be horrendous, and some streets are actually closed to traffic, park in one of the large and inexpensive parking garages near the shopping areas.**

Many small hotel shops post their hours on the door. Expect to find shops in large hotels to be open from 9am or 10am until 5pm or 6pm in the evening.

TRANSPORTATION

Taxis are readily available everywhere in and around San Juan. Taxis are metered in the city, but be sure the meter flag is in the "up" position when starting out. While most drivers are pleasant and honest, you may encounter a few hustlers. Overcharging is sometimes reported in rides from Luis Munoz Marin International Airport. Again, even when traveling from the airport to your hotel or shopping destinations, insist that the driver use the meter regardless of the time of day. The taxi fare is an initial 80 cents plus 10 cents per every additional one-eighth mile. Waiting time costs about $12 an hour, and an additional 50 cents is charged for calling a cab by telephone. Sometimes baggage is charged at 50 cents per piece. These fares apply regardless of the hour for up to four passengers—not per person. Taxis operating outside the normal taxi zones are not metered, but fares are fixed by law. When using an unmetered taxi, be sure to discuss the charge in advance.

Rental cars in San Juan are very convenient and will save you a great deal of money compared to using taxis. The cab fare from many of the hotels, such as the Caribe Hilton, Condado Beach Hotel, and the Clarion Hotel and Casino to the shopping area will be reasonable. However, if you want the cab to wait, the charges can add up quickly. In addition, it is somewhat difficult to carry large packages around with you in the crowded downtown shopping area. Therefore, if you park your rental car in one of the large parking garages centrally located in the shopping district, you will save a great deal of time and energy.

You will find many rental car companies in and around San Juan. If you are planning an island tour it is best to work with the Nationally recognized names who are in a better position to service you on the roads out of town. Some of the larger ones include **Avis** (723-8605, 791-0426, 791-2571), **Budget** (791-3685, 791-0277), **Hertz** (800-654-3131, 725-2027, 791-0840, 721-0303, 724-4410), **Leaseway of Puerto Rico** (788-7272), **Target** (728-1447, 759-8615, 782-6381), **Thrifty** (791-4241, 791-2786), and **Velco Puerto Rico** (792-9292).

Driving in San Juan is an adventure that requires patience and stamina. With an unusually high accident rate and constant traffic jams, city driving can be frustrating even for people with very even temperament. Your best defense in driving in San Juan is a keen eye and good sense of humor. Route numbers are fairly well posted, and roads are referred to by name in the city. Watch for solid yellow lines to the left of one-way streets—these are bus lanes used exclusively by buses traveling in the opposite direction from the normal traffic flow. Double yellow lines across a highway indicate a school zone.

If you drive to the island of Old San Juan, you will be entering on one-way streets on the northern side of the peninsula. Remember to stay out of the bus lanes. To reach the shopping areas of Old San Juan, take Munoz Rivera Avenue, which offers a spectacular ocean view as you approach the old city. You will see the walls of Old San Juan for the first time just beyond the buildings of the Department of Natural Resources and the State Capitol.

Turn left between the Natural Resources Department building and the modern House of Representatives office building, which has a fountain in front of it. If you stay on the street for about two blocks, you will enter the intersection with Paseo Covadonga. Just past the Treasury Department, you will find the Covadonga garage on your left at the intersection of Harding Street. This is the best place in Old San Juan to park for shopping since the garage is open 24 hours a day and a free shuttle service is available throughout the old city. If the Covadonga garage is full, continue on down the same street for approximately two more blocks to the Municipal Parking Garage on Recinto Sur Municipal or to the La Puntilla parking lot. The parking garages are clearly marked on the maps that are included in the local visitor brochures. The Recinto Sur Municipal garage is open in the evening but is not serviced by the free trolleys and minibuses, nor is it open 24 hours a day. The trolleys do, however, serve La Puntilla parking lot, but it is only open during the day.

If you get stopped for a major traffic violation in and around San Juan, the police normally confiscate your license on the spot. You must then return to the district where you received the ticket to pay your fine and retrieve your driver's license. Since the police are extremely attentive in and around San Juan, it is easy to get a speeding ticket on some of the freeways leading into the old city.

Speed limits are posted in miles per hour, but distances are given in kilometers. Road signs may be confusing initially although shapes and colors are familiar. "Pare" (stop) appears on the familiar red octagon sign, but many signs will baffle you and could be dangerous. If you are planning to drive, pay close attention to the road signs, especially those indicating bus only lanes.

Keep in mind that traffic jams in and around Old San Juan can be horrendous, and some streets are actually closed to traffic. Your main destination should be the large parking garages near the shopping areas. Parking fees are extremely reasonable, and it is very easy to get in and out of these parking garages.

The bus system in San Juan is efficient and inexpensive. The fare on all regular city buses in San Juan is 25 cents. Make sure that you have the exact change because the drivers do not make change. Bus stops (paradas) are found three to five blocks apart and can be identified by (1) tall metal standards with or without a sign showing a silhouette of a bus, (2) a wide yellow band painted around the telephone pole with the word "paradas," (3) a small concrete yellow oblique with "parada" or "parada juajua" on it, or (4) a covered waiting area with a bench. Exclusive bus lanes marked off by yellow and white lines travel against the traffic on one-way thoroughfares. A new fare is charged each time you change buses. The main bus terminals in Old San Juan are at the Plaza de Cologne and in the dock area near the craft shops. For information on the city bus routes and fares, call 767-7979.

For convenient door-to-door transportation to just about anywhere, you can call a service known as "la linea." La lineas are on call 24-hours a day and the fares are considerably lower than what regular taxis charge—depending on your destination. A long list of la lineas companies are found under lineas de carros in the Yellow Pages of the telephone directory.

Public van and passenger cars—called "publicos" and identified by the letters "P" or "PD" following the numbers on their license plates—regularly journey between the town plazas of different communities. Publicos are hailed like taxis. Their routes—the two connecting areas—are clearly advertised on the windshield. Fares in town average about 50 cents.

RESOURCES

You will find several tourist type newspapers available at the hotels, airport, and other information centers. One of the best is a publication called ***Que Pasa***, which is the official visitors guide to Puerto Rico.

In San Juan and throughout the island, the Puerto Rico Tourism Company (PRTC) maintains several regional information centers. Many municipalities also have their own centers. The PRTC offices in and around San Juan include the Luis Munoz Marin International Airport, Ilia Verde (791-1014, 791-3443, or 791-2551), the Condado Convention Center (723-3135 or 722-1513), and the Casida Rosada near the docks (722-1709). City Hall has its own tourism office (724-1227 or 724-7171). You can also write directly to the Puerto Rico Tourism Company for information: PO Box 4435, Old San Juan, PR 00905. PRTC offices in the United States are listed in Chapter Three.

WHERE TO SHOP

Although there are thousands of shops all over the island, the main shopping districts are Old San Juan, the Condado area, Isla Verde, and the large shopping centers.

Historic Old San Juan is the place to shop for Puerto Rican products. In addition to housing some of the city's finest art galleries (**Galeria Botello**) and jewelry shops (**Bared and Sons**), and an incredible assortment of specialty shops, you will find an endless array of stores offering local crafts and gifts. Some streets seem to have similar types of shops—Fortaleza and San Francisco Streets offer many stores specializing in precious gems, gold jewelry, crystal, and china, while Cristo Street seems to have the largest collection of clothing stores, crafts, and museums.

The main shopping area of Old San Juan begins at the Plaza La Marina, across the street from the pier where the cruise ships dock. If you continue up San Justo to Sol, turn left and walk three blocks to Cristo, turn left on Cristo and continue back down towards the water to Fortaleza, and then turn left again on Fortaleza for three blocks back to San Justo, you will encircle the area where most shops are located.

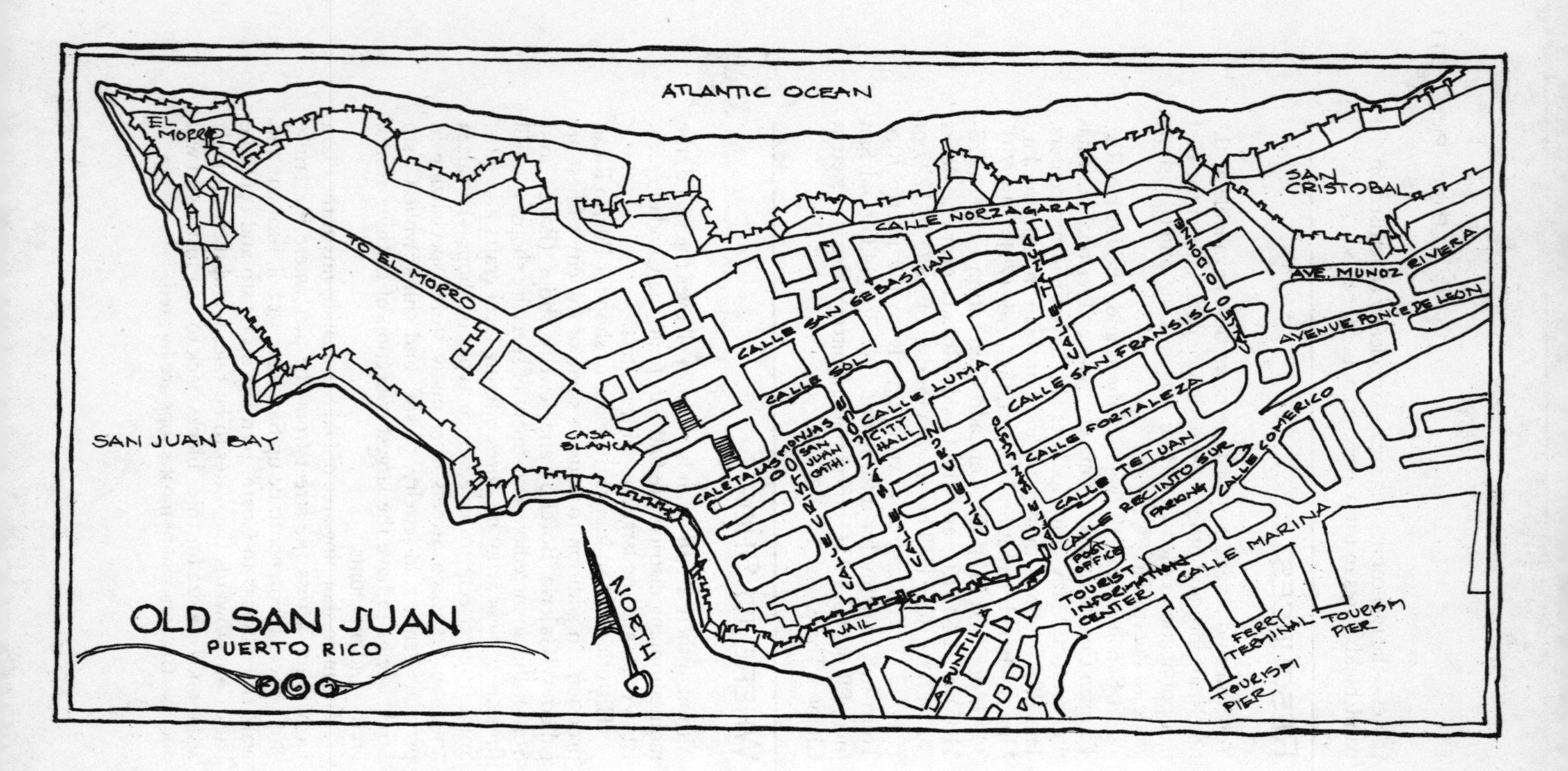
ATLANTIC OCEAN
EL MORRO
TO EL MORRO
SAN CRISTOBAL
CALLE NORZAGARAT
CALLE SAN SEBASTIAN
CALLE SOL
CALLE LUNA
CALLE SAN FRANSISCO
CALLE FORTALEZA
CALLE TETUAN
CALLE RECINTO SUR
CALLE COMERICO
CALLE MARINA
CALLE O'DONNEL
AVE. MUNOZ RIVERA
AVENUE PONCE DE LEON
CALLE CRISTO
CALLE SAN JOSE
CALLE CRUZ
CALLE SAN JUSTO
CALETA LAS MONJAS
SAN JUAN CATH.
CITY HALL
CASA BLANCA
POST OFFICE
PARKING
TOURIST INFORMATION CENTER
FERRY TERMINAL
TOURISM PIER
LA PUNTILLA
JAIL
SAN JUAN BAY
NORTH
OLD SAN JUAN
PUERTO RICO

About two or three miles east of Old San Juan is the high-fashion shopping area of **Condado**. Before the construction of the Puerto Rico Convention Center, this area was exclusively a wealthy residential community. When the emphasis shifted to conventioneers and tourists, many hotels and shops opened. The Condado shopping area, located along Ashford and Magdalena Avenues, is now the center for elegant women's apparel boutiques and other types of specialty shops. Most shopping is within walking distance of the Condado Plaza Hotel, the Regency Hotel, Ramada San Juan, Condado Beach Hotel, La Concha Hotel, the Dutch Inn Hotel, and the Dupont Plaza Hotel. The Radisson Normandie Hotel and the Caribe Hilton are nearby, but a taxi or car may be the best way to go. Although the distance does not seem to great, it is about a one half mile walk from these two hotels to the shopping area.

Just east of Condado, not far from the airport is **Isla Verde**. This is one of San Juan's top centers for tourism, with many miles of beaches, elegant hotels, and many fashionable boutiques. Most of the exclusive shops are within walking distance of the Travel Lodge Hotel, Carib Inn, Plazoleta Isla Verde, the Sands Hotel, El San Juan Hotel, and El San Juan Towers. In fact, many of the more exclusive shops are actually located in the shopping arcades of the hotels.

Ponce and Mayaguez, Puerto Rico's second and third largest cities are just beginning to be noticed for shopping. Armstrong's department store in the Santa Maria Shopping Center, Ponce, has been there for over 20 years. You will also find the Ponce Mall and the Mayaguez Mall here. In addition, one of the largest shopping centers in the Caribbean is being built in Ponce.

Plaza Las Americas, off the Las Americas Expressway and the near the San Juan banking district of Hato Rey, is ultra modern and the Caribbean's largest shopping center. Over 190 retail outlets are found here. In addition to the full array of department stores, men's shops, women's boutiques, and record stores, it has dozens of fast food restaurants, five movie theaters, and plenty of parking. It can get crowded on Saturdays and near the holidays, but it offers one-stop shopping for just about everything Puerto Rico has to offer.

Another very large shopping mall is **Plaza Carolina** with over 160 retail outlets. It is located about 20 minutes east of San Juan and has shops similar to Plaza Las Americas.

SHOPPING IN SAN JUAN, CONDADO, ISLA VERDE, AND PONCE

Visitors find Old San Juan a delightful place to shop. Truly an international shopping center, here you can purchase fine Thai silk; linen and cotton dresses and suits; Spanish antique furniture and reproductions; sundry items such as kettles, ladles, candle sticks; paintings and sculptures from Haiti; hand made wall coverings from Columbia; Kapok table mats from the Philippines; pure silk saris and hand woven cotton bedspreads from India; and diamonds, emeralds, pearls.

Foremost among Puerto Rico's traditional crafts is the carving of **Santos**, small wooden figures depicting a religious scene or representing a Saint. Artisans also fashion **mundillo**, hand made bobbin lace which is worked on a mundillo frame into bands, doilies, collars, tablecloths and other dainty items. **Cuatros**, a guitar type instrument with five double strings and simple **guiros** which date back to the Indian times, are two of several musical instruments which are hand hewn. Island **masks** include coconut vejigantes, which are used in Loiza's St. Festivities and papier-mache masks popular during the carnival festivals.

Although Old San Juan is the center for shopping, you will also find other large shopping centers in the surrounding areas such as the Plaza Los Americas, Plaza Carolina, Plaza Rio Hondo, Mayaguez Mall, Aguadilla Shopping Center, and a new center in Ponce. Other retail locations offer refuge from the large crowds and cheaper prices. Several shopping areas offer inexpensive clothing along with fine boutiques and designer clothing shops—without the discomfort of large crowds and the problems of finding parking space.

WHAT TO BUY

JEWELRY AND WATCHES

Shops in Puerto Rico offer the largest and most exclusive selection of jewelry and watches in the Caribbean—the streets of San Juan and surrounding areas are literally lined with jewelry stores. Although prices are not as low as in other shopping areas, such as St. Martin/Sint Maarten, merchandise is brought into the island duty-free and thus you pay no duty when arriving back in the U.S. Shops such as **Maximimo Jewelers**, located in the Sands Hotel & Casino, Isla Verde, offer fine gems, including rubies, sapphires, emeralds, aquamarines, topazes, tourmalines, and amethysts, as well as handmade settings in 14K and 18K gold. **Juan Abislaiman Jewelers,** a family operated jewelry salon at the corner of San Justo and Tetuan Streets in Old San Juan, has a wide selection of 14K and 18K gold jewelry, diamonds, and semiprecious stones at reasonable prices. They are also the exclusive dealer for Audemars Piguet and Pulchra Swiss watches by Bertolucci.

Other shops that specialize in exquisite jewelry and watches include **N. Barquet Jewelers**, 201 Fortaleza Street, Old San Juan (precious stones, gold jewelry and watches by Chopard, Juvenia, Daniel Mink and Eterna); **Joyeria Riviera**, 205 Cruz Street, Old San Juan (diamonds, emeralds, gold and watches by Rolex, Movado, and Patek Philippe); **Barrachina**, 104 Fortaleza Street, Old San Juan (good prices on one of the Caribbean's largest selections of precious and semiprecious stones).

Puerto Rico has many jewelry stores that specialize in exclusive and unusual designs. **M. H. Reingold & Daughters** (1015 Ashford Avenue, Condado) features the designs of DeBeers award winners David Yurman, M & J Savitt, and Angela Cummings. They also carry Robert Lee Morris and other designers that can be found nowhere else. For lower priced, but no less beautiful jewelry, there are also shops that offer a full line of merchandise made from fabricated diamonds set in 14K gold or silver. **Replicas** (El San Juan Hotel & Casino, Isla Verde) specializes in hand cut and set fabricated gems in various colors as well as finely crafted jewelry.

ART AND CRAFTS

Puerto Rican art has exploded onto the world scene in recent years, and it includes works in oils, water colors, ceramics, sculpture, photography, and graphics. **Galeria Costa Azul** (corner of Sol and Cruz Streets in Old San Juan) offers information on a wide range of Puerto Rican art and resident artists. Many items found here attained international recognition. The graphic art is high quality and reasonably priced; it's an especially good value for collectors or decorators. **Galeria Colibri** (158 Cristo, Old San Juan) only handles graphics, some produced by local artists. Larger galleries, such as **Galeria Botello**, primarily promote local art. They display primitive and other works of art in oils and acrylics as well as bronze sculpture, ceramics, drawings, prints, and posters. The gallery features many artists, but some, such as Botello, Velazquez, Roche, Baez, Espinosa, and Lindsay Daen are exhibited on a permanent basis. **Galeria Botello** has three locations—208

Cristo, Old San Juan; Plaza Las Americans, Hato Rey; and shopping mall at the Caribe Hilton. They are all open every day. The following galleries display a wide range of local art:

- **Casa Candina**: 14 Candina, Condado. Open Monday through Saturday, 9am to 5pm. Tel. 724-2077.
- **Galeria Caliban:** 51 Cristo, Old San Juan. Open Monday through Saturday 10am to 6pm, and Sunday, 12 noon to 6pm. Tel. 722-4443.
- **Galeria Coabey:** 101 San Jose, Old San Juan. Open Monday through Saturday, 10am to 5pm. Tel. 723-1395 or 723-1018.
- **Galeria Diego**: 51 Maria Moczo, Ocean Park. Open Monday through Friday, 10am to 6pm, and Saturday, 9am to 12 noon. Tel. 728-1287.
- **Galeria Espiral**: 68 Navaro, Hato Rey. Open Monday through Friday, 9am to 6pm, and Saturday, 9am to 2pm. Tel. 758-1078.
- **Galeria Fragio**: Cristo and Sol, Old San Juan. Open Monday through Saturday, 10am to 6pm. Tel. 723-7415.
- **Galeria Liga de Arte**: San Jose, Old San Juan. Open Monday through Saturday, 9am to 4pm. Tel. 722-4468.
- **Galeria Luigi Marrozzini:** 56 Cristo, Old San Juan. Open Tuesday through Saturday, 11am to 6pm. Tel. 755-2840.
- **Galeria Palomas:** 207 Cristo, Old San Juan. Open Monday through Saturday, 10am to 6pm. Tel. 724-8904.
- **Taller Galeria Andres:** Condominio El Centro II, 500 Munoz Rivera, Hato Rey. Open Monday through Saturday, 8am to 5pm. Tel. 759-7155.

Puerto Rico is also famous for its native arts and crafts known as "naif" art. One of the most important traditional crafts is the carving of **santos**. The techniques and styles used by the local santeros are passed on for generations within the same family. Even though the same santos figure may have been made by different artists, those produced by father and son will be very similar in design, detail and color.

Local artists also fashion **mundillo**, handmade bobbin lace which is worked on a mundillo frame into bands, doilies, collars, tablecloths, and napkins.

The **cuatro**, a lute type instrument with five double strings, and the simple gourd **guiros** are two of several musical instruments made from native trees. Both of these instruments date back to the Taino Indians, the original inhabitants of Puerto Rico. Cuatros can be purchased in a number of shops, but **Ole** (105 Fortaleza, Old San Juan) probably has one of the best selections of these handmade instruments.

Colorful **masks** of all sizes, colors, and shapes are used to celebrate many special holidays. The island's masks include the coconut vejigantes used in the Loiza Aldea's patron saint festivities and the papier-mache masks that are very popular during the carnival festivities in Ponce. Local artists also make masks from metal, ceramics, and wood.

The following centers offer visitors an opportunity to see a variety of traditional items made by the island's skilled craftspeople.:

- **Aguadilla en San Juan**: 352 San Francisco, Old San Juan. Open Monday through Saturday, 9am to 6pm. Tel. 722-0578.
- **Artesania Camui**: Route 3, Km 15.1, Canovanas. Open Monday through Saturday, 8:30am to 6pm.
- **Beachcomber**: Route 304, La Parguera. Open daily 8am to 6pm.
- **Galeria Cohoba Cialena**: Route 149, Km 9.1, Ciales. Open daily, 6am to 10pm. Tel. 854-8537.
- **Galeria Epoca en Turismo**: La Casita Information Center, Old San Juan. Open Monday, Wednesday, Friday, Saturday, and Sunday, 2pm to 11pm. Tel. 722-1709.
- **Mercado Artesnia Carabali**: Sixto Escobar Park, Puerta de Tierra. Open Tuesday through Saturday, 9am to 5pm. Tel. 722-0369.
- **Mercado de Artesanias Plaza de Hostos**: Recinto Sur,

Old San Juan. Open weekends only in the afternoon and evening.

- **Mercado de Artesania Puertorriquena, Hermandad de Artesanos**: Munoz Rivera Park, Puerta de Tierra. Open Sunday, 9am to 5pm.

- **Plazoleta del Puerto**: Marinia, Old San Juan, Open daily, 9am to 6pm. Tel. 722-3053.

- **Puerto Rican Arts and Crafts**: 204 Fortaleza, Old San Juan. Open Monday through Saturday, 9am to 6pm. Tel. 725-5596.

- **Centro de Artes Populares:** Plaza San Jose on Cristo Street, Old San Juan. Open Monday through Saturday, 10am to 5pm. Tel. 724-6250.

In addition, you can visit artisans' shops outside the normal shopping areas. These include hammock makers in San Sebastian, cuatro makers in Utuado or Corozal, basket weavers in Jayuya, and santeros in Ponce. For information on artisans who open their workshops to visitors, contact the Centro de Artes Populares (Tel. 724-6250) or the Tourism Artisan Office (Tel. 721-2400).

Some of the most unique items in Puerto Rico are the butterfly art at **The Butterfly People** (152 Fortaleza Street, Old San Juan). Here, butterflies from all over the world are dried and mounted in lucite cases. The gallery is located in an 18th Century building that was the birthplace of Munoz Marin, the first elected Governor of Puerto Rico. The butterflies are displayed in a number of rooms on the second floor surrounding a courtyard. Also located on the second floor is The Cafe, which offers drinks and both Puerto Rican creole and continental cuisine. Shopping here is not only unique, it's also one of the most relaxing atmospheres of any gallery or shop in the Caribbean. Each display is made from master designs, and each composition is signed. The Butterfly People accept commissions to design one-of-a-kind creations in just about any size and color. Some larger designs containing hundreds of butterflies are made of several separate boxes hung in groups. While you can see some of the displays from the street, a visit to the gallery itself on the second floor is a must if you are looking for something beautiful and unique in art. Take a shopping break and stop at the small Butterfly People Cafe for a cool drink and a light lunch on the second floor.

FASHIONS

A design center in the Caribbean, Puerto Rico contributes to the world of fashion through the talents of many well-known local designers, and also offers some of the best fashions from around the world. Hundreds of boutiques in Old San Juan, Condado, and the Plaza Las Americas shopping center showcase the clothing that incorporates traditional designs into contemporary attire. Throughout the island you can find unique fashions at good bargains. The *bargains* on exclusive designs are relative, but you will save from 10% to 15% on some of the more expensive items.

One of the best known Puerto Rican couturiers is **Fernando Pena**, whose designs can be found at 1409 Ponce de Leon, San Juan and 1400 Madalena, Santurce. In addition to being able to see the Pena designs at several other shops, you will be able to find handcrafted batik floral clothing at **Java Wraps** (206 Cristo, Old San Juan); Lanvin, Christian Dior, Oscar de la Renta and Calvin Klein designer clothing at **Velasco** (Plaza Las Americas, Hato Rey); and the fashions of Flora Kung, Norma Kamali and Cheryl Tiegs at many locations. For the more adventurous fashion shopper, Puerto Rico is now offering some relatively unknown, but progressive design manufacturers. One of the newer shops is **Incognito** (1112 Ashford Avenue, Condado) which offers the fashions of Marithe Girbaud, Radio, Lust, Z. Cavaricci, and Betsey Johnson.

If you are shopping for the big and/or tall man, San Juan has shops to fit just about anyone. One of the best stocked stores is **Hombre Grande** (135 Ashford Avenue, Condado). Here you will find formal suits, sport jackets, shirts, casual wear, and accessories by such designers as Givenchy, Christian Dior and Lanvin. Sizes are available from XL to XXXXX in shirts, 38-60 in slacks and shorts, 44-60 in suits, and 10-15E in shoes.

Although the full range of shops and fashions are too numerous to mention, a few clothing outlets should not be missed. **Polo/Ralph Lauren Factory Store** (201 Cristo, Old San Juan) has a broad selection of apparel for men, women, and children; fragrances; clothing accessories; and furnishings for the home. You will find savings of up to 50% on most items, but keep in mind that many are factory seconds and should be checked carefully. This is especially true for shirts that are displayed on large tables. Many are excellent buys, but you will find some with noticeable blemishes and areas of discoloration.

The **Hathaway Factory Outlet** (203 Cristo, Old San Juan) features Jack Nicklaus sportswear at savings of up to 50%. Expect savings of up to 60% on Hathaway and Hathaway for

Her as well as comparable savings on Christian Dior shirts, neckwear, accessories, and Chaps by Ralph Lauren.

The **Bass Shoe Factory Outlet** (206 Cristo, Old San Juan) offers excellent savings on their full range of shoes.

Shopping at these three shops usually results in the purchase of another suitcase or sports bag! It's amazing how much room three pair of shoes, five shirts, six belts, a bathrobe, and a number of golf shirts take, especially if you have either shopped another island first, or have spent the previous day shopping in and around San Juan.

CHINA, CRYSTAL, AND CERAMICS

Although more expensive than elsewhere in the Caribbean, the emphasis here is on buying quality china, crystal, and ceramics. Look for unique Dominican handmade ceramic Lime figurines at **Lime, Inc.** (200 Cristo, Old San Juan); many specialty items from Europe and Asia at **Casa Cavanagh** (202 Cristo, Old San Juan); and a large collection of Baccarat, Lalique, Lladro, Hummel, Rosenthal, Waterford, and Wedgwood at **Bared and Sons** (Fortaleza and San Justo Streets, Old San Juan). The only way to become familiar with these products is to browse through the many shops along the streets in Old San Juan as well as in hotel shopping arcades and shopping centers.

SPECIALTY ITEMS

Puerto Rico excels with specialty items. You will find thousands of specialty shops and stores on the island offering hand-made straw hats and baskets, silk-screened T-shirts, handpainted souvenirs, and unique jewelry. Again, the only way to find these products is to walk the streets and shopping centers. You will be pleased with both the quality and prices.

SPECIAL TIPS FOR CRUISE SHIP PASSENGERS

All cruise ships tie up at one of the piers in Old San Juan. When you exit your ship, you're only steps from the Tourist Information Center which is to the left. Pick up a copy of ***Que Pasa*** and a map of Old San Juan there. While there are some small artisan shops directly across the street from the ships, save them for last, and if you have time.

You will be able to see most jewelry, local craft, and clothing street from the Tourist Information Center) and walk up the hill on San Justo to Fortaleza (will be listed as Calle La Fortaleza on some maps). Turn left at Fortaleza and walk towards Cristo. You'll find shops on both sides of the street, with the **Butterfly People** in the second block on the left. Turn right on Cristo and you will be able to cover both sides of the street for three or four blocks, which will include the outlet shops for **Polo, Hathaway and Bass Shoes**. If you have time, turn left on San Francisco when you are coming back down Cristo. There are many shops around a plaza about half way back to San Justo. You can easily do all this within two hours. If you have time left however, spend some of it in the shops on San Jose, La Cruz, and Luna.

If you are in port for more than one day, you may want to visit the exclusive boutiques in and around the large hotels in Condado and Isla Verde.

The traffic can get very heavy around the Isla Verde area, so be sure to allow at least an hour to get back to the ship if you venture that far away. However little time you have in Old San Juan, you will definitely not be disappointed in the vast selection of clothing, jewelry, gems and local crafts.

ENJOYING YOUR STAY

THE SITES

There are almost as many sites to see around Puerto Rico as there are around some of the large U.S. cities, and all in a tropical setting. No trip would be complete without a visit to **Castillo San Felipe Del Morro**, the multi-level fortress within walking distance of Old San Juan known as ***El Morro***, or one of the many other forts located throughout the island. A walking tour around **Old San Juan** is an excellent way to discover the full history of the island.

Sports, including some of the best golf courses in the Caribbean, are available year round. The local newspapers and guidebooks list what is going on the week you are there.

A trip to the **El Yunque rain forest** is wonderful. Located inland, it's a good break from the beach and the crowded shopping areas.

ACCOMMODATIONS

There are hundreds of hotels in Puerto Rico representing every price range. Some of our favorites include:

- **Casa San Jose:** Tel. 809-723-1212. 809-723-7602. Calle San Jose 159. The place to stay in the historic district of Old San Juan. Restored in 1991, this three-story building has five suites and four rooms—all with bath, mini bar and air-conditioning. Black and white marble floors and European antiques help create the elegance along with the interior patio with plush and colorful plantings. Double-pane windows keep out the noise of the street below while affording a close-up look at the architecture and life of the old town area. A continental breakfast is served in this stylish establishment. Young children are not accommodated. Parking is provided.

- **Caribe Hilton:** Tel. 809-721-0303. San Jeronimo Street, San Juan. The only large hotel near Old San Juan. Major renovations have put this hotel back in excellent condition. Shopping is available in the hotel. It is also located just a few blocks from the Condado area and about a 20 minute drive to Isla Verde.

- **Condado Plaza Hotel & Casino:** Tel. 809-721-1000. Fax 809-253-0178. Located at 999 Ashford Avenue, Condado. Very busy with all the facilities to keep you at the hotel. On the water with good restaurants and shops.

- **Radisson Ambassador Plaza Hotel & Casino:** Tel. 809-721-7300. Fax 809-723-6151. Expensive look with high drama. Beautiful chandeliers and marble floors. Full services with a 24-hour concierge and business center for the busy executive.

- **El San Juan Hotel & Casino:** Tel. 809-791-1000. Route 187, Isla Verde. Located in the upscale Isla Verde area near the airport. Recently renovated, the rooms have a tropical decor, but the lobby with its marble, brass, and polished wood appear straight out of European grandeur. Excellent beach, lush grounds, fine restaurants, casino, and theater. Sister hotel to Condado Plaza Hotel & Casino with a shuttle bus service to enjoy both facilities.

- **Holiday Inn Crowne Plaza Hotel & Casino:** Tel. 809-253-2929. Fax 809-253-0079. Opened in 1991, the resort has become a favorite of travelers. Right on the ocean with a soft marble lobby and pastel colors give a serene feeling to the visitor. Located near the airport, but very quiet due to soundproofing. All facilities and services are available.

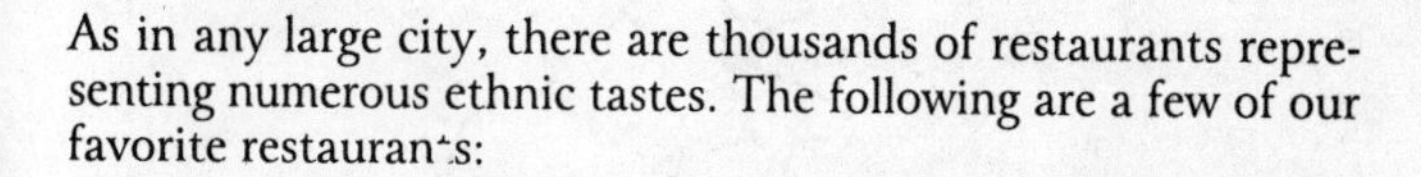

RESTAURANTS

As in any large city, there are thousands of restaurants representing numerous ethnic tastes. The following are a few of our favorite restaurants:

- **Los Galanes**: Tel. 722-4008. 65 San Francisco, Old San Juan. Open for dinner only Tuesday through Saturday. Excellent Spanish food with a good wine list. Expensive.

- **Restaurant Amadeus**: Tel. 722-8635. 106 San Sebastian, Old San Juan. Good Spanish and Caribbean dishes in the heart of the old city.

- **The Cafe at the Butterfly People**: Tel. 723-2432. 152 Fortaleza, Old San Juan. In the heart of Old San Juan on the second floor of an old mansion. Open from 11am to 6pm, this is an excellent place to relax for lunch, listen to music, and to look at the magnificent butterfly displays.

- **El Patio de Sam**: Tel. 723-1149. 102 San Sebastian, Old San Juan. Another casual but excellent place for lunch in Old San Juan.

- **Ramiro's**: Tel. 721-9049. Elegant Spanish restaurant with fresh local ingredients. It is considered one of the most distinguished dining on the island. Save room for their famous "four seasons" chocolate dessert.

- **Dar Tiffany**: Tel. 791-7272. Open for dinner only. The Hollywood stars dine here when visiting. Very tropical. Maine lobster and prime steaks are the popular menu items. Located in the El San Juan Hotel & Casino.

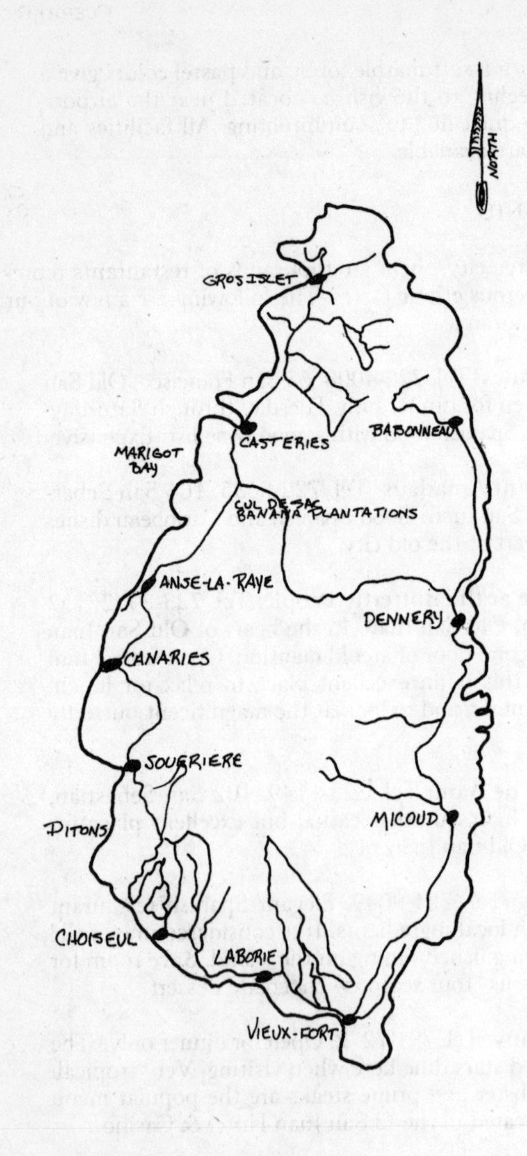
NORTH
GROS ISLET
BABONNEAU
CASTERIES
MARIGOT BAY
CUL DE SAC
BANANA PLANTATIONS
ANSE-LA-RAYE
DENNERY
CANARIES
SOUFRIERE
MICOUD
PITONS
CHOISEUL
LABORIE
VIEUX-FORT
ST. LUCIA

15

St. Lucia

St. Lucia is one of the Caribbean's most recently discovered treasures. There are magnificent rain forests waiting to be explored, secluded beaches, exotic blossoms to rouse your senses, primeval mountain peaks and colorful little fishing villages that time forgot. One of the most dramatic sights to be seen in all of the Caribbean is the half mile high twin Pitons that introduce St. Lucia to visitors. This is truly a tropical volcanic island which rivals scenery associated with such South Pacific islands as Tahiti. Winding roads loop around displaying a nature lover's paradise, and sheer cliffs drop magnificently into rich blue waters. It is a sailor's dream trip to start a journey from this island with its dramatic views of the mountains—and many do. Dozens of inlets line the coast and the famous St. Lucia Green Parrot is found in the huge rain forest reserve. There is a drive-in entrance to the volcano at Soufriere where steamy clouds pour from hot springs bubbling with temperatures of 350 degrees Fahrenheit.

Many delights await your discovery in St. Lucia. In the capital harbor of Castries with its French influence, just about every kind of floating vessel can be seen and all types of shops and street vendors are at the market place. Visitors can also set out for a day of exploration to absorb the natural beauty, breathtaking scenery and the local culture. Pigeon Island at Gros Islet is forty acres filled with history, the Diamond Baths and Diamond Falls make for spectacular sightseeing, and the Maria Islands Nature reserve located on the Atlantic side of Vieux Fort is home to exotic birds, a rare species of ground lizard and Couresse snake.

GETTING TO KNOW YOU

St. Lucia has spent a good part of its past 300 years being pulled between Great Britain and France. Both countries fought to a bloody draw over control of the West Indies.

The peaceful Arawak Indians spent some time on St. Lucia in their attempt to escape the Carib Indians, whose restless expansion across the Caribbean was like a plague of locusts to other indigenous Indian groups. Remains of their villages have been found on Pigeon Point, just off St. Lucia's northern tip which is joined to St. Lucia by a causeway. However, it was the Carib Indians whom the Spanish found when they discovered the island and it was also the Carib Indians who sold some of their huts to the unfortunate English who tried to settle on the island in 1605. That lasted just a few weeks before the remaining settlers fled in a Carib boat. A second attempt by the English to settle in 1639 was also unsuccessful and the settlers who were not killed were driven out. The French arrived in 1651 having purchased the island, but disputes over ownership ensued. In 1746 Soufriere, a French settlement was established and twelve other towns developed over the years bringing the sugar industry to St. Lucia. Slave labor from West Africa worked the fields. In 1778 England attacked the island after declaring war on France for aiding the American Revolution. A naval base was put in place at Gros Islet. The French surrendered the island to the British in 1814. The coal industry was developed in the late 1800's and indentured Indians arrived to help in the mining process. Coal, sugarcane and bananas became the major source of income until tourism arrived after St. Lucia became an independent state within the British Commonwealth of Nations in 1979.

This turbulent past creating a late economic development has enabled St. Lucia to remain unspoiled and has allowed a more controlled environment for tourism. On February 22, 1979, St. Lucia became an independent state within the British Commonwealth of Nations, with a resident governor-general appointed by the Queen. English is the official language, but there are still many relics of French occupation, most notably the island patois which is spoken everywhere; and it is found in the Creole cuisine and the names of the places and even the people. The island's main sources of revenue are now tourism and bananas. The St. Lucian's are working to retain a good mix of making the island welcome to visitors, while retaining and diversifying their agriculture so that the economic base is solid. "Make your lime The Lime!" is the main theme on the island and it means hanging out with friends and most of all having a good time—and that is how St Lucia's magic really begins.

THE BASICS

LOCATION AND GEOGRAPHY

St. Lucia, only 27 miles long and 14 miles wide, is located in the windward portion of the Lesser Antilles, which are included in the West Indies. It is situated 24 miles north of St. Vincent and 25 miles below the southern tip of Martinique, with Florida being approximately thirteen hundred miles to the Northwest. 150,000 St. Lucian's occupy this 238 square mile paradise, which contains a diverse topography ranging from black sand beaches to soaring twin volcanic peaks.

CLIMATE, WHEN TO GO, WHAT TO WEAR

In winter, temperatures range between 65 and 85 degrees Fahrenheit (19-30 C), and during the summer between 75 and 95 degrees Fahrenheit (24 to 35 C). Summers tend to be a little rainy, but winters are dry. Located just 14 degrees north of the equator, the sun sets in St, Lucia at approximately the same time every day. The famous "green flash" that occurs at the very last second before the sun sets is something that every sailor tries to witness while visiting St. Lucia.

Light weight clothing is worn all year (cottons are prevalent). Women will want to take blouses and skirts, shorts, and slacks for daytime wear, and long skirts with caftans for the evening. As on most every Caribbean island, short shorts or bathing suits should not be worn in town or in any of the shops. Men favor casual resort wear for the daytime. Jackets and occasionally ties are required in the evening at the larger hotels and a few restaurants during winter season.

St Lucia is on Atlantic Standard time all year round, so it is one hour ahead of New York during Eastern Standard time, and the same as New York during Eastern Daylight Savings time.

GETTING THERE

St. Lucia has two airports. Most international flights land at Hewanorra Airport at Vieux Fort in the south, about 45 miles from Castries, with BIA offering the widest variety of departure points from the east coast of the US and Canada. American Airlines flies from Miami daily and from New York several times a week. Air Canada and British Airways also provide service. Vigie Airport is the most convenient airport since it is just outside Castries, but it can only handle inter-island flights and lighter aircraft. American Eagle flies into Vigie from San Juan, Puerto Rico. Air Martinique, Liat and Helenair also connect to other islands nearby. Inter-island flights by Eastern Caribbean Helicopter, Ltd. offers shuttle service from both airports to many of the island's hotels. Small plane charters can also be arranged with some of the carriers.

Pointe Seraphine at Castries is served by many cruise lines, including Celebrity, Commodore, Cunard, Diamond, Holland America, Norwegian, Regency, Royal, Seawind, Silversea, Windjammer and Windstar.

Although many sailing enthusiasts begin their journey from St. Lucia, the island is one of the more famous stopping points for sailors because of the many docking facilities and magnificent scenery.

DOCUMENTS

US and Canadian citizens need only a passport or other proof of citizenship (birth certificate, voter's registration card and a form of a photo ID). As with most of the islands in the Caribbean, an on-going or return ticket is also required. Visitor/visa permits are issued upon arrival at the airports and other areas of entry, with the presentation of the proper documents.

ARRIVAL AND DEPARTURE

Arrival at any of the ports of entry is very easy and quite orderly. St. Lucia immigration, while thorough, is accomplished very quickly. Customs Officials at both airport maintain a high profile, but are very helpful to the visitors. Drugs are one of the items the inspectors look for in St. Lucia, and they will inspect all prescription items very carefully. Be sure to always have all prescriptions properly labeled. Although there are many visitors passing through both immigration and customs daily, we have never experienced any delay with either.

Taxis are plentiful at the airports and cruise ship port, but are rather expensive. Taxis are not metered, but the rates are fairly standard. A one way fare from Hewanorra Airport to Castries will be about $55; while a one way trip to Castries from either Vigie Field or Pointe Seraphine is about $5.

Car rentals are also available from several rental companies. All you need to drive in St. Lucia is a valid drivers licence. Temporary three month permits can be obtained from the immigration office at both Hewanorra and Vigie airports, the police station and the major car rental agencies.

The normal departure tax from St. Lucia is $11 (EC 27), unless you are flying to a nearby island, then it is $8 (EC 20). From time to time, some airlines will also impose a $5 fuel surcharge.

Whether you return to the US by air or sea you must declare to the US Customs Official at the point of entry everything you have bought or acquired while in the Caribbean. The duty-free allowance is $600.00 per person for St. Lucia. Duty-free craft items, a system which allows you to exceed your duty-free exemption as long as the purchases are eligible for the GSP Status (a system of preferences to help developing nations improve their economies through exports) must be declared even though they are exempt. Items made from an endangered species will not pass a Custom's Inspector and the item will be confiscated. An example is tortoise shell products. There are certain items that are duty-free up to a certain limit. Individuals are allowed one carton of cigarettes (200), 100 cigars and one liter of liquor or wine. This allowance is for travelers over the age of 21. Alcohol above this allowance is liable for both duty and Internal Revenue Tax. Antiques must be 100 years or older with proof from the seller. Also duty-free are paintings and drawings if done entirely by hand.

CURRENCY, TRAVELER'S CHECKS, CREDIT CARDS

St. Lucia uses the Eastern Caribbean Dollar, generally referred to as "Eecee." The exchange rate is $1.00 US to about$2.70 EC. Money can be changed in hotels and stores, but banks give the best rates. Island banking hours are from 8am to 1pm Monday through Thursday, 8am to 12pm and 1pm to 3pm on Fridays. US and Canadian Dollars are accepted at hotels, stores and restaurants as are traveler's checks and most major credit cards. EC Dollars will generally be given in change. Even though foreign exchange facilities are not available at the airports, this should not pose any problems getting to the hotel or town.

TELEPHONE

When calling from the US, dial 809 (access code) plus 45 (island code) and then the local number. If calling from another island, contact the local operator for the area code. On St. Lucia use only the local number unless otherwise stated. You can access a portable phone by dialing 809-462-5051.

CURRENT

Electricity is 220-230 volts, 50 cycles, AC. Most hotels have provisions for electric shavers; however, converters are required for hair dryers and other small appliances.

TIPPING

A 10% service charge for the hotel is normally included on all hotel bills, and some hotels will include this when they quote a rate. There is also an 8% Government tax added to the bill. Extra tipping is called for only if some special service is rendered. Restaurants add a 10% service to the check which covers the waiter's tip. Cab drivers should be tipped about 10% of the fare. Airport porters depend on tips for a substantial portion of their income, with tips of 50 cents per bag and a $1.00 minimum being the norm.

LANGUAGE

English is the official language of the Island and it is spoken by all of the inhabitants. A slightly different speech pattern keeps your attention. A French-Creole patois similar to Guadeloupe and Martinique is also spoken.

BUSINESS HOURS

Weekdays from 8am to 12:30pm, 1:30pm to 4pm and 8am to noon on Saturdays. Castries Market, where there is fresh produce available, is open from 6am to 6pm, Monday through Saturday.

TRANSPORTATION AND TOURS

Taxi are unmetered but rates are fixed by the government and the Taxi Association, and a list of point-to-point fares is available from the tourist office. However, rates may vary from driver to driver, and it is always a good idea confirm the fare in advance. It is also very important to establish whether the quote is in US or EC dollars.

Car rental costs run about $55 to $65 per day, plus mileage. Usually the first 3 to 50 miles are free. Rates drop slightly in the off season which is April 15-December 15. Agencies with desks at the airport for pickup and drop-off include Avis, National, Budget, Courtesy, CTL St. Lucia Ltd., Inter-Island Car Rental and Dollar. Other agencies are located elsewhere, but most offer pick-up and drop-off service. For example, ABC Cars, St. Lucia Yacht Service Car Rentals are local agencies which may not be advertised at the airports. Several agencies also have desks at the hotels and resorts. All take MasterCard and a few accept other credit cards. An International driver's license or St. Lucia driver's license is required. If you don't have one, it can be obtained through most car rental agencies for about $14.00 and is valid for three months. You must present a valid US, Canadian or UK drivers license.

- **Car rental costs run about $55 to $65 per day, plus mileage.**
- **An International driver's license or St. Lucia driver's license is required.**
- **Tour operators offer all-inclusive day trips to other islands.**
- **Most shops close for lunch and by noon on Saturday.**

RESOURCES

For tourist information, contact The St. Lucia Tourist Board (820 Second Avenue, 9th Floor, New York, NY 10017) Tel 212-867-2950: Fax 212-370-7867. They will be pleased to supply information, literature and maps. On St. Lucia, the Tourist Board Office is located at Pointe Seraphine, Castries. It is open Monday through Friday from 8am to 4:30pm. (P.O. Box 221, Castries, St. Lucia, Tel 452-5978). Visitor information centers are located at each airport and on Bay Street in Soufriere.

Three local newspapers operate in St. Lucia: the ***Crusader***, ***Voice of St. Lucia*** and the ***Star***. Regionally, ***Caribbean Week*** is of interest; ***Discover St. Lucia*** is a complimentary magazine that is available at hotels and shops around the island. The ***New York Times*** is also available—usually a couple days late.

Radio St. Lucia and Radio Caribbean International broadcast local programming. TV stations HTS and DBS carry local as well as some US programs. Some hotels have satellite TV. Cable TV from Cable and Wireless also comes to the island.

SIGHTSEEING TOURS

There are enough tours available to suit almost any need. Several tour operators in Castries offer guided half and full-day excursions. The travel desk at any hotel can help with arrangements for any of these tours as well as all-inclusive day trips to other islands (Martinique, about $170, Grenadine Islands, about $200). You'll find carriage rides, dinner cruises, walks through the lush rain forest, banana estate tours and shopping tours. Some of the major tour operators include Barnard's Travel (Tel. 452-2214; Fax 453-1394); St Lucia's Representative Service (Tel. 452-3762); and Sunlink International (Tel. 452-8232: Fax 452-0459). A complete list of all tour operators is available from the tourist office.

The most popular **sea excursion** is the day long sail to the Pitons with a shore trip to Soufriere's Sulfer Spring. Lunch, drinks, a swim and snorkeling stop plus steel band music en route. The cost is about $70 per person. The square rigged brig Unicore sails twice a week (Tel. 452-6811). Motor Vessel Vigie (Tel. 452-2333), Endless Summer (Tel. 452-3762) and Surf Queen (Tel. 452-8351) also offer day sails from Castries.

Local Air Services are available for charter or sight seeing. Arrangements can be made through Air Martinique (Tel. 452-2453), Eagle Air (Tel. 452-1900) and Helenair (Tel. 452-7196). Day trips to Barbados can be made through LIAT. Helicopter tours can be arranged through Eastern Caribbean Helicopter, Ltd. (Tel. 453-6952).

DUTY-FREE SHOPPING

Pointe Seraphine, located on the opposite side of the Castries Harbor from the city itself is the duty-free shopping complex and also accommodates the cruise ships. Here you will find jewelry, crystal, perfumes, paintings along with tobacco and liqueur. Familiar name brands include Lladro, Lalique, Waterford, Swarovske and Hoya for crystal; Fendi and Salvatore Ferragamo for leather bags and accessories; Polo by Ralph Lauren for clothes; and Tag Heuer and Swatch for watches. Columbia Emeralds is also represented here.

Late evening hours are in effect for the convenience of cruise ship passengers. Goods are delivered to the airport or cruise ship. Keep your airline ticket and passport with you so you are eligible to purchase at low duty-free prices.

As St. Lucia grows in tourism, so does its shopping facilities not only at Pointe Seraphine, but in Castries, Soufriere and

Viex Fort. Remember, however, that most shops close at lunch and by noon on Saturdays.

Shopping in St. Lucia can lead to the discovery of unique treasures. Big names such as Benetton and Columbia Emerald are found in many areas, and there are hundreds of small boutiques specializing in clothing, swim wear and paintings. If you would prefer to find souvenirs with a more local flavor you should travel around the island.

For clothing with that truly tropical design, Bagshaw's silkscreening factory and the Caribelle batiking factory exhibit wide selections. At both factories, you can watch the fashions being created. The Bagshaw's silkscreening studio and factory, located at LaToc, was started by Sydney Bagshaw, a retired art director for Reader's Digest. The designs are his originals based on the beauty of St. Lucia. The Caribelle batik factory, overlooking Castries on Old Victoria Road features freehand art works, predominately of floral design. The selection at both of these outlets feature clothing for women, men and children, as well as wall hangings, bags, and hand painted woodwork.

As the Hill of Good Luck, or Morne Fortune, descends to the south, the road passes two of St. Lucia's's well known art studios. One is operated by the St. Omer family and displays the work of Dunstan Omer, who designed the St. Lucia flag, and has painted the interior of many of the churches on the island. A short way further along the ridge is the Eudovic Woodworking Studio. A small shop displays many souvenir works, but the main studio on the opposite side of the driveway holds the real treasures. The island's most well known wood carver, Eudovic has created masterpieces that are shipped all over the world. His favorite wood to work with is the Laurier Cannelle, a species no longer found growing on the island. The wood is only available from the trunks of monstrous trees that were cut down nearly two hundred years ago. When you visit the Eudovic studios, be sure to also inquire about some of the woodcarvings done by his young son. We have works by both Eudovic and his son proudly displayed in our home.

In the small coastal village of Choiseul, the Choiseul Art and Craft Center keeps alive the traditional skills of the Carib Indians. The crafts displayed include hand molded pottery, and baskets of wicker, khus khus grass, screw pine and sisal. New techniques of bamboo working have been recently introduced by a Taiwanese instructor, which blends perfectly with the Amerindian designs.

Other items, such as Windjammer Clothing, sold all over the Caribbean, but based in St. Lucia, are also great buys.

Finding all these St. Lucian treasures is an exciting cultural experience. Visiting each of these locations also enables you to see much of the work as it is done. Many of the tour excursions include stops at the studios and factories mentioned above, and any of the taxi drivers can give you a private tour.

WHERE TO SHOP

The main areas to shop are Castries, Pointe Seraphine, Soufriere and Vieux Fort. Castries has the largest selections, including **J.Q. Charles,** the main department store.

From appliances to souvenirs, the shops of Castries can provide everything you will need to make your stay on St. Lucia even more enjoyable. **A-1 Collections**, located at the intersection of Jeremie and Cadet Streets, opposite the police station, offers locally screen painted beach wear and a wide range of ladies' formal and casual clothing. **Abyssinia House**, on Chaussee Road offers reggae music, audio and video cassettes, arts and crafts, hats, shoes, health items, oils, incense and show promotion items. **Bagshaw Studios**, just outside of downtown Castries features hand printed fabrics and garments from original designs. **The Book Salon** on the corner of Jeremie and Laborie Streets has an excellent selection of books, maps and stationery supplies. The **Caribbean Perfumery**, located at the Green Parrot on Morne Fortune, blends fragrant tropical oils into its own line of perfumes and colognes for both women and men. **Caribelle Batik** has various locations throughout Castries featuring cotton shirts, beach wear, and wall hangings. **Citizens'** on St. Louis Street offers gold and silver jewelry, watches, handbags, and clocks. **Cox & Co., Ltd.**, on William Peter Boulevard has a wide selection of gift items for special occasions, including Aynskey, Royal Grafton, Royal Worcester and Poole china; Royal Brierley crystal; and jewelry. These are only a few of the many shops and boutiques in Castries. Most of the main shopping is on The Boulevard and around Columbus Square.

At **Castries Market** you will find an assortment of fruits at the front, vegetables and spices lining the sidewalk. Go inside to find all the local handicrafts such as baskets, pottery and wood carvings piled almost to the ceiling. This is one of the few places in St. Lucia where you may bargain.

The shopping at **Pointe Seraphine** is cool, comfortable and duty-free. The Spanish-style complex is within an easy walk from downtown Castries and Vigie Airport, or you can take a taxi for just a few dollars. If you have arrived on the island by cruise ship, you must present a cruise pass to the shopkeeper to take advantage of the duty free prices. If you have arrived by air, you must present a passport or identification card as well as your airline ticket. Upon completion of your purchase, you will be given two copies of the sales invoice; the white copy is yours, the pink copy is handed to Customs when leaving St. Lucia. You will be able to take all purchases with you when you leave Pointe Seraphine, except for spirits and tobacco products. These will be delivered to the cruise ship or the airport where you may collect them just prior to departure. At Pointe Seraphine, in addition to **Bagshaw Studios, Bennetton, J.Q. Charles, Ltd., Columbian Emeralds International** and the **Windjammer Trading Company**, you will also find other very special shops. **The Gallery** features a varied selection of Haitian and St. Lucian oil paintings, wood carvings, African wall hang-ings, carved wooden jewelry boxes and Jamaican handbags. **Images** carries a wide selection of fine fragrances from Oscar de la Renta, Yves St. Laurent, Chanel, Christian Dior and Given-chy; and is the authorized dealer on St. Lucia for Seiko, Citizen, Canon, Minolta, Gucci, YSL, Valentino and Monet. **Island Connection Boutique** stocks a wide variety of designer casuals for men and women, as well as their own line of 100% cotton shirts, sweatshirts and polo shirts. At **Meli** you will find elegant gifts of Lladro, Lalique, Waterford and Hoya crystal; leather bags by Fendi, Salvatore Ferragamo and Ted Lapidus; watches by Tag Heuer and Swatch; and 14 to 22 karat gold jewelry. **Noah's Arcade** carries a large selection of locally handcrafted items; **Simon & Bird** features designer clothing and swim wear; the **St. Lucia Philatelic Bureau** supplies standing orders of stamp collections, including mint sets, canceled sets, first day covers and commemorative issues; and **A Touch of Class** offers an excellent selection of Jewelry, leather goods and books.

In Soufriere there are many small shops and craft outlets, but the **J.Q Charles Ltd.** dry goods and grocery store on Sir Arthur Louis Street, and the hardware store on Bridge Street offer a wide selection of items. In addition, the **Hummingbird Boutiques** in the Hummingbird Beach resort is a tie-dye batik studio featuring wall hangings, sarongs, bikinis, shirts and napkins in Sudanese cotton.

The Choiseul Arts & Crafts Center in Choiseul is a must shopping stop. It offers a delightful range of locally made straw, wood and clay items. Although the Center has all these items for sale in its shop, it will also take personal orders for specially designed pieces.

In addition to the main shopping areas, many hotels and resorts have outlets of the more well known studios and stores.

Rodney Bay Marina near Gros Islet also has a small shopping arcade with boutiques, including **Ermas of St. Lucia** featuring a wide variety of crafts and clothing.

SPECIAL TIPS FOR CRUISE SHIP PASSENGERS

For quick, but quality, shopping, Pointe Seraphine is located next to the cruise ship dock The shops are kept open later for the convenience of the cruise ship passengers, and duty-free items can be found in the many shops with a wide selection of handcrafted items and fine jewelry. **Little Switzerland** has jewelry, watches, fine crystal and china. **Columbia Emeralds International** has two shops filled with beautiful emeralds and diamonds. A branch of **Bagshaw Studio's** internationally known silk-screen prints fashioned into clothing and placemats and other gifts (all made locally in St. Lucia) is there, as well as many speciality shops such as **Noah's Arcade** which displays local handcrafted merchandise.

Quick tours can be arranged for an aerial view of the island by Eastern Caribbean Helicopter, Ltd. (Tel. 453-6952). There are also a variety of sightseeing excursions for a half-day or a few hours. Whether it be hiking, shopping, or simply enjoying the island, several companies can arrange what you need. Remember that the taxis are unmetered, so be sure to agree on a fare before you take off for a quick tour. To avoid misunderstanding, ask the taxi driver to quote the fare in US dollars.

ENJOYING YOUR STAY

THE SITES

Castries (housing one third of the population) is a great place to start sightseeing. It overlooks a beautiful harbor which is on the northwest coast of the island. The interior part of St. Lucia is sugar and banana plantations. The towering Pitons are on the west coast and along the way are the hot springs of Soufriere (the oldest settlement on the island). Given the wealth of St. Lucia's natural wonders and the remnants of its eventful history, taking some time to explore the entire island is very rewarding. You can either rent a car and tour at your own pace and agenda, or have your hotel arrange a guided tour by car or boat.

- High off to the southern side of Castries is Morne Fortune. The road that snakes up the slopes offers spectacular views of the town and harbor of Castries, Vigie Peninsula and the northern coast of the Island. It is a great spot for photos.

- Heading south from Morne Fortune, you will wind downhill into the Cul-de-Sac valley, which is filled with mile after mile of green banana plants. A few miles beyond is Marigot Bay, one of the most beautiful anchorages in the Caribbean. This was the setting for the movie Dr. Doolittle, and today plays host to a major sailing center operated by The moorings.

- Further south, the road runs down into Roseau Banana Plantation and then climbs through the picturesque towns of Anse La Raye and Cannaries to the rain forest. Due to the density of the rain forest, it is only possible to enter with a guide. Full day excursions to the forest can easily be arranged and the experience is unforgettable.

- Further south is Soufriere, a town of delicate French architecture nestled at the base of the Pitons. The twin towing peaks can be climbed. Guides are available and the climb is rated as difficult by mountaineers.

- Not far from the Pitons are the Sulphur Springs, a seven acre crater often billed as the world's only drive-in volcano. Nearby are the Diamond Botanical Gardens Waterfall and Mineral Baths, originally built in 1785. The baths have been restored, and for a small fee you can tour the gardens and enjoy a steaming bath.

- North of Castries is Pigeon Island National Park, near Gros Islet. Its 40 acres are dotted with forts, ruins and caves. In 1550, it was the hideout of a notorious French privateer.

ACCOMMODATIONS

There is much to enjoy in St. Lucia, including its range of accommodations. From first class hotels, to villas by the sea, apartments or all-inclusive resorts where meals and almost everything else is included, the island offers all price ranges. Some are very secluded and small, but all are very friendly and accommodating. Most are along the Caribbean coast where the water is calm. High season stays in wintertime need advance reservations.

- **Anse Chastanet Beach Hotel:** Tel. 809-459-7000. Fax 809-459-7700. Located on the north side Soufriere. Almost all the cottage like rooms face the Pitons. It is built on a steep hillside that comes right down to a golden beach. The rooms are very large with sweeping views of the mountains and the Caribbean. The hotel is secluded and quiet and it is fun to arrive by a boat from Castries rather than the challenging winding road. There are a lot of steps and no televisions in the rooms, but the gorgeous sunsets, the lush natural beauty, or fantastic snorkeling along the reefs are a romantic tranquil escape from life's stresses. Very expensive.

- **Ladera:** Tel. 809-454-7323. Fax 809-459-5156. Very exclusive with only 7 villas and 12 beach side suites in a lush setting. Views of the Pitons can be seen through open walls and mosquito netting protects you from the outside elements. It is considered the most outstanding small resort on the island. Very restful, no TV, but Jacuzzi and individual pools come with the villas and a larger pool for all guests. A shuttle is provided to the beach. Expensive.

- **Le Sport:** Tel. 809-450-8551. Fax 809-450-0368. All-inclusive resort spa. A health resort with seawater massages, plenty of exercise, three pools, golf and tennis located on the far north side of the island at Anse de Cap beach. Expensive.

- **The Royal St. Lucian:** Tel. 809-452-9999. Fax 809-452-9639. Luxury and pampering for those who want the full range of services found in plush hotels all over the world, but rare in the Caribbean Islands. All 98 Suites face the sea. They contain air-conditioning, phones, cable and local TV, music, separate shower and tub, fully stocked mini bar, radio, scales, bathrobes, hair dryers, private patios overlooking the gardens or beach, but most of all fast service. Very expensive.

- **Jalousie Plantation:** Tel. 809-459-7666. Fax 809-459-7667. Located in Soufriere in the shadow of the Pitons is this all-inclusive resort. Horseback riding, tennis,

Olympic size pool, with the greathouse the center for the restaurant and lounges. A very quiet setting. Expensive.

- **Sandals St. Lucia:** Tel. 809452-3081. Fax 809-453-7089. Couples only resort that took over the Cunard La Toc and La Toc Suites in 1993 with complete renovations. There are private pools and a large pool with a bar you can swim to, as well as an outstanding fitness center, and a nine-hole golf course and tennis courts. Expensive.

- **Candyo Inn:** Tel. 809-452-0712. Fax 809-452-0774. Rodney Bay's new small hotel. Close to the beaches and restaurants with a pool, bar and lush grounds. The rooms are sparkling white with air conditioning, phones, TV and some with a kitchenette. Inexpensive.

- **Windjammer Landing:** Tel. 809-452-0913. Fax 809-452-9454. Americans love to stay here at Labrelotte Bay. The Villas (some with plunge pools) are air-conditioned with rattan furnishings, TV, VCR, stereo, microwave, and coffee maker. Give the "island feel" right down to the straw mats on the floor. Dinner can be prepared for you in your villa. Transportation is always available from the shops and main complex to the villas on the hillside. There are swimming pools, a mini-mart, a fitness center and all types of water sports, entertainment and children's programs. Expensive.

RESTAURANTS

Food in St. Lucia is another dimension to be explored and savored. Local dishes go back to the days of the Amerindians, The Arawaks brought yams, dasheen (delicate flavor tubors), and arrowroot to the island. Pepperpot's beginnings were derived from the cassava root's juice. Pepperpot is still a main staple in St. Lucia. As cultures blended, the coal pot was introduced from Africa and adapted to the Caribs pottery style. So was rice and spices and the banana. Flying fish, cray fish, crab back and dolphin (the flat faced fish—not the mammal)are the local delicate dishes from the sea. The national dish is salt fish and green fig (bananas and spiced fish). Of course world class continental cuisine is in the finest restaurants as well. Our favorite is L'Epicure at the Royal St. Lucian Hotel.

- **Green Parrot Restaurant and Bar**: Tel. 452-3300. "Parrot-style!" creole food is served from 7am until the last customer leaves. High on the hill overlooking Castries with a view that can take your breath away. Ever present is Chef Harry who also sings with the Lighting Stars on Saturday nights. Don't under estimate the cuisine—Chef Harry was trained at Claridge's in London and serves some of the most delicious food on the island. Lots of fun. Live shows with limbo Mondays and Wednesdays and Jazz on Fridays. Expensive.

- **Chak Chak**: Tel. 454-6260. A great variety of local creole style cooking. In Vieux Fort near Hewanorra Airport. A tropical courtyard with two bars is spacious enough for group functions. Entertainment some evenings. Moderate.

- **Chez Paul** (formally **Rain**): Tel. 452-3022. A favorite spot in the heart of Castries to take in the atmosphere. Local dishes as well as American food. Very busy due to its powerful rum punches. Delightful Victorian building that overlooks Derek Alcott Square. Moderate.

- **Dasheene Restaurant & Bar**: Tel. 454-7323. Dinner with breathtaking views of the Pitons and the Caribbean waters at the Ladera Resort. Exquisite food and entertainment. Very expensive.

- **The Lime**: Tel. 452-0761. Locals love to gather here and "lime" (hang-out). Casual, fun and very reasonable. No credit cards. Inexpensive.

- **L'Epicure**: Tel. 452-9999. Located at the Royal St. Lucian Hotel. The most elegant restaurant in St. Lucia with over a hundred wines from all over the world. High standards for classical cuisine with expert presentation. Very expensive.

16

Martinique

Martinique is more than a "touch of France." In the French West Indies, Martinique is France! Since this semi-tropical island of flowers has never sought independence, the inhabitants are French citizens and part of the Republic.

People from Africa and the many cultures of the West Indies have settled here. While they brought a rich heritage with them, make no mistake, this is predominately a French island. Because of this, the people have developed their own personality. The Creole women are reputed to be some of the most beautiful women in the West Indies, and it was the home of the Empress Josephine, wife of Napoleon Bonaparte. Indeed, a small museum at La Pagerie at Trois-Islets displays her humble beginnings along with some of her personal effects, including a copy of her divorce decree from the great Emperor. In her extravagance and self indulgence to protect her family's holdings, she convinced Napoleon to keep slavery in Martinique for years after it was abolished in France.

Fort-de-France, Martinique's capital city is rather like a combination of Nice and New Orleans with its narrow streets and iron grill balconies. The banks many of the shops and some of the great restaurants of the island are located there.

NORTH

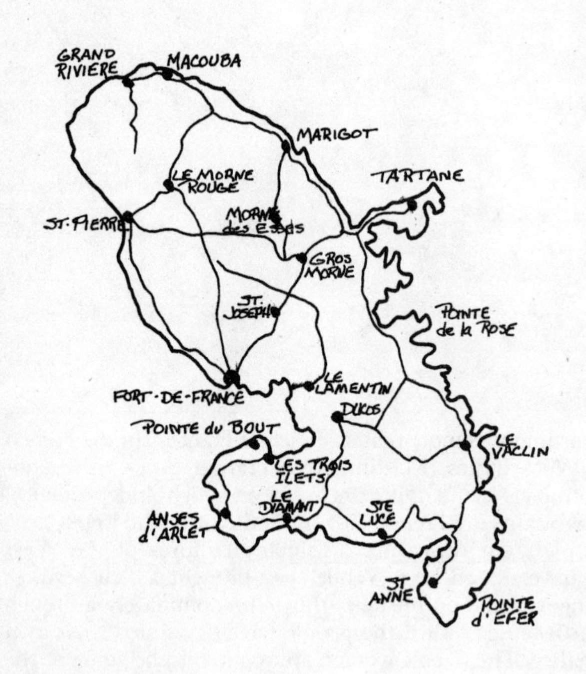
GRAND RIVIERE
MACOUBA
MARIGOT
TARTANE
LE MORNE ROUGE
MORNE des ESSES
ST. PIERRE
GROS MORNE
ST. JOSEPH
POINTE de la ROSE
LE LAMENTIN
FORT-DE-FRANCE
DUCOS
POINTE du BOUT
LES TROIS ILETS
LE VACLIN
LE DIAMANT
ANSES d'ARLET
STE LUCE
ST ANNE
POINTE d'EFER

MARTINIQUE

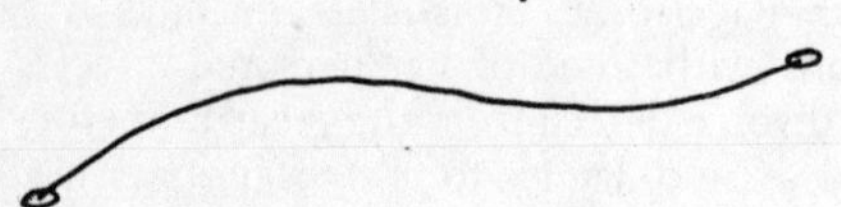

In the heart of the city is La Savane, a large park with benches, walks and playing fields. A statue of Josephine is also locate here—a statue dedicated in 1859, but mysteriously beheaded in 1991. The myths as to why are as plentiful as the beautiful trees that surround the park.

The northern part of the island is dominated by volcanic mountains, and the land climbs steeply from the sea to the cone of Mt. Pele, an active volcano. The central part of Martinique is mountainous, but also home to fields of bananas, sugarcane and pineapples. The southern region is dry, flat and bordered by white sand beaches.

All this is part of an exotic combination of the Caribbean and France that makes Martinique's character so unique and unforgettable.

By day fill your life with the sun, the sea, the museums, all of the wonderful shopping, or ride aboard the little train around the volcanic ruins of Saint-Pierre; and by night fill your evening with piano bars, jazz clubs, casinos, and discotheques or the latest popular music called the zouk. If you are looking for a foreign flavor to your vacation, you will love Martinique.

GETTING TO KNOW YOU

Columbus first spotted Martinique in 1493 and subsequently explored it in 1503. In 1635 the French claimed the island and began the first permanent settlement. Martinique became the perfect spot for untitled aristocracy to settle. Even today, descendants take great pride in their colonial heritage and many continue to grow sugar cane for the production of rum. In 1762 the British conquered the island, but gave it up within the year in order to acquire Canada in the Treaty of Paris. Large plantations with grand houses produced sugar cane and expanded over the rich fertile areas. Slavery was not abolished until April 27, 1848. The decline in sugar production brought banana and pineapple plantations into existence, and those plantations flourish even today.

The famous French painter Paul Gauguin arrived for a five month stay in 1887. Copies of some of his paintings are in the Art Center and Museum along with unpublished material on his family history. Some of his works produced on the island are: "The Mango Harvest" and the "Beach and the Raisiner Trees."

1902 brought the eruption of Mount Pelee down on the city of Saint-Pierre, the capital of the island. It took 3 minutes to destroy the lives of 30,000 people. Only one person survived—a prisoner jailed in a building with three foot thick walls. Rather than try to rebuild the city, the capital of Martinique was moved to Fort-de-France. Today the new capital keeps its very European atmosphere with colorful buildings adorned with wrought iron balconies and its narrow streets.

Tourism arrived later here and has been building over the last twenty-four years. Now, over 350 cruise ships visit annually and passengers get a friendly welcome and patient directions from the Gendarmes when they are trying to find the numerous boutiques, or to determine where they can best quench their thirst with the famous "Petit Punch" (white rum with water splashed with sugar syrup and a lime).

Martinique's charms are enjoyed to the fullest if you speak French. If not, bring a good phrase book. The island is striving for more English to be spoken to help with tourism, and everyone is friendly and willing to assist—even if it is communicating by hand gestures. There are free guide booklets and brochures in English at the Tourist Office. The major hotels, restaurants, shops and tour taxis employ English speaking staff.

THE BASICS

LOCATION AND GEOGRAPHY

As part of the Windward Islands, Martinique lies between St. Lucia and Dominica in the Antilles portion. It is 47 miles long and 22 miles wide. The Island is all mountain and valley with one plain large enough to hold the airport. Rugged and lush, filled with beautiful plants and flowers, its highest point is the top of volcanic Mt. Pelee (elevation 4,656). The location of all sites is within a day's drive, from the crashing Atlantic Ocean on the eastern shores to the seductive Caribbean Sea on the west-ern side. The best beaches are on the south coast at Sainte Anne, and volcanic sand has created black beaches on other shores.

CLIMATE, WHEN TO GO, WHAT TO WEAR

A lovely breeze fills the air so the temperature is always pleasant year round. It does get cooler in the mountains. 79 degrees F is about the average with 69-72 at night.

Since Martinique is like most Caribbean islands, the busy season of the year is the winter, with the period between mid December and mid April being the busiest. Reservations need to be made in advance for this period to ensure that there are rooms available anywhere on the island—but especially in those hotels near Trois-Islet. The summer months bring many tourists from France, however, the island is not crowded as it is during the winter months.

You will need light casual clothing on your trips around the island. In most places, dress is more reminiscent of Europe than of most of the other Caribbean islands, since the cities and towns are very cosmopolitan, and a sweater or jacket is a necessity for the higher elevations. Bathing suits and short shorts are for the beach areas only, and will not be seen in any of the shopping areas or marinas. Women tend to dress for the evening. Jacket and ties for men are only required at a few places such as some of the casinos and a few restaurants.

Martinique is on Atlantic Standard time all year round, one hour later than Eastern Standard during part of the year, the same as Eastern Daylight Savings time during the summer.

GETTING THERE

Air France and American Airlines provide daily service from US ports of Miami and San Juan, and Air Canada provides service from Montreal and Toronto. LIAT flies from the nearby islands.

More than 350 cruise ships arrive annually in Martinique, and by ship is one of the most popular methods of arriving. The cruise ship lines that currently service Martinique are Carnival, Celebrity, Commodore, Costa, Cunard, Diamond, Dolphin, Holland America, Norwegian Princess, Regency Royal, Royal Caribbean, Silver Star Windjammer and Windstar. In most cases the departing ports are Miami or San Juan.

Martinique is also a very popular port of call from privately owned yachts, and you will see hundreds in the bay near Fort-de-France as well as in the marinas at Trois-Ilets.

DOCUMENTS

Since the population on Martinique is comprised of French citizens, all French citizens may enter with their national identity card. US and Canadians are allowed to enter with proof of citizenship. This can be a passport, voter's registration card, birth certificate (with an official seal) and an official photo ID such as a driver's license. All British citizens are required to have a passport.

A visa is only required if your stay is going to be longer than three months. The easiest form of identification and proof of citizenship is, of course, a passport.

ARRIVAL AND DEPARTURE

All flights arrive at Lamention International Airport which is located about 15 minutes from Fort de France, and about 45 minutes from the hotels that are located on the Trois-Ilets peninsula. Immigration and customs are very well organized and you will experience no delays at either. Since the airport is large by Caribbean standards, and very busy, taxis are always available. The rate for taxis is regulated by the government, however, the fares are still quite high. The rates are listed in brochures and at the airport tourist office, but you should always try to agree on the rate before you depart. The fare from the airport to Fort-de-France will be about $15, but it's almost $30 to Pointe du Bout. There is a 40% surcharge in effect in the evening and on Sunday, so it may be better to rent a car. There are many car rental agencies available, and you will only need a valid drivers license for rentals of up to 20 days. For rental periods longer than that, you will need to obtain an International Driver's License. Rental rates for most agencies will average about $60 to $70 per day.

All cruise ships arrive in Fort-de-France, not far from the center of the city. Taxis and guides are readily available at the port . If you do not speak French, it advisable to inquire about the possibility of obtaining an English speaking driver. This is very important if you want to do a little sightseeing on the way to a shopping area or a restaurant.

There is no departure tax to be paid on your way out of Martinique—it has been included in your ticket at the time of purchase.

CURRENCY, TRAVELER'S CHECKS, CREDIT CARDS

The legal currency is the French Franc and the conversion rate is quoted daily. At present it is about 5 francs to the US$1. US and Canadian dollars are accepted as well as credit cards, but it's best to convert enough money into francs for convenience. Traveler's checks are well received and many shops will give a discount for using them. Several shops we visited offered a discount of up to 20% for the use of traveler's checks or credit cards, but some banks will provide a better exchange rate for US currency. Francs are the best to use for meals, taxi fares and other small purchases.

The banks generally offer the best exchange rate and are usually open from 7:30am to 4:30pm. Many banks do close for lunch between the hours of noon to 2:30pm, however.

To benefit from purchases made in Martinique, a tax refund

is available if you are a non-national. The shopkeeper will furnish you with a receipt indicating the date of purchase along with your name and permanent address and local residence (hotel, villa, cruise ship, etc.) during your stay. This will enable you to get a refund of duties and value added taxes on many items.

French francs can be converted back to dollars only at banks, including the one at the airport, and it is less expensive to do it before you depart Martinique.

Electricity

Electricity on the island is 220 volts A.C., 50 cycles, the same as that used on the French mainland. Some hotels have converted the voltage and outlets in the bathrooms, but many have not. You may want to bring your own transformer/converter and adapter with you to make sure that one is available when you need it.

Tipping

It is just like France. A 15% service charge is automatically added to your bill at most all of the restaurants. When you wish to tip for exceptional service, do so in cash. The hotel staff who assists you with your bags usually expect about $1 per bag.

Taxi drivers also will expect a 10% to 15% tip to be added to the fare.

Language

French is the official language of the Martinique. This is one Caribbean Island where a language dictionary will be helpful. English is understood in town and in some hotels and shops. Slightly off the beaten path and you are on your own with French or Patois (French Creole—a mixture of French, Spanish. English and African Languages).

Business Hours

Shops are open Monday through Friday from 8:30am to 6:00pm and Saturdays from 8:30am until noon. Banks open early at 7:30am to noon, close for lunch and reopen at 2:30 until 4:00pm.

TRANSPORTATION AND TOURS

Martinique has a large fleet of taxis. They are relatively expensive and include a 40% surcharge after 8:00pm. Most drivers speak French only, so be prepared for that, or try to find a driver who speaks English. The largest taxi stands are at the airport and in front of the major hotels. Sightseeing taxi tours can be arranged for a reasonable price and an English speaking driver usually can be provided. You can make private arrangements as well. A wonderful English speaking tour driver, who also works privately, is Bernadette Ducteil; her telephone number is 596-51-31-87. She can be located at TI-Marie A 4, Place d'Armes 97232 Lamentin.

Rental cars are available from many different agencies. You should be prepared, however, for the narrow streets in towns, and mountainous country roads with sharp curves. When driving outside of the Fort-de-France area, be sure to take a map with you. A map that is general and illustrates the major roads can be obtained at the tourist office which shares a building with Air France on the boulevard Alfassa. That office also has many other helpful brochures that you will find useful during your stay. A more detailed map is available at most of the bookstores.

For hikers, the rain forest is exciting. Organized tours can be arranged very reasonably through parc Naturel Regional de la Martinique (596-73-19-30). Be aware of where you step. There are poisonous snakes that are not tourist shy in some of the undergrowth. Look around for the red signs put out to indicate you are near the Mancenillie tree. It is gorgeous with little green fruits that look like apples. It is very poisonous and even a drop from the sap will blister the skin.

There is constant ferry service from downtown Fort-de-France to Pointe du Bout, and return.

RESOURCES

The Martinique Tourist Office (Tel. 63-79-60) in the Air France building on boulevard Alfassa can provide fast and easy access to the happenings on the Island. It is located right on the waterfront of Fort de France, and is open Monday through Friday from 7:30am to 12:30pm and from 2:30pm to 5:30pm. There is a branch at the airport that stays open until the last flight has landed. Many pamphlets and booklets are available, and the staff is most helpful. ***Une Histoire d'Amour Entre Ciel and Mer*** is printed in English as well as French.

France-Antilles, the daily newspaper, is published in French.

The *International Herald Tribune* is printed in English and is only one day old upon arrival.

SHOPPING IN MARTINIQUE

The narrow streets, French style buildings, and all the sophisticated boutiques and shops filled with fine French goods give Martinique a flavor so French that it is reminiscent of shopping in Nice or Paris. Shoes, clothing, crystal and porcelain are all made in France. Prices here are lower than some of the shops in Paris, especially if you use traveler's checks, which can save you another 20% off the normal 30% to 40% savings.

WHAT TO BUY

Rum is Martinique's most famous product. Several rum factories offer tours and you may purchase directly from their distilleries. **St. James** is the best known and even has a local museum to see. The rum can be purchased in various colors from very dark to white. The collectors like to acquire the deeper colors that have been aged several years.

Local jewelry made of gold (some as slave chains), the unique Martinique and the Martiniquais dolls in national dress can be remembrances or souvenirs of your visit.

The very best buys are French imports such as china, crystal, designer scarves and especially new perfumes that arrive in Martinique about six months before stateside. Stop at one of **Roger Albert's** shops for these advance fragrances that are for children as well as adults. You can also pick up leather goods, watches, cosmetics and other gift items. The shop is also open at lunch time and discounts further on items purchased with an international credit card. One of the largest shops is located on rue Victor Hugo in the heart of the shopping district. A delightful shop to enjoy is **Salines** with clothing even for children and sporting a small lagoon to stroll around and cross. This location is just down the street from **Roger Alberts**. Gold and silver jewelry can be found at **Albert Venutolo**, **Thomas de Rogatis** and **Cadet Daniel**, all right down town. **Forum Africain** has very colorful batik clothing, leather goods and African accessories to choose from—rue Victor Hugo. Parisian fashions that are fun as well as Martinique island fashion can be seen at **Othello** on rue St. Germain and **L'Univers** on rue Perinon. French sizes are cut differently than US clothing so be sure to try on items you purchase. The shopkeepers are very helpful in converting sizes. **Carmbole** has an excellent selection of crafts and art works by locals and Caribbean artists including Haitian. They are both located downtown on rue Victor Hugo and rue Ernest De Proge—each shop has different artifacts to see. **Boutique Michel Montignas**, at 77 rue Blenac, is the place to pick up wonderful preserves, jellies, pastries, chocolates, special vinegars, and, of course, French breads. **The Galerie d'Art** located on rue Victor Hugo excels in Haitian art, paintings, sculptures and other local handicrafts. **Les Petites Floralis** on rue Blenac and **MacIntosh** on rue Victor Hugo have flowers that can be brought back to the states—and lobster packaged for shipping.

WHERE TO SHOP

The main shopping district is in downtown Fort-de-France near the cathedral and on rue Victor Hugo, rue Moreau de Jones, rue Antione Siger and rue Lamartine. The are also some shops in the hotels and on the streets surrounding the hotels not far from the ferry landing in Pointe du Bout.

Forte-de-France also has three shopping centers on the edge of town (de Cluny, de Bellevure and de Dillon), and in Le Lamentin La Galleria has more than 50 shops. There are branches of boutiques in resorts and hotels and small shops around the island. One delightful market we enjoyed is located near Morne des Esses and was filled with many beautiful baskets of all shapes—some we had not seen elsewhere. Remember to take a French Dictionary when you venture out of Fort-de-France.

SPECIAL TIPS FOR CRUISE SHIP PASSENGERS

Many ships have limited time in Fort-de-France but the parks, museums, shopping and eating are very close to the docks in Fort-de-France. Many shops and restaurants are located downtown, and there is limited shopping next to the port. It takes only 20 minutes by ferry to Pointe du Bout, however. Most of the larger resort hotels are located there with many restaurant selections and some shopping. If you do have some time, there are many ways to explore the island, bicycling, boating, (with special fees for cruise ship visitors), hiking, tennis, sailing and beautiful beaches to roam. The Tourist Office is located right on the waterfront down towards town from the dock. There you can also hire a driver for a private tour if you want to see many areas in a short amount of time.

ENJOYING YOUR STAY

The Tourist Center, one block from the Ferry dock on Boulevard Alfassa, has updated information with pamphlets in English, and is a good place to visit first. Nearby is a beautiful view of **Fort-de-France Bay** and **La Savane** park with its public gardens, tropical shrubs and open areas. **A statue of Empress Josephine** (wife of Napoleon) facing Les Trois-Islets, where she was born, is located in the park. The market place at the edge of the park has crafts from many areas of the Caribbean. It is right next to La Savane park. Other places of interest to visit are:

- The **Musee Departmental de la Martininque**, located in a restored colonial house on the west side of La Savane, contains artifacts from pre-Columbian cultures and representations of the island's everyday life during the colonial period. Two similar galleries are the **Musee del'Esclavage**, on Route de Didier just north of town, with an excellent collection of the history of slavery; and **Archival Services of Martinique**, Tarten-son, rue St. John Perse, with displays of maps and engravings from the 16th and 17th centuries.

- **Sacre Coeurde Balata** can be seen high in the hills above Fort-de-France. It is a sister church to Sacre-Coeur in Paris and can be toured.

- **Les Trois-Islets**, where Empress Josephine was born, also has the **Musee de la Pagerie** that depicts how Josephine lived and contains many articles of clothing and items of furniture that she used.

- **St. Pierre**, once known as the Paris of the West, is the site of the May 1902 eruption of Mt. Pelee which killed 30,000 people. A museum displays pictures and relics, and there is submarine nearby which enables you to view the bottom of the bay that serves as graveyard for dozens of sailing ships and steamboats that sunk during the volcanic eruption.

- **Ceron Plantation**, located near Le Precheur on the northwest coast of the island, is a beautiful restored estate that was once a sugar plantation. It includes the main house, a restaurant (the old sugar refinery) and well-preserved ruins of other buildings.

- **Carbet**, where Columbus landed in 1502, and where the artist Paul Gauguin lived for five months in 1887, is a small fishing village. Nearby is the **Jardin Zoologique Amazona**, home to nearly 60 different animal species; and the **Vallee des Papillons, a** steep ravine containing over 1,500 species of butterflies.

- Two miles off the southern coast is **Diamond Rock** at Diamond Bay. It is the only rock in history to be declared a warship. In the early 19th century, **the British** landed two hundred sailors with cannons and other arms **on** the rock, declaring it **HMS Diamond Rock.** There were able to hold the French at bay for nearly 18 months. Nearby is **Le Diamant** one of the oldest villages on the island.

- One of the most unusual sights to see occurs on Sundays when the Amicale Folklorique Martiniquais Society's famous fighting cocks are pitted against each other at the Marador located outside Fort-de-France. Take an English guide if you do not speak French to explain betting. This is a fiercely combative blood sport to the death—not for the sensitive. It usually occurs between December and July.

ACCOMMODATIONS

Martinique offers a wide variety of accommodations from small country inns to four-star properties and furnished flats. Most of the major hotels are found on the other side of Fort-de-France in Trois-Islets district at Point du Bout, an extensive seaside area with beautiful beaches. It is generally expensive to stay in Martinique. Off season rates in the summer are up to 35% less than winter prices. The Villa Rental service of Martinique can locate excellent homes to rent (Tel. 596-63-79-60).

- **Le Bakoua**: Tel. 596-66-02-02. Fax 596-66-00-41. Decorated with lively Caribbean colors in white stucco buildings, all rooms have patios or balconies facing the garden areas or the water. A four-star hotel complete with air-conditioning, telephones, TVs, and hair dryers in the baths. The pool is located on the terrace level over looking the beach with water cascading to give the appearance it flows right into the sea. The hotel is the center of the social life at Point du Bout with nightly entertainment that incorporates Les Grands Ballets de la Martinique. The cocktail lounge off the lobby provides a spectacular view of the sunset. Very expensive.

- **Le Meridien Les Trois-Islets:** Tel. 596-53-60-60. Fax 596-53-50-58. Life evolves around the pool all year long. Over 200 rooms with views of Fort-de-France. Rooms are air conditioned with telephone and TV, built in hair dryers and duty free shops. Two tennis courts, white sand beach and many activities, even deep sea fishing trips. La Case Creole restaurant has excellent local food. The location is excellent to the marina and ferry dock at Point du Bout. Very expensive.

- **PLM Azur-Carayou:** Tel. 596-66-04-04. Fax 596-66-00-57. The swimming pool is the absolute center of attention with rooms built around it in a very tropical setting. TV's, telephones, air-conditioning and mini bars in the rooms make life very pleasant. A younger active crowd stays here. Restaurants, tennis courts and water sports plus a private beach. Very informal and located at Point du Bout. Expensive.

- **Habitation Lagrange:** Tel. 596-53-60-60. Fax 596-53-50-58. An experience to remember. Located in the northeast in the jungle area with only 17 rooms. An old sugar plantation filled with tropical gardens. The house is filled with antiques. The Creole style four poster bed guest rooms have telephones, TVs, and mini bars. Includes a pool and tennis courts. The staff dresses in 18th century costumes and a horse-drawn carriage transports guest around the facilities. Expensive.

- **Les Islets de l'Imperatrice:** Tel. 596-53-60-60. Fax 596-53-50-58. Two private islands, each with its own guest house in the Creole style. A secluded place without air-conditioning, TV, or telephones. Five guest rooms and staffed with a maid, boatman and cook. You can truly remove yourself from the frays of life. All inclusive and very expensive.

RESTAURANTS

The phrase "eating your way through France" certainly applies to Martinique. Every eatery has delicious food from haute cuisine to local establishments. The major hotels prepare classic French dishes and take the presentation seriously. The very best local fare is found outside of Fort de France along the mountains and it is exotic and wonderful. Your French phrase book is necessary if you do not speak French. Everyone is very helpful and the hotel can make reservations and give you a few tips on ordering the specialities. Don't let this stop you from exploring and enjoying Martinique's local flavors. There are many local specialities. Some from the sea are: ecrevisses (freshwater crayfish), langouste (Caribbean lobster), lamb (conch), arsine (sea urchin), chatru (octopus), crabs farcis (stuffed deviled crab), accra (cod cakes) and soudons (sweet clams). Some from the land are: colombo (curry with meat such as goat), boudin (local blood sausage), blaff (spicy stew with fish), and all types of wonderful thick soups. Fresh tropical fruit or flambe bananas are excellent dessert choices. Don't forget to enjoy the favorite island drink, petit punch also known as ti punch (white rum with sugar syrup, water and a fresh lime). One of the island rums makes a wonderful conclusion to the meal. Take time to explore, discover, and enjoy the variety of excellent restaurants.

- **Leyritz Plantation**: Tel. 596-78-53-92. A great feel for the country and a magnificent view of Mont Pelee. This restored Colonial plantation is located in Basse-Pointe and features Creole food. It is very popular and reservations are a must. Expensive.

- **La Matadore**: Tel. 596-66-05-36. Located in Point du Bout. Creole food is wonderful and can even include turtle steak. Expensive.

- **Davidiana**: Tel. 596-66-00-54. Right at Trois Islets and in the midst of the fun and marinas. A nice varied menu to help you try a little of everything—including a piano bar. Expensive.

- **Club Nautique** Tel: 596-54-31-00. A very informal atmosphere right on the beach with delicious fresh food right out of the sea and very well prepared. The lobster is exquisite. Since it is located in Le Francois, it's a good idea of make reservations. Expensive.

- **Le Pointe De Vue:** Tel. 596-74-74-40. Extraordinary Creole food with a breathtaking view from the mountain top to be enjoyed while dining outside in this covered porch restaurant. Habitation Panor Morne Gommier at Le Marin. Reservations are essential. Expensive.

- **La Fontane:** Tel. 596-64-28-70. Jacket and tie required as well as reservations in this elegant antique filled private home with a very fine French and Creole menu. Just north of Forte-de-France. Expensive.

- **Le Coq Hardi:** Tel. 596-71-59-64. Steak tartare is a speciality here, but if you just need a good steak, T-bone or prime rib, this is the place in Martinique. Right in Fort-de-France. Expensive.

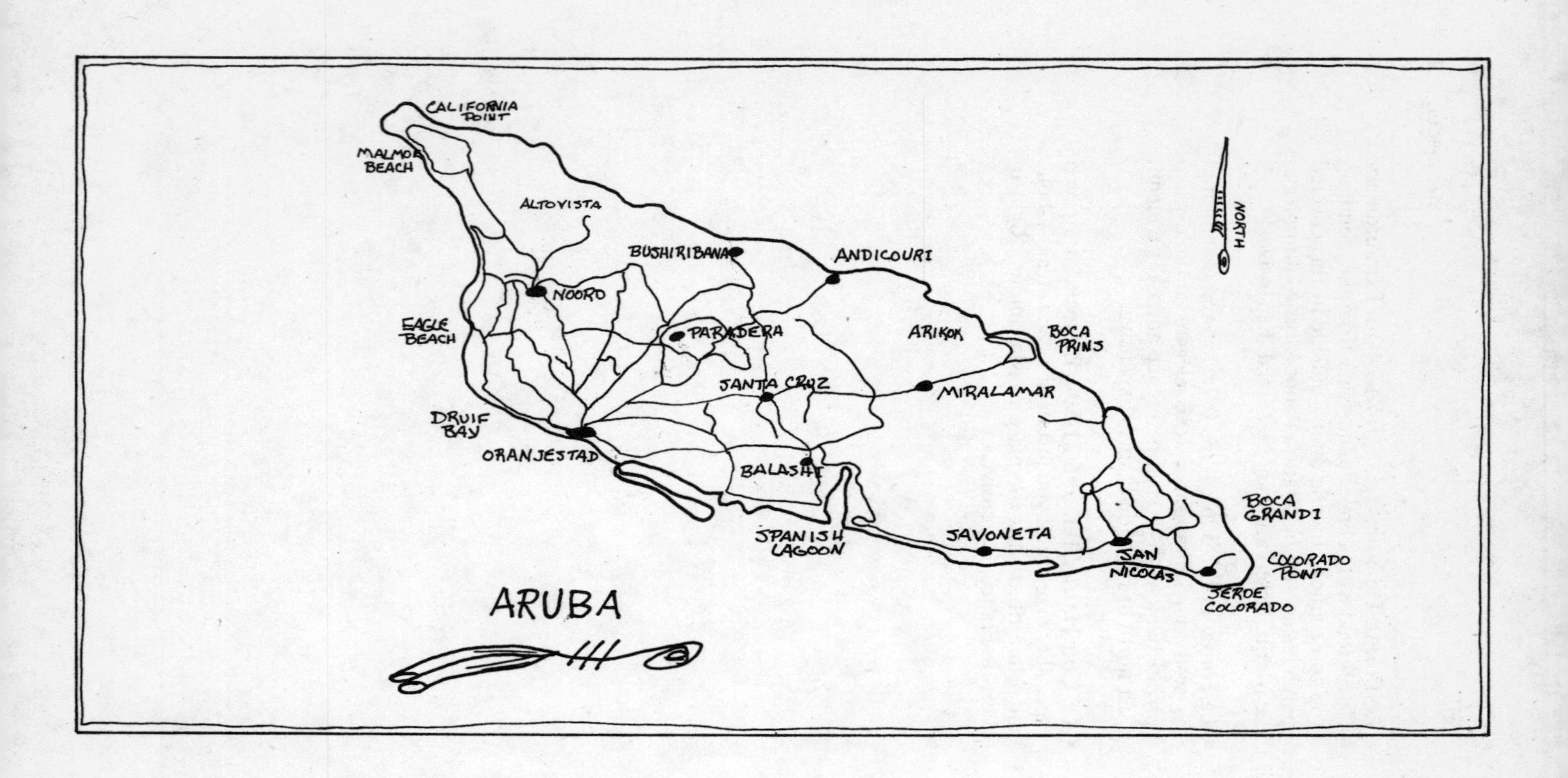
CALIFORNIA POINT
MALMOK BEACH
ALTOVISTA
BUSHIRIBANA
ANDICOURI
NORTH
NOORD
EAGLE BEACH
PARADERA
ARIKOK
BOCA PRINS
SANTA CRUZ
MIRALAMAR
DRUIF BAY
ORANJESTAD
BALASHI
SPANISH LAGOON
SAVONETA
BOCA GRANDI
SAN NICOLAS
COLORADO POINT
SEROE COLORADO
ARUBA

17

Aruba

To first picture Aruba is to envision legendary beaches that stretch for miles along the coast. Lush tropical plants are imported to this semi-arid island with its divi divi trees that have a dramatically blown look from the continuing trade winds. It has deserts which hug boulders and cactus that meet secluded coves which contain shallow waters and caves with prehistoric drawings. Coral reefs surround the island making for great snorkeling, and windsurfing is a popular sport because of the trade winds. The island is dotted with windmills and red roofed houses rich to its Dutch heritage. Late in the development for tourism, Aruba has attracted full-fledged resorts with world class gambling casinos that have lavish entertainment, contain fine restaurants, shops with duty-free merchandise, and has still managed to maintain some old world charm. The commitment to tourism is 100% since it is the major industry today. Visitors are welcome with open arms and friendly smiles. English is spoken everywhere even though Dutch is the national language.

GETTING TO KNOW YOU

Inhabited by the Amerindians from South American as early as 2,500 B.C., recent archaeological excavations indicate that the Arawak Indians were one of the first inhabitants of the island. In the late 1400's Spain claimed it and even though the island didn't seem that interesting or important, Spain still struggled with Holland until the Dutch finally prevailed, and in 1636 sent their first governor, Peter Stuyvesant. During the Napoleonic Wars the English invaded and controlled the island for eleven years, but the Dutch returned in 1816 and have held it ever since. In 1824 gold was discovered and mined through the next century. Even today an occasional nugget is discovered. Oil was the base of the economy after its discovery in the 1920's and the island began to prosper as never before. In 1985 the oil refinery closed and left Aruba without a major industry. In January 1, 1986, Aruba left the Netherlands Antilles and became a separate entity under the Dutch crown. Although still protected by the Netherlands in defense and foreign affairs, Aruba has been able to now direct its energy to developing other sectors of its economy. Tourism has become the industry of Aruba and it has mushroomed over the years. It is still growing with new hotels and resorts being added every year. "Carnival" goes on for one month at the peak of the winter season, and half a million people visit year round to enjoy fun in the sun, gambling and duty-free shopping. Casinos now enliven the night, and almost 40 hotels sit side by side down one major strip along the southwestern shore.

THE BASICS

LOCATION AND GEOGRAPHY

Aruba is one of the three Dutch Leeward islands (Bonaire and Curacao are nearby) and they are known as the ABC islands. Located just off the coast of Venezuela, Aruba is 7 miles wide and only 20 miles long. Here, on an island whose symbol is a tree (the divi-divi), very little vegetation and very little rain (some in November) make this an ideal climate to enjoy the sun. Seventy thousand people with Dutch, Spanish and Carib Indian cultures live here. Rugged eastern shores where the winds blow in from the Atlantic are the buffer for the northern side of the island's calm waters and white beaches. The trade winds keep the air clear and comfortable.

With education, housing and health care financed by an economy based on tourism, the island's population of 70,400 recognizes vicitors from all parts of the world as valued guests.

The island's beauty lies in its distinctive countryside—a landscape full of deserts, rock formations, divi-divi trees, and beaches with crashing waves.

Although there is some rain in November, fresh water on the island comes from desalination plants that convert salt water, and due to the lack of rainfall during most of the year, Arubans have become committed to energy and water conservation.

Aruba is on Atlantic Standard time all rear, so the island is one hour ahead of New York during the winter months, but on the same time as the US converts to Daylight Savings time.

CLIMATE, WHEN TO GO, WHAT TO WEAR

With its low humidity and an average temperature of 82 degrees F., Aruba has the climate of a paradise. It does rain occasionally in November, but most of the year is dominated by cooling trade winds. Consequently any time of the year is the perfect time to visit.

Dress ranges from casual at the less expensive restaurants to the elegant at some of the resorts. Few restaurants, however, require more formal wear than a jacket for men and a dress for women. The air conditioning does get rather cold in some of the establishments, so it may be wise to always plan on something to cover your arms. If you plan to eat at one of the many outdoor restaurants, remember to take insect repellant for those times when the winds drop to keep the mosquitoes away.

GETTING THERE

Since Aruba is only about 3 hours away from Miami and 4 hours from New York it is very easy to find a convenient flight to the island. Daily flights leave from both Miami and New York, with connections from other US cities and San Juan, Puerto Rico. **Air Aruba** is the official airline and flies from Newark, NJ five days a week and daily from Miami. **American Airlines** has non-stop service from JFK and Miami daily. There are also connecting flights from San Juan, Puerto Rico. **ALM** flies from Miami five days a week. **VIASA** out of Venezuela offers non-stop flights from Houston three times a week.

Cruise ships also service the island daily, and all the ships dock at the west side of Oranjestad, the capital, less than a half mile walk to the town center, and within walking distance from the main shopping area. The island is currently served by Carnival, Celebrity, Crystal, Cunard, Dolphin, Holland America, Norwegian, Regency, Royal, Royal Caribbean, Sewing, Sun and Windstar.

DOCUMENTS

US and Canadian citizens need to have a passport or other proof of identification, such as a birth certificate, naturalization certificate, green card, a valid nonquota immigration visa, visa or a valid voter's registration card. A driver's license is not acceptable without additional identification. A valid passport is the easiest method, most other nationalities are required to have one. An ongoing ticket is also needed.

ARRIVAL AND DEPARTURE

Queen Beatrix Airport is only a mile south of Oranjestad, so it is very convenient to get to your accommodations. Immigration and Customs are handled very efficiently, although it should be remembered that drugs are not tolerated. Custom agents usually use dogs to check all incoming baggage. Taxis are prevalent at the airport so there is no problem getting to your hotel quickly. Taxis are also available at the port to meet arriving ships, or they can be requested by telephone from the taxi dispatch office. Taxis are expensive unless you plan to share a ride with others. The taxis are unmetered, but the rates are fixed for most destinations. It is always a wise idea, however, to agree upon a fare in advance. Tipping is optional, but expected when the driver assists with your baggage. Car rentals are available at the airport and it is best to make reservations in advance for the best rates.

Local buses are available and certainly can be recommended. All the drivers speak English, and are very helpful. Bus stops are marked **BUSHALTE**. a one way fare is about $1, and can be paid in US currency.

US Customs allows an exemption of $600 worth of merchandise from Aruba to be brought back into the US.

The departure tax is $12.50 per person.

CURRENCY, TRAVELER'S CHECKS, CREDIT CARDS

The official currency is the Netherlands Antilles florin or guilder (Naf.). US dollars are accepted everywhere so there is no need to change to the local currency. In fact the Islanders do not like to take their own money from tourists. The rate is 1.80 Naf to the US $1.00. Credit cards are widely accepted and shopkeepers do not normally grant discounts for cash, traveler's checks or credit cards.

Tipping and Taxes

Hotels collect 5% government tax and 11% surcharge on rooms. Many restaurants add 10% to 15% to the bill. If a service charge is not added 10% to 15% will cover the tip.

Airport baggage handlers expect 50 cents per bag. Taxi drivers accept tips for special services and heavy luggage.

Language

Dutch is the official language of the island, but English is spoken almost everywhere. Local language is a patois (Papiamento) which evolved from the Portuguese slave traders, Dutch, and many African dialects. You many hear such patois phrases as "bon dia" (good morning) or "masha danki"(thank you).

Business Hours

Shops are open Monday through Saturday from 8am to 12pm (many closing for lunch) and 2pm to 6pm. Some stores close Tuesday afternoons. Banks are open 8am to 4pm during the week days. The Alhambra Bazaar is open until midnight.

Transportation and Tours

It is very easy to get around in Aruba. Visitors need only to show a valid US or Canadian driver's license when renting a car. The hotel can make arrangements if you should decide to rent a car after your arrival. Many national car rentals are here: **Budget** (Tel. 28600), **Hertz** (Tel. 24545), **National** (Tel. 21967), and **Dollar** (Tel. 22783). Local agencies include **Hedwinas** (Tel. 37393). Check the insurance policy, there are exceptions on a collision damage waiver. You may have to draw from your own policy for complete coverage. $10.00 a day is usually the charge for the insurance. Although the road system is not marked as well as you may be accustomed to, the major sites are easy to locate. You may need a guide for any off -the-beaten-track-touring, however.

Mopeds and motorcycles are available for rental in Oranjestad and Noord: **George's Scooter & Cycle Center** (Tel. 25975) and **Semver Cycle Rental** (Tel. 26851, Noord). Mountain bikes are at **Pablitos Bike Rental** (Tel. 75010).

The buses are convenient to use. The **yellow bus** is very efficient for a Caribbean island and runs every 20 minutes daily (except Sunday and Holidays). Visitors use it from town to the beaches. One way is $1.00 and round trip $2.00. If you ask the bus driver he will sell you a round-trip bus card for $1.60, but you must ask. A **"free" shopping tour bus** departs every hour from the Holiday Inn starting at 9:15am until 3:15pm and picks up passengers from various hotels along the way into town. It is easy to spot because it is so colorful, but it is best to check with your hotel in regard to the stop nearest to where you are staying. Be prepared to find another way back to your hotel since the bus does not provide return service.

Taxi tours are available (Tel. 21604). All drivers are knowledgeable of the island and charge about $30.00 for a short tour. There are no meters so agree to the fare before the trip.

For an organized fun day try one of **De Palm Tours** activities (Tel. 24400). This includes beach barbecues, snorkeling, island trips, a glass bottom boat trip as well as sailing adventures. **Corvalou Tours** (Tel. 21149) offers archaeological and botanical trips that last about five hours. If you want a guided tour of the caves call **Aruba Friendly Tours** (Tel. 25800).

At Seaport Village the **Atlantis Submarine** (Tel. 36090) has a one hour tour dropping 140 feet below the surface that come face-to-face with shipwrecks, the coral reefs and beautiful tropical fish.

RESOURCES

Aruba Tourism Authority is located at 172 Lloyd G. Smith Boulevard, Oranjestad. (Tel. 23777). If you have not gathered enough information at the airport or from your cruise ship, it is worth a stop to pick up maps, brochures and guidebooks, all in English. They are open during the weekdays only. ***Aruba Holiday*** is a monthly guide filled with the island activities and shopping information and is in almost all hotel lobbies and at the airport. The local newspapers are in English and come out daily except Sundays. The newsstands have ***The New York Times*** and ***The Miami Herald*** the same day they are published.

SHOPPING IN ARUBA

Duty-free shopping is promoted although Aruba really is not a freeport. However, the duty is only 3.3% and that makes for fun shopping and bargain hunting among a wide collection of merchandise from all over the world.

China and crystal are available in many shops, especially from the **Aruba Trading Company**, a large department store with a large selection, and **Little Switzerland**, one of the mainstays in the Caribbean.

Clothing and accessories are available from the many boutiques, with high fashions being one of the specialties of **Studio Italia** and **Maggy's**. Both carry Dior and other designer labels.

Every shopping complex in town and at the resort hotels has a perfume shop, but the **Aruba Trading Company, D'Orsy's** and **Sardini's** have the largest selections.

Leather is available at prices about 20% lower than US prices at many shops selling Louis Vitton-type handbags and luggage. You need to be familiar with the specific manufacturers goods, however, to determine if these are the genuine item or merely good replicas. If you do not know, or do not care, there are very good buys. **Gucci** does have its own store, however, with its own merchandise.

Jewelry from **Kado, Gandelman** and **Lucor Jewelers** is of high quality, art from **Artishoc** and **Gaspirito** and crafts from the **Artesania Crafts Center** round out some of the best buys in town.

Edam and Gouda cheese is available at many shops, and you may bring back up to one pound to the US. Dutch chocolates can be purchased most everywhere, including the airport.

Most shops are open from 8am to 6pm, some closing for lunch from 12pm to 2pm. Most of the larger shops have branches at the major hotels and resorts.

Bargaining on prices in Aruba is not considered polite—even in the many bazaars.

WHERE TO SHOP

The main shopping area in Aruba is **Gaya G.F. BeticoCroes**, almost half a mile long in Oranjestad. **Artistic Boutique** is definitely international with its gold and silver jewelry, local embroidered linens, Persian carpets and porcelains from Spain. Perfumes, cosmetics, clothing, and jewelry are all found at **Aruba Trading Company**. **Little Switzerland** has a branch store here complete with its famous watches and 18 karat gold jewelry. **New Amsterdam Store** is the major department store in Aruba and carries a wide selection of Delft pottery, among its clothing (swimsuits) leather goods and shoes. **J.L. Penha & Son's** displays designer clothing and cosmetics. Try **Gandelman's Jewelers** for coral necklaces and Swatch watches. They also carry Gucci accessories. **De Witt** has toys and other gift items. Crystal can be found at **Palais Oriental**.

Shopping malls are a way of life in Aruba. **Seaport Village Mall** is close to the cruise terminal and has over eighty stores to fit any shopping list or budget. The **Holland Aruba Mall, Strada I** and **Strada II** designed with Colonial Dutch architecture, are also located in Oranjestad with many boutiques and delightful stores. **The Alhambra Bazaar** lives up to its international flavor with cafes and shops that can become the entire evening's entertainment. It is open from early afternoon until midnight. At **Harbourtown** at Swain Wharf you can find linens from China and handmade pottery from Venezuela. **Port of Call Marketplace** has a variety of shops with batiks, leather goods, boutiques with jewelry and perfumes.

Local crafts can be found at several shops. **Artesania Arubiano** (next door to the Aruba Tourism Authority) has a wide selection, of pottery, wall hangings and local art. T-shirts that are silk-screened are also sold here. Miniature divi divi trees can be found at **Creative Hands** located at Scotorolaan, but the real surprise at this shop is beautiful Japanese dolls.

SPECIAL TIPS FOR CRUISE PASSENGERS

Since the ships dock at the port in Aruba, shopping and other things to do are mere steps away. Here you will find several nice shopping malls offering a wide range of resortwear, souvenirs, jewelry, and handicrafts—Port of Call Market Place, Seaport Village, Holland Aruba Mall, Harbourtown Market. The most upscale shopping area is Seaport Village which includes two floors of good quality shops as well as a casino. Just behind Seaport Village is the main shopping street with its colorful buildings and well respected shops, such as Little Switzerland, Boolchands, Spitzer and Fuhrman, Gandelman Jewelers, and Benetton.

Taxis are at hand at the port to take you anywhere on the island. Tours are also available by jeep or minibus to take you to some of the less accessible parts of the island, and windsurfing lessons are available at many of the hotels along Palm Beach

The capital city of Oranjestad is neat and clean, and can be easily covered in an hour or two. From the port, you can walk along Smith Boulevard to the Aruba Tourist Bureau where you can obtain a copy of **Aruba Holiday**, a free monthly tourist brochure. **Harbourtown**, an attractive shopping mall with boutiques and cafes is also a short walk away.

ENJOYING YOUR STAY

There's a lot to see and explore in Aruba. Because the island is so small, it is easy to slip away for a few hours and enjoy the countryside. Many visitors like to drive to the interior and see the divi divi trees with their branches dramatically swept to the side by the constant trade winds. There are very few places to get refreshments and with facilities, so plan your day trip accordingly.

- The **Natural Bridge** located on the northern coast has been created by the strong splashing surf. It is enjoyable to walk across. There is a small cafe and souvenir shop for convenience.

- Hooiberg has Aruba's highest landmark called **"The Haystack."** It is a 541 foot hill with steps that can take you all the way to the top. On clear days Venezuela can be seen. Northeast of Hooiberg stand magnificent boulders at **Ayo** (ancient Amerindian drawings are found here) and **Casibari** (where you can climb up and see a great view of Aruba). South of Hooiberg are the **Caves of Canashito** where you can see drawings on the walls and ceilings.

- **San Nicolas** is Aruba's oldest town and was at the height of its glory during the oil boom. Nearby is the **Spanish Lagoon**, once a haven for pirates.

- **Oranjestad** offers shopping as the main appeal, but **Schooner Harbor** is very colorful with its boats and fish market, **Wilhelmina Park** is a quiet stroll along the water.

- There are three museums: Museo Arubano—in Fort Zoutman displays artifacts from the history of the island's early times. The Fort is the oldest building on

Aruba. **Archeological Museum** has Pre-Columbian artifacts discovered on the island, tools, skeletons and pottery, some over 1,000 years old. The **Numismatic Museum** contains J.M.Odor's coin and paper currency collection from more than 400 countries.

- There are always fairs, crafts shows and other such events in Aruba. Check with your hotel or cruise ship for the latest information. Carnival festivities beginning a week or so before Lent is also something that should not be missed.

ACCOMMODATIONS

Since Aruba is a recent entrant to the tourist industry almost all the major hotels are resorts with a variety of activities and amenities, some with all inclusive vacation features. However all types of facilities are available including guest houses that book early in the season. Off season rates (May through November) can drop as much as 40%. In the winter season a room can be hard to come by so always be sure you have reservations. When calling from the US dial 011 international code+ 297 the country code + (8) the city code + the local number.

- **Aruba Marriott Resort & Casino:** Tel. 8-6900 or 1-800-228-9290. Aruba's newest resort has the most spectacular view on the island. The fully appointed guest rooms have balconies with a panoramic vista of the ocean. The pool has cascading waterfalls. It contains a health club, tennis courts, golf course and the casino rounded out with elegant service. Located at Palm Beach. Expensive.

- **Hyatt Regency Aruba:** Tel. 8-31234 or 1-800-233-1234, Fax 8-21682. Considered the most glamorous resort on the island with extensive gardens and exotic birds, the resort is centered around a magnificent pool with slides and waterfalls cascading at three different levels. The hotel is pure Caribbean with high ceilings, rattan furniture with special pieces carved by artisans from Central and South America. In the lounge continental breakfast and afternoon cocktails are served. The resort has a variety of restaurants and bars. The Casino Copacabana is located here. Just outside of Oranjestad. Expensive.

- **Aruba Hilton Hotel & Casino:** Tel. 8-6466 or 1-800-HILTONS. Hilton completely renovated the Concord hotel after purchasing it in the early 1990's. Soft island colors predominate throughout the resort, and all of the amenities, including safes in the rooms, and 24 hour concierge services are available. Balconies all have views of the ocean, and there is a beautiful pool with fountains. The Casino Casablanca has a Sultan's tent atmosphere. Located at Palm Beach. Expensive.

- **Divi Aruba Beach Resort:** Tel. 8-23300 or 1-800-22DORAL, Fax 8-34002. An informal Caribbean hotel that captures the essence of a carefree tropical life on one of the longest stretches of soft white beach in Aruba. Among the palm trees by the ocean all rooms have a view of the water from either a patio or balcony. Air-conditioning, radio, and TV, but no room service. Totally renovated in 1993, the resort's focal point is a large elevated pool with a thatched roof dining area. A full range of water sports (including wind surfing) and tennis are available. Adjacent to the Alhambra Casino and Bazaar on Druif Beach. Moderate.

RESTAURANTS

Dining is international in Aruba. Asian, Indonesian, and especially Chinese restaurants abound. French Cuisine has a large presence and European and South American cuisine are available. The Dutch have some local specialities such as funchi (cornmeal), an bati (pancake), Ajaka (Chicken in banana leaves) and many more delights to try. The food is taken seriously and well prepared. Credit cards are widely accepted. Some favorites are:

- **Chez Mathilde:** Tel. 34968. Havenstraut 23. French. The chef is island famous for his bouillabaisse. This is haute cuisine in an elegant setting with superb service. Live piano music rounds out the ambience. Reservations are important. Expensive.

- **Bali Sea Palace Floating Restaurant:** Tel. 22131. Lloyd. G. Smith Boulevard in Oranjestad's Harbor. Rijstaffel (21 dishes with rice) is the speciality of the house. The Hot Sambol is served on the side. It is open for Lunch and Dinner and has a wonderful atmosphere. Reservations are a must during high season. Inexpensive.

- **Boonoonoonoos:** Tel. 31888. Wilhelminastraat 18. Jamaican flavor abounds here with a menu absorbing Caribbean foods from different islands. Pumpkin Soup, Pepperpot, Trinidad Curried Chicken, but most of all Jamaican jerk ribs. Inexpensive

- **Le Petit Cafe**: Tel. 33716. At the corner of Schlepstraat and Main street. A great stop for lunch while shopping. Food is cooked on hot stones and makes an inexpensive quiet spot to relax. Also serve sandwiches. Open for Lunch and Dinner. Inexpensive.

- **De Olde Molen (The Old Mill):** Tel. 620060. J. E. Irausquin Boulevard. A landmark structure shipped from Holland in 1804 and reconstructed, a gift from the Queen. Now a restaurant with Aruban food. Try the Red Snapper with Creole sauce. An easy walk from most Palm Beach Hotels. Moderate.

- **Valentino's**: Tel. 62700. Located in Noord at Caribbean Palm Village. If Italian food is on your mind, this visit is worth the trip. The menu is drawn from all regions of Italy and it is refreshing and excellent. Open for dinner only and reservations are recommended. Expensive.

Index

More Treasures and Pleasures

The following "Impact Guides" can be ordered directly from the publisher. Complete the following form (or list the titles), include your name and address, enclose payment, and send your order to:

IMPACT PUBLICATIONS
9104-N Manassas Drive
Manassas Park, VA 22111 (USA)
Tel. 703/361-7300
Fax 703/335-9486

All prices are in U.S. dollars. Orders from individuals should be prepaid by check, moneyorder, or Visa, MasterCard, or American Express number. If your order must be shipped outside the U.S., please include an additional US$1.50 per title for surface mail or the appropriate air mail rate for books weighting 24 ounces each. We accept telephone orders (credit cards). Orders are shipped within 48 hours.

Qty.	TITLES	Price	TOTAL
__	Shopping and Traveling in Exotic Asia (5 countries)	$16.95	______
__	Shopping in Exciting Australia and Papua New Guinea	$13.95	______
__	Shopping the Exotic South Pacific	$16.95	______
__	Treasures and Pleasures of the Caribbean	$16.95	______
__	Treasures and Pleasures of Hong Kong	$14.95	______
__	Treasures and Pleasures of Indonesia	$14.95	______
__	Treasures and Pleasures of Singapore and Malaysia	$14.95	______
__	Treasures and Pleasures of Thailand	$14.95	______

Available in mid-1996:

__ Treasures and Pleasures of India	$14.95	______
__ Treasures and Pleasures of Italy	$14.95	______
__ Treasures and Pleasures of Morocco	$14.95	______
__ Treasures and Pleasures of Paris and the French Riviera	$14.95	______
__ Treasures and Pleasures of the Philippines	$14.95	______

SUBTOTAL $ ______

Virginia residents add 4.5% sales tax $ ______

Shipping/handling ($4.00 for the first title and $1.00 for each additional book) $ ______

Additional amount if shipping abroad $ ______

TOTAL ENCLOSED------------ $ ______

SHIP TO:

Name ______________________

Address ______________________

____

____

PAYMENT METHOD:

❑ I enclose check/moneyorder for $ __________ made payable to IMPACT PUBLICATIONS.

❑ Please charge $ __________ to my credit card:

❑ Visa ❑ MasterCard ❑ American Express

Card # ______________________

Expiration date: ______/______

Signature ______________________